Frontier Soldiers of New France

Volume 2: Campaign Clothing, Armament, and Equipment of the Colonial Troops in North America (1683–1760)

Kevin Gélinas

Helion & Company

Helion & Company Limited
Unit 8 Amherst Business Centre
Budbrooke Road
Warwick
CV34 5WE
England
Tel. 01926 499619
Email: info@helion.co.uk
Website: www.helion.co.uk
X (formerly Twitter): @Helionbooks
Facebook: @HelionBooks
Visit our blog at http://blog.helion.co.uk/

Published by Helion & Company 2025
Designed and typeset by Mach 3 Solutions (www.mach3solutions.co.uk)
Cover designed by Paul Hewitt, Battlefield Design (www.battlefield-design.co.uk)

Text © Kevin Gélinas 2025
Illustrations © as individually credited
Cover: 'We Dined in a Hollow Cottonwood Tree', by Robert Griffing. © Paramount Press

ISBN 978-1-804516-79-9

British Library Cataloguing-in-Publication Data.
A catalogue record for this book is available from the British Library.

For details of other military history titles published by Helion & Company Limited, contact the above address, or visit our website: http://www.helion.co.uk

We always welcome receiving book proposals from prospective authors.

Contents

Preface

This project was born from a shared vision between Francis Back and me, a collaboration deeply rooted in our mutual passion for the material culture and history of New France. The idea first took shape in Francis Back's garden in Montréal, during the early days of June 2012, where our conversations and shared dedication to this rich heritage brought us together. We envisioned a comprehensive volume that would detail and preserve the unique blend of French and Indigenous influences that shaped this territory, with each of us bringing our expertise to the project.

Francis, whose legacy as a historical illustrator, author, and researcher is unmatched, pioneered the study of New France's material culture with unparalleled dedication. His work was meticulous as he examined notarial records, judicial archives, and merchants' account books with a dedication to period accuracy that inspired me deeply. His research and his passion for understanding New France's clothing led to approximately 50 articles published in various local and international journals.

When we discussed merging our expertise, my focus being on fur trade goods, weapons, and equipment, and his on clothing, it was clear that together, we could create a comprehensive book on the subject. Though Francis had amassed an impressive body of documentation, I saw an opportunity to expand our research further by exploring unexamined archival collections. I took on the task of documenting all relevant notarial records from Montréal and Trois-Rivières and combing through other archives across Canada, Europe, and the United States. This also involved reviewing thousands of probate records from Québec and the Illinois Territory, uncovering significant and previously unknown records. My research also took me to archaeological sites across North America, where I photographed French-era artifacts at Fort Ticonderoga, Fort Michilimackinac, Fort de Chartres, Fort Ouiatenon, Fort Senneville, and in Parks Canada collections. To further enrich the project, we invited Michel Pétard, whose expertise and skill in line drawing brought added depth to our work.

We were particularly captivated by the distinct identities that emerged between the French-Canadians, known as Canadiens, and their European counterparts.[1] The Canadiens' adaptability to varied environments revealed a unique blend of French and Indigenous influences, shaping local fashion, customs, and notably, the military practices of French colonial forces. To bring these connections to light, I undertook the task of matching specific French or colonial terms in period documents with the corresponding weapons, objects, and clothing, terms that were either lost or whose meanings had evolved to the point where today their exact interpretations are often uncertain. This endeavour proved both challenging and immensely rewarding. I thereafter set out to uncover the origins of these items, exploring whether they were imported or crafted locally.

In the wake of Francis's passing in 2017, I was filled with a profound resolve to undertake the writing of this volume, though I deeply regret that neither volume could be completed in collaboration with him. This second and final instalment in our series represents the culmination of years of meticulous research into the non-regulation clothing, weapons, and equipment used by colonial troops in French North America between 1683 and 1760, with a particular focus on those stationed in Canada and the Great Lakes region.

In honouring Francis's legacy and our collaboration, my hope is to provide readers with a richer understanding of French culture and its enduring influence on North America, seen through the lens of New France's military life: 'From the fork to the musket.'

---

1   In the eighteenth century, Canadians (with the English spelling) began to refer more broadly to the inhabitants of Canada after the British took control of New France. However, it was still not used in the same inclusive way as it is today.

Acknowledgements

To my two incredible daughters, Geneviève and Dominique, whose unwavering support and inspiration have guided me throughout this journey that began in 2012. This book is also dedicated to the memory of my father, Paul Gladysz, and my grandfather, Rolland Gélinas, both of whom passed away in recent years. Their values, influence, and legacy remain a profound part of all that I do.

I owe my deepest thanks to Michel Pétard, whose encouragement and sage advice gave me the strength to persist with the research and writing of this book. Without his support, this project might never have reached completion. I also wish to honour the memory of René Chartrand, my former co-author and mentor, whose wisdom and passion for history were both a guiding light and an enduring source of inspiration.

Finally, I extend my heartfelt gratitude to everyone whose work, research, and generosity contributed to the creation of this book. In particular, I want to thank Christian Back, Ryan Gale, Ken Hamilton, Joseph Gagné, Gilles Havard, Christian Lemasson, Jeff Pavlik, Donald F. Shaffer, Robert Speelman, Don Troiani, Louis Valiquette, Mark B. Wilson, and Thomas Wojcinski for their invaluable contributions and support.

Key to Cited Manuscript Sources

AC: Archives nationales d'outre-mer, Colonies (Aix-en-Provence, France).

AG: Archives de la Guerre (Service Historique des Armées, Vincennes, France).

AM: Archives de la Marine (at the Archives Nationales, Paris, France).

ANMT (Les Archives nationales du monde du travail, Roubaix, France.)

AR: Archives du port de Rochefort (Rochefort, France).

BAnQ-M: Bibliothèque et Archives nationales du Québec (Centre d'archives de Montréal, Montréal, Canada).

BAnQ-Q: Bibliothèque et Archives nationales du Québec (Centre d'archives de Québec, Québec, Canada).

BAnQ-TR: Bibliothèque et Archives nationales du Québec (Centre d'archives de Trois-Rivières, Trois-Rivières, Canada).

BNF: Bibliothèque Nationale de France (Paris, France).

BRH: Le Bulletin des Recherches historiques.

TNA: The National Archives, (Kew, United Kingdom).

HCA: High Court of Admiralty. Prize Papers; WO: War Office.

KM: Kaskaskia Manuscripts (at Randolph County Courthouse, Chester, Illinois, USA).

LAC: Library and Archives Canada (Ottawa, Canada).

LOC: Library of Congress (Washington, DC, USA.)

RAPQ: Rapport de l'archiviste de la Province de Québec.

PRDH: Programme de recherche en démographie historique.

SHAT: Service Historique de l'Armée de terre (Vincennes, France.)

SHD: Service Historique de la Défense (Vincennes, France).

UMCB: Université de Montréal, Collection Baby, Université de Montréal, Division des archives, Collection Louis Francois-Georges Baby (Montréal, Canada).

Introduction

Throughout the Intercolonial Wars, or 'French and Indian Wars,' the guerilla warfare tactics employed by the military forces in New France allowed them not only to keep the British in New England's settlements on the defensive but served to overcome hostile Native nations with the purpose of achieving control over the major transportation and trade routes in the interior.[1] While the French had huge disadvantages in manpower and resources in these Intercolonial Wars, they had a clear advantage in frontier warfare because of their adoption of la petite guerre, a way of conducting war in the Native style, which consisted of surprise ambushes and raids followed by immediate withdrawals from the battleground.

During the early years of the colony, the French living in the St Lawrence Valley learned that la petite guerre was the method preferred by Native enemies, namely the Iroquois, who engaged in this type of warfare continuously and without mercy. This approach was thereafter adopted by the French settlers when militia units were established for the defence of the colony. In the early 1640s, Paul Chomedey de Maisonneuve, Governor of Montréal, pursued the enemy into the forest and 'placed his men behind the trees as the enemy did and they began firing at will,'[2] which reveals the beginning of adaptations in tactics, which would have been seen as utterly dishonourable in the eyes of European soldiers. The year 1669 marked the official birth of the Canadian militia (milice Canadienne), where every male between the ages of 16 and 60 fit to bear arms was compelled to join the milice. In essence, this militia was an auxiliary force to the regular troops stationed in New France. Many of these men were already well acquainted with wilderness survival skills, such as long canoe trips, encampments, and hunting. In 1709, Jacques Raudot, Intendant of New France, observed that 'The Canadian is very brave; we cannot doubt it by the different parties in which he took part. He is also an exceptional marksman, surpassing other nations in this skill. It is to hunting, which occupies him from his most tender youth and which he loves passionately, that he owes

this.'[3] Even so, miliciens could not replace professional soldiers drilled in orthodox manoeuvres to defend settlements, forts, and outposts, since militiamen were first and foremost 'Habitants', or civilians.

When relations with the Iroquois deteriorated in the 1680s, Governor de la Barre submitted a formal request for military reinforcements from France. The troops that disembarked at Québec in 1683, known as the Compagnies franches de la Marine, were an ensemble of autonomous infantry units attached to the Marine royale bound to serve in the colony on a permanent basis. Initially, the King used these companies to defend his control of the fur trade in North America and to protect civilians from raiding parties. The French officers who first arrived in Canada in the 1680s quickly recognised that their military knowledge and experience were useless in the colony. Since there was no road network in New France before the 1730s, fighting forces had to travel using snowshoes during winter and birch bark or dugout canoes in summer. The lack of roads and heavily forested land made field artillery and cavalry impossible to move and deploy. Over time, many officers came to realise that Native tactics were far better suited to the North American environment, and especially when combined with European military discipline. On the frontier, soldiers taking part in raids were required to act more independently while still following a chain of commands and obeying and executing orders as on a European battlefield. They had to move fast in small units, scout enemy positions, approach them undetected, strike, and then withdraw with equal haste. The effectiveness of this approach was a result of the combined Native-style attack with organised and coordinated efforts that necessitated discipline and unity such as is found in European troops.[4]

---

1 The term Native will be used to refer to the Indigenous peoples/First Nations/Native Americans
2 François Dollier de Casson, *Histoire du Montréal, 1640-1672, Numéros 1–5* (Paris: Imprimerie Nati.nale, 1871), p.30.
3 Camille De Rochemonteix, *Relation par lettres de l'Amérique septentrionale (années 1709 et 1710)* (Paris: Letouzey et Ané, 1904), pp.5–6.
4 René Chartrand, 'Hertel and Canada's first tacticians in the seventeenth century', in Bernd Horn and Roch Legault (eds), *Loyal Service, Perspectives on French-Canadian Military Leaders, Hertel and Canada's First Tacticians in the Seventeenth Century* (Montréal: McGill-Queen's University Press, 2007), pp.19–52.

While the French employed la petite guerre to contain or repel enemies, they also conducted large-scale wilderness operations that resembled regular European warfare. Notable examples include the 1687 expedition against the Iroquois, as well as the 1715 campaigns against the Fox and the 1739 expedition against the Chickasaw nation.

Organizing equipment and clothing for raids and expeditions was quite different from the military practices established in France. Colonial soldiers contended with harsh terrain and extreme climates – hot, humid summers and brutally cold winters – which necessitated significant environmental adaptations. They needed to adopt equipment and clothing better suited to North America, much like those already in use by the local militiamen. While colonial soldiers wore their European-issued regulation uniforms during duties, reviews, inspections, parades, and ceremonies, when participating in small detachments and expeditions, they left these uniforms behind, progressively adopting Canadian-style civilian wear and elements of wilderness equipment tried and tested by the Canadian militia. This habillement à la Canadienne (traditional Canadian clothing style) laid the foundation for non-regulation campaign attire worn by the colonial troops throughout this entire period.

Hence, the purpose of this study is to shed light on the various items of wilderness campaign clothing, arms, and equipment used by the colonial troops serving in New France between 1683 and 1760 using the most current research information available. It is important to note that only a limited number of French colonial records related to Canada's military and commercial affairs have survived; however, those that remain offer valuable insights into the types of supplies colonial troops received and carried during various military operations over the years. Determining the items specifically issued to the colonial troops using existing equipment lists, which are scattered and fragmentary, was a complex undertaking. Many of the same articles were intended for several recipients (militiamen, Native warriors and soldiers), making the task of distinguishing what article was provided to whom quite challenging. The quantity and quality of each item to be supplied to each man appear to vary based on rank, and the length and the nature of each military operation, which varied over time due to several factors, including availability, and changes in trends. While certain finished articles were imported from the mother country, many were made directly in the colony. Combined with an extensive amount of complementary period sources (period accounts, memoirs, journals, published works, judicial and notarial records), period iconography, extant pieces, and archaeological evidence, a more complete picture of each of these objects begins to take shape.

'Canadianization' of the Clothing and Equipment of the Colonial Troops

Before the large army of French regulars arrived in Canada in 1755, it was customary for colonial officers and soldiers to receive standard campaign-issue supplies prior to expeditions, campaigns, detachments, and voyages, or when garrisoned in forts and outposts. Certain items were specific to winter or summer campaigns and the quantities issued to each man varied based on several factors, such as rank, length and instance of each military action, and the season. Intendant Bigot made it very clear that '…. besides the regulation uniform, which the troops had, they were provided as well as the Canadians and Natives, with winter and summer equipment.'[5]

Table 1. Conjecture of the winter and summer equipment generally issued to officers and soldiers of the colonial troops based upon surviving supply lists ranging from 1755 to 1760. (See Appendix)

Summer equipment	Winter equipment
1 capot	1 gilet waistcoat
2 cotton shirts	2 pairs of wool slippers (chaussons)
1 cloth breechcloth	2 pairs of foot-cloth wraps (nippes)
1 pair of cloth mitasses leggings	1 pair of mittens
1 pair of breeches and a caleçon	1 tarpaulin (per 4 men)
1 pair of tanned moccasins (per month)	1 deer skin to make moccasins 2 pairs of deerskin moccasins
1 wool blanket	1 bearskin (usually for officers)
1 wool stocking cap	1 sealskin (to cover supplies on the toboggans and for soldiers to sleep on)
1 casse-tête tomahawk	1 large axe (per 2 men)
1 gun case	2 Siamois knives
1 boucheron knife	1 covered kettle (for officers)
1 cooking pot (for each officer)	1 kettle (per 4 or 5 men)
2 skeins of thread	1 pair of snowshoes
6 sewing needles	1 toboggan
1 awl	1 tumpline
1 fire steel	
6 gunflints	
1 gun worm	
1 comb	

Besides a few standard-issue articles, such as gunflints or combs, the metropolitan Marine troops serving at sea or in the ports in France did not receive the types of

---

5   François Bigot, *Mémoire Pour Messire François Bigot, ci-devant Intendant de Justice, Police, Finance & Marine en Canada, Accusé: Contre Monsieur le Procureur-Général du Roi en la Commission, Accusateur: Contenant l'Histoire de l'Administration du sieur Bigot dans la Colonie, & des Réflexions générales sur cette Administration* (Paris: Prieur, 1763), p.39.

campaign equipment that were issued to the troops serving in North America. Surprisingly, most of the non-regulation supplies issued to the autonomous infantry units in North America were identical to those offered in the fur trade or to the Native nations allied to the French. The same articles were also handed out to the militia and Native allies detached alongside the colonial troops. Some items were direct adaptations to the North American climate and environment, while others were adopted from Native practices, including breechcloths, Native leggings, tumplines, toboggans, snowshoes, tomahawks, butcher knives, and awls for making moccasins. These adaptations highlight the significant cross-cultural interaction between the French and the Indigenous communities living in New France. According to the Swedish botanist Pehr Kalm, 'When the French are traveling about in this country, they are generally dressed like the natives; they wear then no trousers, but do not carry Indian weapons.'[6]

By the turn of the eighteenth century, colonial soldiers had fully embraced the 'à la Canadienne' kit when taking part in wilderness expeditions. Initially, the outfit answered a utilitarian purpose, which was to ward off the cold. François Bigot, last Intendant of New France, went so far as stating that 'each soldier or militiaman needed a waistcoat, a capot, mittens and a blanket, otherwise they would freeze.'[7] The first French settlers were ill dressed for Canadian winters and adopted some warm-weather clothing items from local Native Americans and French West Coast mariners.[8] This combination of French sailor attire and Native clothing styles and designs was especially popular among the coureur de bois, or voyageurs, men who worked in the fur trade and travelled deep into the interior using canoes, and who were seen as freshwater sailors.[9] King Louis XIV went so far as to qualify this 'Canadian-style clothing' as made 'in the fashion of the coureurs de bois.'[10] Fundamentally, the further into the interior one went, the more common the Native interaction, and thus the adoption of additional Native clothing and practices.

As early as 1705, for instance, French colonial soldiers serving in the Newfoundland expedition were said to be dressed à la Canadienne, '...that is, a tapabord cap, a gun, a powder horn, and a shoulder-strapped bullet pouch, snowshoes strapped on their feet.'[11] Three years later, the

men who participated in the raid on Haverhill, which included 100 militiamen and soldiers, were described as wearing a distinctive type of dress:

> The ordinary dress of the Canadians is a type of hooded coat which overlaps at the front in the way of a buff leather justaucorps, the sleeves are tight-fitting and closed like those of a vest. The Canadians … do not wear hats, but tapabords, which are English-style caps. When they go to war, they carry their swords slung over their shoulder, or under their arm, as well as their fusil [musket or gun]; the gunpowder in a horn which serves as a fourniment [powder reserve], and the lead balls in a type of pouch.[12]

This is attested some 40 years later by the author of a captivity journal, which reveals that French officers and soldiers dressed as the Natives did when raiding New England settlements:

> It is Notorious that the French Themselves not only Soldiers but Officers During the Present War when they Come upon the British Settlements with Indians (as they too frequently doe) they Dress and Paint in the same Manner as the Indians doe Nay the Rev'd John Norton Assured me that When he was beset and Taken att Fort Massachusetts he Could not Distinguish the one from the other but the French Appear'd in all respects like the Indians not only in their Dress but in their Gesture and Hellish Din the Indians make at an Assault.[13]

A few years later, colonial officer Jean-Daniel Dumas, who served in Canada from 1750 to 1760, observed that when taking part on wilderness expeditions, colonial soldiers sometimes adopted the clothing of the Canadians or Natives: 'at a certain time, we were falsely persuaded that to travel in the woods, one had to be dressed à la Canadienne [in the Canadian manner] or like the Sauvages [Natives].'[14] This myth is even perpetuated in Aubert de Gaspé's historical novel *Les Anciens Canadiens*, whose grandfather was a French colonial officer during the Seven Years War: '...not only the soldiers, but the very officers of the French army, when they waged war in the forests, wore the costume of the Natives: short capots, Native leggings, breechcloth and deerskin shoes. This flexible and light outfit gave them a

6   Pehr Kalm, *Voyage de Pehr Kalm au Canada en 1749* (Montréal: Pierre Tisseyre, 1977), folio 929, p.547.
7   Bigot, *Mémoire Pour Messire François Bigot*, p.77.
8   Francis Back, 'S'habiller à la canadienne', *Cap-aux-Diamants*, 24 (1991), pp.38–41; Francis Back, 'The Dress of the First Voyageurs, 1650–1715', *Museum of the Fur Trade Quarterly*, 36 (Summer 2000), pp.3–17.
9   Francis Back, 'Le costume des coureurs des bois: le mythe et la réalité', *Cap-aux-Diamants*, 76 (2004), pp.15–17.
10   RAPQ, 1927–1928, p.86.
11   *Le mercure galant* (Paris: Chez Michel Brunet, 1706), p.85.

12   *Le mercure galant* (Paris: Chez Michel Brunet, 1709), p.56.
13   Isabel M. Calder, *Colonial Captivities, Marches and Journeys* (New York: The Macmillan Company, 1935), p.96.
14   Archives départementales du Tarn-et-Garonne à Montauban, Cote 20J, 12 à 141, *Fonds de la Société archéologique, Papiers du Général Dumas, Réflexion politiques et militaires sur le Canada pour servir à son rétablissement* (Montauban: Archives Départementales, n.d.).

great advantage over enemies which were always dressed in European clothes.'[15]

Mismanagement and Quality of Supplies

By the 1750s, Intendant Bigot estimated that between 25,000 and 30,000 sets of summer equipment were distributed to the fighting forces in Canada, apart from what the Governor General of New France gave as presents to the Native families.[16] Dumas had established that the distribution and logistical system of what was provided to the colonial troops was severely flawed, which led to excessive abuse and tremendous expenditures on behalf of the King of France. According to this officer, carelessness and waste among the troops was widespread and appeared to be the leading cause of constant shortages of certain goods and supplies:

> I have seen soldiers receive four blankets over the course of a year by the few rules set in place for these types of supplies. The same holds true of campaign equipment such as pots, tools, etc. which are provided from the King's storehouses without anyone concerned with their conservation.[17]

An account of the Battle of Lake George authored by Bigot in 1755 provides further evidence of the squandering of weapons and equipment by the fighting forces, especially when retreating:

> There was an extraordinary consumption of food, clothing, and muskets in Mr. Dieskau's action. His army, consisting both of Natives and others, had been newly equipped with muskets, to the reserve of the soldiers. Those who took part in this action have all lost or broken them. They have also left in the woods when retreating, food for ten days' worth, and their clothing. They were compelled to do so, as they claim, to carry the injured and to lighten their loads.[18]

Considering this situation, Dumas pleaded for the complete removal of the campaign dress, arguing that the colonial soldier could serve on expeditions while wearing his official soldier's uniform, and declared it to be 'a source of a continual thievery to the soldier whom the King provides clothes every two years. He [colonial soldier] can

serve everywhere without any other clothes.'[19] Lastly, an undated memoir, likely written by French army officer François-Charles de Bourlamaque after 1760, seems to reaffirm this point of view: 'the soldier's dress shall be as in France. We will only provide a waistcoat and a blanket every two years, a pair of wool cloth gaiters, a pair of mittens and six pairs of tanned oxhide shoes every year,' while adding 'this expense has always been very considerable and unnecessary. A soldier does not need two sets of clothes.'[20]

Arrival of the Metropolitan Infantry Troops: Regulation-Issued Supplies

After the arrival of metropolitan troops in Canada in 1755, official lists of equipment to be issued to officers and soldiers of the colonial troops were closely controlled and regulated for each campaign. Intendant Bigot, summarized the way in which equipment was administrated prior to and after the arrival of the French Troupes de terre in 1755:

> Previously, in the marches and in the army, the Canadians and the Natives were provided with everything they needed for their subsistence. But as they were not regulated by rations, they were not provided with a supplement for what we had not given them. Instead, once the regular French troops had arrived, war was waged in Canada in the European manner: every officer or soldier having an allowance and regulation equipment. What was not supplied to them as a handout was granted to them in the way of money. In order to understand the enormous quantities of goods required for the service, it must be known that the King provided to the [colonial] troops, to the Canadians, and to the Natives, all the necessary campaign gear, such as tents, kettles, and weapons; and that the soldiers would throw them out and leave them in the retreats, rather than take charge and carry them, being assured that we would be required to supply them with replacements. Besides the regulation clothing which the troops had been given, they were provided, as well as the Canadians and the Natives, with winter and summer equipment. That officers and domestiques were to receive the same treatment.[21]

Details included in a dissertation written by Jean-Guillaume Plantavit de La Pause de Margon, who served as *capitaine* of the Régiment de Guyenne in Canada,

---

15   Aubert de Gaspé, *Les anciens Canadiens* (Québec: Desbarats et Derbishire, 1863), p.399.

16   François Bigot, *Mémoire Pour Messire François Bigot*, p.39.

17   Archives départementales du Tarn-et-Garonne à Montauban, Cote 20J, 12 à 141.

18   LAC, F3, vol.14, p.1, f.203.

19   Archives départementales du Tarn-et-Garonne à Montauban, Cote 20J, 12 à 141.

20   LAC, MG18, K9, vol.6, f.95–96.

21   François Bigot, *Mémoire Pour Messire François Bigot*, pp.38–39.

establishes that the distribution of supplies was closely monitored by military officials serving under Louis-Joseph de Montcalm, commander of the forces in North America during the Seven Years War. The passage below describes in detail the amounts and types of supplies issued to the troops serving in Canada during the conflict:

> We give to all those who are instructed to campaign, either officers, domestiques, regular or colonial soldiers, or militia and Natives (often these militiamen have only a portion and often nothing)...to each a capot of 5 aunes of Cadis or... molleton, 2 cotton shirts, a woollen blanket, an aune of molleton to make gaiters or mitasses, a wool bonnet, a breechcloth, and instead for the soldiers a pair of breeches, 2 skeins of threads, 6 needles, an awl, a fire steel, 6 gunflints, a gun worm, a comb, a gun case, a tumpline, a knife and, in addition, for winter campaigns, a sealskin pelt as much as possible to sleep with and one to shelter food, a pair of snowshoes, two pairs of deerskin moccasins, two pairs of slippers, two pairs of nippes, a hatchet, an oil cloth per four men, a kettle, a large axe and food for the number of fixed days, corn, bread or other food. The colonial soldiers have only one sol, for a day's wage, they are clothed every two years, and, besides the equipment, they receive each year a vest, breeches, a hat, two shirts, a pair of stockings, two pairs of shoes and a collar. In addition to the equipment above, the troops receive tents, pots, bowls, water cans and all the campaign equipment and useful tools. The officers also receive tents and campaign gear and a camp bedstead to sleep. Powder and balls are given as needed.[22]

Michel-Jean-Hugues Péan, a *capitaine* in the colonial regular troops and adjutant at Québec, reaffirms in his memoir that with the arrival of the Troupes de terre in 1755, the way in which war was waged in Canada drastically changed: 'It will be observed that until now, that is to say, up to the time of the last campaigns [the Seven Years War], war had been waged in Canada only in the Native style; the soldiers carried their bundles on their backs ... but when the European troops arrived, we changed our ways. We had to have tents, crews, rations... '[23]

---

22 RAPQ, 1933–1934, p.210.
23 *Mémoire pour Michel-Jean-Hugues Péan, chevalier, capitaine-aide-major des ville & gouvernement de Québec & des troupes détachées de la Marine, chevalier de l'Ordre royal & militaire de Saint-Louis, accusé, contre M. le Procureur-général du roi en la Commission, accusateur* (Paris : Imprimerie de Guillaume Desprez, 1763), p.100.

These arms once hung in Québec City, serving as powerful symbols of French sovereignty and empire. From 1725 onward, colonial officials displayed the Royal Arms on town gates and public buildings. Commissioned in 1727 by royal engineer Gaspard-Joseph Chaussegros de Léry and crafted by master sculptor Noël Levasseur, this painted wooden cartouche adorned one of the city gates of Québec until 1759. (Coat of Arms, CWM 19940024-001, Canadian War Museum)

Map of New France about 1750 overlaid on modern political boundaries (Creative Commons)

The Raid on Deerfiled, Massachusetts – In the pre–dawn hours of 29 February 1704, a force of about 300 French and Native allies led by the colonial officer Jean-Baptiste Hertel de Rouville, launched a surprise attack on Deerfield, Massachusetts. (Francis Back © Raphaëlle and Félix Back)

The march to Canada – The group of over 400 prisoners and attackers made a swift march toward the Saint Lawrence Valley, equipping captives with snowshoes and moccasins to aid their trek through the wilderness. (Francis Back © Raphaëlle and Félix Back)

Campaign Clothing of the Colonial Troops

Regulation Uniform

Essentially, regulation uniforms for troops posted in New France were supplied each year on an alternating basis. The practice of issuing the Grand Habillement (grand clothing) one year and the Petit Habillement (small dress) the following year had been the norm for quite some time and remained essentially the same over the course of several decades (see Volume 1). By the early eighteenth century, the basic European-issued regulation uniform of the Compagnies franches de la Marine consisted of the following:

- a long collarless single-breasted justaucorps uniform coat of grey-white cloth with a blue lining and facings
- a thigh-length long-sleeved waistcoat
- knee breeches
- a shirt
- a cravat
- a tricorn with braiding of false gold
- buckled shoes

A buff leather waist belt with a brass buckle was attached to a double frog, which held the sword and bayonet. A red-brown leather gargoussier cartridge box that held nine cartridges was attached to the waist belt, and a small brass-mounted powder-horn or leather-covered powder flask suspended from the shoulder by a strap, termed a fourniment, completed the equipment. When serving in forts and posts on the frontier, the basic daily working uniform was the small clothes which could vary depending on the regiment, social status, and specific military needs.

Campaign Clothing

During wilderness expeditions, the regulation justaucorps was replaced by a Canadian-style capot probably of brown or blue wool, or made from a point blanket or an old coat, and featuring an unlined, hooded design with a single shoulder button to cross the front flap over the chest. Capots for colonial troops were worn with regulation buff waistbelts, while officers wore fashionable sword belts. Some men may also have adopted Native-style finger-woven sashes when joining small war parties accompanying allied Native American warriors.

Besides their regulation vests, colonial soldiers often received a short waistcoat known as a gilet as part of the winter campaign supplies; this was likely worn as an undershirt and probably featured sleeves. Instead of their regulation hats, these soldiers wore red caps (bonnets) and opted for low-cut moccasins in the summer, while in winter they wore high-cut moccasins to accommodate snowshoes, prevent snow infiltration and better protect from the cold. Native-style breech-cloths (brayets) made from wool cloth were occasionally issued to both officers and soldiers of the colonial troops for summer and winter campaigns. However, by 1755, evidence suggests that soldiers may have preferred their regulation breeches, as the newly arrived soldiers of the Troupes de terre, unfamiliar with breechcloths, would have viewed them as unconventional or undignified. Alongside stockings and breeches, Native American gaiters, or mitasses, often recorded in blue molleton fabric in records, were used by soldiers in the field. They not only protected the legs from bushes, thorns, and insects but also provided warmth during the colder months. These tubular leggings were held up using strips of fabric or, more commonly, with Native finger-woven garters tied below the knee.

The Capot: A Standard Issued Garment of the Wilderness Dress

From the very beginnings of the colony there was a need to adequately dress soldiers for winter campaigns and standing guard in freezing weather. This sometimes required the authorities to provide additional clothing to compensate for uniforms ill-suited for Canada's climate. Colonial records reveal that colonial soldiers and officers quickly adopted capots and wore them on top of, or instead of, their regulation justaucorps. By the 1740s, capots were contracted out and dispensed through the King's storehouses for the colonial troops. Capots were mostly made of woollen cloth termed Cadis, Mazamet, and occasionally Dourgne and molleton, while some accounts mention the use of blankets or salvaged wool fabric from regulation uniforms. Although these relatively well-tailored over-coats came in a myriad of variations (short, long, hooded or without a hood), most of these were made with hoods although by the mid-eighteenth century, some were made with collars. A late seventeenth-century engraving shows a Canadian militiaman in snowshoes wearing a capot having mariners cuffs, a style of cuffs which was described on the capots worn by the French fighting forces at Haverhill in 1708 described as tight-fitting sleeves, '…and closed like those of a veste…'[1] The Troupes de terre, which arrived in 1755, probably had capots made with cuffs that matched their regimental facing colours whereas no currently known record indicates that this was also the case with the colonial troops.[2]

Origin and Definition of the Canadian Capot

Originally, the capot was a long coat with a hood that French sailors wore in harsh maritime conditions. The word capot comes from the Latin word caput (head), referring to clothing that covered the head, and this mari-ner's overcoat was designed like a large cape with sleeves and a hood. The first settlers in New France adapted this convenient but crude-looking garment into one that was more fitted and elegant.[3] After taking part in a mili-tary campaign against the Iroquois in 1666, René-Louis Chartier de Lotbinière noted that the blue capots worn by Canadians 'are made like justaucorps at the top of which there are hoods in which they place their heads to protect them from the wind.'[4] According to the Mercure Galant for November 1708, 'The ordinary dress of the Canadians is a type of hooded coat which overlaps at the front in the way of a buff leather justaucorps, the sleeves are tight-fit-ting and closed like those of a veste.'[5] A few years later, the Jesuit missionary Lafiteau remarked that the coats look like 'a French-style justaucorps.'[6]

During the Seven Years War, the young lieutenant Jean-Baptiste d'Aleyrac, who served in the Régiment de Languedoc, provided a detailed description of this garment, which may have had either a collar or a hood: 'The ordinary Canadian does not wear clothing made in the French-style, but rather capots that are a type of waist-coat with cuffs, which overlaps at the front, the collar and buttons are of another colour; these are always fastened around the waist. This type of dress is plain and very convenient.'[7] An equipment list dated to 1756 indicates that the capots issued as part of the summer equipment for the troops serving in New France had hoods, as they are described as resembling a 'volant with a hood,'[8] a volant being a type of waistcoat without cuffs or pockets worn overtop the justaucorps.[9] A memoir written by the Chevalier Péan described the capot as 'a type of unlined and pocketless surtout (frock coat) which the Canadians and sometimes the Natives wear.'[10]

A few years after the conquest of New France, Pierre Droz, a Swiss watchmaker who travelled to Canada, observed that 'the men in the villages and in the country wear a short capot that they close over with a sash. There is at the neck area, a hood, that they wear, or let hang, according to the cold they feel.'[11] Francis Back's Le capot canadien: ses origines et son évolution aux XVII et XVIIIe siècles and René Chartrand's The Winter Costume of Soldiers in Canada remain the most comprehensive studies on the subject.[12]

Soldier's Capots

Historic accounts reveal that capots were issued to the armed forces prior to wilderness campaigns throughout much of the French period in Canada. As early as 1665, French soldiers of the Carignan-Salières regiment were provided with moccasins, chaussons (slippers), mittens,[13] and probably capots since Capitaine François de Tapie de Monteil received them for his company that year prior to an upcoming military campaign against the Iroquois.[14] Before embarking on an expedition against the English on Hudson's Bay in 1686, each of the 31 colonial soldiers under the command of the Chevalier de Troyes received '1 capot of blue woollen cloth, trimmed in lace.'[15]

For a short period during the 1690s, capots replaced the regulation issued justaucorps for the whole of the colonial

1   Le mercure galant (Paris: Chez Michel Brunet, 1709), p.56.
2   BAnQ-QQ, TL5, D1960, Procès criminel contre Jonas Mathé (Matey) dit Tranquille, 31 ans, natif de Neufchâtel en Suisse, soldat du régiment de la Reine, compagnie de D'Asserat, accusé de vol avec effraction chez Marie-Françoise Sédillot, veuve de Charles Maufait (Mauffet), demeurant au faubourg Saint-Jean à Québec, 24 février–13 mars 1758.
3   Back, 'S'habiller à la canadienne', pp.38–41; Francis Back, 'Le capot canadien, origines et évolution aux XVII et XVIIIe siècles', Canadian Folklore/Folklore canadien, vol.10, no.2 (1988), pp.99–128.
4   BAnQ-Q, P1000, S3, D374, Poème sur le gouverneur de Courcelles par René-Louis Chartier de Lotbinière, p.5.
5   Le mercure galant (Paris: Michel Brunet, 1709), p.56.
6   Jean-François Lafiteau, Moeurs des Sauvages Amériquains…, tome 2 (Paris: Chez la Veuve Desaint, 1724), p.31.
7   BAnQ-M, ZF8, Fonds Jean Baptiste d'Aleyrac.
8   SHAT, Dossier A1, 3417, Pièce 144.
9   François A. de Garsault, Art du tailleur (Paris: Chez Saillant & Nyon, 1769), pp.9, 19.
10   Michel-Jean-Hugues Péan, Mémoire pour Michel-Jean-Hugues Péan, Chevalier, Capitaine Aide-Major des Ville & Gouvernement de Québec, accusé, contre M. le Procureur Général du Roi, accu-sateur (Paris: Guillaume Desprez, 1763).
11   Pierre Droz, L'aventurier Suisse ou les voyages surprenans de Pierre Droz (Amsterdam : 1786), p.135.
12   Back, 'Le capot canadien: ses origines et son évolution', pp.99–127.
13   RAPQ, 1930-1931, p.107.
14   R. Le Blant, 'Le Livre de raison de François de Tapie de Monteil, capitaine au régiment de Poitou (1661–1670) (suite)', Revue d'his-toire de l'Amérique française, 14 (1960), p.109.
15   LAC, MG1-C11A, vol.8, f.278v.

A detachment of colonial soldiers wearing their wilderness campaign attire, led by a Canadian officer. (Francis Back © Raphaëlle and Félix Back)

troops serving in Acadia and Canada. Perhaps as a cost-saving measure to address the significant expense of providing colonial soldiers with new regulation clothing every two years, the King announced in a letter dated 7 April 1692, that soldiers' clothing would henceforth be made and sent in the style of the coureurs de bois, following a specific model.[16] The following year, a number of these garments were sent to Acadia to dress the troops: '40 complete outfits, while observing that these items of clothing are in the Canadian-style [à la Canadienne], and whose officers who are at Rochefort, will provide the model.'[17] In a letter addressed to Intendant Bégon at Rochefort that same year, an official at Versailles requested '90 capotes' along with mittens, blankets, and powder horns for 50 soldiers that were to return from the Boston Prison.[18] Two years later, the soldiers of the Compagnies franches de la Marine stationed in Canada would receive 900 items of clothing each consisting, among other items, of a capot made of greyish-white Romorantin twill trimmed with blue Aumale serge and with cuffs and buttons.[19] However, a statement of clothing for Canada dating to 1696 reveals a shift back to regulation European-style clothing, where the capot is replaced by a greyish-white justaucorps lined with blue Cadis.[20]

In Acadia, this garment was supplied until 1701, since a memoir informs us that 'For the soldier's clothing, a ready-made justaucorps and breeches along with the rest, as usual. The Canadian-style capot is no longer necessary here.'[21] Military authorities appear to have reverted to the former practice of maintaining a metropolitan-style uniform, no doubt more becoming for soldiers, that would be supplemented, if necessary, by Canadian-style clothing issued before leaving for a campaign. Consequently, we may speculate that the regulation uniform clearly distinguished the soldier from the private citizen and helped establish a strong social identity among soldiers. This regulation outerwear helped to create an esprit du corps and was part of a push to instil discipline in soldiers.

Between 1715 and 1717, capots, breechcloths, and leggings were supplied to the men participating in the Fox War,[22] whereas during the Chickasaw campaign of 1739, 12 capots were intended for the reserve corps, to be traded to buy food, to wage war, or other party needs.[23] In 1749, a large detachment of men sent to the Saint-Jean River, which included colonial soldiers and officers, were provided with a few dozen capots.[24]

Other instances of on-duty soldiers wearing capots in garrison towns may have included occasions where their regulation clothing had not arrived. For example, in October of 1749, Intendant Bigot had a number of capots made locally in Canada for newly recruited soldiers since 'no clothing was sent this year for the new recruits, which were in great numbers, so that most of them are reduced to a single veste.'[25] Three years later, the equipment intended to outfit a very large military expedition headed to La Belle-Rivière (Ohio) totalling 2,200 colonial troops, militiamen, and Native American allies, included capots.[26]

During the Seven Years War, capots were distributed to both colonial and metropolitan troops before departing on summer and winter wilderness campaigns. In 1755, a general statement of what was needed for the French regular battalions under the command of maréchal de camp Dieskau included 3,577 capots that were requested by Intendant Bigot and which were to be drawn from the King's storehouses at Québec. This suggests that they were made in the colony rather than in France.[27] Capitaine Pouchot of the regiment de Béarn remarked that whenever Canadian troops went on campaign that 'they were provided with…a capot,'[28] whereas a report written in July of 1756 at Fort Carillon by capitaine François Frédéric Leduchat of the Régiment de Languedoc specified that one capot was provided to each officer, soldier, and domestique of the regular and colonial troops for each campaign.[29] This is repeated in an account of goods that were to be issued to soldiers of the Troupes de terre battalions, as well as those of the colony anticipated for each month of the campaign of 1757.[30] That March, a soldier at Fort William-Henry reported that both colonial and regular soldiers were issued hooded capots: 'Each man had … one watch coat or Great coat with a cap [hood]…'[31] Additionally, a letter published in the Boston Gazette declared that every man in the French army attacking Fort William-Henry was equipped with, among other items, '1 large overcoat,' which certainly points to a capot.[32] At Fort Carillon, '152 capots, for

16 RAPQ, 1927–1928, p.86.
17 LAC, MG1-B, vol.16, f.139.
18 LAC, MG1-B, vol.16, f.6 (74).
19 LAC, F1A, vol.8, f.207.
20 AR, 1E, Liasse 599, 19 mars, 1696.
21 LAC, F1A, vol.10, f.1/80, 1701.
22 LAC, MG1-C11A, vol.38, f.161–164.
23 LAC, MG1-C11A, vol.71, f.165.

24 LAC, MG1-C11A, vol.119, f.9.
25 LAC, MG1-C11A, vol.93, f.316.
26 LAC, MG1-C11A, vol.98, f.276.
27 LAC, MG1-C11A, vol.100, f.263v.
28 Pierre Pouchot, Mémoires sur la dernière guerre de l'Amérique septentrionale entre la France et l'Angleterre (Québec: Les éditions du Septentrion, 2003), p.28.
29 AG, MG 4, B 1, série A1, vol.3417, f.383.
30 Centre d'histoire La Presqu'île, P03/F.089, Fonds De Beaujeu, 28 novembre 1756.
31 LOC, Colonial Office 5 folio 47, E. of Loudoun's Letter of April 25th. 1757, Declaration of two Prisoners taken the 23.d March 1757 at Fort Wm. Henry, Information of John Victor and Guillaume Chasse, two French Prisoners, Fort William Henry March 25th.
32 Boston Gazette, 'From a Letter Dated March 26th, 1757: 'Every Man in the French Army That Came Against Fort William

A soldier on guard duty wearing a watchman's capot, while another soldier, seen on the right wearing small-clothes and wooden clogs, performs fatigue duty. (Francis Back © Raphaëlle and Félix Back)

men' as well as '6 ditto, old' were inventoried in 1757, indicating that capots were stockpiled at military outposts for outfitting troops on campaign and in garrison.[33]

Officer's Capots

Firsthand accounts highlight the adoption of capots by officers during frontier raids, demonstrating their popularity and practicality in combat situations. While fighting in the battle of Grand Pré, for instance, Louis Liénard de Beaujeu de Villemonde commented that 'they immediately fired three or four shots at me which only passed through my capot.'[34] Ten years later, colonial officer Thomas-Philippe Dagneau de La Saussaye was wearing a capot when ambushed by a party of Catawbas on his

---

Henry, Was Equipped in the Following Manner, viz. … 1 Large Overcoat.'

33   LAC, MG18, K9, vol.6, f.458.

34   Joseph Gagné, 'Fidèle à Dieu, à la France, et au Roi' Les retraites militaires de La Chapelle et de Beaujeu vers la Louisiane après la perte du Canada 1760-1762 (Master's thesis, Université Laval, 2014), p.47.

return to Montréal from Fort Cumberland. A voyageur from Montréal testified that 'he thought he could distinguish and recognise Sieur de La Saussaye by his long, blond hair, by his capot, (that was next to him, all tore up, his body lying naked).'[35]

Furthermore, capots worn by colonial officers and NCOs may have been adorned with false gold or silver braiding, which would have denoted rank in the French military hierarchy. In 1747, a post-mortem inventory of goods belonging to *sergent* Dubois at Québec included 'an old capot of Mazamet with a very old gold braid plate,' which may have represented his military service capot rather than his personal one.[36] A few years later, 'an old capot of Cadis with a thin silver braid edge' was found in the personal possession of officer Louis D'Amour, Sieur de Louvière, at Montréal,[37] while four years earlier a detachment of soldiers sent to the Saint-Jean River was provided with '60 plain capots' as well as '10 braided capots,' the latter probably being intended for the officers.[38]

Ordonnance Capots

Several sources dated to the 1750s use the term capot d'ordonnance as part of on-duty outerwear worn by colonial soldiers standing guard at Fort Duquesne and Fort le Bœuf.[39] With regards to clothing, the *Dictionnaire universel* defines the term ordonnance as such: 'We call habit d'ordonnance, the uniform clothing that officers and soldiers are required to have in each regiment, or in a certain company of the regiment.'[40] In other words,

these particular capots may have been a standardised and distinctive dress worn by colonial soldiers standing guard at certain frontier forts. In 1754, for instance, Michel Marchand dit Deslauriers, a colonial soldier stationed at Fort Duquesne, was seen 'standing guard wearing an ordonnance capot,'[41] while a witness observed that the soldier Rousselière dit Sanscartier at Fort le Bœuf was 'standing guard in his ordonnance capot.'[42] We may wonder if the term capot d'ordonnance employed by colonial authorities did not, in fact, represent a sentry's capot (capot de sentinelle), a large watch coat often made of greyish or white Lodève cloth. These will be discussed later.

Probate Records: Soldiers and Officers' Personal Capots
Civilian-style capots were certainly worn by both colonial soldiers and officers in off-duty situations, since they are often included as part of their personal belongings. In 1688, Jacques Frémont dit Laverdure, a colonial soldier in garrison at Sorel, had set aside his capot as payment for a debt he owed,[43] while in 1703, *capitaine* De Joibert was the owner of an 'old capot of ratine, coffee [colour].'[44] Some two years later, *lieutenant* Antoine de Planiol of Saint-François was the owner of 'an old capot, patched up.'[45] In 1707, '2 capots, one old and one half-new' belonged to Delisle, a married soldier at Fort Pontchartrain.[46] Six years later, Monsieur de Rané, an officer at Montréal, paid a large sum of money for a rather fine tailored capot equipped with pockets made using 7 *aunes* of fine woollen cloth ⅓ in width, ½ *aune* of grey Coutil fabric at 3 livres 5 sols to make pockets.[47] Considering the quantity of cloth,

35 BAnQ-M, TL4, S1, D6300, Sollicitation de Marie-Anne De Verchères pour obtenir confirmation du décès de son mari, Thomas-Philippe Dagneau de LaSaussaye, officier, 18 avril 1760.

36 BAnQ-Q, Greffe du notaire Claude Barolet, Vente en inventaire des biens de C. Dubois, décembre 1747.

37 BAnQ-M, Greffe du notaire Pierre Panet. No 5, Inventaire et vente des meubles de la communauté des biens entre feu Louis D'Amour, Sieur de Louvrière et Geneviève Catalogne, Montréal, 27 février, 1755. 7

38 LAC, MG1-C11A, vol.119, f.9.

39 BAnQ-M, TL4, S1, D5667, Procès devant le Conseil de guerre contre François Boirond dit St-François, Caporal de la compagnie de Croizille, Henri Davoud dit Lasonde, soldat de la Compagnie Croizille, chirurgien, et Pierre Beauvais dit Léveillé, soldat, accusés de désertion, 10 janvier–1 février 1752.; BAnQ-M, TL4,S1, D5877, Procès devant le Conseil de guerre contre Michel Marchand dit Deslauriers, Pierre Gressignolet dit Breton, et Étienne Darny dit Bellehumeur, tous soldats du Fort Dusquesne, accusés de désertion, 17 avril–4 juin 1754.; BAnQ-M, TL4, S1, D5904, Procès devant le Conseil de guerre contre François Lissot dit Fleury, tambour de la Compagnie de Herbin, accusé de désertion, 23 juillet–31 juillet 1754.; BAnQ-M, TL4, S1, D5894, Procès devant le Conseil de guerre contre Rousselière dit Sanscartier, soldat de la Compagnie de Lamartinière, accusé de désertion, 5 juin–17 juin 1754.

40 *Dictionnaire universel françois et latin* (Paris: la Compagnie des libraires associés, 1752), vol.5, p.199.

41 BAnQ-M, TL4, S1, D5877, Procès devant le Conseil de guerre contre Michel Marchand dit Deslauriers, Pierre Gressignolet dit Breton, et Étienne Darny dit Bellehumeur, tous soldats du Fort Dusquesne, accusés de désertion, 17 avril–4 juin 1754.

42 BAnQ-M, TL4, S1, D5894, Procès devant le Conseil de guerre contre Rousselière dit Sanscartier, soldat de la Compagnie de Lamartinière, accusé de désertion, 5–17 juin 1754.

43 BAnQ-M, Baillage de Montréal, 11572, 39, Interrogatoire de Jacques Frémont dit Laverdure, soldat de la Cie du Sr de Mines en garnison à Saurel, 21 ans, menuisier de son métier, 25 juin 1688.

44 BAnQ-Q, Greffe du notaire Louis Chamballon, inventaire des biens de feu M. Jacques de Joibert, chevalier, seigneur de Soulanges, enseigne sur les vaisseaux du Roi et capitaine d'une compagnie franche des troupes du détachement de la marine, 2 mai, 1703.

45 BAnQ-TR, Greffe du notaire Jean-Baptiste Pottier, … à la requête de damoiselle Charlotte Giguière, veuve de défunt le Sieur Antoine de Plagnyol, écuyer lieutenant d'une compagnie de détachement de la marine vivant demeurant en la seigneurie de Saint-François près du lac Saint-Pierre, 2 mai 1705.

46 Timothy J. Kent, *Ft. Pontchartrain at Detroit: A Guide to the Daily Lives of Fur Trade and Military Personnel, Settlers, and Missionaries at French Posts* (Ossineke, Mich: Silver Fox Enterprises, 2001), vol.2, p.1043.

47 BAnQ-M, Greffe du notaire M. Lepailleur, Monsieur de Rané (Rassé), officier des troupes doit à Soummande, marchand de Montréal, 29 août 1713.

this coat must have been lined using the same fabric, and we may presume that the pockets were placed on the skirt of the coat as on a justaucorps. In 1714, Montréal notary Lepailleur took note of 'an awful capot, all torn up of no value' as part of the personal belongings of Sieur de La Moillerie, an ensign in the colonial troops.[48] Prior to his departure to the Baie-des-Puants post (Green Bay, Wisconsin) in 1739, officer Joseph Marin de La Malgue purchased a 'capot de voyage (travel capot) from the merchant Monière.[49]

It is unclear if the capots in the possession of soldiers stationed at frontier forts were standard campaign-issued garments or if they were personally acquired, repurposed, or locally made. For example, the clothing belonging to *sergent* Jacques Bonin dit Laforet, who was accused of robbery at Chambly, included 'an old capot of Mazamet [fabric],'[50] while 'an old blue capot of molleton' was found in a wooden case belonging to St-Léger, a grenadier of the Régiment de la Sarre at Fort St-Jean in 1758.[51] That same year, a 'pair of breeches and a capot' were found in the prison cell at Fort Carillon that held Jean-Baptiste Gadoux dit Sansfaçon of the Régiment de Béarn.[52]

Manufacturing Sources of Capots for the Colonial Troops

Besides a few shipments of 'Canadian-style' capots from the mother country in the 1690s and some cloth requested for Acadia to make capots for soldiers in 1692,[53] it would seem the majority of capots intended for colonial troops and militiamen serving in Canada were contracted out and issued through the King's storehouses. Military-issued capots were made by the King's tailor and colonial seamstresses around Montréal. In times of haste, the Sœurs-Grises (Grey Nuns) of the Hôpital-Général were called on

to make capots for the Magasin royal.[54] Military sewing contracts were seemingly based on a specific price list, termed tarif in French, which was managed by the storekeeper appointed by the King in Canada. The term storekeeper (garde-magasin) refers to the individual responsible for overseeing and managing the storage and inventory of goods in a warehouse or store.[55] For instance, this contract was granted to the Montréal storekeeper Jean-Baptiste Martel by Jean-Victor Varin, commissary and controller of the Marine, 'since the King's Tailor could not supply all of the capots that were to be made for the soldiers and militiamen.'[56] Varin noted that the sewing jobs included 'capots and mantelets with which the soldiers and militiamen were equipped,'[57] while according to a memoir written by Martel, he and his wife were responsible for all the King's sewing contracts, which included capots:

> The King's storekeeper in Montréal had always been responsible for having sewing work done, and was paid for it, like a contractor, at the rate set by Monsieur Hocquart; a rate, as I have previously noted, that I had reduced in 1745 by Monsieur de Villebois, commissaire-ordonnateur. My wife arranged for part of this work to be done at our home by local workers, whom she paid slightly above the rate allocated to me, except for certain items for which we employed the Sœurs de l'Hôpital when the work was urgent, and they were paid according to the same rate...[58]

Surviving statements of expenditures incurred during 1745, however, show that capots were made for the King's storehouses by seamstresses and tailors working out of both Montréal and Québec. For example, a seamstress in Québec named Marianne Metivier was paid 30 sols for each plain capot (capot uni) she had made and 3 livres for braided ones (capot galonné),[59] and a tailor in Montréal named François Picard was paid 3 livres 10 sols per braided capot.[60] Some capots supplied by the munitionnaire

48 BAnQ-M, Greffe du notaire M. Lepailleur, Inventaire des effets de feu Louis Mallerais, écuyer, Sieur de La Moillerie, enseigne en pied dans les troupes, blessé d'un coup d'épée en travers le corps par les Sieur d'Argenteuil, 20 décembre 1714.

49 BAnQ-M, 06, M-P 218, Jean-Alexis Lemoine-Monière, Livres de comptes du 27 juin 1739 au 8 janvier 1751, Film M 641.1,14 août 1739.

50 BAnQ-M, TL4, S1, D1864, Procès contre Jacques Bonin dit Laforet, sergent de la compagnie d'Esgly, accusé de vol d'argent chez le trésorier de la marine à Québec, 19 février–19 mai 1716.

51 BAnQ-M, TL4, S1, D6208, Procès contre Laurent Croze dit Provençal, boulanger du fort St-Jean, Jean Cailla dit Petitjean, boulanger au fort St-Jean, Jean-Baptiste Quercy, habitant de St-Jean, Jacques-Frédéric Raymon dit Bonvivant surnommé Lesuisse, caporal, Joseph Gaillard dit Sansfaçon surnommé Mandrin, soldat de Raymond, et Pierre-Joseph Cheval, boulanger, accusés de vol dans le magasin du roi du fort St-Jean, 5 février–31 mai 1758.

52 BAnQ-M, TL4, S1, D6241, Procès contre Jean-Baptiste Gadoux dit Sansfaçon, soldat de la Compagnie de Vassal, au camp Carillon, et Armand Janot dit Laréole, demeurant au fort Carillon, accusés de vol de porcelaines, 18 novembre 1758–20 janvier 1759.

53 LAC, MG1-B, vol.16, f.74.

54 LAC, MG 18, h 45, Mémoire pour le Sieur Jean-Baptiste Martel. Garde-magasin à Montréal, Canada (Grand et Lacharest, 1764), Provenant des papiers de M. Léopold de Martel de Saint-Antoine, descendant de Jean-Baptiste Martel, demeurant à La Roche Martel, à Louestault, près de Tours.

55 Journal de jurisprudence: dédié à son Altesse sérénissime électorale palatine, Juin 1763 (Bouillon: De l'Imprimerie du Journal, 1763), p.121.

56 Jean-Baptiste Martel, *Mémoire du Sieur Martel dans l'affaire du Canada* (Paris: f.Cellot, 1763), pp.45–46.

57 Anon., *À Monseigneur de Sartine, lieutenant-général de police, Et à Nosseigneurs les gens tenant le Châtelet de Paris, commissaires du Conseil en cette partie* (Paris: De l'imprimerie Moreau, 1763), p.17.

58 Jean-Baptiste Martel, *Mémoire pour Jean-Baptiste Martel, ecuyer, ci-devant Garde des Magasins du roy à Montréal. Commission du conseil pour les affaires du Canada* (Paris: De l'Imprimerie Knapen 1763), p.25.

59 LAC, MG1-C11A, vol.115, f.159.

60 LAC, MG1-C11A, vol.115, f.163.

(purveyor general to the French forces in Canada) during the Seven Years War were apparently made too short, too small, or made of inferior cloth, based on the observations made by Louis-Antoine de Bougainville.[61] Some capots were apparently made onsite at forts, as revealed in a 1746 list of goods delivered to the store clerk at Fort St-Frédéric, likely intended as winter supplies for the posted soldiers. The inventory included 165 *aunes* of Dourgne fabric, two gross and six dozen buttons (360), and 2 *livres* of thread from Rennes to make 30 capots, indicating that each capot had 12 buttons.[62]

Fabrics (Cadis, Mazamet and Molleton)

By the 1740s, an average of 5 to 6 *aunes* of cloth was needed to make a man's size capot, with Cadis and Mazamet emerging as the most popular types of woollen fabrics used for the military forces in Canada. In 1740, for instance, M. de Sabrevois, commander of a detachment fighting in the 1739 Chickasaw campaign, was given '5½ *aunes* of Mazamet, as a capot.'[63] A few years later, the Sieur Portneuf, cadet in the colonial troops, was provided with '5½ *aunes* of Cadis' to replace his capot 'which he wore out during the campaigns in which he served for the King's service.'[64] Additionally, a 1747 list of food and equipment issued to Monsieur de La Chauvignery and two Frenchmen for martial purposes included '16½ of Cadis, 4 *onces* of Rennes thread, for making 3 capots.'[65] That same year, two cadets participating in war parties were forced to exchange their capots with Native Americans, which were replaced with '12 aunes of Cadis, in making two capots with hoods.'[66] A portion of the supplies provided to a war party at Fort St-Frédéric in 1747, which was composed of militiamen, Native American warriors, and colonial regulars, included '3 capots from 16½ *aunes* of Mazamet.'[67]

During the Seven Years War, capots made of Cadis, Mazamet, and occasionally molleton were distributed to both colonial and metropolitan troops before their departure on campaigns. In 1755, the officer Anne-Joseph-Hippolyte de Maurès de Malartic noted that the equipment distributed to each officer and soldier of the Régiment de Béarn serving in Canada consisted of 'one capot of Cadis,'[68] while *capitaine* Jean-Guillaume Plantavit de La Pause de Margon of the Régiment de Guyenne mentioned

Missionary priest Father Claude Chauchetière illustrated what are likely two French voyageurs in 1686 near Montréal, wearing capots with mariner's cuffs, as opposed to the long 'boot cuffs' seen on justaucorps. (Claude Chauchetière, *Les Sauvages Vont S'établir à la Prairie de la Magdeleine avec le François*, Manuscript, p.23)

that each fighting man was issued 'a capot of 5 *aunes* of Cadis or molleton.'[69] Intendant Bigot noted that the winter campaign equipment for the colonial troops and Canadian militia consisted of '1 capot of Cadis' for the officers and capots made of Mazamet for soldiers, militiamen, domestiques, and Natives.[70]

According to Guillaume Estèbe, storekeeper at Québec (1740–1753), the garments made of woollen cloth issued to the colonial troops in Canada were made using Cadis de montagne, whereas the Native Americans were given Cadis d'Aignan:

> The King supplies to his troops and to the Natives onsite, two types of cloth known as Cadis d'Ourgue (Dourgne) or de Montagne and Cadis drapé or d'Agnian (d'Aignan). The latter, which is thinner, is worth, for example, 8 livres per aune and is given to the Natives that we wish to be bound to France; it is also used for the regular clothing in the colony. The first type [Cadis Dourgne or de Montagne], which is thicker, is worth 4 livres the *aune* and serves for our troops.'[71]

Savary des Brûlons describes Cadis as 'a type of light-weight twilled woollen cloth, which is nothing more than

61   Louis-Antoine Bougainville, *Écrits sur le Canada: mémoires-journal-lettres* (Sillery, Québec: Les éditions du Septentrion, 2003), pp.297–298.
62   LAC, MG1-C11A, vol.88, f.216v.
63   LAC, MG1-C11A, vol.72, f.201.
64   LAC, MG1-C11A, vol 86, f.213v.
65   LAC. MG1-C11A, vol.117, f.196–196v.
66   LAC, MG1-C11A, vol.117, f.216.
67   LAC, MG1-C11A, vol.117, f.26v.
68   Gabriel de Maurès de Malartic, Paul Gaffarel (eds), *Journal des Campagnes au Canada de 1756 à 1760 par le comte de Maurès de Malartic* (Dijon: L. Damidot, 1890), p.13.

69   RAPQ, 1933–34, pp.210, 225.
70   Bigot, *Mémoire Pour Messire François Bigot*, pp.39–40.
71   Martel, *Mémoire du Sieur Martel*, p.24.

An engraving depicting a Canadian militiaman from around 1690, wearing a capot fastened by a sash at the waist. The sleeves feature simple mariner's cuffs instead of large cuffs, a more practical design for canoe travel. The illustrator did not include a hood, although its presence is well-documented in period sources. (Claude-Charles Le Roy Bacqueville de La Potherie, *Histoire de l'Amérique Septentrionale*, 1722. Canadiens en raquette allant en guerre sur la neige, Creative Commons)

a very narrow and light sergette, which has only two *pans* in width, measure of Languedoc, which amounts to half an *aune* less a twelfth [*aunes*], Parisian measure. Cadis pieces usually had 30 to 31 *aunes* in length, also following Parisian measure.'[72]

The type of woollen fabric known as Mazamet was produced in Mazamet, France, and was referred to as Cordelats in the mother country. Each piece measured 30 *aunes* in length and was made using local wool for the use 'of the country and of the French colonies.'[73] Once fulled, the pieces measured half an *aune* and one twelfth in width.[74] According to the *Dictionnaire universel de commerce*, four thousand pieces of Cordelats were produced yearly in white and brown (muse).[75]

Capots Made from Munition Coats or Cloth

Several sources dealing with militiamen and civilians mention 'munition capots,' or capots made using munition cloth or fabric. According to the 1740 edition of the *Dictionnaire de l'Académie Françoise*, the word munition refers to 'materials of war necessary in an army or in a stronghold.'[76] Hence, we may assume that these coats were made using either old soldier's regulation justaucorps or regulation cloth and may represent a form of standardized or homogeneous capot in use among the fighting forces

72 Jacques Savary des Brûlons, *Dictionnaire universel de commerce, tome premier, A-E* (Paris: Jacques Estienne, 1723), p.514.

73 Jacques Peuchet, *Dictionnaire universel de la géographie commerçante...* , (Paris: Blanchon, 1799), p.750.

74 Jacques Savary des Brûlons, *Dictionnaire portatif de commerce, contenant la connoissance des marchandises de tous les païs, etc,* (Copenhague: Chez les Frères C. & A. Philibert, 1761), vol.2, p.469.

75 Jacques Savary des Brûlons, *Dictionnaire universel de commerce: Commerce & compagnies* (Genève: Chez les Frères Cramer & Claude Philibert, 1750), p.268.

76 *Dictionnaire de l'Académie Françoise, Tome second, L-Z* (Paris: Chez Jean-Baptiste Coignard, 1740), p.169.

in Canada. In 1703, 'two old awful capots d'amonition [de munition], worn out and patched up' were found in the personal belongings of Jacques Moliés, a mason living at Québec.[77] Ten years later, Jacques Lhuissier, a colonist living in Varennes, was the owner of a 'munition capot.'[78] In 1747, another 'old munition capot' was found among the belongings of Joseph Dagenest, a Habitant of Côte Saint-Michel,[79] which may suggest that this type of capot may have been issued to some militiamen during the War of the Spanish Succession (1701–1714) and King George's War (1744–1748). During the Seven Years War, militiamen who were called to campaign received capots,[80] some of which were apparently made using ordonnance woollen fabric, such as the 'capot of munition cloth' valued at 4 livres owned by Jean-Baptiste Lesieur dit Desaunier of Yamachiche in 1756,[81] or the 'capot of munition fabric' valued at 10 livres, which was found some two years later at the home of Charles Lebeau at Chambly.[82]

It is interesting to point out that civilian capots were sometimes made using salvaged soldiers' uniform coats. A woman living in Montréal in the early 1690s had a number of soldiers' clothing items, including 'the justau-corps belonging to Beauvais and Jean-Guy that she disas-sembled to make a capot.'[83] In addition, her husband acquired 'a uniform belonging to M. Godefroy as well as a justaucorps from a soldier' that he made use of by 'selling one to a sauvage [Native American] and making a capot for himself with the other.'[84] The only known refer-ence to a capot made from a soldier's uniform which has been found thus far, dates to 1752, when Henri Davoud dit Lasonde, a colonial soldier and deserter from the Fort Sandusky garrison, declared that he only had with him 'a capot made from an old munition coat.'[85]

Blanket Capots

Colonial soldiers and officers also used capots de couverte made from wool blankets, a thicker and warmer fabric well suited to Canada's cold winters. Primary docu-ments indicate that the first blanket coats were primarily intended for the fur trade and thereafter adopted by the coureurs de bois before spreading among the Canadian population during the last quarter of the eighteenth century. A memoir allegedly written by Antoine-Denis Raudot around 1705 describing the way Canadians trav-elled in wintertime, mentioned that they were 'wrapped in their blankets which serves them as bedding at night, and during the days, as a surtout (overcoat),' which may point to an early use of blanket coats in Canada.[86]

In fact, historic probate records indicate that the popu-larity of these coats may have spread to Canada from the Illinois Territory, since references to them frequently turn up around Kaskaskia in the late 1740s,[87] but only begin to appear in post-mortem inventories at Montréal, Trois-Rivières, and Québec in the late 1750s. We may presume that the capots de couverte were made using wool blan-kets, especially those termed couvertes à points (point blankets), such as the '1 capot de 1 couverte en 3 points' sold by the merchant Monière in 1744.[88] These blankets will be explored further in Chapter 2. While blanket coats were traded as early as 1746 by both the French and British,[89] in 1747, the colonial soldier Jean-Baptiste Leroy, stationed at Montréal, remarked that he and a fellow soldier 'laid a buffalo pelt with a blanket capot and their uniforms beneath them to sleep on.'[90] Five years later, Jean-Bernard Bossu, an officer of the Compagnies franches de la Marine, described his capot as being 'made from a wool

77 BAnQ-Q, Greffe du notaire Louis Chamballon, Inventaire des biens de Jacques Moliers, maçon habitant cette ville (Québec) et de feu Margueritte Quevillon sa femme, 4 et 5 juin 1703.

78 BAnQ-M, Greffe A. Adhémard, 16 mars, 1713.

79 BAnQ-M, Greffe G. Hodiesne, Inventaire des biens de Joseph Dagenest, 15 janvier, 1747.

80 De Malartic & Gaffarel (eds), *Journal des Campagnes au Canada*, p.39.

81 BAnQ-TR, Greffe J. Leproust, Inventaire des biens de la commu-nauté de Marguerite Lamy, veuve de Jean-Baptiste Lesieur dit Desonier, de Yamachiche, 21 juillet, 1756.

82 BAnQ-M, Greffe du notaire Antoine Grisé, Inventaire du défunt Charles Lebeau, habitant de Chambly… , 25 février 1758.

83 BAnQ-M, Baillage de Montréal, 11576, 22, Interrogatoire de Marie Moitié, 41 ans, femme de Jean Magnan dit L'espérance, cabaretier, accusée de recel…, 15 avril 1692.

84 BAnQ-M, Baillage de Montréal, 11576, 22, Interrogatoire de Marie Moitié, 41 ans, femme de Jean Magnan dit L'espérance, cabaretier, accusée de recel…, 15 avril 1692.

85 BAnQ-M, TL4, S1, D5667, Procès devant le Conseil de guerre contre François Boirond dit St-François, Caporal de la compagnie de Croizille, Henri Davoud dit Lasonde, soldat de la Compagnie Croizille, chirurgien, et Pierre Beauvais dit Léveillé, soldat, accusés de désertion, 10 janvier–1 février 1752.

86 LAC, MG1-C11A, vol.122, f.155–155v.

87 Kaskaskia Manuscripts (Randolph County Courthouse, Chester, Illinois), Inventaire à la requête d'Antoine Bienvenu, demeurant en cette ville, tuteur de Charles Braseau, enfant mineur de feu Charles Braseau et feue Marie-Françoise Melot, 23 janvier 1747.; Kaskaskia Manuscripts (Randolph County Courthouse, Chester, Illinois), Inventaire de ce que le nouvel époux, Charles Phillipot, amène à la communauté avant le mariage avec la dite veuve, 8 février 1747.; Kaskaskia Manuscripts (Randolph County Courthouse, Chester, Illinois), Testament d'André Roy, malade chez le Sieur Joseph Mathieu… , 26 septembre 1747.

88 BAnQ-M, 06, M-P 218, Jean-Alexis Lemoine-Monière, Livres de comptes du 27 juin 1739 au 8 janvier 1751, Film M 641.1, 9 septembre, 1744.

89 H. Ellis, *A Voyage to Hudson's-Bay, by the Dobbs Galley and California, in the years 1746 and 1747* (Dublin: George and Alexander Ewing, 1749), p.86.

90 BAnQ-M, TL4, S1, D5321, Procès contre Guillaume-Jacques Wouters dit Duchâteau, soldat de la Compagnie de LaGauchetière, Jean-Baptiste Leroy dit St-Jean, soldat de la Compagnie de Longueuil, Charles Érard dit Tranchemontagne, soldat de la Compagnie de Noyan, Jean Jouffard dit St-Médard, soldat de la Compagnie de Noyan, et son épouse Marie-Anne Cardinal, accusés de distribution de fausses ordonnances, 30 juin–12 août 1747.

blanket, and looks like a hooded cloak.'[91] Near Québec in March of 1760, colonial officer Nicolas Renaud d'Avène des Méloizes wrote to his wife, 'Please give my blanket capot to the courier Barain who promised to bring it to me.'[92]

Even French metropolitan and militia officers adopted them, as attested by the inclusion of a 'blanket capot' valued at 60 livres in the 1760 after-death inventory of Joseph Fournierie, a *lieutenant* in the Régiment Royal-Roussillon residing in Montréal.[93] That same year a 'blanket capot, half worn out' was recorded as belonging to Antoine Sauvé, a militia *capitaine* incorporated into the Compagnies franches de la Marine.[94] A circular letter from *Brigadier* Lévis to battalion commanders during the Saint-Foy campaign of 1760 strictly forbade soldiers from making capots 'using their blankets,' suggesting either a shortage of ready-made capots or the popularity of the blanket capot among troops due to its warmth and suitability for the cold Canadian climate.[95]

Capot Colours
Capots issued to soldiers in the seventeenth century were typically made of blue woollen cloth, but by the 1740s, colonial records suggest that brown had become the dominant colour. It is to be noted that, at the present time, there is no concrete evidence regarding the colour of wool fabric used for capots provided by the King's storehouses to colonial troops and Canadian militia between 1700 and 1760. However, a 1746 requisition for replenishing the King's depots in Québec included '3,500 *aunes* of brown Mazamet.'[96] Given that Mazamet and Cadis were the most common types of woollen cloth used for capots for the King's troops in Canada, this suggests that the brown Mazamet could have been intended for such garments. Additionally, another '6,000 *aunes* of brown Mazamet' were requested for 1747,[97] excluding the 607⅓ *aunes* of

A watercolour circa 1730 depicting a Canadian voyageur wearing a short capot with a hood. The mid-thigh-length coat features mariner's cuffs, likely making it more practical than longer coats for traveling in rugged terrain and canoeing, as it would help prevent the fabric at the skirt area from getting soaked. (Habillemens des Coureurs de Bois Canadiens, no. 2, Anonymous, c. 1730, Beinecke Rare Book and Manuscript Library, Yale University Library, New Haven, CT, USA, WA MSS S-2412)

brown Mazamet supplied by private merchants for the war effort.[98] While the Cadis fabric records did not specify colours, the following year, a merchant named Mariette of Montauban was contracted to supply 1,000 *aunes* of purple (violet) molleton, 1,000 *aunes* of brown Mazamet, and 1,000 *aunes* of brown Dourgne for Canada.[99] This further points to brown fabric being a popular choice for military clothing during this period.

91   Jean-Bernard Bossu, *Nouveaux voyages aux Indes Occidentales; contenant une relation des différens peuples qui habitent les environs du grand fleuve Saint-Louis, appellé vulgairement le Mississipi, etc.* (Amsterdam: Chez D.F. Changuion, 1769), vol.1, p.98.

92   Archives du Séminaire de Québec, P32/002/093, Mme Nicolas Renaud d'Avène des Méloizes informe Claude-Pierre Pécaudy de Contrecœur, qu'elle est allée voir son … , 19 mars 1761.

93   BAnQ-M, Greffe du notaire Pierre Panet, Inventaire des biens d'entre Dame Marie-Louise Decouagne et feu Joseph Fournierie (Royal-Roussillon, Archives judiciaires, boîte C6 MT1 1/169, C HEM, septembre 1760), vivant lieutenant d'infanterie en garnison à Montréal, 30 septembre 1760.

94   BAnQ-M, Greffe du notaire Thomas Vuatier, … à la requête du Sieur Antoine Lalonde, capitaine de milice à Ste-Anne en haut de l'île de Montréal… , 23 février 1760.

95   Henri-Raymond Casgrain, *Lettres du Chevalier de Lévis concernant la guerre du Canada 1756–1760* (Québec: Imprimerie de L.-J. Demers & Frère, 1889), p.281.

96   LAC, MG1-C11A, vol.86, f.279.

97   LAC, MG1-C11A, vol.86, f.13.

98   LAC, MG1-C11A, vol.117, f.114.

99   AR, 1E, vol.143, État des étoffes à fournir pour le Canada en 1748 par les Sieurs Mariette de Montauban,15 décembre 1747. :

The following decade, the Gradis family, who was involved in supplying the storehouses and the King's armies in Canada, shipped substantial amounts of fabric to Québec between 1755 and 1757, which included Mazamet, frequently described as 'brown and vineux (burgundy),'[100] along with Cadis, which was labelled 'drapé,' 'de montagne' (Cadis of a larger width),[101] or 'd'Aignan' (Cadis made at a manufacture established by David d'Aignan in Montauban).[102] According to numerous merchant and post-mortem inventories, in the St Lawrence Valley dating from 1730 to 1763, Cadis de montagne was most often recorded in brown, burgundy-red, and black. The inventories also listed Cadis d'Aignan in brown, light brown, grey, and black; Cadis ras in brown, burgundy-red, white, and black; Cadis frisé in brown, light-brown, grey, and burgundy; and Mazamet in brown, white, blue, cinnamon, and yellow. A 1753 inventory from a Québec-based merchant offers further details about the colours of Cadis and Mazamet fabrics imported to Canada:

> From Montauban, 20 half-pieces of 20 *aunes* for each Cadis…for their colour, let there be 15 pieces of the aforesaid which are brown, although with variations in colour, and the other 5 remaining pieces, 3 light brown and the other 2 burgundy-red…10 pieces, Mazamet, grey, 4 pieces brown, 2 pieces, brown, but a little lighter in colour.[103]

Based on this, by the 1740s, we may surmise that brown woollen fabric was one of the most widespread colours used to make capots for the troops. This is further supported by specific examples, such as a colonial soldier who frozen to death near Montréal in 1737, found wearing a brown capot of 'Mazamet or Cadis' along with his munition hat,[104] while in 1752, Alexis Lacour, a soldier serving in the Compagnie de Lorimier, was seen 'wearing a half-worn brown Cadis capot … trimmed with goat hair buttons.'[105] Six years later, a 'brown capot, unlined' was found in a chest belonging to Jacques Frédéric Raymond dit Bonvivant, a *caporal* accused of stealing flour at Fort

French officer wearing a surtout (frock coat). L'Art du tailleur defines the surtout as a type of justaucorps worn over the veste, featuring no buttons or buttonholes along the front opening, but with buttons on the cuffs and three buttonholes on each side of the rear vent. Sometimes, a collar is added. Canadian officer Michel-Jean-Hugues Péan described the capot as '…a type of unlined and pocketless surtout which the Canadians and sometimes the Natives wear.' (Man in officer's dress, with sword hanging at left hip, shown in frontal view with his head turned toward the left, trees beyond, Louis Desplaces, After Antoine Watteau French, ca. 1700–1739, MET)

St-Jean.[106] That same year, a militia *sergent* at St-Pierre (île d'Orléans) testified in a criminal trial that he saw a soldier of the Régiment de la Reine 'wearing a brown capot, white buttons, and red facings … with a collar of the same colour [red].'[107] Additionally, domestiques in

100 LAC, MG 18, H63, Fonds famille Gradis.

101 Jules Lépicier, *Archives historiques du département de la Gironde* (Paris: Alphonse Picard et fils, 1918), vol.52, p.117.

102 Édouard Forestié, *Notice historique sur la fabrication des draps à Montauban, du XIVe siècle à …* (Montauban: Imp. et Lith. Forestié, 1883), p.9.

103 BAnQ-Q, P908, P9, Mémoire à accomplir par les frères Rouffio et Romagnac pour l'année 1753 relativement aux commandes de marchandises auprès de négociants de France et de Hollande, destinées à être envoyées au Québec… , 1752.

104 BAnQ-M, TL4, S1, D4394, Constat du décès de Laliberté, soldat de la compagnie de Repentigny, tanneur de profession, 28–29 janvier 1737.

105 BAnQ-M, TL4, S1, D5662, Procès contre Alexis Lacour, soldat de la Compagnie de Lorimier, accusé de vol de vêtements, 24 décembre 1751–8 janvier 1752.

106 BAnQ-M, Doc. Jud. Boîte 06MT1–1/168, Procureur du Roi vs Jacques Frédéric Raymond dit Bonvivant surnommé Suisse, 27 ans, caporal de la Cie de Courtemanche, en garnison au Fort St-Jean, accusé de vol de farine, 19 février 1758.

107 BAnQ-Q, TL5, D1960, Procès criminel contre Jonas Mathé (Matey) dit Tranquille, 31 ans, natif de Neufchâtel en Suisse,

Above: Short capots worn by Breton sailors in the 1840s, featuring red bonnets, striped sashes, and double gilets, illustrating the strong influence French sailors had on 'Canadian-style' clothing. The man on the right could easily be mistaken for a Canadian Habitant. (François-Hippolyte Lalaisse, Le Fanal. Sept maquettes de costumes anonymes, Marin de Plougastel, 1849. Creative Commons)

Above: right: A Breton sailor dressed in shore attire as part of a study of mariners' clothing from Kerlouan. The hooded coat is described as 'Caugoul (cagoule) en molleton'. The cagoule was a garment commonly used for protection against the cold. Typically made of wool or thick fabric, it was a regular part of everyday wear in colder climates. (François-Hippolyte Lalaisse, Le Fanal. Sept maquettes de costumes anonymes, Habitant de Kerlouan en costume de grève,1849. Creative Commons)

Right: Colonial soldier dressed for a winter campaign, c. 1695. From 1693 to 1696, colonial authorities replaced the soldiers' justaucorps in Canada with Canadian-style capots made of greyish-white serge, trimmed with blue serge, with cuffs and buttons. (Francis Back © Raphaëlle and Félix Back)

Left: A Nipissing Native wearing what appears to be a simple brown unlined capot (without cuffs), tied at the waist with a sash featuring a thin red collar. In this depiction, one can also see the single button where the capot is closed at the collar area. Notably, this depiction also shows a rare occurrence of the mitasses being tied just over the heel, a practice that may have been adopted by Canadians and members of the colonial troops. Hoodless capots, known as capots à collet, are documented in the Saint-Lawrence Valley starting in the mid-eighteenth century. In 1758, a soldier from the Régiment de La Reine was seen near Quebec wearing a brown capot with white buttons, red facings, and a matching collar. (Canadian Indian, 1732. Library of Congress, <www.loc.gov/item/2021668134/>)

Right: This Canadian Habitant was painted in 1778 by *Kapitän* Friedrich Von Germann. He is wearing a white blanket coat (capot de couverte) with a blue stripe near the skirt, adorned with blue piping and ribbons. His coat is fastened in three places by ribbons, which closely matches a known description from 1776. His capot is fastened at the waist by a 'ceinture fléchée' (arrow sash), one of the earliest depictions of this item. ('Ein Canadischer Bauer. 1778', The New York Public Library Digital Collections)

Ex-voto of Notre-Dame-de-Liesse from the first half of the eighteenth century, depicting three Canadian civilians who may have been militiamen during a raid or possibly involved in a hunting accident. The kneeling man on the right wears a dark brown capot, the man lying down wears a light brown capot, and the man in the background is dressed in grey. The coats resemble justaucorps with three buttons on large boot cuffs and are fastened at the waist with sashes, similar to descriptions from a trial in Montreal that detailed three work capots owned by a colonist: one dark brown with a hood, another brown with a collar, both with boot cuffs. A witness from the trial noted, '...he was wearing a brown capot...of Cadis de Montagne,' and described the sleeve as having 'a brown boot cuff of Cadis, old, with four buttons.' BAnQ-Q, TP1, S777, D176,14 mai-7 juin 1752. (Photo Kevin Gélinas. Fabrique de Rivière-Ouelle)

Circa 1700–1750 sash made of wool, beads, and hemp. Sashes like this would have been wrapped tightly around the waist as a belt. Intricately woven without a loom, it features a flat braid pattern with white 'seed' beads forming a decorative design. This sash was reportedly given by Eunice Kanenstehawi Williams and her husband Arosen to Eunice's brother, the Reverend Stephen Williams of Longmeadow, Massachusetts. Both Eunice and Stephen had been captives of the 1704 raid on Deerfield, Massachusetts by the Canadians, but Eunice chose to remain with her Kanienkehaka (Mohawk) family in Kahnawake, Canada. L: 182.8cm. W: 7.6cm. (Courtesy Pocumtuck Valley Memorial Association's Memorial Hall Museum, Deerfield, MA.)

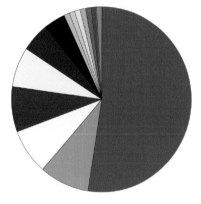

Graph showing the distribution of capots colours from probate records in Montreal, Trois-Rivières, Quebec, and Kaskaskia between 1730–1763.

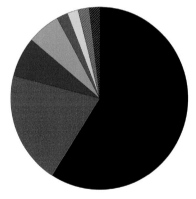

Graph showing the colours of men's sashes (1723–1764) in Trois-Rivières, Montreal, Quebec, and the Illinois Country taken from probate records

Possibly one of the earliest depictions of an arrow sash. Detail of Jean-Moyse Raymond wearing the uniform of Collège Saint-Raphaël (later Collège de Montréal), consisting of a blue capot with white piping and a chevron or arrow-patterned sash. Raymond attended the school from 1798 to 1805. (Montreal Museum of Fine Arts, Jean-Moyse Raymond, anonymous, c. 1800. Photo René Chartrand)

From Garsault's L'Art du tailleur, plate XIII, showing a tailor taking measurements and seamstresses assembling and sewing various pieces. Many capots for colonial troops were made by Montréal-based seamstresses subcontracted by the King's storekeeper.

the Régiment de Guyenne were issued capots made from brown fabric, while the valets received white capots with red facings that matched their regimental colours.[108] This colour distinction likely served both to identify these different personnel within the regiment and to keep track of their respective quantities, ensuring that each group was properly accounted for and managed. Even British soldiers stationed at Québec wore coats made from Cadis, as confirmed by a deserter reported in October of 1761, who was wearing 'an old brown capot of Cadis and a light infantry bonnet.'[109] According to Francis Back's capot study, more than half of the capots worn in the St Lawrence Valley from 1650 to 1715 were blue.[110]

Capot colours according to Francis Back (1650-1715)
Blue – 52.1%
White – 10.3%

Blue and red – 9.9%
Gray – 9.0%
Brown – 6.0%
Red – 5.6%
Red and black – 1.2%
Reddish-brown – 1.2%
Cinnamon – 0.4%
Musk – 0.4%
Black – 0.4%
Olive – 0.4%
Doe belly (Fawn) – 0.4%
Green – 0.4%
Wine red – —[111]

However, an analysis of 211 probate records referencing capots and their respective colours relating to the Montréal, Trois-Rivières, Québec, and the Illinois Territory (Kaskaskia manuscripts) from 1730 to 1763 shows that more than half of the capots (55 percent) were made from woollen fabric described as brown or chestnut, blue hues (10 percent), and white (8 percent), while red or dark red hues (burgundy, cinnamon and red) made up a total of 14 percent, followed by black, grey, and ginger.

soldat du régiment de la Reine, compagnie de D'Asserat, accusé de vol avec effraction chez Marie-Françoise Sédillot, veuve de Charles Maufait (Mauffet), demeurant au faubourg Saint-Jean à Québec, 24 février–13 mars 1758.

108 RAPQ, 1933–34, p.68.
109 Mémoires de la Société Historique de Montréal, *Règne militaire en Canada*, cinquième livraison. (Montréal: Des Presses à Vapeur de la Minerve, 1870), p.205.
110 Francis Back, *Le capot canadien, origines et évolution*, Canadian Folklore canadien, vol.10, no.2 (1988), p.119.

111 f.Back, *Le capot canadien: ses origines et son évolution aux XVIIème et XVIIIème Siècles*, Ethnologies, 10 (1–2), p.119.

Capot colours (1730-1763)
Brown (brun) – 54%
Blue (bleu) – 9%
White and off-white (blanc, blanchâtre, blafard) – 8%
Cinnamon (canelle) – 8%
Yellow (jaune) – 7%
Burgundy (vineux) – 5%
Black (noir) – 4%
Bluiesh (bleuâtre)- 1%
Ash grey (cendré) – 1%
Grey (gris) – 1%
Iron grey (gris de fer) – 1%
Red (rouge) – 1%
Ginger (roux) – 1%
Chestnut (marron) – 1%

Left and above: Studies of soldiers holding muskets and wearing capes by Watteau, c. 1710. The long watch-coats worn by these sentries were shared among soldiers on patrol and often referred to as capot de sentinelle or cape de sentinelle in New France. (Private collection, France.)

Lastly, the adventurer and traveller Claude Lebeau, who stayed in Canada from 1729 to 1730, observed that Canadians living in villages wore capots that were 'made in a similar way and almost all are of the same colour', which was more than likely brown, based on the evidence stated above.[112]

Watchmen's Capots
By the eighteenth century, greatcoats, often referred to as watch coats and termed capot or capote in period French dictionaries (not to be confused with the colonial term capot), were issued to French soldiers on sentry duty in poor weather and at night. Though not provided for general use, these greatcoats formed part of the shared guardhouse kit and were issued when needed. Made of wool or waterproof material, watchmen's capots were, by the 1740s, commonly made from Lodève cloth, a grey-white woollen fabric. In 1760, Louis de La Noue de Varo, commandant of the Volontaires de l'armée, recommended that watchmen's capots be made using 'approximately 2½ aunes of cloth, and shall not extend beyond the calf, shall have a hood or at least a piece of square fabric which serves as a covering, and when raised, covers the head and thus acts as a hood.'[113]

---

112 Claude Le Beau, *Avantures du Sr. C. Le Beau, avocat en parlement, ou, Voyage curieux et nouveau parmi les sauvages de l'Amérique septentrionale...* (Amsterdam: Uytwerf, 1738), p.65.

113 Louis de La Noue de Varo, Comte de Stanillas, *Nouvelles Constitutions militaires avec une tactique adaptee ...* (Francfort: Knoch et Eslinger, 1760), vol.2, p.88.

Origin and Definition of the Watchmen's Capot

Colonial records contain several terms that may have been used interchangeably for watch coats, including capot à sentinelles (sentries' capot), capot pour sentinelles (capot intended for sentries), cape à/de sentinelles (sentries' cloak), and cape pour sentinelles (cloaks intended for sentries). The 1740 edition of the *Dictionnaire de l'Académie Françoise* states that 'when soldiers stand sentry (en sentinelle), they usually wear capots.'[114] In the 1758 edition of the *Dictionnaire Militaire*, a capote (spelled with an 'e') is defined as 'clothing made in the shape of a hooded robe, which the sentries wear in winter in the places.'[115] *Le grand vocabulaire François* describes the word capot as 'a type of cape or large cloak of coarse fabric, on which a hood is attached and which are used by on-duty soldiers to ward off the cold.'[116] Minutes drawn up regarding the inspection of 'capottes' for the Landau garrison in the winter of 1739/1740 reveals that repairs to these coats required '...thread and buttons...',[117] while the 1754 military study *La Medecine d'armée* urged a soldier to 'pull down the hood of his capotte' when transitioning from a warm to a cold environment.[118] And finally, the 1783 edition of the *Encyclopédie méthodique* defines the capot de sentinelle (sentries' capot) as a 'type of great coat made of heavy fabric for the sentries.'[119]

Watchmen's Capots in New France

Watchmen's capots were worn at most French frontier outposts, as indicated by a 1689 payment to a man named des Bergères for waxcloth he supplied to make 'capots for the soldiers at Niagara.' This likely refers to watch coats or capes made from waxed canvas, designed to be waterproof and suitable for rainy or snowy conditions.[120] At the turn of the century, '6 capots de sentinelle for the two forts, of good cloth and well lined' were requested for Plaisance while another two coats were intended for Acadia.[121] At the same time, two capes à sentinelles (sentry's cape) valued at 3 livres were accounted for at Fort Frontenac.[122]

By the 1700s, greatcoats made of wool cloth were frequently supplied to the colony of Île-Royale, where the climate was often cold and damp. For instance, a quantity of '6 capots of Lodève [cloth], greyish-white, for sentinels, conforming to the model at 24 livres' were included on a statement dated 1744, revealing that this particular shipment of coats was made from a specific model back in France.[123] The following year, '30 capots for sentinels' at 24 livres each were supplied by a French merchant named La Louvray for the troops stationed at Louisbourg.[124] In 1750, 12⅝ aunes of blue cloth was requested to make capes de sentinel, which also indicates that they were probably made onsite,[125] while a few years later, '40 capots of woollen fabric for the sentinels' were once again requested from France.[126]

These outer garments were occasionally listed in the King's storehouses in the St Lawrence Valley and other frontier posts, with one or two coats typically issued to frontier forts, but provided in greater numbers in towns such as Québec and Montréal. In 1738, for example, one sentry's coat (cape de sentinelle) was itemised at Fort Niagara[127] while two years later two capes pour sentinelles were inventoried as part of the clothing and armaments of the troops stationed at Fort Saint-Frédéric.[128] Three years later, '30 aunes of semi-Lodève cloth for capes à sentinel' was sent to Québec as part of the Petit habillement, suggesting that these watch coats were fabricated onsite in the colony using that particular type of fabric.[129] The town of Lodève, France, was known to make white and grey woollen cloth for the troops' clothing.[130] Two of these coats were also itemised at the Forges du Saint-Maurice near Trois-Rivières in 1748, where a handful of soldiers were stationed.[131] Another six capes à sentinelles were accounted for in the King's storehouses at Montréal in 1752 for the outings, trips, and services of the storehouses, and another four were inventoried at Québec as part of the clothing and armament of the troops there.[132] Ten years earlier, an officer testified that he found 'the musket and cape (watch coat)' of François Marteau dit Lespérance, a colonial soldier at Montréal who was on watch at the poudrière (powder magazine) as a sentry.[133]

114   *Dictionnaire de l'Académie Françoise* (Paris: chez Saillant & Nyon, 1740), vol.1, p.222.

115   François-Alexandre Aubert de La Chesnaye, *Dictionnaire Militaire, Portatif: Contenant Tous Les Termes Propres A La Guerre; Sur ce qui regarde la Tactique, le Genie, l'Artillerie, la Subsistance, la Dicipline des Troupes, & la Marine ...* (Paris: Chez Gissey, 1758), p.345.

116   *Le grand vocabulaire françois* (Paris: Chez C. Pankoucke, 1768), vol.4, p.596.

117   François de Chennevières, *Détails Militaires Dont la connoissance est nécessaire à tous les Officiers, & principalement aux Commissaires des Guerres, Tome troisième* (Paris: Chez Charles-Antoine Jombert, 1750), pp.438–439.

118   Guillaume Mahieu de Meyserey, *La Medecine d'armée* (Paris : Chez la veuve Cavelier, 1754), vol.1, pp.404–405.

119   *Encyclopédie méthodique. Marine...* (Paris: Panckouke, 1783), vol.1, p.264.

120   LAC, MG1-C11A, vol., f.16.

121   LAC, MG1-B, vol.22, f.33, 41.

122   LAC, C11A, vol.20, f.260v.

123   LAC, F1A, vol.35, f.10.

124   LAC, MG1-B, vol.27, f.87.

125   LAC, C11B, vol.28, f.233.

126   LAC, MG1-B, vol.37, f.212.

127   LAC, MG1-C11A, vol 69, f.275v.

128   LAC, MG1-C11A, vol.73, f.339v.

129   LAC, MG1-C11A, vol.75, f.303.

130   Jacques Savary des Bruslons, *Dictionnaire Universel De Commerce...* (Genève: Cramer-Philibert, 1742), vol.1, pt.2, p.268.

131   LAC, MG1-C11A, vol.112, f.290v.

132   LAC, MG1-C11A, vol.98, f.234v.; LAC, MG1-C11A, vol.98, f.239.

133   BAnQ-M, TL4, S1, D4905, Procès devant le Conseil de guerre contre François Marteau dit Lespérance, soldat de la Compagnie de LaGauchetière, accusé de désertion, 8 décembre–11 décembre, 1742.

In 1755, 200 capots de sentinelle were to be loaded aboard ships bound for Québec to outfit the battalions of French regulars, indicating that they were to be shared between each regiment during that year's campaign.[134] An undated memo addressed to an officer named D'Hebecourt at Carillon, likely from 1757, noted that sentries relieved every half hour during the night must have '…capotes and mittens… Orders are given to the sentries to call out every quarter hour, "Prenez garde à vous!"'[135] That same year, the merchant Lemoyne of Rouen, a prominent supplier of goods for Canada, was offering 'capots de sentinelle of cloth.'[136] These coats were even found as far inland as the Illinois Territory, as 'A Sentinel's capot' was recorded in an inventory of effects and merchandise moved from Fort de Chartres to the present city of St Louis, Missouri in 1765.[137]

Sashes (Ceintures)

Capots worn by French colonists or Native Americans were usually bound around the waist with a woollen sash called ceinture in French. In warm weather, many militiamen donned sashes over their shirts to carry their casse-tête tomahawks, slit pouches and tobacco bags. By the early 1700s, sashes worn by Canadian militiamen were viewed as similar to those traditionally worn by French sailors termed écharpe à la matelote,[138] while 30 years later, Claude Lebeau observed that Canadians living in villages wore capots 'by means of a Native-made sash decorated with porcupine quills.'[139] Colonial records reveal that the majority of sashes, sometimes referred to as ceintures sauvages (Native-made sashes), were finger-woven/braided, of black yarn, interwoven with beads (rassades) or decorated with porcupine quills, and most likely handcrafted by Native American women living in the various Native missions in the St Lawrence Valley. In fact, Lebeau remarks that Native American woman used porcupine quills to decorate 'sashes that they sell to Canadians.'[140] Others were made on looms or simply cut from cloth. It is possible that some colonial troops replaced their standard-issued ceinturon waist belt with sashes when detached in small war parties. Some officers may have also worn sashes on wilderness raids, but they most probably wore a

leather waist belt with a frog that allowed them to carry a sabre or hunting sword.

Probate Records

Records indicate that colonial troops in Canada owned sashes, which probably served to close their civilian capots rather than their standard-issued ones, which they likely wore with their ceinturon waistbelt. This was the case of a colonial soldier named Laliberté, who was found dead on the Chemin du Roy (King's Road) in 1737 'wearing a capot of Mazamet or of brown Cadis, a wool porcupine sash, leather breeches, a soldier's hat, a silk scarf, a cotton handkerchief around the neck, wearing French shoes.'[141] In 1747, the Montréal merchant Monière sold a porcupine quill sash to a soldier for 3 livres,[142] while three years later, Louis Audet de Pierrecot, junior officer in the colonial troops, owned 'a beaded sash' esteemed at 15 livres.[143] Similarly, in 1754, Paul Bécard was found to have 'a beaded wool sash' in his possession[144] whereas the post-mortem inventory drafted following the death of Chevalier de La Corne in 1762 included 'a uniform of white cloth with blue facings' and '… one woollen cloth capot, very old' as well as 'a beaded sash' valued at 3 livres.[145]

Based on 287 references to men's sashes (ceintures) gathered from hundreds of probate records at Québec, Trois-Rivières, Montréal, and the Illinois Territory from 1723 to 1764, the majority (65 percent) were described as finger-woven sashes made of yarn wool or buffalo hair, while the remainder were made on a loom (one percent) or from fabrics (34 percent), such as Taffetas, Calmande, soie, Damas, Grenade, Droguet, serge, Carisé, Camelot, satin, laine du pays, and étamine. There was also a single reference to a leather-made belt. Sashes found in merchant records were not included in this count.

134 LAC, MG1-C11A, vol.100, f.283v-284.
135 LAC, MG18, K9, vol.6, f.137.
136 LAC, MG7, 1, A 2, vol.11336, f.48.
137 Frederic L. Billon, *Annals of St Louis in Its Early Days Under the French and Spanish Dominations* (St. Louis: G.I. Jones and Company, 1886), p.49.
138 *Le mercure galant* (Paris: Michel Brunet, 1709), p.56.
139 Claude Le Beau, *Avantures du Sr. C. Le Beau, avocat en parlement, ou, Voyage curieux et nouveau parmi les sauvages de l'Amérique septentrionale…* (Amsterdam: Uytwerf, 1738), p.65.
140 Le Beau, *Avantures du Sr. C. Le Beau*, p.43.

141 BAnQ-M, TL4, S1, D4394, Constat du décès de Laliberté, soldat de la compagnie de Repentigny, tanneur de profession, 28–29 janvier 1737.
142 Marie Gérin-Lajoie, *Montréal Merchant's Records Project* (microfilm copy of M496 Montréal Merchants Records Project, Research Files, 1971–1975, 1 roll — St. Paul: Minnesota Historical Society Library Copy Services), Monière, microfilm M-849, ledger 1740-47, vol.9, fol. 130.
143 BAnQ-M, Greffe du notaire Antoine Foucher, Inventaire des biens de feu Pierre Cot, vivant lieutenant d'une compagnie des troupes de détachement de la marine, écuyer de Bailleul et Seigneur de la paroisse de l'Assomption, 7 janvier, 1750.
144 BAnQ-Q, TP1, S777, D178, Procès de Pierre de Monferand (Montferrand) dit Chevalier, 23 ans, chirurgien, soldat de la compagnie de Paul Bécard, sieur de Fonville, natif de La Châtre en Berry, aucune demeure fixe, étant arrivé cet automne de France à Louisbourg, accusé du meurtre, par un coup de fusil, de Louis Chel dit Saint-André, à la Pointe-à-la-Caille, paroisse Saint-Thomas, 17 novembre 1754–17 mai 1755.
145 BAnQ-M, Greffe du notaire Pierre Panet, Inventaire des biens de la communauté d'entre dame Marie-Anne Hubert, veuve de Sieur Chevalier de la Corne, dit Sieur De la Corne, vivant chevalier de l'ordre Royal et militaire de St-Louis, capitaine d'infanterie de sa majesté, 19 avril 1762.

Detail from Duhamel du Monceau's treatise, showing two men wearing mariner's waist sashes, conversing in a seaport town over freshly arrived fish. (Duhamel du Monceau, *Traité Général des Pêches*, Part 1, Section 3, Plate 9, Fig. 3)

Besides those made of fabric or on a loom, 34 percent of all sashes had beads interwoven, 24 percent were simply listed as handwoven, while the remaining descriptions mention porcupine quillwork or buffalo hair. In essence, 65 percent of the sashes were made in the Native style, which confirms Claude Lebeau's observation that French Canadian colonists wore Native-made or style sashes.

Table 2. Men's sashes found in probate records (Illinois, Montréal, Trois-Rivières, Québec), 1723–1764 (taken from a total of 287 references of men's sashes).

Description	Total	%
Various fabric (Taffetas, Calmande, soie, Damas, Grenade, Droguet, serge, Carisé, Camelot, satin, laine du pays, étamine, etc)	99	34%
Wool yarn sashes decorated with beads (ceintures de laine garnies de rassades)	97	34%
Wool yarn sashes – unspecified (ceintures de laine)	70	24%
Native-made sashes – unspecified (ceintures sauvages)	8	3%
Wool or Native-made sashes decorated with porcupine quill (ceintures sauvages ou de laine garnies de porc-épic)	6	2%
Buffalo yarn sashes (ceintures de poil de bœufs ou Illinois)	5	2%
Sashes made on a loom (ceintures faites au métier)	2	v1%
	287	100%

Colours of Finger Woven Sashes in Canada

Probate records that note the colour of sashes are rare, but a sample of 55 records indicates that the majority were black, with two appearing to be multicoloured, such as the 'red, yellow and blue wool sash' owned by Joseph Garneau in 1755,[146] or the 'black and red beaded wool sash' included in the personal possessions of Louis Vachon of Beauport two years later.[147]

Table 3. Colour of men's sashes found in probate records (Illinois, Montréal, Trois-Rivières, Québec), 1723–1764.

Black	59%
Red	20%
Blue	7%
Green	6%
Brown	2%
Yellow	2%
Red, yellow and blue	2%
Black and red	2%

Most of the black sashes were probably made using black wool yarn designed to resemble bison hair, a material traditionally used by allied nations located south-west of Canada. In fact, numerous French records spanning over 100 years document this practice, particularly along the Mississippi River, where these ceintures were likely traded with eastern tribes through established trade routes. When Father Marquette visited the Illinois country in 1673, he was presented with 'belts, garters, and articles made of the hair of bears and cattle [bison], dyed red, yellow, and grey.' while, interestingly, the chiefs were distinguished from the warriors 'by wearing red scarves [sashes]. These are made, with considerable skill, from the hair of bears and wild cattle [bison].'[148] Additionally, De Sabrevois, the commandant at Fort Pontchartrain had observed that the Illinois women made 'garters, belts [sashes], and cords for powder-horns…they spin the Wool of the buffalo and make with it all these articles.'[149] Jean-Bernard Bossu remarked that the Arkansas women spin the bison hair 'which is a very fine wool, with which they make sashes.'[150]

In his memoirs, *capitaine* Pierre Pouchot wrote that Native American men 'wear a belt about six inches

146 BAnQ-Q, Greffe du notaire Pierre Parent, …à la requête du Sieur Joseph Garneau, habitant de la Seigneurie de Beauport, au nom et comme tuteur aux enfants mineurs de feue Louise Touchet, Évangéline Chrétien…, 7 avril 1755.

147 BAnQ-Q, Greffe du notaire Pierre Parent, …à la requête de Élisabeth Campagnat, veuve de feu Louis Vachon, vivant habitant de la Seigneurie de Beauport…, 4 juillet 1757.

148 Louise Phelps Kellogg, *Early Narratives of the Northwest 1634–1699* (Baltimore: Genealogical Publishing Company, 2009), pp.242–244.

149 *Wisconsin Historical Collections* (Madison, Wisconsin: State Historical Society of Wisconsin, 1902), vol.XVI, p.374.

150 Jean Bernard Bossu, *Nouveaux voyages dans l'Amérique septentrionale, contenant une collection de lettres écrites sur les lieux par l'auteur, à son ami M. Douin, chevalier, capitaine dans les troupes du roi, ci-devant son camarade dans le Nouveau-Monde, Nouvelle édition* (Paris: Chez la Veuve Duchesne, 1778), p.104.

[pouces] wide, made of wool of different colours, which the Indian women make very neatly, with flaming designs,' which may refer to one of the earliest records of waist sashes with arrow or flame designs.[151] More importantly, in 1757, a Montréal-based merchant trading at the Fort des Deux-Montagnes, a fortified Native mission established in 1721 near present-day Oka, kept '4 black sashes,' '3 red sashes,' '2 sashes par fleche (with arrows)' and '1 sash en rée (netted-design sash)' in his stores.[152] The sashes described as having par fleche designs may prove to be the earliest mention of an arrow sash, the precursor to the standard nineteenth century 'Assomption sash' pattern. The most recent studies on the subject reveal that the first written references to arrow sashes date back to 1798, when a voyageur was described as wearing 'une jolie cinture à flesche,' or the 'deux cintures à flesches' included in the after-death inventory of Mrs Chaboillez.[153] Considering this, it is feasible that Canadians were already producing or trading arrow sashes as early as 1757. George Townshend's sketches from 1758 vividly depict a Native American war chief adorned with a powder horn strap and medal band, featuring arrow designs that reflect the artistry of arrow sashes. This serves as solid evidence that arrow designs were already in use by Native Americans fighting alongside French forces during the Seven Years War, highlighting their cultural significance.

The Gilet Waistcoat

The gilet was part of the standard winter equipment issued to colonial and regular soldiers serving in Canada. Based on French published works of the period, a gilet was defined as a small waistcoat without skirts. The term appears to have been interchangeable with the word camisole, which referred to a type of under-waistcoat or under-shirt, unlike regulation waistcoats (veste) such as what a colonial soldier would have worn under their justaucorps. An after-death inventory at Québec included 'seven old camisoles or gilets of white molleton fabric, whereas four are sleeveless,' confirming that in the colony the two terms were probably synonymous.[154]

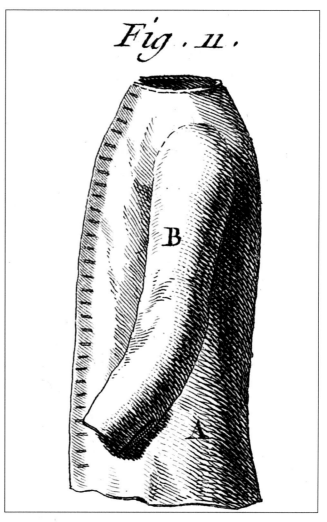

Taken from Diderot's Encyclopédie, showing a gilet described as '...a small waistcoat without skirts,' in fashion around the mid-eighteenth century. (*Encyclopédie*, Tailleur d'Habits et Tailleur de Corps, Planche V, II)

A mid-eighteenth century French military medical treatise suggested that soldiers stationed in cold climate regions wear a camisole to avoid several types of chest-related ailments. The treatise advise: 'To avoid these illnesses, and the sad consequences that they bring on, one must cover their chest with a camisole or a good double-breasted veste, or at least well buttoned up,' and added, 'it is cautious to wear, on one's chest, a piece of woollen or cotton cloth, or a wool cap, or a folded handkerchief; one must favour a good double-breasted camisole.'[155] Probate records relating to the French settlers living in the St Lawrence Valley indicate that garments termed gilets were made with or without sleeves, lined or unlined, single- or double-breasted, and using a number of different fabrics. Those issued to the troops in Canada during the 1750s were apparently made of wool or flannel and had sleeves.

151 Pierre Pouchot, *Memoir Upon the Late War in North America, Between the French and English, 1755–60* (W. Elliot Woodward, Mass: 1866), vol.2, p.192

152 BAnQ-M, Greffe du notaire Thomas Vuatier, Inventaire des biens et effets de feu Joseph Lemaire (Lemer) dit St-Germain, marchand négociant au Lac des deux montagnes et défunte Marie-Josephe Ducharme, 3 août 1757.

153 Monique Genest LeBlanc, '*Une jolie cinture à flesche*'. *Sa présence au Bas-Canada, son cheminement vers l'Ouest, son introduction chez les Amérindiens* (Québec: Presses de l'Université Laval: 2003), pp.34–35.

154 BAnQ-Q, Greffe du notaire Claude Barolet, Inventaire des biens de la communauté d'entre le feu Joseph Roussel et Marie-Madeleine Gauvreau, 21 février 1758.

155 De Meyserey, *La Medecine d'armée*, vol.1, pp.404–405.

Origin and Definition of the Gilet

Le dictionnaire des arts et des sciences defines a gilet as 'a small vest without sleeves, made of wool in wintertime and using cotton in summertime,'[156] while the *Dictionnaire de Trévoux* mentions a 'kind of sleeveless camisole, of wool or Bazin, that we wear under or over a shirt to protect against the cold.'[157] However, the most comprehensive description of a gilet or camisole can be found in Garseault's *Art du tailleur*, which states:

> The camisole, otherwise gilet, is worn either on the skin or over the shirt. When worn [directly] on the skin, it is only made of flannel. If it is worn over the shirt, it is made using many warm and light fabrics. It can be made with or without sleeves and can be cut roughly like a waistcoat from which the basques (tabs) would have been removed. The back side is almost straight. It is unlined, we simply add two bands of the same fabric at the front because of the buttons and buttonholes which run from top to bottom. Only small flat buttons should be used … the camisole is, so to speak, an under-jacket, that one wears immediately over the skin: it is made with sleeves and without sleeves; the latter is called gilet.[158]

Equipment Lists

The colonial soldiers that accompanied de Troyes on his expedition to Hudson Bay in 1686 may have been provided with an earlier type of gilet or camisole, since each man was provided with a chemisette of red cloth,[159] a piece of clothing defined as 'a diminutive of chemise, a sort of garment that is worn over the shirt … some wear this flannel shirt against their skin.'[160] In 1750, '75 camisoles' were distributed to the soldiers and militiamen serving at the Rivière St-Jean and Shediac,[161] while during the 1755 campaign, Malartic noted that soldiers were 'issued for winter equipment, above what is given in summer … one gilet.'[162] A few supply lists document gilets for the winter expeditions in 1756,[163] with officers at Fort Niagara, provided with a gilet valued at 16 livres, while their domestiques were given the same garment estimated at 10 livres, suggesting a difference in the quality of the fabric.[164] In the winter of 1757, Montcalm and Bougainville both mentioned that one gilet was provided as part of the winter equipment to the troops camped at Fort St-Jean.[165] An important declaration of two French soldiers dating to April of 1757 noted that they wore 'one flannel waistcoat with sleeves, a blue coat vest & breeches, one upper coat,' revealing that the sleeved flannel waistcoat would have therefore corresponded to the standard-issued gilet.[166] Intendant Bigot clearly specified that 'the summer equipment for the officer, the domestiques, the soldier, the militiaman and the Native American, was the same as that of winter, except that we removed the woollen gilet and the bear hide.'[167]

Countless other judicial records referenced gilets in the possession of, or worn by, colonial soldiers as attested by a 1714 account in which the body of a drowned man 'dressed in a soldier's waistcoat, a pair of canvas breeches and another one of white cloth underneath, wearing white stockings and French shoes' was found wearing 'a white gilet of Carisé under the waistcoat.'[168] At Pointe-à-la-Chevelure (Crown Point) in 1735, Pierre Coulo dit Jolicoeur, accused of desertion, left the fort with a few shots of lead, powder, a waistcoat, and a gilet.[169] In 1751, two worn-down gilets were found in a cassette belonging to a soldier of the Compagnie de Beaujeu,[170] while that same year, a *sergent* of the colonial troops, who was engaged in a sword duel, was recorded wearing 'a gilet of satin with a white and linseed grey background' along with a shirt, waistcoat, and justaucorps.[171] The following year, 'a gilet of espagnolette, the fronts of which are covered in flower-covered satin with a pink and green background' was found in a chest belonging to a *caporal* named Louis

156 *Le dictionnaire des arts et des sciences, tome premier* (Paris: Chez Jean-Baptiste Coignard, 1732), p.512.

157 *Dictionnaire universel François et Latin, vulgairement appelé Dictionnaire de Trévoux Contenant la Signification et la Définition des mots de l'une et de l'autre Langue* (Paris: Par la Compagnie des libraires associés, 1771), vol.4, p.509.

158 François A. de Garsault, *Art du tailleur* (Paris: Chez Saillant & Nyon, 1769), p.9.

159 LAC, MG1-C11A, vol.8, f.278v.

160 *Dictionnaire de l'Académie Françoise* (Paris: Chez Jean-Baptiste Coignard, 1740), vol.1, p.269.

161 LAC, MG1-C11A, vol.86, f.122v

162 De Malartic & Gaffarel (eds), *Journal des Campagnes au Canada*, p.96.

163 SHAT, Dossier A1, 3417, pièce 144.; Centre d'histoire La Presqu'île, P03/F.089, Fonds De Beaujeu, 28 novembre 1756.

164 RAPQ 1933–1934, p.78.

165 Henri-Raymond Casgrain, *Journal du marquis de Montcalm durant ses campagnes en Canada de 1756 à 1759* (Québec: Impr. de L.J. Demers & frère, 1895), p.156; De Bougainville, *Écrits sur le Canada*, p.168.

166 LOC, Colonial Office 5 folio 47, E. of Loudoun's Letter of April 25th. 1757, Declaration of two Prisoners taken the 23.d March 1757 at Fort Wm. Henry, Information of John Victor and Guillaume Chasse, two French Prisoners, Fort William Henry March 25th.

167 Bigot, *Mémoire Pour Messire François Bigot*, pp.39–40.

168 BAnQ-Q, P1000, S3, D812, Certificat de sépulture de Jean Garreau, 19 mai 1714.

169 BAnQ-M, TL4, S1, D4202, Procès devant le Conseil de guerre contre Pierre Coulo dit Jolicoeur, natif du Périgord, soldat de la Compagnie LaFresnière, accusé de désertion, 4 janvier–7 mai 1735.

170 BAnQ-Q, TL5, D1640, Procès criminel contre Claude du Retour (Duretour) de Monsy, seigneur de Neuville et autres terres, environ 31 ans, soldat de la compagnie de Beaujeu, et Louis Daurizon (Dorizon) dit Larose, soldat de la compagnie de Beaujeu, environ 39 ans, pour falsification d'ordonnances, 1er janvier 1749–5 novembre 1751.

171 BAnQ-M, TL4, S1, D5571, Procès contre feu André Deville, sergent de la Compagnie de Muy, et Delmas, sergent, accusés de duel, 11 janvier–21 mars 1751.

Bonin.[172] Espagnolette is a type of wool fabric mainly produced at Darnetal, France, and used 'for men's waistcoats, ladies' habits, etc. The wool is generally from Spain and Berri, but not first-quality Spanish wool.'[173] As part of a criminal trial involving soldiers stationed at Fort Saint-Frédéric in 1754, 'a sleeveless gilet of Carisé with the fronts of amaranth-coloured satin trimmed with very old gold buttons' was in the possession a colonial soldier accused of stealing from the King's storehouses.[174]

Gilets were also popular among colonial officers, many of which were made of Carisé (Kersey) and espagnolette. The after-death inventory of René Legardeur de Beauvais, *capitaine* in the colonial troops, listed an 'old gilet of Carisé croisé,' which was a doubly crossed threaded kersey woollen cloth, esteemed at 15 sols.[175] Sieur de Minouville, reformed (retired or discharged) *lieutenant* at Montréal, was the owner of 'an old gilet of Carisé'[176] while the famous French explorer and officer Sieur de La Vérendrye had a total of eight gilets following his death in 1749. These included 'two gilets of Carisé and flannel,' 'two gilets of espagnolette, trimmed, with their liners of cloth,' and finally 'four gilets of Bazin, very old.'[177] Six years later, 'a gilet of Carisé, covered with yellow damask' was part of the personal belongings of Louis Damour de Louvière, écuyer in the colonial troops,[178] whereas a few months later, a probate record relating to Sieur François de Sarrobert, *enseigne*, referenced 'an old capot of Cadis and an old sleeve gilet of Carisé,' priced together at 4 livres.[179] In the ensuing years, gilets owned by colonial officers were mostly referenced as

being made using espagnolette, a popular and fashionable fabric for this type of undergarment.[180]

Breechcloths (Brayets)

Breechcloths, part of the wilderness dress adopted by colonial troops in New France, are simple garments consisting of a strip of cloth or leather that hangs from the waist, secured with a belt or sash, covering the hips and extending to the upper thighs. While on duty in towns, posts, and forts, soldiers would have worn their regulation-issued breeches, but brayets (breechcloths), or the cloth to make them, were provided to colonial troops prior to wilderness expeditions and campaigns. These rectangular pieces of cloth were probably devoid of any decorations such as beadwork or quilling and to date, no primary sources have been found that identify the colour of the cloth used to make government-issued breechcloths for the Compagnies franches de la Marine. By the Seven Years War, both regular and colonial soldiers began receiving European-style breeches and drawers instead of breechcloths, which may imply that they may have rejected breechcloths in favour of breeches. An aversion to wearing breechcloths by some enlisted men may have already been around for some time, considering that 'two munition [soldier's] breeches,' instead of breechcloths, were provided to two presumed soldiers taking part in a war party against New England in 1747.[181]

While brayets may have had financial advantages for the King, being inexpensive to make and helping prevent wear and tear on the soldier's regulation breeches, they may not have been socially acceptable to some European-born soldiers serving in New France. Others, on the other hand, saw the benefit of their use, as breechcloths were well adapted for the summer months, when the legs were ordinarily bare, and were less constricting than breeches, allowing full movement of the legs. According to the officer d'Aleyrac: 'we wear these [brayets] without breeches to walk more freely in the woods,'[182] while Pehr Kalm observed that one could not persuade the Native Americans to use breeches 'for they thought that these

172 BAnQ-Q, TL5, D1667, Procès criminel contre Louis Bonin, caporal de la compagnie de Lanaudière et soldat congédié; et Denis Lemoine dit Parisien, 14 ans, soldat de la compagnie de Lanaudière en garnison à Québec, logé à la caserne Dauphine, et complices, accusés de vol.- 17 février 1752–6 août

173 Arthur Young, *Travels During the Years 1787, 1788, & 1789 Undertaken More Particularly with a View of Ascertaining the Cultivation, Wealth, Resources, and National Prosperity of the Kingdom of France* (London: W. Richardson, 1794), vol.1, p.553.

174 BAnQ-M, TL4, S1, D5921, Procès contre Menin Pouteau dit Parisien, sculpteur, soldat d'Herbin, Michel Dufeu dit Flame, soldat de la Compagnie de Villemonde, et Guillaume Goursol dit Lagiroflée, soldat de la Compagnie Debonne, accusés de vols dans la chambre de distribution du fort Saint-Frédéric, 9 septembre 1754–26 février 1755.

175 BAnQ-M, Greffe du notaire Danré de Blanzy, Inventaire des biens de feu René Legardeur de Beauvais, capitaine d'infanterie et de Louise Lamy son épouse, 8 janvier 1743.

176 BAnQ-M, Greffe du notaire Antoine Foucher, Inventaire des biens de feu Jean-Baptiste Boucher, écuyer Sieur de Minouville, vivant lieutenant réformé d'une compagnie des troupes du détachement de la marine, 1er juillet 1748.

177 RAPQ, 1949–1951, pp.53, 55, 57.

178 BAnQ-M, Greffe du notaire Pierre Panet, Inventaire et vente des meubles de la communauté des biens entre feu Louis Damour Sieur de Louvrière et Geneviève Catalogne, 27 février 1755.

179 BAnQ-M, Greffe du notaire Danré de Blanzy, Inventaire des biens de feu Sieur François de Sarrobert, enseigne d'infanterie, 8 janvier 1756.

180 BAnQ, Greffe du notaire Danré de Blanzy, …Louis Coulon écuyer Sieur de Villiers, capitaine d'infanterie demeurant Montréal rue Saint-Paul, 17 novembre 1757.; BAnQ-M, Greffe du notaire Pierre Panet, Inventaire des biens d'entre Dame Marie-Louise Decouagne et feu Joseph Fournerie (Royal-Roussillon, Archives judiciaires, boîte C6 MT1 1/169, C HEM, septembre 1760), vivant lieutenant d'infanterie en garnison à Montréal, 30 septembre 1760.; BAnQ-Q, Greffe du notaire Jean-Claude Panet, Inventaire de la communauté de Madeleine Coulon de Villier, veuve de Joseph Damour de Plaine, écuyer, de la rue Sous le Fort, 1er mars 1768.

181 LAC, MG1-C11A, vol.117, f.182.

182 BAnQ-M, 06M, ZF8, Fonds Jean Baptiste d'Aleyrac, 1793.

BRAYER

Est un morceau d'Étoffe de toutes Couleurs qu'il passe à une ceinture de corde tant par le devant que par le derriere

Detail from Baron de Lahontan's 1703 edition of *Nouveaux Voyages dans l'Amérique septentrionale*, showing a Native wearing a brayet described as '...a piece of cloth of various colours that he wears over a cord belt, both in front and behind.'

were a great hindrance in walking.'[183] They were also much more convenient than breeches for wearing in canoes, which were the most important means of transportation inland at the time, as breechcloths were less apt to get wet when getting in and out. According to period records, breechcloths worn by the French forces in New France typically measured ¼ *aune* wide and were usually made from woollen cloth (drap), which was lighter than leather and dried more quickly. When wet, they were simply hung up near the fire to dry.

Definition and Origin of the Brayet

Understanding the origin of the term brayet is crucial, as it provides insight into the historical context of the garment and its use, especially considering the various ways the word was written in old French. Found in several French colonial records (also written as braguet, braguette, brayette, brahier, brayer, or bragnier), the term appears to refer to the breechcloths worn by Native American people and adopted by many French settlers. The word brayet, used by Sagard as early as 1609, almost certainly referred to the French term braguette, 'a diminutive of brague. We say brayette in Paris but in most other places in France we say braguette.'[184] According to the *Dictionnaire universel françois et latin*, 'It was not long ago that we said braguette

and it was part of the clothing that held the genitals,'[185] while *The Royal Dictionary* defines the term brayette as 'the Cod-piece,'[186] a covering flap or pouch that attaches to the front of the crotch of men's trousers. In fact, the term brague (or braye) referred to 'clothing that covers from the belt to the knees, such as a hose, breeches ... this is otherwise called brague, brages or brais, from the Celtic words.'[187] The word braie also meant 'the cloths that one puts in the backs of young children who are not clean.'[188]

As part of their summer dress, Canadian militiamen and voyageurs working in the fur trade adopted breechcloths from the Native Americans in replacement of European-style breeches.[189] These loincloths were essentially a long strip of cloth hung front and back from a small cord of gut, which served as a belt around the hips. As early as 1682, Henry de Tonty had noticed that the voyageurs from Louisiana were dressed 'without breeches wearing a simple brayet.'[190] Three years later, the Minister of the Marine ordered Denonville, Governor General of New France, to clamp down on young folks in the colony running in the woods 'naked in the manner of the Natives.'[191] A narrative written by Iberville in 1699 described a scene where a southern Native American tribe is initiated to wool fabric breechcloths and leggings by Canadians: 'Breechcloths are made using 5/4 of fabric, cut in two lengthwise...he [Iberville] ordered that they [Natives] be shown how each item was used. We put shirts on them, their breechcloths and their hats, we sewed their mitasses, which we put on their legs, because our Canadians, of whom I have already spoken, were accustomed to doing such things.'[192]

In 1719, Bishop Saint-Vallier had learned that during hot weather, the Habitants in the Montréal area appeared 'against decorum, in a simple shirt without caleçon

183 Pehr Kalm, *The America of 1750 Peter Kalm's Travels in North America* (Madison, Wisconsin: Wilson-Erickson, 1937), vol.2, p.560

184 Gilles Ménage, *Dictionnaire etymologique ou origine de la langue françoise* (Paris: Anisson, 1694), p.124.

185 *Dictionnaire universel françois et latin, Tome premier* (Nancy: Pierre Antoine, 1740), vol.1, p.1214.

186 Abel Royer, *The Royal Dictionary* (La Haye, Chez Adrian Moetjens, 1702) vol.1.

187 *Dictionnaire universel françois et latin, Tome premier* (Nancy: Pierre Antoine, 1740), vol.1, p.1213.

188 *Dictionnaire universel francois et latin* (Paris: Par la Compagnie des Libraires associes, 1752), , vol.1, pp.1837–1838.

189 Pehr Kalm, *Peter Kalm's Travels in North America; the English Version of 1770, Rev. from the Original Swedish and Edited by Adolph B. Benson, with a Translation of New Material from Kalm's Diary Notes* (New York: Dover Publications, 1964), vol.2, p.560.

190 Henry de Tonty, *Relations de la Louisiane et du fleuve Mississippi...* (Amsterdam: Jean Frederic Bernard, 1720), p.14.

191 *Nouvelle-France: Documents historiques. Correspondance échangée entre les autorités françaises et les gouverneurs et intendants* (Québec: L.J. Demers & frère, 1893), vol.1, p.226.

192 BnF, André Joseph Penicaut, *Relation, ou annale véritable de ce qui s'est passé dans le païs de la Louisiane pendant vingt-deux années consecutifes, depuis le commencement de l'établissement des François dans le païs, par Mr d'Hyberville et Mr le comte de Sugère, en 1699, continué jusqu'en 1721* (Collection numérique : France-Amérique), pp.9–10. (http://catalogue.bnf.fr/ark:/12148/cb39230575v.)

or breeches.'[193] In essence, in the hot North American summer heat, the dress of the voyageur, like that of certain colonists in New France, consisted of a brayet, a shirt or Native-style leggings (mitasses). This was also the same for Canadian militiamen, who did '4 to 5 months of campaign wearing only a shirt, a brayet and a [wool] cap.'[194] *Capitaine* Pierre Pouchot went so far as describing a group of these men as 'all wearing shirts, and their backsides bare in the Canadian style.'[195] Even if it meant breaking with French metropolitan customs and offending the sense of modesty of certain individuals, wearing a breechcloth was a widespread practice for those who had to face the realities of the North American climate.

Equipment Lists

Prior to 1755, few official equipment lists relating to the colonial soldiers serving in New France listed brayets, even though they were almost certainly provided for large-scale wilderness expeditions. For example, a cadet of the colonial troops was given 'a pair of mitasses and a brayet,' both estimated at 12 livres, to replace the ones he had lost when returning from the Chickasaw campaign in 1740.[196] Six years later, '2½ *aunes* of drap, for 10 breechcloths' were sent from the King's storehouses at Montréal to Fort Saint-Frédéric for the fort's needs,[197] while, in 1752, Intendant Bigot planned to include brayets as part of the winter campaign equipment for Native American allies, militiamen, and colonial soldiers as part of the Ohio Valley expedition.[198]

In 1755, '1,200 *aunes* of Drap d'Angleterre (English cloth) for brayets,' were requested by Bigot as part of the clothing needed for the regular troops accompanying Baron de Dieskau.[199] Prior to leaving Montréal for Fort Frontenac that summer, the officer Malartic listed a 'brayer' (breechcloth) as part of the standard-issued campaign equipment supplied to the colonial officers and soldiers and of the Troupes de terre.[200] La Pause took note that officers, domestiques, regular or colonial soldiers, militiamen, or Native Americans taking part in a campaign were usually supplied with breechcloths with the exception of the soldiers that were given breeches instead.[201] The following year, this same officer claimed that 'each officer was given, as well as the previous campaign, an additional blanket,

ditto for their domestiques, and also breeches with caleçon (drawers) instead of breechcloths.'[202] According to Robert Eastburn, a British prisoner returning from an attack against Fort Bull on March 27, 1756, a portion of the French forces, that included the colonial troops and the Canadian militia, wore breechcloths in winter: 'The French carried several of their wounded Men all the Way upon their Backs, and (many of them wore no Breeches in their Travels in this cold Season, they are strong, hardy Men).'[203] At Carillon in July of that same year, *capitaine* Leduchat of the Régiment de Languedoc wrote that officers of the colonial and regular troops were provided, among other items, with 'a brayet,' and added that 'soldiers and the domestiques are treated the same for their equipment.'[204]

At Fort St-Jean in February of 1757, Montcalm and Bougainville both pointed out that soldiers were to receive breeches and drawers for the winter campaign of 1757, rather than breechcloths.[205] However, a declaration by two French prisoners taken on 23 March 1757, at Fort William-Henry stated that breeches were provided to soldiers as part of the standard-issue equipment, without mentioning breechcloths, indicating that colonial soldiers did not wear breechcloths during winter campaigns at that time.[206] On the other hand, a quantity of '224 molleton breechcloths' were inventoried at Fort Carillon in 1757, which were unquestionably intended for the body of troops or militiamen stationed at that military outpost.[207] By 1758, the army officer Bourlamaque took note of the oversupply of regulation breeches which were handed out instead of breechcloths: 'You may be surprised at the stockpile of breeches. In addition to those of the Habillement général, we were each given a pair before taking part in the campaign, instead of a breechcloth.'[208] Lastly, an undated equipment list prepared by Bourlamaque specified that a breechcloth valued at 2 livres 10 sols was provided to each officer for the summer months as well as '1 pair of breeches and drawers' for

193 LAC, MG 11, H 25, vol.2, doc. 24.
194 *RAPQ* 1931–1932, p.75.
195 Pierre Pouchot, *Mémoires sur la dernière guerre de l'Amérique septentrionale, entre la France et l'Angleterre* (Yverdon: F.B. de Félice, 1781), vol.2, p.261.
196 LAC, MG1-C11A, vol.73, f.249.
197 LAC, MG1-C11A, vol.88 f.238v.
198 LAC, MG1-C11A, vol.98, f.276.
199 LAC, MG1-C11A, vol.100, f.263v.
200 De Malartic & Gaffarel (eds), *Journal des Campagnes au Canada*, p.13.
201 RAPQ, 1932–1933, p.210.

202 RAPQ, 1932–1933, p.68–73.
203 Robert Eastburn, *A Faithful Narrative of the Many Dangers and Sufferings, as Well as Wonderful Deliverances of Robert Eastburn, During His Late Captivity Among the Indians* (Philadelphia: William Dunlap, 1758), p.11.
204 AG, MG 4, B 1, Série A1, vol.3417, f.383.
205 De Bougainville, *Écrits sur le Canada*, p.168. Henri-Raymond Casgrain, *Journal du marquis de Montcalm durant ses campagnes en Canada de 1756 à 1759* (Québec, Impr. de L.J. Demers & frère, 1895), pp.156–157.
206 LOC, Colonial Office 5 folio 47, E. of Loudoun's Letter of April 25th. 1757, Declaration of two Prisoners taken the 23.d March 1757 at Fort Wm. Henry, Information of John Victor and Guillaume Chasse, two French Prisoners, Fort William Henry March 25th.
207 LAC, MG18, K9, vol.6, f.457.
208 Henri-Raymond Casgrain, *Collection des manuscrits du maréchal de Lévis, lettres de M. de Bourlamaque au maréchal de Lévis* (Québec: Imprimerie de L.-J. Demers & Frère, 1891), p.208.

the soldiers,[209] while Intendant Bigot confirmed that the winter campaign equipment intended for colonial officers, soldiers, militiamen, domestiques, and Natives American allies included, among other items, '1 breech-cloth of cloth' per man.[210]

Length, Type of Cloth, and Colours

Breechcloths are often referenced in period records as measuring ¼ *aune*, as exemplified by Marie-Andrée Regnard Duplessis, a Nun Hospitaller of the Hôtel-Dieu of Québec, who in 1728 noted that a brayet was 'a small piece of leather or cloth of about a square quarter [of an *aune*].'[211] Meanwhile, the missionary Lafiteau described this item as 'a skin, a *pied* wide and three or four in length. It is passed between the thighs and then carried up over a belt of sinew worn around the waist, with the two ends hanging down about a *pied* or so.'[212] The French soldier, storekeeper at Fort Duquesne, and presumed author of *Voyage au Canada fait depuis l'an 1751*, Joseph-Charles Bonin dit Jolicoeur, remarked that 'a brahier … is a quarter or a third of [an *aune* of] cloth,' where the front flap is longer than the back one,[213] while Pouchot noted that Native Americans wear a breech-cloth 'which is a quarter of an *aune* of cloth.'[214] During the 1740s, breechcloths provided to Native American allies from the King's storehouses generally measured ¼ or ⅔ of an *aune* and were sometimes specified as made using molleton.[215] Colonial commercial records from the 1740s to the 1760s often referenced molleton as being white, blue, red, violet (purple), or occasionally brown. During the Seven Years War, French officers deemed that breechcloths supplied by the munitionnaire du Roi (purveyor general to the French forces in Canada) were obviously made too short, small, or from inferior cloth.[216]

Records relating to military personnel serving in New France contain scarce mentions of breechcloths, and even fewer specify their colour. For example, in 1727, *sergent* Sanspeur purchased '1 brayet' for 2 livres 10 sols from the merchant Nolan-Lamarque before his departure for the Detroit garrison,[217] while Girard, an officer of the colonial troops at Kaskaskia, owned a breechcloth made from Limbourg cloth, which was often referenced in red or blue.[218] According to Dumont de Montigny, Native American men living in Louisiana 'wear a kind of belt, through which they pass a quarter of [an *aune*] a red or blue cloth, which in the country one calls Limbourg.'[219] Gilbert Barbier, a colonist living at Montréal in 1660 was the owner of a 'a breechcloth of gray cloth' valued at 3 livres while in 1757, 'a brayet of red cloth' assessed at 2 livres was listed among the personal possessions of Louis Binet, Habitant of Beauport near Québec.[220] In short, these strips of cloth came in a number of colours and Baron de Lahontan, an officer in the colonial troops who travelled to Canada during the late 1600s, confirmed this, stating that a brayer 'is a piece of fabric of many colours.'[221]

Leggings (Mitasses)

Native gaiters, called mitasses by French settlers using the Native term from the Algonkin languages, were adopted by the colonial troops as part of their wilderness dress to replace their military gaiters or regulation stockings. According to surviving records, those issued to the colonial troops from the Magasins du Roy would have been pre-made without any ornamentation, and mostly using molleton fabric, a type of serge. No official document specifies the colours used in making leggings for the colonial troops, although, based on judicial and probate records relating to soldiers and officers, blue ones appear to be more common. In addition, some men may have chosen to add an edge of lace or tape to prevent the cloth from unravelling or to simply decorate them. Leggings were held by garters below the knee, while a tie extending from the top of the leggings was attached to a belt worn around the waist to hold them up. These economical and practical tubular leg coverings protected the men's lower legs as they marched through branches and underbrush.

209 LAC, MG18, K9, vol.6, f.470.

210 Bigot, *Mémoire Pour Messire François Bigot*, p.39.

211 Archives nationales, Section ancienne, Série T, Séquestre, 1718–1758. MG3, I, série T, carton 77–78, f.6–33, Québec, 17 octobre 1723.

212 *Le voyageur français ou la connaissance de l'ancien et du nouveau monde* (Paris: Chez L. Cellot, 1769), vol.9, p.121

213 Henri-Raymond Casgrain, *Voyage au Canada: dans le nord de l'Amérique septentrionale: fait depuis l'an 1751 à 1761* (Québec: Imprimerie Léger Brousseau, 1887), p.223.

214 Pouchot, *Mémoires sur la dernière guerre de l'Amérique septentrionale*, p.238.

215 LAC, MG1-C11A, vol.86, f.181, 184; LAC, MG1-C11A, vol.115, f.264.

216 De Bougainville, *Écrits sur le Canada*, pp.297–298.

217 BAnQ-M, Livre de compte de C. Nolan Lamarque, 1727–1729, p.22.

218 Kaskaskia Manuscripts (Randolph County Courthouse, Chester, Illinois), 4 juillet, 1723.

219 Jean-François-Benjamin Dumont de Montigny, *Mémoires historiques sur la Louisiane* (Paris: Chez Cl. J. B. Bauche, libraire, 1753), vol.1, p.137.

220 BAnQ-Q, Greffe du notaire Pierre Parent, …à la requête de Madeleine Giroux, veuve de feu Louis Binet, vivant habitant de la paroisse de Beauport…, 2 septembre 1757.

221 Louis Armand de Lom d'Arce baron de La Hontan, *Voyages du baron de Lahontan dans l'Amérique Septentrionale* (Amsterdam: Chez Francois l'Honoré, 1728), vol.1, p.90.

Left: This drawing, executed around 1730, depicts a Fox warrior, tattooed and armed with a bow and arrow. Notably, the warrior is wearing a red brayet with a stripe running along the end, likely made of Limbourg or Stroud cloth. The French officer Dumont de Montigny observed that Native men living in Louisiana wore breechcloths made using red or blue Limbourg cloth. As noted at the bottom of this illustration, 'When they have a shirt, they wear it tied when they have to fight.' (World Digital Library. Control Number: 2021668133)

Right: Despite the disapproval of local clergymen, French colonists living in the St Lawrence Valley would often wear only breechcloths and shirts in the summer heat to work more comfortably in the fields. The shirts modestly covered them down to the knees. (Francis Back © Raphaëlle and Félix Back)

Detail from a 1754 anonymous painting of Cardinal Richelieu, copied from an original dated 1639. In the background are two Huron warriors: one wearing a blue decorated breechcloth, the other in a plain red breechcloth with edging, holding a small axe. (Augustines de L'Hôtel-Dieu de Québec. Photo Kevin Gélinas)

Left: Detail featuring Chief Okana-Stoté of the Cherokee, serving as a *capitaine* in the French forces during the French and Indian War. He is shown receiving a commission from Governor Louis Billouart, Chevalier de Kerlérec, of Louisiana. The Native chief is depicted wearing a blue brayet with a single white stripe, likely made of Limbourg cloth, with red or blue being the colours most often referenced in French records for making brayets. A similar breechcloth from the Eastern Woodlands (1775–1785), made from blue Stroud cloth, is part of the Canadian Museum of History collection (Artifact number: III-X-248). (General Records of the Department of State, Record Group 59; National Archives at College Park, College Park, MD.)

Right: Detail from a watercolour (c. 1750–1780) depicting an Algonquin man wearing a blue breechcloth and leggings. The leggings are shown tied to the waist with a ribbon or tie to keep them in place. These types of leggings (mitasses) were worn for leg protection against underbrush and for warmth. (Archives de la Ville de Montréal, BM7-2_27P004.)

Two of five wax Native dolls from a miniature canoe model. Both male dolls wear traditional clothing representing different nations from the French period in the St Lawrence Valley. Note the red leggings and white garters. According to Michael Galban, the canoe was designed at the beginning of the eighteenth century, although the exact date is uncertain. It is one of the earliest examples of its kind. (Collection du musée des Beaux-Arts de Chartres)

Detail from a rare (1730?) drawing of voyageurs in the fur trade, showing Native-style leggings worn by one of the men dressed for colder weather. Garters are tied below the knees to prevent the tubular leg coverings from slipping down, and the mitasses are tucked into his high-cut moccasins. Interestingly, this coureur de bois appears to be wearing European breeches instead of a breechcloth. (Habillemens des Coureurs de Bois Canadiens, no. 2, Anonymous, c. 1730, Beinecke Rare Book and Manuscript Library, Yale University Library, New Haven, CT, USA, WA MSS S-2412)

Origin and Definition of Mitasses

Observations relating to the equipment issued to the regulars and colonial soldiers as part of the 1756 campaign in Canada mention that a pair of mitasses 'serve as gaiters.'[222] These Native-style leggings, originally made of leather (buckskin, moose hide), were now mostly crafted from wool cloth and made from a long rectangular piece of fabric folded around the leg and sewn along the outside edges, leaving about four finger-lengths of material hanging on either side. Colonial officer Pierre Le Moyne d'Iberville described these types of leggings and how a group of Canadians introduced a Louisiana tribe of Native Americans to mitasses: 'The mitasses are made from ½ aune of cloth, cut in half and sewn like stockings in which they place their legs…We sewed their mitasses that we fitted on their legs, because our Canadians, of whom I have already spoken of, were in the habit of doing such things.'[223] According to Jean-Baptiste d'Aleyrac, the

mitasses issued to a man sent to war or on duty in Canada 'are a type of very wide gaiters, the two sides of which are sewn together at about four fingers from the edge without buttons or buttonholes.'[224] J.C.B., presumably Joseph-Charles Bonin, known as Jolicoeur, a gunner serving in the Compagnie des canonniers-bombardiers of Canada during the 1750s, described the mitasses worn by the French colonists in detail:

> What we call mitasses or mitassonés in the Indian language are a kind of stockings that Canadians made using two halves of an *aune* of cloth, or one yard of molleton separated in two for each leg … there is an excess outside the seam of about four to five *pouces* in width that can be allowed to flutter down the leg at will, or where the leg opening can be tucked in the shoe, if we wish, and is fastened from above using a garter above the calf. When we want to decorate these kinds of stockings, we trim them with ribbons sewn in a row or in a zigzag shape, on the edge of the flap which flutters on the outside.[225]

Equipment Lists

Surviving military equipment lists show that, by the 1690s, officers, cadets, and soldiers of the colonial troops serving in New France were issued mitasses as part of wilderness campaigns or when detached to serve at forts. These are usually referenced as made using 1 *aune* of molleton fabric, which, according to the *Dictionnaire portatif de commerce*, was a type of serge 'which is very warm and very soft, is ordinarily used to make camisoles, petticoats and linings for the winter.'[226] Initially, soldiers of the Compagnies franches de la Marine taking part in small detachments would have worn stockings, probably cut from cloth. For example, the 31 colonial soldiers that accompanied de Troyes from Montréal to James Bay in 1686 were issued '2 pairs of stockings (bas)' rather than mitasses leggings, which were instead issued to the 65 Habitants that took part in the expedition.[227] By 1692, 50 soldiers returning to Acadia from the Boston prisons were to be provided with '150 *aunes* of Mazamet to make 90 pairs of mitasses.'[228] In 1734, '56 pairs of mitasses using 56

222 SHAT, Dossier A1, 3417, Pièce 144.
223 BnF, André Joseph Penicaut, *Relation, ou annale véritable de ce qui s'est passé dans le païs de la Louisiane pendant vingt-deux années*

consecutifes, depuis le commencement de l'établissement des François dans le païs, par Mr d'Hyberville et Mr le comte de Sugère, en 1699, continué jusqu'en 1721 (Collection numérique: France-Amérique), pp.9–10. <http://catalogue.bnf.fr/ark:/12148/cb39230575v>.
224 BAnQ-M, ZF8, Fonds Jean Baptiste d'Aleyrac.
225 Henri Raymond Casgrain, *Voyage au Canada: dans le nord de l'Amérique septentrionale : fait depuis l'an 1751 à 1761 / par J. C. B.* (Québec: Imprimerie Léger Brousseau, 1887), p.79.
226 *Dictionnaire portatif de commerce* (Copenhague: Chez les Frère C. & A. Philibert, 1761), vol.5, p.472.
227 LAC, MG1-C11A, vol.8, f.278v, 279v.
228 *Collection de manuscrits contenant lettres, mémoires, et autres documents historiques relatifs á la Nouvelle-France* (Québec: Imprimerie A. Coté et cie, 1884), vol.2, p.72.

aunes of molleton' were provided to 56 colonial soldiers taking part in the last major campaign against the Foxes,[229] while at Fort de la Pointe-à-la-Chevelure, a quantity of 2 *aunes* of 'molleton for mitasses' were stockpiled for service of the fort for various outings or for replacements for the garrison.[230] Five years later, officers, cadets, and soldiers sent to make war on the Chickasaw tribe were each issued one pair of mitasses.[231]

Numerous records reference mitasses being issued to the troops during King George's War, including a 1746 entry where the officer Le Mercier, detached to Fort Saint-Frédéric, received '1 *aune* of molleton for 1 pair of mitasses,' while officers De Longueuil and Mezière, as well as cadets Porneuf and Dusablé, were given '4 *aunes* of molleton in 4 pairs of mitasses.'[232] That same year, 10 men, including officers, cadets, Canadians, and two soldiers named Roulleau and Lafausse were provided with '10 *aunes* of molleton in 10 pairs of mitasses.'[233] Additionally, equipment distributed to various war parties sent against New England in 1747 also included these leggings using 1 *aune* of molleton fabric.[234] Five years later, Intendant Bigot had planned to distribute leggings to a number of colonial soldiers as part of the equipment required for an important winter expedition in the Ohio Valley.[235]

According to Pierre Pouchot, each time the colonial troops participated in a campaign during the Seven Years War, the King supplied them with a pair of mitasses.[236] In 1755, Malartic observed that these leggings were provided to both officers and soldiers of the Troupes de terre,[237] and the following year, an account of provisions for the officers and soldiers of these battalions as well as those of the colonial troops for each month of campaigning during the summer included '1 pair of mitasses.'[238] Guillaume de Méritens de Pradals, an officer in the Régiment de la Sarre, wrote that during winter campaigns, officers and soldiers received 'one pair of mitts and two pairs of mitasses, which are stockings made from coarse cloth.'[239] Reports by Montcalm and Bougainville confirm that mitasses were distributed in February 1757 at Fort Saint-Jean, with one list valuing them at 5 livres and another at 3 livres.[240] The

following month, a regular and a colonial soldier captured at Fort William Henry both confirmed they were each given 'one pair of Indian stockings or Leg pieces', likely referring to mitasses or possibly gaiters.[241] In 1760, while retreating to Montréal, a shipment of war munitions transferred from the storehouses at Trois-Rivières to Montréal included '12 *aunes* of molleton, made into mitasses', indicating that the wool leggings were pre-made.[242] Lastly, during his trial in 1763, Intendant Bigot noted that the winter equipment issued to colonial officers and soldiers included '1 pair of mitasses of cloth.'[243]

By late 1757, there appears to have been a shortage of some standard-issue items required for winter, including mitasses. A letter addressed to Bourlamaque at Fort Carillon in November 1757 highlights this scarcity: 'The equipment that M. Bigot grants is very modest for a wintering, especially for the stockings, of which the soldiers are completely lacking … if he finds that their gaiters are worn out, I cannot afford to send them mitasses instead.'[244] During the 1760 campaign, a circular letter about equipment availability noted that officers could be given mitasses 'or, instead, a pair of stockings', while soldiers were forced to use these tubular leggings due to the lack of stockings.[245]

Probate Records

Judicial archives reveal that a few colonial soldiers owned mitasses, and those referenced were mostly blue in colour. For instance, as part of an interrogation at Montréal in 1725, Jean-Baptiste dit Guignolet, a colonial soldier, was asked 'where he got the pair of mitasses he wears every day. Said he got them from his mother, who got them from the Seminary.'[246] In 1741, Jean Prétat dit Lajoie, a *caporal* in the colonial troops who was accused of theft at the King's storehouses at Fort Niagara, declared that he

229 LAC, MG1-C11A, vol.62, f.150v.
230 LAC, MG1-C11A, vol.66, f.56.
231 LAC, MG1-C11A, vol.71, f.156–161, 169–169v.
232 LAC, MG1-C11A, vol.88, f.214, 229v.
233 LAC, MG1-C11A, vol.86, f.218v.
234 LAC, MG1-C11A, vol.117, f.191v-192.
235 LAC, MG1-C11A, vol.98, fol. 276.
236 Pouchot, *Mémoires sur la dernière guerre de l'Amérique septentrionale*, p.28.
237 De Malartic & Gaffarel (eds), *Journal des Campagnes au Canada*, p.13.
238 SHAT, Dossier A1, 3417, Pièce 144.
239 R. Douville, 'Le Canada 1756–1758, vu par un officier du régiment de La Sarre', *Les Cahiers des Dix*, 24 (1959), p.116.
240 Henri-Raymond Casgrain, *Journal du marquis de Montcalm durant ses campagnes en Canada de 1756 à 1759* (Québec :

Imprimerie de L.J. Demers & frère, 1895) pp.156–157; De Bougainville, *Écrits sur le Canada*, p.168.
241 LOC, Colonial Office 5 folio 47, E. of Loudoun's Letter of April 25th. 1757, Declaration of two Prisoners taken the 23.d March 1757 at Fort Wm. Henry, Information of John Victor and Guillaume Chasse, two French Prisoners, Fort William Henry March 25th..
242 BAnQ-Q, Greffe du notaire Jean-Claude Panet, Facture des marchandises et munitions qui ont été tirées des magasins du Roi aux Trois-Rivières et chargées sur le bateau le St-Henry, capitaine Laparre pour porter et remettre à Monsieur Fayolle, garde des dits magasins à Montréal, le tout marqué et numéroté comme en marge, 25 août 1764.
243 Bigot, *Mémoire Pour Messire François Bigot*, p.39.
244 LAC, MG18, K9, vol.6, f.458.
245 Casgrain, *Collection des manuscrits du maréchal de Lévis*, p.275.
246 BAnQ-M, TL4, S1, D3159, Procès entre Julien Trottier DesRivières, marchand, plaignant, et Marie-Joachim, panise, esclave de la veuve Biron et Jean-Baptiste Gouriou dit Guignolet, soldat de Blainville, fils du sergent Jean-Baptiste Gouriou dit Guignolet, accusés respectivement de vol et de recel, 17 juillet–17 octobre 1725.

'sold a pair of blue mitasses' as part of what he bartered with several people of the garrison.[247] Thirteen years later, a soldier accused of theft in the distribution chamber at Fort Saint-Frédéric 'recognised the breeches, mitasses and garters belonging to the said Parisian (soldier)', which were described as 'a pair of mitasses, of blue molleton, [edged] with green tape trimmed with white beads.' Another description of the same leggings noted 'a pair of mitasses of molleton violet, trimmed with white beads,' revealing that the colour violet used in this case may have appeared closer to blue than purple.[248]

Probate records show that some colonial officers owned leggings made from a variety of materials, including blue and white cloth, as well as leather. For instance, in 1703, *capitaine* Jacques de Joibert of Montréal owned 'an old pair of mitasses of white finette, worn down', that was estimated at 1 livre 5 sols.[249] Finette was a type of wool cloth manufactured in the Dauphiné Province. Two decades later, the post-mortem inventory of the personal effects of Girard at Kaskaskia included 'a pair of deer-skin mitasses' as well as a 'a pair of blue mitasses.'[250] A few years later at Québec, the officer Philipe D'Amour de La Morendière had 'a pair of mitasses' among his personal possessions.[251] In 1737, 'a pair of brass buckles and a pair of silk garters' as well as 'a pair of mitasses' were inventoried after the death of Joseph Dejourdy de Cabanac, *lieutenant* of the colonial troops.[252] In April of 1760, Jean-Baptiste de Langy, a écuyer in the Troupes de la Marine living in the Outaouais region owned 'an old pair of mitasses of molleton,' likely a standard issue pair of leggings he received prior to a campaign.[253] Exceptionally, Louis de La Corne, who died in the sinking of the *Auguste* in 1761, left behind 'a pair of leather mitasses'[254] while Joseph Damour de Plaine, a écuyer living at Québec until 1768, owned 'an old pair of mitasses of blue molleton', which may have been his King's issue leggings.[255] High-ranking officers of the Troupes de terre concluded that the leggings provided by the munitionnaire du roi during the Seven Years War were obviously made too short, too small, or from inferior cloth.[256]

Legging Colours and Material

As stated above, blue appears to have been one of the most common colours of molleton used for mitasses worn or owned by the members of the colonial troops, as illustrated by numerous judicial and probate records in which they were found recorded. This is further supported by notarial records of French colonists living in the Illinois Territory and in the districts of Montréal, Trois-Rivières, and Québec, which show that blue was the most common colour of mitasses, while red is not mentioned. It is important to note that references to the colours of mitasses in records are exceedingly rare, which accounts for the small number of samples.

Blue – 53%
White – 24%
Violet – 10%
Burgundy – 10%
Brown – 3%

Table 4. References to the colour of mitasses found in probate records, 1730–1763 (Illinois, Montréal, Trois-Rivières, Québec).

District	Blue	White	Violet	Burgundy	Brown	Total
Illinois	1	2	1			4
Montréal	7	1	1			9
Trois-Rivières	1	2				3
Québec	7	2	1	3	1	14
Total	16	7	3	3	1	
%	53%	24%	10%	10%	3%	

247 BAnQ-M, TL4, S1, D4797, Procès contre Claude Pillet, charretier pour le roi à Niagara, et Jean Prétat dit Lajoie, natif de Paris, caporal de la Compagnie de Linctot, et Marie-Suzanne Bissonnet, épouse de Brias, blanchisseuse, respectivement accusés de vol dans le magasin du roi, de complicité et de recel, 11 août 1741.

248 BAnQ-M, TL4, S1, D5921, Procès contre Menin Pouteau dit Parisien, sculpteur, soldat d'Herbin, Michel Dufeu dit Flame, soldat de la Compagnie de Villemonde, et Guillaume Goursol dit Lagiroflée, soldat de la Compagnie Debonne, accusés de vols dans la chambre de distribution du fort Saint-Frédéric, 9 septembre 1754–26 février 1755.

249 BAnQ-M, Greffe du notaire Louis Chamballon, Inventaire des biens de feu M. Jacques de Joibert, chevalier, seigneur de Soulanges, enseigne sur les vaisseaux du Roi et capitaine d'une compagnie franche des troupes du détachement de la Marine…, 2 mai 1703.

250 Kaskaskia Manuscripts (Randolph County Courthouse, Chester, Illinois), 4 et 23 juillet, 1723.

251 BAnQ-Q, Greffe du notaire Jacques Barbel, Inventaire des biens après le décès de la dame D'Amour La Morendière, auparavant veuve du feu Sieur Pierre Gauvreau (vivant armurier)… épouse en secondes noces de Philippe D'Amour, écuyer Sieur de La Morendière, officier des troupes du détachement de la Marine entretenu pour le service du Roi en ce pays, de présent en l'ancienne France, 25 avril 1726.

252 BAnQ-M, Greffe du notaire Charles René Gauchon de Chevremont, Inventaire des biens de feu Sieur Joseph Dejourdy de Cabanac, lieutenant d'une compagnie des troupes de ce pays, 27 mars 1737.

253 BAnQ-M, Greffe du notaire Danré de Blanzy, Inventaire de Catherine d'Ailleboust du Manthet et de Jean-Baptiste ? écuyer Sieur de Langy, officier demeurant aux Outaouais, 26 avril 1760.

254 BAnQ-M, Greffe du notaire Pierre Panet, Inventaire des biens de la communauté d'entre dame Marie-Anne Hubert, veuve de Sieur Chevalier de la Corne, dit Sieur De la Corne, vivant chevalier de l'ordre Royal et militaire de St-Louis, capitaine d'infanterie de sa majesté, 19 avril 1762.

255 BAnQ-Q, Greffe du notaire Jean-Claude Panet, Inventaire des biens de la communauté de Madeleine Coulon de Villier, veuve de Joseph Damour de Plaine, écuyer, de la rue Sous le Fort, 1er mars 1768.

256 De Bougainville, *Écrits sur le Canada*, pp.297–298.

The references to mitasses analysed as part of this research, drawn from hundreds of probate and merchant records, reveal that they were made from various fabrics, including molleton, Mazamet, Carisé, droguet, étoffee du pays, as well as canvas, and leather from sheep, caribou, and deer. In the district of Québec, mitasses made of caribou leather, a material that was readily available in the region, are commonly encountered.

Probate and judicial records sometimes included the colour of mitasses made from molleton, as seen in 1752, when Louis Bonnedeau dit Chatellereau of Québec owned 'a pair of mitasses of violet molleton.'[257] In 1756, a criminal trial at Montréal mentioned 'an *aune* or so of cloth to make a pair of mitasses, and two ribbons, one lemon-coloured the other red.' The cloth is specified later in the document as 'one *aune* or so of violet molleton, one *aune* or so of ribbon, lemon-coloured, another of cherry red.'[258] Three years later, Joseph Greslon dit Laviolette was caught with 'a pair of mitasses of blue molleton, edged with flame-colour and green silk tape with its ties, also edged, for about two thirds of blue cloth.'[259]

Garters (Jarretières)

Garters worn with breeches, referred to as 'jarretières pour culotte' or 'jarretière à culottes' by the French, were made using a variety of fabrics, including domestic wool, common wool, lace, silk, grenade silk, thread, gold thread, similor, silver thread, tape, and leather. However, Canadiens seem to have preferred wearing Native-style garters with their mitasses. Devoid of buckles, these garters were finger-woven using woollen yarn. They are often described in probate records as quilled, beaded, or, by the 1730s, made using bison hair. For instance, 'a quantity of garters of wool, finger-woven (tressée)' along with 'wool netted quilled sashes' were referenced as part of a criminal trial at Montréal in 1742.[260] Pehr Kalm commented on the widespread adoption of Native finger-woven articles by the Canadians in 1749, stating 'the French in Canada, in many respects, follow the customs of the Indians, with whom they converse every day. They make use of the tobacco-pipes, shoes, garters, and girdles of the Indians.'[261] Pouchot observed that, around the time of the Seven Years War, Native Americans 'wear garters of beads, or porcupine quills, bordered four fingers' wide, which are tied on the side of the leg.'[262]

It is probable that a few colonial soldiers or officers might have privately purchased or traded for Native-style garters to use with their standard issue mitasses, as these were not supplied by the King. Alternatively, these men may have also used whatever was readily available, such as common European-style garters intended for military or civilian trousers. In 1721, for instance, the officer Louis Aubert in Québec owned 'three garters decorated with porcupine quills.'[263] Similarly, a cassette belonging to a colonial soldier at Fort Saint-Frédéric in 1754 contained 'a pair of wool garters decorated with rassade beads', 'a pair of blue mitasses', and 'a pair of garters, black Granada silk with a brass buckle attached to each one.'[264] The following year, Pierre de Monferand, a soldier near Québec, had 'a garter of wool with white stripes' and 'two black garters of wool,' which might have been made with bison hair.[265] And lastly, a trial from 1749 to 1751 revealed that a soldier of the Compagnie de Beaujeu owned 'a pair of leather garters', possibly used as straps for military gaiters, and 'a pair of garters, black Granada silk with a brass buckle attached to each one.'[266]

Wool Stocking Caps (Bonnets de Laine)

Initially supplied with tapabord caps, by the mid-eighteenth century, the colonial troops were also issued knitted

257 BAnQ-Q, Greffe du notaire Gilbert Boucault de Godefus, Inventaire de Louis Bonnedeau dit Chatellereau et Marie-Geneviève Chalifour, 28 août 1752.

258 BAnQ-M, TL4, S1, D6078, Procès contre Louise Gouriou dit Guignolet, son époux Joseph Croizau dit Larose, journalier, et Geneviève Loiseau, veuve d'André Dutault, matelot, accusés de vente de boisson aux sauvages, 12 février–5 avril 1756.

259 BAnQ-M, TL4, S1, D6220, Procès contre Joseph Greslon dit Laviolette, transporteur de l'île Chauve, son épouse Marguerite Piton dit Toulouse, Charles Saint-Amant, habitant de l'île Chauve, sa femme, et Louis Greslon dit Laviolette, accusés de vol de marchandises du Roi, 13 juin 1758–23 octobre 1759.

260 BAnQ-Q, TL5, D1307, Procès criminel à la Juridiction royale de Montréal contre les nommés Jean-Baptiste Ceré, père et fils, et Étienne-Michel Ruparon dit Sanspoil (Sans Poil), fils d'Étienne Ruparon, accusés de vols nocturnes, 17 mars–28 avril 1742.

261 Pehr Kalm, *Travels into North America* (London: William Eyres, 1771), vol.3, p.254.

262 Pouchot, *Memoir Upon the Late War in North America*, vol.2, p.187.

263 BAnQ-Q, TL5, D831, L'inventaire des biens dépendants de la succession de feu Louis Aubert écuyer, Sieur du Forillon, demeurant en cette ville de Québec, rue du Sault-au-matelot… , 6 mars 1721.

264 BAnQ-M, TL4, S1, D5921, Procès contre Menin Pouteau dit Parisien, sculpteur, soldat d'Herbin, Michel Dufeu dit Flame, soldat de la Compagnie de Villemonde, et Guillaume Goursol dit Lagiroflée, soldat de la Compagnie Debonne, accusés de vols dans la chambre de distribution du fort Saint-Frédéric, 9 septembre 1754–26 février 1755.

265 BAnQ-Q, TP1, S777, D178, Procès de Pierre de Monferand (Montferrand) dit Chevalier, 23 ans, chirurgien, soldat de la compagnie de Paul Bécard, sieur de Fonville, natif de La Châtre en Berry, aucune demeure fixe, étant arrivé cet automne de France à Louisbourg, accusé du meurtre, par un coup de fusil, de Louis Chel dit Saint-André, à la Pointe-à-la-Caille, paroisse Saint-Thomas, 17 novembre 1754–17 mai 1755.

266 BAnQ-Q, TL5, D1640, Procès criminel contre Claude du Retour (Duretour) de Monsy, seigneur de Neuville et autres terres, environ 31 ans, soldat de la compagnie de Beaujeu, et Louis Daurizon (Dorizon) dit Larose, soldat de la compagnie de Beaujeu, environ 39 ans, pour falsification d'ordonnances, 1er janvier 1749–5 novembre 1751.

bonnets fashioned from yarn, similar to those worn by Canadian Habitants, for both winter and summer campaigns. The bonnets, which originated from the sailors and coastal people of France, were frequently recorded in red or scarlet, while some were two-tone (half in natural wool and the other half dyed in red), or simply white (natural wool). They came in several sizes and in several grades of wool and dyes and, therefore, differed in price. The majority were imported from France as finished articles and were mostly made in the cities of Saint-Maixent, Marseille, and Orléans. During King George's War, wool caps termed bonnets drapés (mill-fulled knit caps) and bonnets à bateau (boat caps) were frequently issued to the colonial troops taking part in wilderness campaigns.

By the Seven Years War, official military supply lists included a bonnet de laine (wool cap), and those stocked at forts for the use of soldiers were frequently recorded as made at Saint-Maixent, France. Although these caps came in a single thickness model, termed bonnet simple in French, the majority were double, meaning they were made in the form of an empty cocoon, with one end tucked into the other to provide additional warmth. The term 'bonnet de laine' either referred to the bonnet drapé or the bonnet à bateau. The latter bonnets à bateau, are believed to have had brims with earflaps, which protected the wearer's ears in cold or windy weather, similar to the ones found on the wreck of the Machault.

Origin and Definition of the Bonnet

Pehr Kalm observed that most colonists living in Canada wore 'red woollen caps at home and sometimes on their journey',[267] while Father Potier noted that 'almost all Canadians have tuques (wool caps).'[268] As early as the 1720s, French colonists living in the St Lawrence Valley nicknamed their wool caps tuques, and in the area surrounding Québec, they were often called fouroles.[269] According to the officer d'Aleyrac, Canadians would say 'a tuque or fourole to designate a red wool cap which they usually wear.'[270] The caps are not to be mistaken with the bonnet de police (fatigue caps) worn on fatigue duty, that is, when on work detail and not under arms.

Equipment Lists

At first, the colonial troops in New France were provided with tapabord caps, wool caps with brims and flaps that covered the back of the head and ears, tied under the chin to prevent it from flying away and when not in use the brim and flaps folded around the cap.[271] Each of the roughly 30 men of the 1686 de Troyes expedition to capture the British forts on James Bay were supplied with tapabord caps as their only head covering.[272] In 1692, a list of supplies intended for the soldiers posted in Acadia included '90 tapabords [caps],'[273] yet four years later, the minister of Marine informed the Intendant at Rochefort that hats were requested for the soldiers at Fort Naxouat instead of tapabord caps, which were formerly issued to the soldiers.[274]

Wool caps, which only occasionally appeared on official regulation clothing lists, were provided to soldiers headed to Plaisance and Acadia in 1687 with 'one bonnet,'[275] and each soldier crossing over to Canada in 1696 was supplied with 'one wool bonnet' (un bonnet de laine).[276] In 1716, officials in France wrote that 'the practice is to provide the recruited soldiers before their departure with … one bonnet', priced respectively at 8 sols.[277] Thirty years later, a quantity of '500 wool bonnets' was sent to various ports along with weapons and clothing for both the metropolitan and colonial troops.[278]

During King George's War, woollen caps termed bonnet à bateau or bonnet drapé were occasionally provided to the colonial troops taking part in wilderness campaigns. According to period dictionaries, the term 'drapé' meant a mill-fulled finish meant to resemble the nap of thick woollen cloth, or woollen items prepared in such a way that they resemble cloth.[279]

Bonnet à bateau, which can be translated as 'boat cap', was likely a style of knitted cap with ear pockets or flaps, such as were found aboard the Machault, a French frigate that sank in 1760 in Baie des Chaleurs. In fact, numerous excavated seventeenth- and eighteenth-century whalers' knitted caps, discovered in Dutch whaling camps in the Arctic, featured ear flaps, highlighting a practical design to protect against the harsh cold.

267 Kalm, *Travels into North America*, vol.3, p.255.
268 Robert Toupin, *Les écrits de Pierre Potier* (Ottawa: Les Presses de l'Université d'Ottawa, 1996), p.480.
269 f.Back, 'Tuque, teuge, toque ou bonnet à la Turque?', *Cap-aux-Diamants*, 53 (1998), p.56.
270 BAnQ-M, ZF8, Fonds Jean Baptiste d'Aleyrac.

271 f.Back, 'Le tapabord', *Cap-aux-Diamants*, 60 (2000), p.50; Isaac Walters, 'The Tapabord Hat in New France: A Cold Weather Alternative', *On The Trail*, vol.13 no.6 November/December 2006.
272 LAC, MG1-C11A, vol.8, f.278v.
273 *Collection de manuscrits contenant lettres, mémoires, et autres documents historiques relatifs á la Nouvelle-France* (Québec: Imprimerie A. Coté et cie, 1884), vol.2, p.72.
274 LAC, MG6, 1E, vol.38, f.170.
275 LAC, F1, vol.3, f.123.
276 AR, IE, 599, Adjudication des marchandises pour Canada faite à La Rochelle par Mr Massiot, conseiller du Roy, commissaire de la marine, 19 mars, 1696.
277 AR, IE, 87, fol. 167.
278 LAC, MG1-B, vol.84, f.71v.
279 *Dictionnaire universel Francois et Latin contenant la signification et la définition tant des mots de l'une et de l'autre langue* (Paris: Par la Compagnie des Libraires associé, 1752), vol.3, p.327.; *Nouveau Dictionnaire François composé sur le Dictionnaire de l'Académie Françoise...* (Lyon: J.B. Delamollière, 1793), vol.1, p.97.

Engraving from Duhamel du Monceau's *Traité général des Pêches*, depicting a French mariner wearing a long stocking cap.

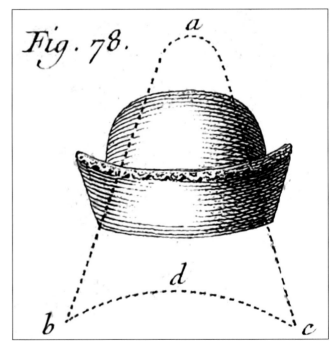

This illustration by Francis Back demonstrates the versatile nature of the tapabord hat, a headgear adaptable to different weather conditions. While its aesthetics may be debatable, its protective qualities are undeniable. The reconstruction is based on European iconography and sketches by missionary Chrestien Le Clercq, who depicted Mi'kmaq wearing tapabords. (Francis Back © Raphaëlle et Félix Back)

The cap featured in L'Art du Chapelier (Figures 77 & 78), referred to as a bonnet de poste, is '…also called a bonnet en bateau [boat-shaped cap]… because of its shape, felted like hats.' While this felted hat does not correspond to the knit stocking caps known as bonnets à bateau, which were shipped in large quantities to New France, its folded appearance, as depicted here by Nollet, resembles a boat – likely inspiring its name. Period dictionaries often describe 'folded-down caps' as bonnet rabattu or bonnet de matelot (mariner's cap), suggesting that the popular bonnet à bateau issued to colonial soldiers in Canada undoubtedly had ear flaps, similar to those worn by French sailors to protect their ears from cold, brisk winds.

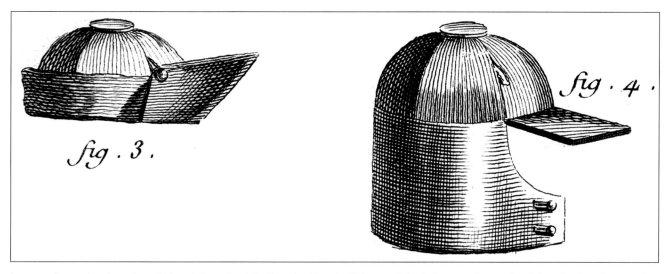

Images of a tapabord cap from Diderot's Encyclopédie (Boursier, Planche III, Figures 3 & 4.), showing the tapabord described as a *bonnet de voyageur*. It is also referred to as a type of *bonnet à l'angloise* [English cap], '...worn at sea, with flaps that fall over the shoulders.'

Detail of an *engagé* in the fur trade wearing the popular tuque stocking cap worn by most colonists in New France. (Habillemens des Coureurs de Bois Canadiens, no. 2, Anonymous, c. 1730, Beinecke Rare Book and Manuscript Library, Yale University Library, New Haven, CT, USA, WA MSS S-2412)

References to bonnets à bateau in Canada date back to at least 1722,[280] and in 1746, a cadet named Duplessis was given '1 bonnet drapé' as a replacement for the one he lost, which was later referred to as a 'bonnet à bateau' in the same document, priced at 4 livres 10 sols, suggesting that these terms were at times interchangeable.[281] That same year '7 bonnets à bateau,' individually valued at 4 livres 10 sols, were purchased from private merchants for the King's storehouses in preparations

for war,[282] while another '20 bonnets à bateau' at 4 livres 10 sols apiece were procured from the Magasins du Roy at Montréal for various parties heading for the coast of New England in 1747.[283] Colonial officers, like the soldiers they commanded, wore knit caps on detachments such as officer Boishébert, wounded in the battle of Grand-Pré in 1747, who 'received a bullet in his bonnet.'[284] Two years later, part of the equipment sent to Acadia for the colonial troops under the command of

280   Houghton Library (Harvard University, Cambridge, Massachusetts), Charles Chadenat collection of manuscripts on French Canada, Inventory of possessions of Pierre Rivet; s. by widow Marie Madeleine Rageot; notary Jacques Barbel, 26 November 1722.

281   LAC, MG1-C11A, vol.115, f.272, 273.

282   LAC, MG1-C11A, vol.88, f.255.

283   LAC, MG1-C11A, vol.117, fol. 315v.

284   Charles Deschamps de Boishebert, *Mémoire pour le Sieur de Boishebert, capitaine, chevalier de Saint Louis, ci-devant commandant de l'Acadie* (Paris: Imprimerie de Moreau, 1763), p.11.

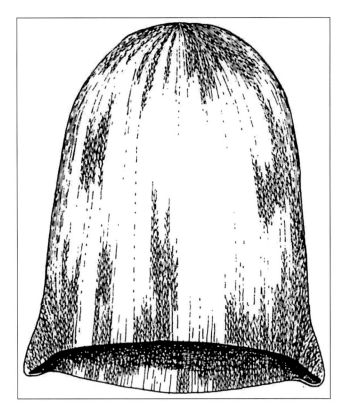

An artist's reconstruction of the headpiece taken from Legacy of the Machault, a collection of eighteenth-century artifacts by Catherine Sullivan. The wearer could fold it back on itself for a double layer of warmth. Additional stitches in the middle of the tube created ear pockets or flaps on the brim of this particular example. The French may have referred to this type of cap as a bonnet à bateau. (Courtesy of National Historic Sites, Parks Canada. Photo Kevin Gélinas)

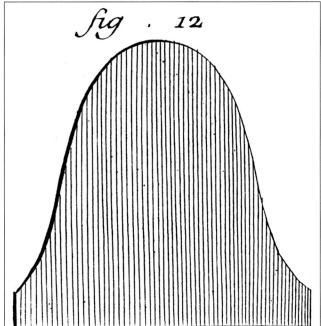

Detail of an engraving by Diderot, part of Bonnetier de la Foule (Hosier), showing a stocking pattern for a common French stocking cap. Wet caps were set to dry over a knitting frame like the one depicted.

Louis de La Corne included '45 bonnets drapés' valued at 2 livres each as well as another '11 dozens and 9 scarlet bonnets' priced at about 2 livres 15 sols per cap.'[285]

During the Seven Years War, the King customarily provided a knitted cap to all metropolitan soldiers, colonial troops, and militiamen taking part in any given campaign, and these were often simply listed as 'bonnet de laine' (woollen cap) on supply lists.[286] For example, an equipment list of goods issued to regular and colonial soldiers for the summer months of 1756 included a 'bonnet de laine,'[287] while an undated list found in the Bourlamaque papers noted that soldiers and militiamen received '1 bonnet de laine' (price unspecified) for the summer months with the bonnets issued to officers were valued at 3 livres, suggesting they were of finer quality.[288]

In the winter of 1757, both Montcalm and Bougainville observed that 'one bonnet de laine' was distributed to each man at Fort Saint-Jean,[289] while a declaration of two soldiers, one of which was a colonial soldier taken captive

at Fort William-Henry that same winter, showed that each man had 'one thick red woollen cap besides their hats',[290] which diverges with a letter published in the Boston Gazette on 26 March claiming that 'Every man in the French army that came against Fort William Henry, was equipped in the following manner…2 caps, 1 hat.'[291] The thick red woollen caps may have referred to the thicker bonnets doubles (double caps), which will be discussed later on. That same year, significant quantities of red woollen caps were purchased at Orléans by the merchant Gradis for the 'militia soldiers', which in truth, was probably intended for the whole army serving in Canada, including the colonial soldiers: '8,000 fulled caps, double, men's size. Be careful that the caps are always narrow by the thickness of the fulling (lavage), and it is necessary that they come in men's or large-cadet sizes, being different, to be of service for the militia soldiers.'[292]

In addition, there appears to have been a shortage of bonnets starting in November of 1757 given that, according to d'Hébécourt, none were available at Fort Carillon: 'The allotted bonnets become useless, since

285 LAC, MG1-C11A, vol.119, f.3v.
286 RAPQ, 1933–1934, p.21.
287 SHAT, Dossier A1, 3417, Pièce 144.
288 LAC, MG18, K9, vol.6, f.469–472.
289 Casgrain, *Journal du marquis de Montcalm*, pp.156–157; De Bougainville, *Écrits sur le Canada*, p.168.

290 LOC, Colonial Office 5 folio 47, E. of Loudoun's Letter of April 25th. 1757, Declaration of two Prisoners taken the 23.d March 1757 at Fort Wm. Henry, Information of John Victor and Guillaume Chasse, two French Prisoners, Fort William Henry March 25th.
291 *New York Military Magazine, Devoted to the Interests of the Militia Throughout the Union* (Labree and Stockton, 1841), vol.1, p.211.
292 LAC, MG 18, H63, Fonds famille Gradis, F-1600, M. Père Aubry, Orléans, 11 octobre 1757.

there are none.'[293] During the siege of Québec in 1759, certain pieces of equipment were in such short supply that militiamen were given money for the items that were not available, such as a bonnet drapé valued at 2 livres 10 sols each.[294] According to Intendant Bigot, colonial officers, soldiers, militiamen, domestiques, and Native American allies were supplied with '1 bonnet de laine' as part of their summer and winter equipment.[295]

Distribution lists during the Seven Years War provide no descriptive details for caps; however, in 1755, bonnets from Saint-Maixent were the only ones requested for Fort Duquesne, and two years later, '8 bonnets from Saint-Maixent' were stocked in the King's storehouses at Fort Carillon.[296] According to La Pause, officers of the Troupes de terre stationed at remote posts were provided with finer wool caps, and the bonnets distributed to the officers wintering at Fort Niagara in 1756, valued at 4 livres, contrasted with those supplied to their domestiques, assessed at 2 livres 10 sols, suggesting that officers likely received wool caps made of finer wool, such as bonnets de Ségovie.[297]

Probate and Judiciary Records

A number of after-death inventories and excerpts from criminal trials held in Canada reveal that many colonial troops were in possession of wool caps, often listed alongside other personal belongings such as clothing and equipment. In 1726, a 'bonnet à bateau' esteemed at 30 sols was found in a trunk belonging to officer Sieur de La Morendière,[298] whereas a few years later, De la Buissonnière, commandant at Fort de Chartres, had among his personal possessions 'six Ségovie wool caps',[299] wool stocking caps made of fine-grade wool from the Spanish city of Segovia.[300] Charles Henry, *sergent* at Fort

de Chartres, left 'two red tuques' in the hands of Madame Saint-Ange in 1741 as a guarantee for merchandise.[301] Two years later, 'a grey tuque' valued at 2 livres 10 sols was recorded as part of the personal belongings attributed to *sergent* Jean Soupras at Montréal.[302] In 1745, a soldier named Brindamour purchased '1 bonnet from St-Maixent' along with a Bizaillon knife and black tape from the merchant-outfitter Monière,[303] while the belongings of a deserter at Québec included 'and old bonnet de laine (wool cap).'[304] That same year, Louis Aubert de la Chesnay, *lieutenant* in the colonial troops at Montréal, left behind 'an old bonnet drapé' as part of his testament[305] and in 1748, Jean-Baptiste Boucher, *lieutenant* of a company at Montréal, owned 'an old tuque'[306] The following year, three wool bonnets were found in a cassette and a chest belonging to Dorizon dit Larose, a colonial soldier accused of counterfeiting,[307] while '19 bonnets drapés, red and whitish, à bateau, men's size' were accounted for as part of the after-death inventory of Christophe Dubois, *sergent* of the colonial troops at Québec.[308] In 1751, another soldier involved in a criminal trial was said to have been wearing 'a bonnet, nearly new, red in colour and gray inside' and later referenced as a tuque in the same document.[309] A munition vest, a dozen brass soldiers buttons, a flint striker

293 LAC, MG18, K9, vol.1, f.273.

294 Aegidius Fauteux, *Journal du siège de Québec, du 10 mai au 18 septembre 1759* (Québec: 1922), p.21.

295 Bigot, *Mémoire Pour Messire François Bigot*, p.39.

296 Archives du Séminaire de Québec, P32/002/164a, Viger-Verreau, Papiers Contrecoeur: État des effets demandés à Montréal pour le Fort Duquesne, 15 janvier 1755.; LAC, MG18, K9, vol.6, f.457.

297 RAPQ, 1932–1933, p.78.

298 BAnQ-Q, greffe du notaire Jacques Barbel, inventaire des biens après le décès de la dame D'Amour La Morendière, auparavant veuve du feu sieur Pierre Gauvreau (vivant armurier)… épouse en seconde noce de Philippe D'Amour, écuyer, sieur de La Morendière, officier des troupes du détachement de la Marine entretenu pour le service du roi en ce pays de présent en l'ancienne France… , 25 avril 1726.

299 Kaskaskia manuscripts (Randolph County Courthouse, Chester, Illinois), inventaire de monsieur (Alphonse) de La Buissonnière (commandant aux Illinois) et dame Marie-Thérèse Trudeau, sa femme, 12 décembre 1740.

300 *Chronicon Rusticum-Commerciale; Or, Memoirs Of Wool etc. Being A Collection of History and Argument, concerning the Woollen Manufacture and Woollen Trade in general … In Two Volumes* (London: John Smith L.L.B., 1747), p.412.; *Encyclopédie Ou Dictionnaire Raisonné Des Sciences, Des Arts Et Des Métiers* (Neufchastel, Chez Samuel Faulcher, 1765), vol.9, p.178.

301 Kaskaskia manuscripts (Randolph County Courthouse, Chester, Illinois), 4 mars 1741.

302 BAnQ-M, Greffe du notaire Jean-Baptiste Adhemard dit St-Martin, Inventaire de feu Jean Soupras et de Marie Elisabeth Vallé, vivant sergent des troupes de la marine, 25 septembre 1743.

303 BAnQ-M, 06, M-P 218, Jean-Alexis Lemoine-Monière, Livres de comptes du 27 juin 1739 au 8 janvier 1751, Film M 641.1, 14 février 1745.

304 BAnQ-Q, TL5, D1778, Information contre René Gautier (Gauthier), déserteur, 13–26 octobre 1745.

305 BAnQ-Q, greffe du notaire Jacques-Nicolas Pinguet de Vaucour,… à la requête de monsieur Henri-Albert de St-Vincent, écuyer, lieutenant des troupes de détachement de la Marine… au nom et comme chargé de l'exécution du testament de feu Louis Aubert Lachesnay, écuyer, vivant lieutenant dans les dites troupes, 25 octobre 1745.

306 BAnQ-M, Greffe du notaire Antoire Foucher, Inventaire des biens de feu Jean-Baptiste Boucher, écuyer, sieur de Minouville, vivant lieutenant réformé d'une compagnie des troupes du détachement de la Marine, 1er juillet 1748.

307 BAnQ-Q, TL5, D1640, Procès criminel contre Claude du Retour (Duretour) de Monsy, seigneur de Neuville et autres terres, environ 31 ans, soldat de la compagnie de Beaujeu, et Louis Daurizon (Dorizon) dit Larose, soldat de la compagnie de Beaujeu, environ 39 ans, pour falsification d'ordonnances , 1er janvier 1749–5 novembre 1751.

308 BAnQ-Q, Greffe du notaire Claude Barolet, Inventaire des biens meubles et immeubles de feue Madeleine Gacien, veuve de Jean-Baptiste Marchesseau en 1ère noce et en seconde de Christophe Dubois, sergent des troupes de la marine en ce pays… (Nicolas Marchesseau, majeur de vingt-sept ans ou environ absent de cette ville pour les pays d'en haut, tous deux habitants à se dire présomptifs héritiers de feu Madeleine Gacien…), 20 décembre 1749.

309 BAnQ-M, TL4, S1, D5662, Procès contre Alexis Lacour, soldat de la Compagnie de Lorimier, accusé de vol de vêtements, 24 décembre 1751–8 janvier 1752.

and an old wool cap were among the article found in a chest in a home where the soldier Louis Bonin was lodged at Québec in 1757[310] and according to a sworn statement made the following year, a colonial soldier by the name of Barthélemy Fouques dit Fouques apparently purchased 'two tuques, one red and the other white.'[311]

Types of Wool Stocking Caps Shipped to New France and their Sources

Among the caps imported to Canada, as detailed in the 1748 import duty roster for goods shipped from France to Canada, were two popular types of wool caps, each valued differently depending on the quality and origin. The first type was described as 'bonnets de laine, doubled, from Ségovie (Fine Spanish wool),' which were priced at 12 livres per dozen for men's size and 9 livres per dozen for cadet's size, reflecting their high quality and fine craftsmanship. The second type, 'bonnets from St-Maixent,' were priced at 11 livres 6 sols per dozen for men's size and 4 livres 6 sols per dozen for cadet's size.[312] These varying prices highlight the differences in quality, size and regional sourcing of wool caps imported into New France.

St-Maixent Bonnets: Common Red Caps

Bonnets made at St-Maixent (France) near the town of Niort were frequently mentioned in colonial records, and an English treaty dealing with the French trade of the period noted that 'At St Maixant (Maixent)…they make abundance of double caps and stockings of wool of the country, and of Limoges.'[313] Numerous bonnets made at St-Maixent were among the goods supplied by private merchants to replenish the King's storehouses at Québec in 1746 and 1747, and based on price and descriptions, they appear to be common double red caps, as opposed to finer-grade scarlet ones made with Segovia wool:

- bonnets, double, fine, scarlet-coloured, 5 dozen-1/2 at 5 livres 10 sols
- double bonnets from St-Maixent, 44 at 3 livres
- Ségovie bonnets, double, fine, scarlet, 12 at 5 livres

- Ségovie bonnets, scarlet, 40 at 5 livres 10 sols
- double bonnets from St-Maixent, 4 at 2 livres 5 sols[314]

These common caps were also fulled (drapé), given that '1 dozen bonnets drapés, men's size, from Saint-Maixent' were sold to Monsieur Sicard by private merchants at Québec in 1754.[315] Additionally, the majority of the caps originating from St-Maixent appear to be red in colour considering that in 1757, the Bordeaux-based merchant Gradis purchased for Canada 2,400 bonnets from St-Maixent, 'the majority red, men's size' along with another 3,600 bonnets from St-Maixent 'men's size' from a man named Chantreuille based in Niort.[316] The previous year, this merchant supplied '100 men's size bonnets, of colour,' suggesting other colours than red.[317] For instance, 'a bonnet from St-Maixent, burgundy colour, for men' was recorded as part of the personal possessions of Joseph Desrocher at Québec in 1751,[318] while a bundle of 'bonnets from Saint-Maixent, of various colours' were stocked in the stores of Sieur Riverin, a merchant bourgeois at Québec in 1756.[319] These types of bonnets were also made with ear flaps, as 'one bonnet à bateau from the St-Maixent factory' belonged to Pierre Lanclet at Québec in 1749,[320] and also came in the simple version, such as the '22 bonnets à bateau from St-Maixent, simple' that were found in the storehouses of Jacques-François Lebé, visiteur au bureau du domaine du Roi at Québec.[321]

Orléans Bonnets: Fine Red Caps

Red fine wool stocking caps imported to New France were also purchased from mills located around Orléans, which were made from 'Spanish wool, wool of Berry, and of the country.'[322] These caps were often termed 'bonnets in the style of Tunis' (the capital of present-day Tunisia)[323] or

310 BAnQ-Q, TL5, D1667, Procès criminel contre Louis Bonin, caporal de la compagnie de Lanaudière et soldat congédié; et Denis Lemoine dit Parisien, 14 ans, soldat de la compagnie de Lanaudière en garnison à Québec, logé à la caserne Dauphine, et complices, accusés de vol, 17 février–6 août 1752.

311 BAnQ-Q, TL5, D1941, Procès criminel de Barthélemy Fouques dit Fouques, Allemand; Jacques Floc dit Beausoleil, 28 ans; et Jacques Bodin dit Potvin, 25 ans, tous soldats de la compagnie de Saint-Vincent, accusés de vol d'ordonnances par Nicolas Han dit Chaussé, de Saint-Sulpice, 21 juillet 1758–6 juin 1759.

312 LAC, MG1-C11A, vol.121, f.183.

313 Malachy Postlethwayt, A short State of the Progress of the French Trade and Navigation, etc. (London: J. Knapton, 1756), p.29.

314 LAC, MG1-C11A, vol.117, f.97v, 104, 108, 111v.

315 BAnQ-Q, Greffe du notaire Jean-Antoine Saillant, Le magasin de Havy & Lefebvre doit Monsieur Gilles Sicard à lui vendu à livrer pour l'exploitation de son poste… , 16 septembre 1754.

316 LAC, MG 18, H63, Fonds famille Gradis, F-1600, M. Chantreuille ainé, Riort, 10 octobre 1757.

317 LAC, MG 18, H63, Fonds famille Gradis, F-1599, M. Chantacaille, aîné, Niort, 7 août 1756.

318 BAnQ-M, Greffe du notaire Danré de Blanzy, Inventaire des biens de feu Joseph Desrocher, 27 février 1751.

319 BAnQ-Q, Greffe du notaire Jean-Antoine Saillant, Inventaire des meubles, effets et marchandises délaissé après de décès de feu Sieur Riverin… , 28 octobre 1756.

320 BAnQ-Q, Greffe du notaire Claude Barolet, Inventaire des biens de la communauté d'entre feu Pierre Lanclet (maître cordonnier en cette ville de Québec) et Charlotte Chaudonnet, sa veuve, 15 décembre 1749.

321 BAnQ-Q, Greffe du notaire Claude Barolet, Inventaire des biens du feu Jacques François Lebé (vivant visiteur au bureau du domaine du Roy en cette ville), 16 février 1756.

322 Postlethwayt, A short State of the Progress of the French Trade, p.30.

323 Essais historiques sur Orléans, ou, Description topographique & critique de cette capitale, & de ses environs (Orléans: Chez Couret de Villeneuve, 1778), p.36.

'bonnets for the Turk's turbans,'[324] or again as red bonnets, serving as a base for turbans worn by Orientals: 'There is an art in the making of these caps, which involves the finishing, the manner in which they are made, and especially in the choice of the raw material which is always a very fine wool.'[325] In fact, the word 'tuque' commonly used in Québec to designate a wool hat, may have been a truncated form of the words 'Bonnet à la turque' (Turkish bonnet).[326]

According to Peuchet, 'Orléans, is the place where we find the most significant manufactories of stockings and fulled caps made on a loom, especially caps, of which a large portion is sold abroad. Almost all of this bonneterie [hosiery], like almost all of which is fulled, is made using two threads.'[327] A Québec-based merchant's memoir from 1752 sheds light as to the types of bonnets imported from Orléans, which included '8 dozen bonnets, men's size, all scarlet, double, and at the lowest price there is; 3 dozen ditto, grand-cadet's size, same; 4 dozen scarlet bonnets, double, buck colour and grey, No 2½; 4 dozen, grand-cadet's size.'[328] A merchandise list seized from the ship *Le Sagitaire* on its way to Québec in 1757 included over 1,000 bonnets from Orléans described as scarlet and 'doubled coloured,' suggesting that both ends were entirely dyed in red.[329] As mentioned previously, '8,000 fulled caps, double, men's size…for the militia soldiers' were purchased from a merchant based out of the town of Orléans.[330]

Marseilles Bonnets: Fine and Common Red Caps

Woollen caps produced in Marseille, Toulon, and in the Provence region were called 'Bonnets de Marseille' and were made in two grades: common and fine.[331] The *Encyclopédie méthodique* mentions that 'the so-called Marseille hats and more commonly Tunis-style hats are woollen hats, which are imitated in France to be sent to the Middle East.'[332] In 1750, 30 wool cap manufactories were in production in Marseille.[333] According to the *Dictionnaire universel de commerce*, the woollen caps (bonnet de laine) made in Marseille were dyed in red.[334]

Bonnet Colours in New-France (1733–1764)

Based on a sizable sample of probate records relating to Canada and the Illinois Territory, the majority (85 percent) of bonnets found in the possession of settlers were dyed using various shades of red (red, scarlet, cinnamon, or red and white). The remaining 15 percent were described as beige, grey, white, or brown, which may point to various shades of natural undyed wool.

Table 5. Colours of the bonnets, tuques or fourolles taken from after-death inventories at Québec, Montréal, Trois-Rivières and Illinois Territory (1733–1764).[335]

	Illinois	Montréal	Trois-Rivières	Québec	Total	%
Red	4	20	6	53	83	58%
Scarlet		15	2	9	26	18%
Red and white		5		7	12	8%
Doe belly beige (ventre de biche)		5		3	8	6%
Grey		3	2	1	6	4%
White		2		2	4	3%
Brown		1		2	3	2%
Cinnamon		1			1	1%
					143	100%

An urban legend has surrounded the colour of tuques for some time. The legend originated from the Cours d'histoire du Canada published in 1865 by l'Abbé Jean-Baptiste-Antoine Ferland. According to the author, during the seventeenth century, the caps of the colonists were said to be blue in the Montréal District, red at Québec, and white around Trois-Rivières. This inaccurate statement was repeated by a multitude of authors. French notarial and judicial records provide solid evidence that red caps were primarily worn by all residents of New France, regardless of their geographic location. The appearance of blue caps, mainly in the region of Montréal, is a nineteenth-century phenomenon, and the white caps of Trois-Rivières is pure fantasy propagated by Ferland.[336]

324 *Journal Oeconomique, ou Memoires, notes et avis sur l'Agriculture, les Arts, le Commerce, & tout ce qui peut avoir rapport à la santé, ainsi qu'à la conservation & à l'augmentation des biens des Familles* (Paris: Chez Antoine Boudet, 1771), p.121.

325 Claude Carlier, *Traité des bêtes à laine* (Paris: Chez Vallat La Chapelle, 1770), p.725.

326 Francis Back, 'Tuque, teuge, toque ou bonnet à la Turque?', *Cap-aux-Diamants*, 53 (1998), p.56.

327 Jacques Peuchet, *Dictionnaire universel de la géographie commerçante, contenant… au change, à la balance de commerce, aux colonies* (Paris: Chez Blanchon, 1798), vol.4, p.273.

328 BAnQ-Q, P908, P9, Mémoire à accomplir par les frères Rouffio et Romagnac pour l'année 1753 relativement aux commandes de marchandises auprès de négociants de France et de Hollande, destinées à être envoyées au Québec… , 1752.

329 TNA, HCA, 32, vol.246, Le Sagitaire, 1757.

330 LAC, MG 18, H63, Fonds famille Gradis, F-1600,M. Père Aubry, Orléans, 11 octobre 1757.

331 Jacques Savary des Brûlons, *Dictionnaire universel de commerce* (Amsterdam: Chez les Jansons à Waesberge, 1732), vol.3, p.95.

332 *Encyclopédie méthodique, Manufactures, arts et métiers* (Paris: Chez Panckoucke, 1790), vol.2, p.19.

333 Louis Chabaud, *Marseille et ses industries, les tissus, la filature et la teinturerie* (Marseille: Barlatier-Feissat,1883), pp.152–157

334 Jacques Savary des Brûlons, *Dictionnaire universel de commerce: contenant tout ce qui concerne le commerce qui se fait dans les quatre parties du monde* (Amsterdam: Chez les Jansons à Waesberge, 1726), vol.1, p.891.

335 It is to be noted that the aforementioned samples do not take into account any references to bonnets, fourolles or tuques included in private merchant's storehouse inventories as with any references to cotton bonnets or simply bonnets without any accompanying colour.

336 F. Back, 'Le bonnet bleu des patriotes', *Cap-aux-Diamants*, 61 (2000), p.62.

Bonnet de Draps or Casque de Fourrure

Winter caps, termed bonnet de casque, were another type of headgear worn by colonial soldiers during the colder winter months. This headpiece featured a long bonnet made of red, scarlet, or black cloth, embellished with a fur ring near the front, made using bear, raccoon, beaver, or rabbit fur. The style was called 'casque' because, during the reign of Louis XIV, French mounted grenadiers, dragoons, and hussars wore similar headgear.[337]

Sergent Christophe Dubois of the Troupes de la Marine owned two such fur hats described as 'a bonnet of coarse red cloth edged with marten fur and a ditto, older.'[338] Some officers' caps were finely decorated, reflecting their rank and status. François de Sarrobert, an *enseigne* in the colonial troops, had 'a Stroud hat lined with bobcat' in his personal possession,[339] while 'an old shroud hat with a small embroidery of false gold lined with bobcat fur' belonged to officer Louis Coulon de Villiers in 1757.[340] In 1760, Joseph Fournierie, an infantry officer serving in the Régiment Royal-Roussillon stationed at Montréal, owned 'a velvet hat edged with gold lace and trimmed with marten fur' valued at the very expensive sum of 50 livres.[341] Even if these hats were never included on official equipment lists, it is possible that the casques (hats) included in the lot of '16 bonnets or casques' sent from Trois-Rivières to Montréal in 1760 when French forces were retreating westwards, and intended for the colonial troops, probably did not refer to winter caps lined with fur.[342]

Fatigue Caps (Bonnets de Police)

Although not a standard-issue item, according to eighteenth-century French military tradition, infantry soldiers were provided with fatigue caps, allegedly referred to as bonnet de tricot in colonial records or known as bonnet de police in official French military works. According to De

Hussar fur-trimmed cap depicted in *L'Encyclopédie* (Boursier, Planche II, Figure 11), which may resemble the popular bonnet de casque worn in New France. The *Encyclopédie Méthodique* mentions these were often trimmed with groundhog fur from Canada.

Bombelles, '…there are still small pleasures which seem to be trifles and which are nevertheless useful…supplying them [infantry soldiers] with bonnets to fetch water, wood, or straw, and the likes, to conserve their hats.'[343] This infantry *colonel* also observed that the caps were fabricated from worn-out uniforms: '…most regiments hand out standardised soldiers caps, which are made out of old uniforms; this small expense is honourable and profitable, in that it conserves the hats.'[344] By the same token, it seems that the Minister of the Marine agreed to issue bonnets to the troops serving at Île-Royale to conserve their tricorn hats. Although approved in 1759, the year following the capture of the fortress of Louisbourg, a letter dispatched from Versailles to M. de Bonnaventure, King's *lieutenant* at Louisbourg, permitted soldier's fatigue caps to be distributed to colonial soldiers: 'we will include a cap, that you deem necessary to conserve the hats and to prevent them from suffering from the bad weather during night factions in wintertime.'[345] In light of this, there is much debate over whether the caps were ever supplied to the Compagnies franches de la Marine units in North America.

However, the French regulars that fought in Canada from 1755 to 1760 appear to have initially been provided with caps termed bonnet de tricot and subsequently supplied with common wool caps (bonnets), such as were stocked at the King's storehouses, prior to each campaign. In fact, the 31 May 1776 ruling concerning the dress of the troops, which described the way the fatigue caps were made in detail, used the terms 'en tricot' to designate them: 'Each soldier shall be supplied with a bonnet de police, made en tricot, lined in canvas in the shape of a pokalem [forage cap],' which reinforces the premise that

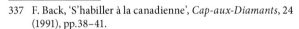

337 F. Back, 'S'habiller à la canadienne', *Cap-aux-Diamants*, 24 (1991), pp.38–41.

338 BAnQ-Q, Inventaire de la communauté des biens d'entre Jean Marcheseau Christophe Dubois (sergent des troupes de la Marine entretenu pour le service du Roi en ce pays…) et Marie Magdeleine Gatien, 22 janvier 1748.

339 BAnQ-M, Greffe du notaire Danré de Blanzy, Inventaire des biens de feu Sieur François de Sarrobert, enseigne d'infanterie, 8 janvier 1756. Stroud refers to a traditional fabric associated with the town of Stroud in Gloucestershire, England.

340 BAnQ-M, Greffe du notaire Danré de Blanzy, Inventaire de Louis Coulon écuyer Sieur de Villiers, capitaine d'infanterie demeurant Montréal rue Saint-Paul…, 17 novembre 1757.

341 BAnQ-M, Greffe du notaire Pierre Panet, Inventaire des biens d'entre Dame Marie-Louise Decouagne et feu Joseph Fournierie (Royal-Roussillon, Archives judiciaires, boîte C6 MT1 1/169, C HEM, septembre 1760), vivant lieutenant d'infanterie en garnison à Montréal, 30 septembre 1760.

342 BAnQ-Q, Greffe du notaire Jean-Claude Panet, 25 août 1764.

343 Henri François de Bombelles, *Memoires sur le service journalier de l'infanterie, Tome second* (Paris: La veuve de François Muguet, 1719), vol.2, pp.58–59.

344 De Bombelles, *Memoires sur le service journalier de l'infanterie*, vol.2, pp.237–238.

345 LAC, MG1-B, vol.110, f.540.

Illustration by Francis Back depicting an officer of the Compagnies Franches de la Marine circa 1745 in his winter campaign gear, wearing a bonnet de casque and identified by the brass gorget around his neck. The officer wears a camail with a collar over his capot. The camail, a small mantle that became fashionable in the early 1730s, was also adopted by members of the bourgeois class in Canada. He is armed with a double fusil, a newly introduced weapon in New France at the time, which further emphasises his position as an officer or a man of status. (Francis Back © Raphaëlle et Félix Back)

the bonnets provided to the battalions in 1755 were in fact fatigue caps rather than stocking caps.[346]

The general supplies Dieskau requested for the battalions heading to Canada in 1755 included 3,200 bonnets, to be supplied by Boisroger. Intendant Bigot requested another 3,522 caps from the King's storehouses at Québec, which would have corresponded to the common stocking cap variety such as the '176 bonnets à bateau or bonnets drapés' fulled caps, priced at 22 livres per dozen, available at the King's depots at Québec in 1752.[347] Those requested by Dieskau, which were to be distributed to the metropolitan troops before leaving France, were listed as such:

- 1,040 white tricot caps with white facings
- 1,040 white tricot caps with blue facings
- 1,120 white tricot caps with red facings[348]

Another 50 caps specified as 'white tricot reserve caps' (bonnet de tricot blanc de reserve) were also added.[349] The all-white bonnets are loaded onto the ships transporting Artois and Bourgogne. Bonnets with blue facings are on the ships transporting Languedoc and Béarn, while those with red facings are on the ships transporting la Reine and Guyenne. Additionally, some red-faced bonnets are loaded onto the ships carrying Artois, Bourgogne, and Languedoc for their tambours. This list clearly shows that the retroussés match the colour of the vestes, not the parements (cuffs).

The following year, the metropolitan soldiers stationed at Louisbourg were exclusively provided with 'white tricot caps with red facings.'[350] De La Chenaye-Desbois observed that the soldiers of the Régiment de la Reine wore 'red caps, lined in blue and edged in white,' while the Régiment de Languedoc had 'blue caps lined in red and edged in white.'[351] In 1758, a deceased soldier of the Régiment de Berry found on L'île d'Orléans was described as was wearing, among other articles, his regulation justaucorps, white breeches, two sets of stockings, new shoes, and in a small canvas bag, un bonnet rouge (a red cap), which may have been either a fatigue cap, since his regimental colour was red, or a common red woollen cap, such as those provided prior to campaigns in Canada.[352] It remains to be determined whether these fatigue caps were

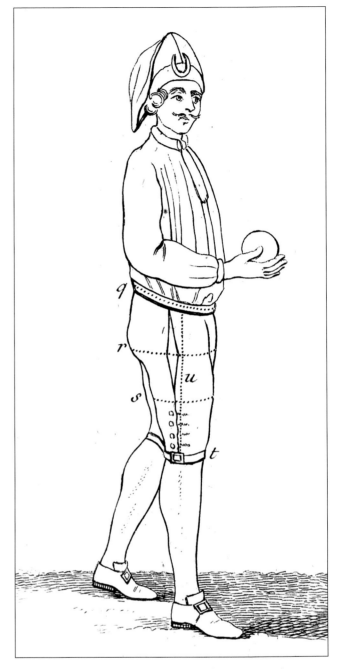

A military man wearing an undress cap, or fatigue cap, with a symbol at the front. While references are often vague and scattered, French armies had been using some form of informal headgear, especially for fatigue duty, since the early eighteenth century. (L'Art du Tailleur, Planche IV, Figure C, 1769)

decorated with a fleur-de-lis or other insignias, but it appears that the appropriate regimental colour was issued to the Troupes de terre units in North America.

In February of 1760, a circular letter addressed to the commandants of each battalion specified that officers could receive 'bonnets de drap' (woollen caps), while the term 'bonnets' (caps) was used for the caps distributed to soldiers who needed them.[353] It is important to understand

346 *Règlement arrêté par le Roi concernant l'habillement et l'équipement de ses troupes, eu 31 Mai, 1776* (Paris, L'Imprimerie royale, 1776), p.17.

347 LAC, MG1-C11A, vol.98, f.243.

348 LAC, MG1-C11A, vol.100, f.269v.

349 LAC, MG1-C11A, vol.100, f.278v-279.

350 AG, MG-4, B1, Série A1, vol 3417, f.805–808.

351 François Alexandre Aubert de La Chesnaye-Desbois, *Dictionnaire militaire* (Paris: Chez David Fils, 1745), vol.2, pp.540, 564.

352 PRDH, volume 32 & 33, Ste-Famille-de-l'île-d'Orléans, 8 juin 1758-06-08.

353 Casgrain, *Collection des manuscrits du maréchal de Lévis*, pp.274–275.

Soldiers of the Gardes Françaises playing cards during a halt. The soldier in the middle is shown wearing a fatigue cap. (Halte des Gardes Françaises, Parrocel, Le Bas, Graveur du Roy, 1736)

the distinction between both terms. On the one hand, a bonnet de drap (cloth cap) probably referred to a fatigue cap, while the ones issued to the soldiers probably referred to simple woollen stocking caps. The bonnet de drap supplied to officers may have had a false-gold edging such as the 'bonnet de drap with a small gold edge' esteemed at 14 livres that was left behind by Joseph Fournierie, a *lieutenant* in the Régiment Royal-Roussillon who passed away at Montréal in 1760.[354]

Mittens (Mitaines)

Mittens, termed mitaines in French, were an essential part of winter clothing for soldiers in New France, providing crucial protection against the harsh cold during military campaigns and daily duties in freezing conditions. Savary des Brûlons defines mitaines as 'certain large gloves … usually made of leather which are stuffed or lined with a warm woollen cloth, the fingers of which are not separated, with the reserve of the thumb.'[355] Primary source records indicate that the mittens issued to the troops

---

354 BAnQ-M, Greffe du notaire Pierre Panet, Inventaire des biens d'entre Dame Marie-Louise Decouagne et feu Joseph Fournierie (Royal-Roussillon, Archives judiciaires, boîte C6 MT1 1/169, C HEM, septembre 1760), vivant lieutenant d'infanterie en garnison à Montréal, 30 septembre 1760.

355 Jacques Savary des Brûlons, *Dictionnaire Universel De Commerce Contenant Tout Ce Qui Concerne Le Commerce Qui Se Fait Dans Les Quatre Parties Du Monde* (Paris: Jacques Estienne, 1723), vol.2, p.749.

were mostly made of wool cloth rather than knitted from woollen yarn, and were mostly made in the colony,[356] while officers often preferred those made from finer wool cloth which served to clearly distinguish them from enlisted men, highlighting their rank and setting them apart from the standard issue items supplied to the soldiers.

Equipment Lists

Unlike in France, soldiers serving in the colder climates of New France, such as Canada and Acadia, were issued mittens to protect against the harsh winter conditions. In 1692, 50 soldiers returning from the Boston prisons were to be given '90 pairs of mittens'[357] and '56 pairs of mittens, using 18⅔ aunes of Mazamet' were issued to the soldiers taking part in an expedition against the Fox nation under the command of de Noyelles in 1734.[358] Two years later, 15¼ aunes of Mazamet fabric for mittens were delivered to the storehouses of Fort de la Pointe-à-la-Chevelure (Crown Point), intended for use by the fort's personnel, various royal service duties, and the changing of the garrison.[359] Mazamet, a town in southern France and a major wool production centre, lent its name to the woollen cloth produced there, which was also known as Cordelats and primarily came in white and brown.[360]

During King George's War, roughly one-third of an aune of molleton fabric was necessary to make a pair of mittens.[361] For instance, at Fort Saint-Frédéric in January of 1746, '1 pair of mittens and 1 pair of chaussons (slippers)' made using ⅔ of an aune of molleton fabric were issued to the officer Le Mercier,[362] while four canonniers (gunner) soldiers sent to garrison at this fort were provided with '4 pairs of mittens, 4 pairs of chaussons (slippers) using 2⅔ aunes of molleton.'[363] That same year, the officer Duverger de Saint-Blin, who accompanied 12 Ottawa and Potawatomi warriors in waging war on the coast of New England, was provided with '...⅔ [of an aune] of molleton for 1 pair of mittens and 1 pair of chaussons (slippers).'[364] In the late 1740s, the mittens issued to soldiers, officers, and colonists in Acadia were often doubled (lined), as shown by the delivery of 302 pairs of 'double mittens' in 1748 to the Habitants, soldiers, and officers of Île St-Jean.[365] Those

at Shediac in 1750 were provided with '50 pairs of mittens, lined with Carisé,' a coarse woollen fabric.[366]

Before leaving Niagara in 1755, the officer la Pause provided wool fabric to soldiers of the Troupes de terre 'to make mittens' which equated to roughly ¼ aune of fabric per man.[367] Throughout the Seven Years War, these hand coverings were distributed to all men involved in winter campaigns, as documented by a supply list from 1756 that was issued to both regular and colonial troops. The list included '1 pair of mittens' for the winter campaign, on top of what was given during summer months,[368] which is repeated in an undated list of equipment prepared by Bourlamaque.[369] Additionally, Bougainville and Montcalm both noted that '1 pair of mittens' were supplied to the soldiers from Fort St-Jean leaving on a raiding parties in February of 1757,[370] while a regular and colonial soldier taken prisoners at Fort William-Henry in March of that year declared that each enlisted man was issued 'one pair of thick worsted mittons for their hands.'[371]

Probate Records

Colonial officers, like their soldiers, relied on mittens to endure the harsh winter conditions of Canada. At the turn of the century, the officer De Joibert was the owner of 'an old pair of mittens made from white finette [wool cloth], worn down,'[372] and in 1714, 'an old pair of mittens of Créseau,' a type of coarse serge fabric, was found in the possession of Louis Malleras, enseigne in the colonial troops at Montréal.[373] In 1737, an old pair of mittens' was recorded by the notary De Chevremont as part of the after-death belongings of Joseph Dejourdy de Cabanac.[374] The last will of the officer Louis Aubert de la Chesnay, drafted in 1745, included 'a pair of wool fabric mittens, lined in Chamois [leather]' valued at 1 livre 10 sols,[375]

356 LAC, MG1-C11A, vol.116, f.99.
357 Collection de manuscrits contenant lettres, mémoires, et autres documents historiques relatifs à la Nouvelle-France (Québec: Imprimerie A. Coté et cie, 1884), vol.2, p.72.
358 LAC, MG1-C11A, vol.62, f.150v.
359 LAC, MG1-C11A, vol.66, f.56.
360 Jacques Savary des Brûlons, Dictionnaire universel de commerce: Commerce & compagnies (Genève: Chez les Frères Cramer & Claude Philibert, 1750), p.268.
361 LAC, MG1-C11A, vol.86, f.200v.
362 LAC, MG1-C11A, vol.88, f.214.
363 LAC, MG1-C11A, vol.88, f.214v.
364 LAC, MG1-C11A, vol.86, f.190
365 LAC, MG1-C11A, vol.92, f.49.

366 LAC, MG1-C11A, vol.119, f.5.
367 RAPQ, 1933–34, p.70.
368 Centre d'histoire La Presqu'île, P03/F.089, Fonds De Beaujeu, 28 novembre 1756.
369 LAC, MG18, K9, vol.6, f.462, f.469–470.
370 De Bougainville, Écrits sur le Canada, p.168; Casgrain, Journal du marquis de Montcalm, pp.156–157.
371 LOC, Colonial Office 5 folio 47, E. of Loudoun's Letter of April 25th. 1757, Declaration of two Prisoners taken the 23.d March 1757 at Fort Wm. Henry, Information of John Victor and Guillaume Chasse, two French Prisoners, Fort William Henry March 25th.
372 BAnQ-Q, Greffe du notaire Louis Chamballon, Inventaire de feu Jacques de Joibert, chevalier et seigneur de Soulanges, enseigne des vaisseaux du roy, capitaine dune Cie des troupes, 2 mai 1703.
373 BAnQ-M, Greffe du notaire Michel Lepailleur, Inventaire des effets de feu Louis Mallerais, écuyer Sieur de la Moillerie, enseigne en pied dans les troupes, 20 décembre 1714.
374 BAnQ-M, Greffe du notaire Charles René Gauchon de Chevremont, Inventaire des biens de feu Sieur Joseph Dejourdy de Cabanac, lieutenant d'une compagnie des troupes de ce pays, 27 mars 1737.
375 BAnQ-Q, Greffe du notaire Jacques-Nicolas Pinguet de Vaucour,... à la requête de monsieur Henri-Albert de St-Vincent,

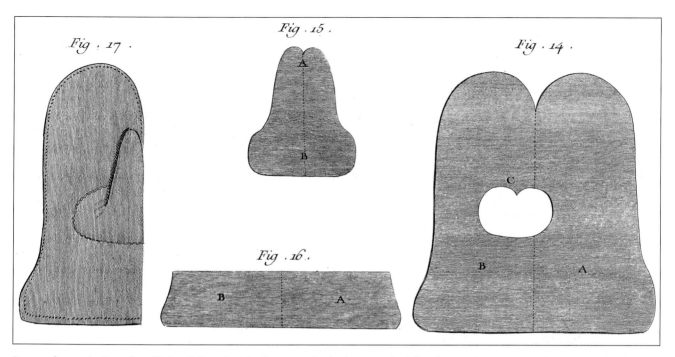

Patterns for men's gloves from Diderot's *Encyclopédie*, showing a finished mitt on the left and pieces for a mitten in the centre and right. The production techniques for gloves and mittens, as shown in these eighteenth-century illustrations, remained largely unchanged for centuries. (Gantier, Planche II, Figures 14-17)

whereas in 1760, Sieur de Langy, a colonial officer living in the Outaouais, had 'a pair of mittens of Carisé [Kersey]' as part of his personal belongings at Montréal.[376]

Probate records and legal records occasionally provide glimpses into the practical winter gear used by soldiers of the colonial troops, including mittens. In 1749, for example, an inventory of goods found in the home of *sergent* Christophe Dubois included 'a pair of mittens, wool cloth, whitish-grey, lined' valued at 15 sols, which may have been a pair of government-issued mittens.[377] Records from a criminal trial held in Montréal in 1749 detailed the contents of a soldier's chest, which included 'two old pairs of mittens.'[378] Similarly, Antoine Sauvé, a

voyageur from Lachine near Montréal and a member of the Compagnies franches de la Marine, was documented as owning 'a pair of raccoon mittens' valued at 2 livres among his personal possessions.[379]

Methods for Wearing Mittens in Winter

Colonial soldiers probably wore their mittens during winter expeditions using a mitten string, a cord or leather strap spanning the wearer's arm length, designed to prevent them from being lost. This string could be draped over the shoulders or threaded through the sleeves of a coat, keeping the mittens securely hanging from the ends of the sleeves. Canadians had likely adopted this practical method from Indigenous peoples, who used similar cords to secure their mittens. This ingenious solution allowed for quick removal while firing a weapon or engaging in hand-to-hand combat, while ensuring the mittens were not misplaced. The officer Pouchot observed that Indigenous peoples had '...mittens of leather or flannel, hung from their necks by a cord; which are better than gloves, since separated fingers are more likely to freeze.'[380] Some Canadians also attached their mittens to their sash, as in the case of Thomas Riveau, who was found drowned near Montréal in 1761 and was described as wearing 'a

écuyer, lieutenant des troupes de détachement de la Marine… au nom et comme chargé de l'exécution du testament de feu Louis Aubert Lachesnay, écuyer, vivant lieutenant dans les dites troupes… en la prévôté de Québec y résidant, somme ci emporté en la chambre où le dit feu sieur Aubert de Lachesnay faisait sa demeure… , 25 octobre 1745.

376 BAnQ-M, Greffe du notaire Danré de Blanzy, inventaire de Catherine d'Ailleboust du Manthet et de Jean-Baptiste ?, écuyer, sieur de Langy, officier demeurant aux Outaouais. (Inventaire des biens de feu sieur Joseph de Langy, écuyer, sieur de Montegros, officier d'infanterie [frère de Catherine d'Ailleboust]… Compagnies franches de la Marine.), 26 avril 1760.

377 BAnQ-Q, Greffe du notaire Claude Barolet, Inventaire des biens meubles et immeubles de feue Madeleine Gacien, veuve de Jean-Baptiste Marchesseau en 1ère noce et en seconde de Christophe Dubois, sergent des troupes de la marine en ce pays…, 20 décembre 1749.

378 BAnQ-Q, TL5, D1640, Procès criminel contre Claude du Retour (Duretour) de Monsy, seigneur de Neuville et autres terres, environ 31 ans, soldat de la compagnie de Beaujeu, et Louis Daurizon (Dorizon) dit Larose, soldat de la compagnie de

Beaujeu, environ 39 ans, pour falsification d'ordonnances, 1er janvier 1749–5 novembre 1751.

379 BAnQ-M, Greffe du notaire Thomas Vuatier, Inventaire des biens de feu Antoine Sauvé, voyageur de Lachine, incorporé dans les compagnies franches de la marine, 23 février 1760.

380 Pouchot, *Mémoires sur la dernière guerre de l'Amérique septentrionale*, p.281.

bougrine of Calmande, a blanket capot and a snowshoe on his foot, a leather work apron, and his mitts attached to his sash.'[381]

Non-Regulation Footwear of the Colonial Troops

Origin of the Souliers Sauvages (Moccasins)

Officers and soldiers of the colonial troops in New France owned both regulation European-style shoes with heels as well as various types of moccasins, commonly referenced as souliers sauvages (Native-style shoes) in historic records. These included low-cut moccasins made from dressed deerskin (deerskin moccasins) or tanned oxhide and sealskin for summer campaigns (tanned-leather moccasins), as well as high-cut moccasins (winter moccasins) designed for winter travel and snowshoeing. Moccasins which were contracted out to supply the King's storehouses, were primarily made of sealskin sourced from the Québec administrative region, while the majority of those made from oxhide were produced around Montréal. From the early 1740s to 1760, soldiers taking part in expeditions or campaigns were generally issued one pair of summer moccasins per month, while part of the additions to the basic summer issue list included dressed deer skins meant for making their own winter moccasins.

Using moccasins instead of European-style shoes on expeditions began among the Compagnies franches de la Marine as early as the 1680s. The practice was as much a matter of adapting to local conditions as it was one of necessity, considering the lack of commercially-made buckled shoes that arrived from France. During the late 1750s, thousands of these shoes never made it to Canada because the ships that carried them were captured by the British Royal Navy. In November of 1757, Montcalm wrote: 'The English having taken 40,000 shoes that were sent to the colony, shoes and leather are lacking; we try to make up for it by making the soldiers shoes with sealskin for the rain and deer skin for the frost [snow].'[382] In 1757, 20 Canadians established themselves at Fort Carillon 'to tan deer hides which we need to make shoes.'[383]

Presumably, moccasins were supplied to the colonial troops to make their annually-issued soldier's shoes last longer, but also because of the advantages they offered. Moccasins were lighter than shoes, and they made less noise when walking. Unlike hard-soled shoes, moccasins allowed the feet to flex, making them suitable for use with snowshoes, and could also be worn in birch bark canoes without damaging the fragile bark and wood sheathing. Moccasins could be relatively cheap and easy to make, but it should not be assumed that every soldier had the knowledge or tools to do so. During the Canadian campaign of 1755, infantry officer La Pause observed that 'the shoes [moccasins] were not ready-made. The soldiers were required to have them made at their expense.'[384] Moccasins were not always a cheaper alternative to shoes, as noted in a 1755 document from the Archives de la guerre addressing military equipment lacking in Montréal, which stated: 'In truth, we provide souliers sauvages (moccasins) for the length of a campaign, but besides that they do not last very long and that it would not be possible for our Frenchmen to use them continuously. They cost the King almost as much. The dealer's asking price is commonly from 2 livres 10 sols to 3 livres.'[385] Bougainville observed that deerskins and tanned-leather moccasins provided by the official purveyor of goods to the French forces during the Seven Years War were of poor quality.[386]

Not all soldiers took to moccasins and according to De Poilly, an engineer who undertook a topographic survey of Île-Royale in the winter of 1757, Frenchmen resorted to wearing shoes, rather than moccasins, on certain terrain: 'it was rough ice and so uneven that after walking for three hours, with my moccasins, we were forced, unable to go any further by the pain we suffered at the soles of the feet, to wear French shoes.'[387] In August of 1760, Bourmalaque wrote to Lévis that 'Mr. Du Roquan, my dear general, is without shoes and is unable to walk. He cannot use tanned-leather moccasins, although he is a good walker. You would give him great pleasure if you could provide him with a pair of French shoes.'[388]

Summer Campaign Footwear

Initially, moccasins distributed during summer campaigns, presumably referring to low-cut moccasins made of dressed deer skin, were provided to the colonial troops in Canada. These sometimes had a folded-down cuff along each side, as per those traditionally made by allied Native nations. In August of 1696, goods needed for 100 soldiers who were to accompany De Villieu to attack Fort Pemaquid included souliers de sauvages, which, in this case, were low-cut moccasins rather than those intended for snowshoe use.[389] Colonial soldiers often had to make souliers sauvages themselves, since the King issued hides

381 PRDH, vol 38, St-Joseph-de-la-Rivière-des-Prairies, 18 juin 1761.
382 Casgrain, *Journal du marquis de Montcalm*, p.317.
383 De Malartic & Gaffarel (eds), *Journal des Campagnes au Canada*, p.125.

384 RAPQ, 1933–1934, p.68..
385 AG, MG-4, B1, Série A1, vol 3405, f.356–359.
386 De Bougainville, *Écrits sur le Canada*, pp.297–298
387 AG, Comité technique du Génie, Bibliothèque, 1751, 1757. MG 4, C 2, Ms in-folio 210f.
388 Casgrain, *Collection des manuscrits du maréchal de Lévis*, p.115.
389 LAC, MG1-C11A, vol.2, fol. 97v.

rather than ready-made articles, such as the '336 livres of deer hides … to make shoes for the soldiers' that were provided to 112 cadets, soldiers, and Habitants sent to wage war against the Chickasaw nation in the summer of 1739.[390] We may assume that the '3 deer hides' listed as part of the equipment provided to M. de Louvigny, as well as the other officers taking part in a military campaign against the Fox nation in the summer of 1716, likely also served to make low-cut summer moccasins.[391]

Oxhide and Sealskin Tanned Leather Shoes (Souliers Tannés)

Moccasins made of oxhide or sealskin, generically called souliers tannés (tanned leather shoes), were often included in lists of equipment issued to the colonial troops. By the 1740s, colonial soldiers were primarily issued tanned leather moccasins made from oxhide, but by the 1750s, those of sealskin became increasingly frequent, and were mainly supplied from the King's storehouses at Québec. Guillaume Estèbe, storekeeper at Québec from 1740 to 1754, claimed that 'the shoes provided to the soldiers were made with tanned oxhide or sealskin leather.'[392]

During the 1755 campaign, the officer Malartic remarked that the ordinary campaign equipment for both officers and soldiers consisted of 'one pair of souliers tannés per month.'[393] The following year, each soldier and officer serving in the colonial troops was to be issued 'one pair of souliers tannés per month' for the summer months.[394] For the year 1757, La Pause noted that one pair of tanned shoes 'per two months' was distributed at the start of that year's campaign, whereas officers and their domestiques were given '2 pairs of tanned shoes.'[395] Intendant Bigot corroborates that one pair of souliers tannés were provided to both officers and soldiers for the summer campaigns.[396] At Fort Carillon in 1757, eight barrels of 'unusable tanned shoes' as well as two barrels of 'tanned shoes, good' were inventoried as part of the Inventaire general des marchandises.[397] While retreating up the St Lawrence River in 1760, 2,690 pairs of tanned moccasins were sent from the King's storehouses at Trois-Rivières to Montréal.[398]

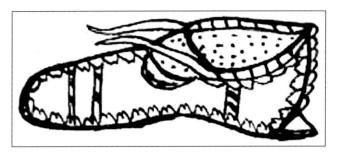

Detail from Plate 19 of the Codex Canadensis, showing a pair of shoes labelled 'makikin soulier' (moccasin shoes) with front cuffs and laces. This undated and unsigned manuscript, attributed to French Jesuit Louis Nicolas and dated between 1664 and 1675, is one of the earliest detailed depictions of Eastern Woodland moccasins. (Creative Commons)

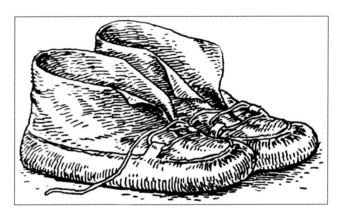

Shoes labelled souliers de bœuf (oxhide shoes) featured in the 1926 edition of the Almanach du peuple Beauchmin. Although laces and an extended upper collar are more modern additions, the basic form and construction of these shoes had not changed in over three centuries. Oxhide shoes in this style were still worn in rural Québec as late as the 1920s.

Tanned Oxhide Shoes (Souliers de Bœuf)

At the outset of King George's War, a particular type of moccasin commonly referred to as souliers de peau de bœuf, souliers de bœuf, or souliers sauvages de bœuf, which can all be roughly translated to Native-style oxhide shoes, was regularly issued to the men serving in Canada. These were moccasins made using thick tanned oxhide rather than softer deer or elk leather, and were intended for heavy use, as the thicker leather soles did not wear out as fast. The thicker leather was also better at repelling water. Father Lejeune suggested that when snow began to melt, tanned leather moccasins would be much better since '…souliers de sauvages take water like a sponge, and leather brought over from France would keep the feet dry.'[399] These souliers de bœuf combined traditional Native American moccasin construction with French shoemaking techniques and were a direct result of the cross-cultural interactions between the French and the Indigenous people.

390 LAC, MG1-C11A, vol.71, f.167v.
391 LAC, MG1-C11A, vol.38, f.188.
392 Anon., À Monseigneur de Sartine, p.17.
393 De Malartic & Gaffarel (eds), Journal des Campagnes au Canada, p.13.
394 Centre d'histoire La Presqu'ile, P03/F.089, Fonds De Beaujeu, 28 novembre 1756.
395 RAPQ, 1932–1933, pp.79, 81.
396 Bigot, Mémoire Pour Messire François Bigot, p.39.
397 LAC, MG18, K9, vol.6, f.462.
398 BAnQ-Q, Greffe du notaire Jean-Claude Panet, État des mémoires et certificats ci-après mentionnés, 25 août 1764.

399 Relations des Jésuites (Québec: Augustin Coté, éditeur-imprimeur, près de l'Archevêché, 1858), vol.1, p.10.

According to Peter Kalm, these Euro-tanned leather moccasins were common among the Canadian peasants living in the St Lawrence Valley: 'The shoes that women wear inside their homes look very much like our Finnish boots. Most men also wear shoes of the same type; the hide is prepared, and the hair is removed; the French have learned this way to make the shoes from the American Natives who, if they do not go barefoot, almost all use such shoes.'[400] In fact, infantry officer d'Aleyrac went into great detail when describing the construction of this type of buckleless footwear: 'souliers de cuir de bœuf are made differently than those made in France, because they have a sole as thin as the top which surrounds the entire foot at the height of the quarters; then, on this piece of leather, one sews a smaller piece of leather covering the top of the foot. It is a Canadian fashion with which to walk more easily in the woods and in the mountains.'[401] These sturdy-leather shoes may also have been treated with grease or oil as a form of waterproofing. Some may have been made with dyed leather, but many were probably left undyed. A French colonist's body found near Sorel in 1757 was described with a pair of '…souliers de bœuf, tanned in white [undyed].'[402]

Equipment Lists

The widespread use of oxhide shoes among soldiers in New France is well-documented, reflecting their practicality and availability for both summer campaigns and garrison life. In 1735, '160 pairs of souliers de cuir de bœuf' at 35 sols a pair were supplied by the King's storekeeper at Montréal for the workers and soldiers employed at Pointe-à-la Chevelure (Crown-Point)[403] Archival records also reveal that by the early 1740s, the enlisted men were regularly issued pre-made tanned oxhide shoes when participating in campaigns during the summer months. For instance, 1,358 pairs of oxhide shoes (souliers de peaux de bœuf) were distributed to various war parties that headed to the coast of New England in 1747.[404] Three cadets taking part in a party headed by the Chevalier de Niverville were given '3 pairs of oxhide leather shoes' along with '3 deer hides,' which may have served to make winter moccasins.[405] In August of that same year, '169 oxhide shoes' were enumerated on a statement of expenditure of a war party commanded by M. Rigaud de Vaudreuil, including officers, cadets, soldiers, and militiamen.[406] This type of footwear was also worn by soldiers serving at various forts such as Fort Châteauguay, where '30 pairs of oxhide shoes' were sent for 'the service of the garrison of the said fort.'[407]

By the Seven Years War, the Native-style shoes issued to the colonial troops were specifically made of oxhide. A 1756-dated list of supplies for the officers and soldiers of the battalions and those of the colony mentions 'one pair of tanned shoes per month', which were described as 'oxhide shoes' in the margin.[408] Bourlamaque proposed in a 1762-dated memoir that 'six pairs of tanned oxhide shoes' be provided annually as part of the soldier's regulation clothing, corresponding to one pair every two months.[409] As such, the King's storehouses in Montréal had to stock large quantities of oxhide shoes during wartime to meet the demands of military campaigns. In 1745, 150 pairs were included as part of the war supplies delivered to Fort St-Frédéric,[410] whereas, two years later, 1,441 pairs of souliers de peau de bœufs (oxhide shoes) were purchased from the King's storehouses for the war preparations and other needs.[411]

Tanned Sealskin Shoes (Souliers de Loup Marin)

Numerous military records reference moccasins made from tanned sealskin being issued to troops, valued for their waterproof and pliable qualities, making them ideal for wet and snowy conditions. Charlevoix described sealskins as excellent for crafting waterproof footwear:

> When they are tanned, they have almost the same grain as Moroccan leather… They are made into very good shoes, and boots, which do not take on water. These skins are tanned here with spruce bark, and in the dye, which is used to blacken them, a powder is mixed, which is obtained from certain stones, found on the banks of rivers.[412]

The importance of seal hide tanning in the Québec area is evident in a 1732 inventory of M. Bégon's tannery, which included a variety of processed seal hides and footwear, such as blackened and tanned seals, 52 pairs of sealskin shoes, and 42 raw sealskins awaiting further treatment.[413] Montcalm remarked in 1757 that due to a shortage of munitions shoes that year, a number of individuals in the colony were 'making soldiers shoes with sealskin for

400 Pehr Kalm, Jacques Rousseau, Guy Béthune, & Pierre Morisset, *Voyage de Pehr Kalm au Canada en 1749* (Montréal, Québec: Pierre Tisseyre, 1977), p.379.
401 BAnQ-M, ZF8, Fonds Jean Baptiste d'Aleyrac.
402 PRDH, volume 41, St-Pierre-de-Sorel, 15 mai 1757.
403 LAC, MG1-C11A, vol.70, f.49.
404 LAC, MG1-C11A, vol.117, f.318v.
405 LAC, MG1-C11A, vol.117, f.192v.
406 LAC, MG1-C11A, vol.117, f.30.

407 LAC, MG1-C11A, vol.117, f.226.
408 SHAT, Dossier A1, 3417, Pièce 144.
409 LAC, MG1-C11A, volume 105, f.372v.
410 LAC, MG1-C11A, vol.85, f.390v.
411 LAC, MG1-C11A, vol.117, f.166.
412 Pierre-François-Xavier de Charlevoix, *Histoire et description generale de la nouvelle France, avec le journal historique d'un voyage fait par ordre du roi dans l'Amerique septentrionnale* (Paris: Chez Pierre-François Giffard, 1744), vol.3, pp.145–146.
413 BAnQ-Q, ZE25, P113, Inventaire des effets trouvés en la tannerie de M. Bégon après le décès du sieur Hurel, 10 novembre 1732.

the rain.[414] According to Pierre Pouchot, each time the Canadian troops went off to war, each man was supplied with 'one pair of sealskin shoes per month,'[415] while *capitaine* Leduchat of the Régiment de Languedoc stationed at Fort Carillon in 1756, noted that 'Native-style shoes (souliers sauvages), in other words, of sealskin,' were distributed to the officers and soldiers of the regular and colonial troops per campaign.[416]

Equipment Lists

Few summer expedition equipment lists from the 1740s include sealskin moccasins, although by the 1750s, their numbers increase dramatically. In 1743, Jean Soupras, *sergent* in the Troupes de la Marine at Montréal, was the owner of '30 pairs of tanned sealskin shoes,' each priced at 15 sols per pair,[417] while 11 years later, a cassette belonging to a soldier stationed at Fort St-Frédéric contained 'two pieces of tanned sealskin fit to make shoes.'[418] Based on expense reports, it would seem that most of these waterproof shoes were made by artisans or supplied by merchants working out of the Québec administrative area, where sealskins were readily available. In 1745, '11 pairs of shoes' were delivered from the King's storehouses at Québec for the war effort,[419] whereas the following year, '281 sealskins for shoes' were purchased by Sieur de Beaujeu on account of the King.[420] In 1747, a single document listed 1,387 pairs of sealskin moccasins provided by two Québec-based merchants, in addition to hundreds of extra tanned sealskins.[421] In 1750 alone, '1,200 pairs of tanned sealskin shoes' were sent from the King's storehouses at Québec to the Rivière Saint-Jean and Shediac for the service and subsistence of the troops, Native Americans, and Acadians.[422]

Production Source of Oxhide and Sealskin Shoes

The sealskin or oxhide moccasins issued to colonial soldiers were supplied by local sources, such as shoemakers around Montréal and Québec. In 1748, for example, 233 pairs of oxhide shoes were purchased from the Montréal-based shoemaker Joseph Guyon dit Després.[423] According to King's storekeeper Estèbe, the King's storehouses were supplied by a Montréal merchant named Despins, possibly referring to Jacques-Joseph Lemoine Despins, as well as a Demoiselle Ramezay and a man known as Barselou, a leather tanner at Côte-des-Neiges.[424] During the Seven Years War, as demand surged, orders extended beyond local suppliers to merchants in France. In 1757, '20,000 pairs of tanned oxhide shoes, thin [leather], for men, plain, red, and similar to the sample sent last year' were to be made for Canada by M. Banchereau of Tours, France.[425] This record suggests that the souliers de bœuf made in the colony probably used thin, reddish leather.

Winter Moccasins of the Colonial Troops (Souliers de Chevreuil or Souliers de Peau de Chevreuil)

Initially issued ready-made moccasins for winter campaigns or expeditions, colonial soldiers by the late seventeenth century were instead provided with deer hides to craft their own footwear prior to winter expeditions, during the journey or upon arrival at a fort or outpost. In 1680, the colonial officer Lahontan observed that while trekking overland at the end of winter, the usual equipment consisted of 'dressed hides to make Native-style shoes, which often last only a day, those which are worn in France, being of no use in these western countries.'[426] During the Seven Years War, one deerskin was generally issued for the winter equipment of each soldier serving in New France 'to be used to make shoes in the manner of the Natives.'[427] Soldiers had to either make their own high-cut winter moccasins or pay to have them made by locals, such as the Canadians who made souliers de peau de chevreuil for the soldiers in March of 1757 at Fort St-Frédéric.[428] In colder months, European-style shoes, or tanned leather moccasins, were replaced with tall moccasin made of soft leather, a type of footwear adopted from the Native Americans commonly termed souliers de chevreuil or souliers de peau de chevreuil in colonial records.

These types of 'Native-style boots' were commonly worn by the first French colonists as early as the second quarter of the seventeenth century, becoming essential

414 Casgrain, *Journal du marquis de Montcalm*, p.317.

415 Pouchot, *Mémoires sur la dernière guerre de l'Amérique septentrionale*, p.28.

416 AG, MG-4, B1, Série A1, vol.3417, f.383.

417 BAnQ-M, Greffe du notaire Jean-Baptiste Adhemard dit St-Martin, Inventaire de feu Jean Soupras et de Marie Elisabeth Vallé, vivant sergent des troupes de la Marine, 25 septembre 1743.

418 BAnQ-M, TL4, S1, D5921, Procès contre Menin Pouteau dit Parisien, sculpteur, soldat d'Herbin, Michel Dufeu dit Flame, soldat de la Compagnie de Villemonde, et Guillaume Goursol dit Lagiroflée, soldat de la Compagnie Debonne, accusés de vols dans la chambre de distribution du fort Saint-Frédéricm 9 septembre 1754–26 février 1755.

419 LAC, MG1-C11A, vol.84, f.138.

420 LAC, MG1-C11A, vol.117, f.49.

421 LAC, MG1-C11A, vol.117, f.100, 109v.

422 LAC, MG1-C11A, vol.96, f.124v.

423 LAC, MG1-C11A, vol.116, f.108v.

424 Anon., *À Monseigneur de Sartine*, pp.17–18.

425 LAC, MG 18, H63, Fonds famille Gradis, F-1600, M. Panchereau, Tours, 11 octobre 1757.

426 Louis Hennepin, *Description de la Louisiane, nouvellement découverte au sud-ouest de la Nouvelle France* (Paris: Chez Amable Auroy, 1688), pp.173–174.

427 SHAT, Dossier A1, 3417, Pièce 144.

428 De Bougainville, *Écrits sur le Canada*, p.172.

for winter survival. In 1634, Father le Jeune wrote that 'the French never wear any others [shoes] in winter, since one cannot go out except with snowshoes under one's feet (and) to walk on the snow one cannot use French shoes.'[429] The flexibility of the sole made winter moccasins suitable for use with snowshoes, which required the feet to bend, while their larger size compared to summer moccasins allowed for feet wrapped in strips of cloth (nippes), and they were typically crafted from frost-resistant deerskin. Montcalm took note that deerskin moccasins were made 'for the frost,' in other words, made to be used in sub-zero temperatures.[430] The upper panels covered the calves and were tightly bound to the leg of the wearer by two long leather strips, which were wrapped around each panel and tied in front, effectively preventing snow from entering the boot. According to Lafitau: 'Some of them [Natives] make their shoes go up to mid-leg, to be less bothered by snow, and the manner in which they bind these resembles very much the shoes which were worn by the ancient heroes and the warriors of the Roman legions.'[431] By the nineteenth century, French Canadians living in the St Lawrence Valley adapted these boots by making them out of oxhide leather, calling them bottes sauvages, a tradition that persisted in more rural or isolated areas of Québec until the second quarter of the twentieth century.

Government-Issued Souliers de Chevreuil

Winter moccasins, worn with snowshoes, were used on military campaigns in New France as early as the 1660s, highlighting their practicality, as shown by accounts of souliers sauvages issued for wilderness expeditions. In 1666, René-Louis Chartier de Lotbinière, who had composed a poem of Monsieur de Courcelles' trip into the Iroquois country, described them as 'made like animal skin slippers to tie them [snowshoes] onto.'[432] The colonial soldiers commanded by Chevalier de Troyes who set off from Montréal to Hudson's Bay in March of 1686 were each issued 'two pairs of Native-style shoes', which meant they were ready-to-wear.[433] At Fort Frontenac in 1702, '11 pairs of souliers sauvages' priced at 20 sols each were allocated for the needs of the garrison and were likely intended to be worn with snowshoes.[434] In 1706, Cadillac requested 'four deer hides for making shoes for

Line drawing made from a mannequin representing an Innu (Naskapi) taken from a catalogue published in 1709 showing the bottes sauvages construction style with a vamp, uppers and a cord wrapped around and tied at the front. (Courtesy of Francis Back)

the soldiers' to equip a winter expedition consisting of one officer and four soldiers, tasked with preventing several allied nations from going to war.[435] A few years later, the goods needed for a plan to deal with the Foxes proposed by officer Payen de Noyan included '500 pairs of souliers sauvages',[436] while during de Noyelle's 1735 winter expedition against the Sauk and Foxes, 'many soldiers were forced to eat their souliers sauvages'.[437]

By the 1740s, winter equipment lists typically allocated two deerskins per man, undoubtedly intended for making winter moccasins. In 1740, '90 livres of deer skins' were distributed to a detachment of Habitants and soldiers

429 Relations des Jésuites contenant ce qui s'est passé de plus remarquable dans les missions des pères de la Compagnie de Jésus dans la Nouvelle-France (Québec: Augustin Côté, 1858), vol.1, p.48.
430 Casgrain, Journal du marquis de Montcalm, p.317.
431 Joseph-François Lafitau, Mœurs, coutumes et religions des sauvages américains... (Paris: Librairie d'éducation de Perisse Frères, 1845), vol.1, p.200.
432 BAnQ-Q, P1000, S3, D374, Poème sur le gouverneur de Courcelles par René-Louis Chartier de Lotbinière, p.4.
433 LAC, MG1-C11A, vol.8, f.278v.
434 LAC, MG1-C11A, vol.20, f.262.

435 LAC, MG1-C11A, vol.24, f.290.
436 LAC, MG1-C11A, vol.56, f.314.
437 LAC, MG1-C11A, vol.63, f.243v.

who participated in the Chickasaw campaign.[438] Seven years later, cadets Langy and St-Blin were issued '4 deer skins weighing 10½ livres' as part of their winter equipment to 'go to war on the coast of New England with a party of Abenakis Natives from St-François,'[439] whereas Monsieur de la Chauvignery and two Frenchmen were issued '6 deer skins weighing 17 livres.'[440] A supply list of goods issued to colonial soldiers in 1756 included 'for the winter campaign in addition to the summer one … 1 deer skin and no tanned shoes.'[441] The following year, both Bougainville and Montcalm recorded '2 pairs of deer-skin shoes' as well as '1 deer skin, passée' distributed to each man at Fort St-Jean in the winter of 1757.[442] The term 'passé,' designating tawed leather.[443] According to a declaration of two French soldiers taken prisoners at Fort William-Henry in March of 1757, each man had 'two pair mocassans or Indian shoes' as well as 'one pair of Snow Shoes.'[444] According to Intendant Bigot, the standard winter equipment issued to officers, soldiers, militiamen, and Native American allies included '1 deer skin,' likely for making winter moccasins to wear with snowshoes, and '1 pair of tanned shoes per month,' presumably for everyday use.[445]

King's Storehouses and Forts

Records pertaining to the King's storehouses at Montréal and nearby forts reveal the importance of winter moccasins when patrolling, hunting or moving about in winter. At Pointe-à-la-Chevelure (Crown Point) in 1734, 'deer skins to make Native shoes' were sent from Montréal for the garrison's use.[446] In 1740 and 1743, both deerskins for making Native shoes as well as 100 pairs of ready-made Native shoes priced at 30 sols each were sent to Fort Saint-Frédéric.[447]

The amount of deerskin required to produce moccasins varied depending on their size, as shown in records from the Montréal storehouses in 1746. At the Montréal storehouses in 1746, 1½ livre of deerskin was used to make two pairs of souliers sauvages,[448] whereas another '1¾

Detail of snowshoes and vamp-style winter moccasins worn by a colonial soldier or militiaman during King William's War (1689-1697). This engraving, published in 1722, provides evidence of the use of wider vamp-style moccasins with snowshoes, allowing for the inclusion of blanket strips and woollen liners for warmth. (Claude-Charles Le Roy Bacqueville de La Potherie, *Histoire de l'Amérique Septentrionale*, 1722. *Canadiens en raquette allant en guerre sur la neige*, Creative Commons)

livres of deer skin' was needed to make a similar number of pairs.[449] That same year, a party of eight Canadian militiamen were provided with 13 *livres* of deer hides to make 16 pairs of winter moccasins 'in replacement of two pairs of souliers sauvages each, which they supplied,'[450] whereas an itemised list of expenses incurred for Fort Saint-Frédéric included 230 *livres* of deer skins in making 264 pairs of Native shoes.[451] In 1746, a cadet named Robital was issued one deer skin weighing 2¾ *livres* for his garrison at Châteauguay,[452] while colonial officer Charles de Montesson and cadets Duburon and Boiclerc received 'three deer skins weighing 7½ *livres*' from the Montréal storehouses for their garrison at [Fort] Ste-Thérèse.[453]

Supply Sources

Initially, Native shoes were supplied by Native American allies, but French colonists soon began tanning their own deer, moose, and seal hides, learning to craft a variety of Native-style moccasins. Despite this, the colonists and military continued to rely on their Indigenous allies for hides to meet growing demand. For example, in 1748, the Hurons around Québec supplied 400 deer hides valued at 15 sols each to the King's storehouses.[454] Québec-based merchants like Chalet and Charly supplied large quantities of deer hides,[455] some of which were used to make winter moccasins for the troops, while Jacques Hubert provided 401 pairs of souliers sauvages at 19 sols 4 deniers each,[456] and Christophe Dubois delivered 41 pairs at 32 sols each to replenish the

438 LAC, MG1-C11A, vol.117, f.196v-197

439 LAC, MG1-C11A, vol.117, f.184v.

440 LAC, MG1-C11A, vol.17, f.196–196v.

441 Centre d'histoire La Presqu'ile, P03/F.089, Fonds De Beaujeu, 28 novembre 1756.

442 Casgrain, *Journal du marquis de Montcalm*, p.156; De Bougainville, *Écrits sur le Canada*, p.168.

443 Joseph Jérôme Le Français de Lalande, *Art du tanneur* (Paris: Desaint & Saillant, 1764), p.40.

444 LOC, Colonial Office 5 folio 47, E. of Loudoun's Letter of April 25th. 1757, Declaration of two Prisoners taken the 23.d March 1757 at Fort Wm. Henry, Information of John Victor and Guillaume Chasse, two French Prisoners, Fort William Henry March 25th.

445 Bigot, *Mémoire Pour Messire François Bigot*, p.39.

446 LAC, MG1-C11A, vol.66, f.56.

447 LAC, MG1-C11A, vol.73, f.155v.; LAC, MG1-C11A, vol.82, f.170.

448 LAC, MG1-C11A, vol.88, f.215.

449 LAC, MG1-C11A, vol.86, f.224v.

450 LAC, MG1-C11A, vol.86, f.229v.

451 LAC, MG1-C11A, vol 88, f.216v.

452 LAC, MG1-C11A, vol.86, f.227.

453 LAC, MG1-C11A, vol.86, f.223v-224.

454 LAC, MG1-C11A, vol.116, f.99.

455 LAC, MG1-C11A, vol.115, f.174, 175.

456 LAC, MG1-C11A, vol.116, f.82v.

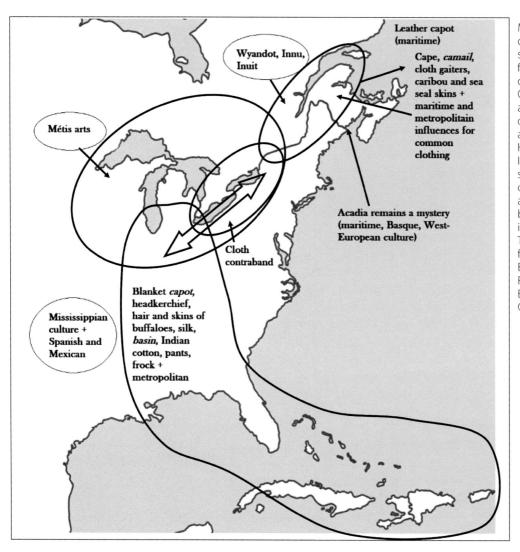

Leather capot (maritime)

Cape, _camail_, cloth gaiters, caribou and sea seal skins + maritime and metropolitain influences for common clothing

Wyandot, Innu, Inuit

Métis arts

Acadia remains a mystery (maritime, Basque, West-European culture)

Cloth contraband

Mississippian culture + Spanish and Mexican

Blanket _capot_, headkerchief, hair and skins of buffaloes, silk, _basin_, Indian cotton, pants, frock + metropolitan

Map illustrating the diverse cultural influences that shaped French colonial fashion across the regions of New France, including Canada, Acadia, the Illinois and Louisiana territories during the seventeenth and eighteenth centuries. Highlights include Indigenous contributions such as leather and blanket capots, Métis craftsmanship, and the use of materials like buffalo hides, seal skins, and imported cotton fabrics. The map underscores the fusion of local, maritime, and European styles that defined French colonial clothing. Based on research by Kevin Gélinas and Francis Back.

King's storehouses at the onset of King George's War.[457] At Montréal, 1,631 _livres_ of 'deer hides for souliers sauvages' were set aside in preparation for war in 1744.[458] Some 15 years later, the storekeeper at Fort Machault paid a man named Gaudebœuf the sum of 549 livres for 244 pairs of deer hide shoes (souliers de chevreuil), while at Fort le Bœuf, four pairs of souliers de chevreuil were purchased from a Lajeunesse for 9 livres.[459] Lastly, during the Montréal campaign of 1760, the dealer Jacques Hervieux supplied 3,654 livres of dressed deer hides for the needs of the service.[460]

Wool Slippers (Chaussons) and Cloth Wraps (Nippes)

Blanket strip liners and woollen cloth slippers were essential components of the winter equipment issued to

colonial troops. These low, slipper-like coverings, called chaussons, were used to line the inside of deerskin winter moccasins and were crafted from popular French woollen fabrics such as Carisé, Mazamet, and molleton. According to the engineer Franquet, who travelled to Canada between 1752 and 1753, when Canadians travel in winter, they 'take Indian moccasins with them, which are made only of deerskin and lined on the inside with wool slippers (chaussons).[461] The _Dictionnaire universel Francois et Latin_ defines them as 'what is used to cover the sole of the foot and that we insert in shoes under the stockings.'[462] In 1734, the 56 colonial soldiers accompanying de Noyelles in his campaign against the Fox nations each received a pair of these slippers, requiring 18⅔ _aunes_ of Mazamet fabric.[463] Eleven years later, Joseph Marin de La Malgue, leading a war party of colonial officers and cadets, distributed 233 pairs of slippers made from Carisé (Kersey) at a

457 LAC, MG1-C11A, vol.115, f.163v.

458 LAC, MG1-C11A, vol.82, f.186.

459 LAC, Archives de la marine, G-239, Bobine F-1516, Pièces numéro 14 & 23, 1767.

460 LAC, MG1-C11A, bobine F-104, vol.115, f.395.

461 Louis Franquet, _Voyages et mémoires sur le Canada en 1752–1753_ (Québec: Imprimerie générale A. Coté et cie, 1889), p.131.

462 _Dictionnaire universel Francois et Latin avec des remarques d'érudition et de critique_ (Paris: Par la compagnie des Libraires associés, 1752), vol.2, p.648.

463 LAC, MG1-C11A, vol.62, f.150v.

cost of 40 sols per pair.[464] A small contingent of gunners sent to Fort Saint-Frédéric in 1746 was issued four pairs of mittens and four pairs of slippers crafted from 2⅔ *aunes* of molleton fabric, demonstrating that wool liners were also supplied to men stationed at forts in the interior.[465] In 1751, 'five pairs of wool slippers' were found in a chest belonging to Dorizon dit Larose, a soldier in the Compagnie de Beaujeu, suggesting that they may have served as extra pairs of liners that were replaced when his feet got wet.[466] According to a number of senior officers, the standard government-issued equipment distributed to colonial and regular troops serving in Canada for winter campaigns throughout the Seven Years War included 'two pairs of wool slippers.'[467]

Nippes were strips of unusable blankets used to bind one's feet, and were worn in conjunction with chaussons, inside high-cut winter deerskin moccasins for additional warmth. Nippes, from the primitive word nip, meaning water, was a familiar eighteenth century French expression, usually denoting clothes, garments with which one is always clean and that can be washed.[468] In a colonial context, it specifically referred to 'pieces of wool cloth to put in shoes',[469] and the practice of wrapping one's foot was attested by Father Lejeune as early as 1634:

> They make them [moccasins] large and very resistant, especially in winter, to protect them against the cold; they usually use a hare's skin, or a piece taken from a blanket, folded in two and three, double lined… and then having wrapped their feet in these rags, they put on their shoes, and sometimes two pairs, one on top of the other.[470]

Pouchot also observed this practice among the Natives: 'They wrap pieces of blankets around their feet and the sides of the shoe form a tight fit with the ankle that prevents the snow from entering.'[471]

Probate records reveal that discarded blankets in the colony were commonly repurposed to wrap around the feet when wearing winter moccasins, a practice that made use of every available resource. These worn-out blankets, often too tattered for other uses, were transformed into strips of fabric, which provided additional insulation inside souliers sauvages. For instance, 'two old wool blankets, completely worn out and completely unserviceable … which can only serve to make nippes for souliers sauvages' were in the possession of Guillaume Deguise dit Flamand, while Jean-Baptiste Grenille (Greenhil), storekeeper at Fort de La Présentation, was the owner of 'an old wool blanket fit to make nippes', valued at 2 livres.[472]

By the time of King George's War, small blankets known as couvertes à berceau (cradle blankets), typically measuring ½ *aune*, were issued to each colonial soldier. These blankets were likely torn into two or more strips to bind each foot before putting on winter moccasins. In 1745, the equipment for a war party led by Marin de La Malgue to Acadia included 547 cradle blankets.[473] Similarly, in 1746, '1 cradle blanket for nippes' was issued to colonial officer Le Mercier, stationed at Fort St-Frédéric.[474] That same year, '10 2-point blankets, unsound, for nippes' were provided to M. de Montesson and two cadets for their garrison at Fort Ste-Thérèse, where they commanded a detachment of 74 Native warriors.[475] The use of nippes is further documented in a 1756 supply list for colonial troops, which explicitly mentioned 'nippes for the shoes.'[476] In 1757, Montcalm noted the distribution of 'half a cradle blanket' and 'nippes for shoes' to soldiers at Fort St-Jean[477] whereas Intendant Bigot, during his trial at the Bastille, also referenced '1 cradle blanket for nippes, to wear inside the shoes,' emphasizing that such items were standard winter equipment for both colonial officers and soldiers.[478]

464 LAC, MG1-C11A, vol.84, f.147–150.

465 LAC, MG1-C11A, vol.88, f.214v.

466 BAnQ-Q, TL5, D1640, Procès criminel contre Claude du Retour (Duretour) de Monsy, seigneur de Neuville et autres terres, environ 31 ans, soldat de la compagnie de Beaujeu, et Louis Daurizon (Dorizon) dit Larose, soldat de la compagnie de Beaujeu, environ 39 ans, pour falsification d'ordonnances, 1er janvier 1749–5 novembre 1751.

467 *Journal du marquis de Montcalm durant ses campagnes en Canada de 1756 à 1759* (Québec: Imprimerie de L.-J. Demers & frère, 1895), p.156.; SHAT, Dossier A1, 3417, Pièce 144.; Centre d'histoire La Presqu'île, P03/F.089, Fonds De Beaujeu, 28 novembre 1756.; 1757–Montcalm « 2 paires de chaussons »;

468 Pierre-Joseph-André Roubaud, *Nouveaux synonymes françois* (Liège: Chez C. Plomteux, 1786), vol.3, pp.258–261.

469 De Malartic & Gaffarel (eds), *Journal des Campagnes au Canada*, p.95.

470 *Relations des Jésuites, cont. ce qui s'est passé de plus remarquable dans les missions des pères de la compagnie de Jésus dans la Nouvelle-France* (Québec: Augustin Côté, 1858), vol.1, p.48.

471 Pierre Pouchot, *Memoirs on the late war in North America between France and England* (Youngstown, NY: Old Fort Niagara Association, 1994) p.458.

472 BAnQ-Q, TL5, D1829, Inventaire des biens de Guillaume Deguise dit Flamand, vivant entrepreneur d'ouvrages de maçonnerie, de Québec, et de Marie-Anne Rouillard, sa femme, 23 décembre 1756. ; BAnQ-M, Greffe du notaire Antoine Loiseau dit Chalons, Inventaire des biens de Jean-Baptiste Grenille, vivant garde-magasin au Fort de la Présentation, 22 février 1759.

473 LAC, MG1-C11A, vol.84, f.148.

474 LAC, MG1-C11A, vol.88, f.214v.

475 LAC, MG1-C11A, vol.88, fol. 224.

476 SHAT, Dossier A1, 3417, Pièce 144.

477 Casgrain, *Journal du marquis de Montcalm*, pp.156–157.

478 Bigot, *Mémoire Pour Messire François Bigot*, p.39.

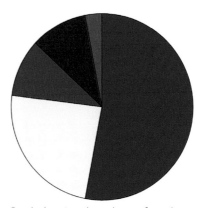

Left: A painting by Father Chauchetière of Kateri Tekakwitha, created between 1682 and 1693, shows her wearing lightly decorated dark blue wool leggings. Her moccasins, with a pucker-toe centre seam construction, appear to be quilled along the opening. (Creative Commons)

Graph showing the colours of men's mitasses (1723–1764) at Trois-Rivières, Montréal, Québec, and the Illinois Country taken from probate records.

Detail from a watercolour showing an Abenaki man wearing blue mitasses with what appears to be silk ribbon edging. (Archives de la Ville de Montréal, BM7-2_27P002)

Above left: Rare depiction of a Canadian 'Habitant' or colonist wearing the common red knit cap, known as a tuque in Montréal and Trois-Rivières, and as a fourolle around Québec. Shown as part of a votive of the shipwreck at Lévis. Anonymous, 1754. (Musée Historique, Basilique Sainte-Anne. Courtesy of Joseph Gagné)

Above centre: Detail from Claude-Joseph Vernet's Moonlight, showing a French sailor wearing a red wool cap, likely similar to those issued to colonial troops in New France. (Courtesy of the National Gallery of Art, Washington)

Above right: Sailor wearing a red cap and a mariner's sash, from Vue du Port de La Rochelle, Prise de la Petite Rive (1762), by Joseph Vernet. (Courtesy Musée de la Marine, Paris. Photo Kevin Gélinas)

Left: One of three Canadians painted by a German immigrant between 1775 and 1785 wearing a white capot trimmed in blue and fastened by a red, yellow and blue sash. Note the presence of boot cuffs as well as greenish coloured mitasses lined with red silk. He is also wearing a two-tone tuque, of red and white. (With permission of the Royal Ontario Museum © ROM)

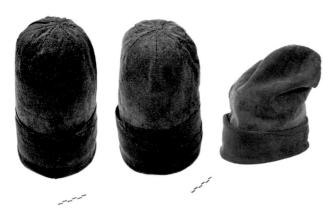

A stocking cap knitted in a long, seamless tube, closed at both ends, recovered from the Machault, an eighteenth-century frigate loaded with supplies for New France, which sank in 1760 in the Restigouche estuary. (Courtesy of National Historic Sites, Parks Canada. Photo Kevin Gélinas)

This rare artifact, a soulier de bœuf (oxhide shoe), dates from between 1770 and 1800 and originates from the Saint-Henri-des-Tanneries site. Barselou, a tanner from nearby Côte-des-Neiges, is recorded as having supplied Estèbe, the storekeeper in Montréal, with these shoes for the King, a portion of which was likely intended for the colonial troops. This example likely resembles the type of leather footwear worn by colonial soldiers during summer campaigns. (Pointe-à-Callière, Montreal Archaeology and History Complex, Sébastien Martel, 2022. BiFj-118-26J4-297)

Detail from a watercolour by James Peachy, 1781, showing a man wearing a yellow, collarless capot and moccasins with long extensions (hausses) reaching up to just below the knee, secured by a tightened cord. This type of footwear would have been highly practical for walking in deep snow, providing added protection and warmth. (Courtesy of Library and Archives Canada, James Peachy, View of the Falls of Montmorency with his Excellency General Haldimand's Country House, 1781)

Detail from a 1756 painting by Jean-Joseph Kapeller, depicting a luxurious longboat in Marseille harbour, used for the river transport of senior officials during maréchal duc de Richelieu's 1756 campaign against the island of Minorca. The soldiers rowing the boat are wearing blue and red fatigue caps. (Photo Jean Bernard. Musée des Beaux-Arts, Marseille, France. © RMN-Grand Palais/Art Resource, NY)

Top to bottom (c. 1750–1780) Detail from an image of an Algonquin couple, both wearing cuffed centre-seam moccasins. (Archives de la Ville de Montréal, BM7-2_27P004) Close-up of cuffed moccasins worn by a Wendat woman (left) and a man (right). The woman's moccasins feature a centre seam running down the vamp, while the man's have a wider, rounded-toe vamp style. (Archives de la Ville de Montréal, BM7-2_27P003) Moccasins worn by an Abenakis couple, showing the centre-seam style. These moccasins are typically made from a single piece of leather, sewn together at the vamp and featuring collars. (Archives de la Ville de Montréal, BM7-2_27P002)

Detail of a circa 1700–1750 votive painting depicting two dead Canadiens, likely militiamen, and a survivor giving thanks to the Blessed Virgin Mary. The deceased are wearing high-cut winter moccasins tied around the legs with long leather thongs, a style commonly used by colonial troops during winter expeditions. (Photo Kevin Gélinas. Fabrique de Rivière-Ouelle)

69

2

Summer Campaign Equipment and Hand-Held Weapons of the Colonial Troops

By the eighteenth century, the common soldier of the Compagnies franches de la Marine was, by regulation, armed with a musket, sword, and bayonet, in addition to a cartridge box and sword belt. The use and detailed specifications of these weapons, including their muskets, swords, and bayonets, are covered in Volume 1. These soldiers also carried a gargoussier waist box when on duty, whether in towns, forts, trading posts, or during campaigns, which also doubled as a practical holder for spare gunflints and lead balls. While colonial officers conceivably carried Canadian-style powder horns and Native-style slit pouches, enlisted men were equipped with the regulation-issued fourniment powder flasks.

In the field, colonial soldiers preferred to carry casse-tête tomahawks rather than swords, which were cumbersome in the densely forested terrain of North America. These tomahawks were likely tucked under the buff leather regulation ceinturon at the back, rather than carried in the waist belt's frog, to ensure they stayed firmly in place and to prevent accidental cuts from the blade. The casse-tête was a versatile tool, used not only as a formidable weapon but also for practical tasks such as splitting wood, breaking ice, and performing camp chores. Some colonial officers carried this type of hatchet, along with a sabre, cutlass, or hunting sword, as a replacement for the small sword more common in European theatres. Enlisted men also commonly carried a boucheron knife, a long butcher knife typically worn in a leather sheath around the neck, which was inspired by their Native allies. In bush warfare, the regulation bayonets proved almost useless, as they were designed for large infantry formations and were often left behind. These practical adaptations in the field stand in sharp contrast to the standard armament of French officers and soldiers on European battlefields or during naval engagements.

The Casse-tête: the Colonial Soldier's Tomahawk

Adopted early on by the militiamen and rapidly embraced by the colonial troops in Canada, the common casse-tête (tomahawk) increasingly replaced the bayonet and sword on wilderness campaigns against the British and their Native allies.[1] In part, this shift occurred because one of the main drivers of the bayonet's adoption, protection against cavalry, was not a concern in the forests of New France. The casse-tête eventually became standard-issue equipment for colonial soldiers, officers, and cadets on both winter and summer campaigns. Unlike in France, where axes or hatchets were reserved for specialised units such as grenadiers, cavalry, or as boarding axes on ships, in New France these lightweight hand-held axes proved far more practical. They were ideal for navigating dense forests and served as highly effective weapons in hand-to-hand combat during 'la petite guerre'.

Origin and Definition of a Casse-tête

The term casse-tête, which can literally be translated as skull-cracker, is derived from the North American Native use of war clubs, proven as an effective striking weapon. By the eighteenth century in New France, this term became synonymous with the common iron hatchet provided as a trade item or distributed to arm allied Native Americans, militia, and colonial troops. An account of Braddock's defeat published in *The Scots Magazine* provides us with a factual period English interpretation of this term: 'Led on by this new commander [M. Dumas], they [Natives], and the Canadians rushed furiously upon the enemy, without giving them time to charge again, and with their little hatchets, which they call scull-crackers, made a great slaughter of the English troops.'[2]

---

1   Kevin Gladysz (Gélinas) and Ken Hamilton, 'Axes in New France, Part III: Casse-têtes (French Tomahawks)', *Journal of the Early Americas*, vol.II, Issue 6 (December 2012/January 2013), pp.6–19.
2   James Boswell, *The Scots Magazine* (Edinburgh: Sands, Brymer, Murray and Cochran, 1755), vol.17, p.503.

Detail taken from the Baron of Lahontan's 1703 edition of *Voyages du baron de Lahontan dans l'Amérique septentrionale* depicting an 'Axe called small casse-tête' the likes of which was issued to every colonial soldier serving in Canada.

Shown here is a late 1690s Canadian militiaman on snowshoes carrying a casse-tête through his sash. (Claude-Charles Le Roy Bacqueville de La Potherie, *Histoire de l'Amérique Septentrionale, 1722. Canadiens en raquette allant en guerre sur la neige*, Creative Commons)

The French writer Guillaume Thomas François Raynal described the evolution of the casse-tête from a Native war club to an iron hatchet, noting: 'Before the arrival of the Europeans, it was only a small club made from a very hard wood, having a round face with a sharp side. Today it is a small axe.'[3] French military officials in North America during the Seven Years War provided us with short but insightful descriptions of the adopted term casse-tête. For instance, a French *lieutenant* in the Languedoc regiment wrote in 1756 that when the Natives Americans living in Canada left for war they were armed with 'a fusil, a small axe that we call casse-tête, and a lance [spear]',[4] while the following year, a French officer who was campaigning at Île-Royale (Cape Breton Island) described this weapons as 'a casse-tête (this weapon looks like a small axe).'[5]

Usefulness of the Casse-tête in New France

From an early period in New France, the casse-tête served many uses such as a utilitarian tool or a striking and throwing weapon, while also replacing the soldier's bayonet and sword in combat. In 1716, the Minister of the Marine proposed giving Louisiana troops hatchets hanging from narrow shoulder belts rather than swords or

sabres.[6] In a 1749 letter to the minister in France, Intendant Bigot emphasised the importance of the bayonet to defend or force an entrenchment while adding 'I do not wish that the casse-tête be deducted because of its usefulness in the marches for the encampments', revealing the advantages of such a tool in such circumstances.[7] Some five years later, Louisiana Governor Kerlerec proposed that the bayonets used by the soldiers be altogether replaced with casse-têtes when fighting against the Native Americans, judging that they also doubled as a camp tool:

> I have then considered that the casse-tête, which is a little hand hatchet, would be in every way more proper inasmuch as it is a good defensive arm, and it is very useful for a soldier for cutting firewood or the pickets for his cabin; it serves to cut him a trail in many circumstances or to make him a boat in other emergencies or finally to chop down the pickets of an intrenchment which they want to capture.[8]

At the outset of the Seven Years War, French regulars arriving in Canada quickly adopted tomahawks, or casse-têtes, during campaigns, recognising their versatility as both a practical tool and an effective replacement for the bayonet in defensive situations. For instance, 3,522

---

3   Guillaume Thomas François Raynal, *Histoire philosophique et politique Des Etablissemens & du Commerce des Européens dans les deux Indes* (Amsterdam: 1773), vol.6, p.37.

4   Élie-Catherine Fréron, *Journal Etranger: Ou Notice Exacte et Détaillée des Ouvrages de Toutes les Nations Étrangères, en Fait d'Arts, de Sciences, de Littérature, &c. Mars 1756, Numéro 3* (Paris: Chez Michel Lambert, 1756), p.141.

5   RAPQ, 1931–1932, p.381.

6   LAC, 13A, vol.4, f.117.

7   LAC, MG1-C11A, vol.93, pp.255–258.

8   Theodore Calvin Pease; Ernestine Jenison, *French Series, vol.III, Illinois on the eve of the Seven Years War, 1747–1755* (Springfield, Ill.: The Trustees of the State Historical Library, 1940), pp.885–886.

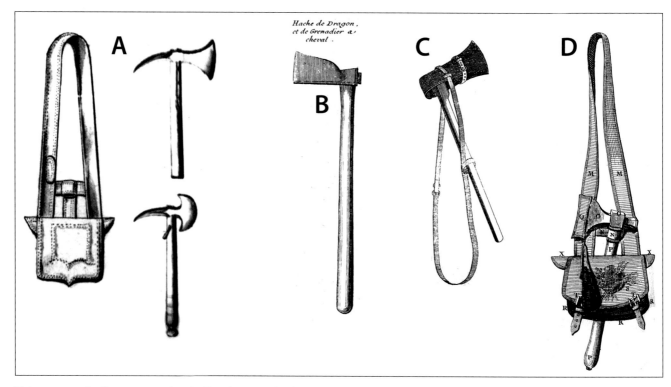

Various types of military axes used in the French marine, by the cavalry or grenadiers. The boarding axes used in the marine had a cutting blade opposed by a spike for boarding purposes, while those used by the ground troops were equipped with hammer-poll axes that were used for certain war operations and to overthrow palisades. Campaign axes were also issued to each infantry company for encampments, which are described as well as their cases and strap in the 17 February 1753 ordonnance. The casse-tête issued to the troops in New France was very different to the military hatchets in use in France. A) Detail from a c. 1703 illustration showing two types of marine axes for the use of the grenadiers or sailors aboard the Royal French Galleys along with their pouch and frog. (Document Archives Nationales, Archives de la Marine, France, Série G). B) Dragoon or Horse Grenadier's axe, c.1697, taken from Surirey de Saint-Remy's *Mémoires d'artillerie*. C) French dragoon's axe with its strap and case, which was carried on the right side of the horse instead of the pistol with dimensions as per 17 February 1753 ordonnance. (M. de La Porterie, *Institutions militaires pour la cavalerie et les dragons*, plate 11). D) French infantry grenadier pouch and axe frog, c.1697, from Surirey de Saint-Remy.

casse-têtes were included in a statement of supplies necessary for the battalions of the Troupes de terre that were to cross over to Québec in 1755.[9] Prior to the Battle of Carillon in the summer of 1758, orders were issued for soldiers to 'bring a few axes', which likely referred to casse-têtes, so that 'the first sentinels of the line could use them on those who would climb entrenchments, if they could not use bayonets in a more convenient way.'[10]

Casse-têtes proved invaluable for cutting down the palisades of enemy forts, as noted by the La Pause during the 1756 storming of Fort Bull: 'The order was executed so quickly that the English had barely time to close the gate that we tried in vain to break through with small axes called casse-têtes.'[11] That same year, *capitaine* de Villiers of the colonial regulars commented on his men after smashing numerous boats taken from a British convoy during that year's campaign, that they would have demolished many more but for 'the terrible quality of the casse-têtes provided by the magasins [King's storehouse].'[12]

Equipment Lists

The practice of equipping colonial soldiers with hatchets can be traced back to the seventeenth century, such as in 1688 when '200 small axes' from La Ferrière were included in a war expenditure report for the conflict against the Iroquois.[13] Eight years later, a report outlining projected expenses for an operation against Fort Pemaquid that involved one hundred colonial soldiers detached from Québec included 'one hundred haches d'armes', referring in this case to hatchets.[14]

Throughout the 1730s, colonial troops carried small axes (petites haches) as part of their campaign equipment, with every officer and soldier under *Capitaine* Nicolas-Joseph de Noyelles being issued one during the 1734 campaign against the Foxes.[15] Five years later, during the Chickasaw campaign, '14 casse-têtes' were allocated to the officers, while '112 casse-têtes' were distributed among the cadets, soldiers, and volunteers.[16]

9   LAC, MG1-C11A, vol.100, f.265v.
10   RAPQ, 1932–1933, p.355
11   RAPQ, 1932–1933, p.320.
12   De Bougainville, *Écrits sur le Canada*, p.107.

13   LAC, MG1-C11A, vol.10, f.131v.
14   LAC, C11C, vol.2, f.98.
15   LAC, MG1-C11A, vol.62, f.150-150v.
16   LAC, MG1-C11A, vol.71, f.159, 161.

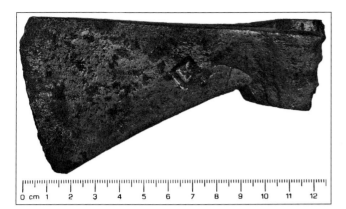

Casse-tête found at the Fort Carillon site (Fort Ticonderoga) bearing a single stamp on the left side of the blade representing what appears to be two initials within a square cartouche. (Collection of the Fort Ticonderoga Museum, New York. Photo Kevin Gélinas)

One of the only known casse-tête excavated from a very tightly dated French fort (1751–1756), and likely used by one of the 150 colonial soldiers garrisoned at Fort Gaspereau (New Brunswick). Note that the poll on this axe head is flattened, and its blade is slightly bent out of shape. (Courtesy of National Historic Sites, Parks Canada. Artifact number: 1E2G1-18. Photo Kevin Gélinas)

Hatchet excavated at the Maison Milot in Quebec City and likely corresponding to a mid-eighteenth century French colonial-made casse-tête. (Catalog number: 1QU-2150-glacière-373. Ministère de la Culture, des Communications et de la Condition féminine du Québec. Laboratoire et Réserve d'archéologie du Québec. Photo Kevin Gélinas)

King George's War saw the widespread issue of casse-têtes to equip officers and soldiers at forts and outposts, as well as to arm officers and cadets leading attacks and pursuing the enemy. In 1746, the colonial soldiers Roulleau and Lafausse were each given one casse-tête prior to being detached to Fort Saint-Frédéric on the occasion of the war.[17] The following year, casse-tête tomahawks were issued to a small contingent of soldiers composed of one *sergent* and six soldiers who were to garrison at Fort de Châteauguay,[18] while the officer François-Marc-Antoine Le Mercier was issued '1 casse-tête'.[19] Around this time, a total of 60 casse-têtes were delivered to Monsieur de Lavaltry, *capitaine commandant* at the Sault Saint-Louis Fort, for the service of the guard house and other needs, indicating that casse-têtes would also probably served for practical purposes around the fort, such as preparing kindling or breaking ice.[20] The casse-tête was also a vital weapon in raiding operations, valued for its versatility and effectiveness in close combat. Between 1746 and 1747, a colonial officer, two cadets, and two Canadian volunteers were equipped with casse-têtes for a raid into New England[21] while Jacques Legardeur de Saint-Pierre and his men used casse-têtes to pursue an Iroquois war party near Montréal.[22]

By the Seven Years War, casse-têtes were issued to the colonial and regular troops as part of their summer and winter equipment. In 1757, Montcalm wrote that one casse-tête was to be distributed to all men at Fort Saint-Jean for the winter campaign.[23] This is supported by a similar account recorded by Bougainville,[24] while the

French officer Bourlamaque reported that officers and soldiers alike were issued one casse-tête for the summer months.[25] A list of supplies published as part of Intendant Bigot's trial reiterates that these weapons were issued to colonial soldiers and officers as part of the winter and summer equipment.[26] In March 1757, a soldier of the Compagnies franches de la Marine taken prisoner at Fort William Henry reported that each French soldier carried 'one Tomahack,' omitting any reference to a sword, suggesting that the casse-tête had supplanted swords in New France's frontier campaigns.[27]

17   LAC, MG1-C11A, vol.86, f.218v.
18   LAC, MG1-C11A, vol.117, f.206.
19   LAC, MG1-C11A, vol.88, f.214–215.
20   LAC, MG1-C11A, vol.117, f.108–109.
21   LAC, MG1-C11A, vol.86, f.202v-203.
22   LAC, MG1-C11A, vol.117, f.228-228v.
23   Casgrain, *Collection des manuscrits du maréchal de Lévis*, p.156.
24   De Bougainville, *Écrits sur le Canada*, p.168.

25   LAC, MG18, K9, vol.6, f.469–472.
26   Bigot, *Mémoire Pour Messire François Bigot*, p.39.
27   LOC, Colonial Office 5 folio 47, E. of Loudoun's Letter of April 25th. 1757, Declaration of two Prisoners taken the 23.d March 1757 at Fort Wm. Henry, Information of John Victor and Guillaume Chasse, two French Prisoners, Fort William Henry March 25th.

Colonial Officers Armed with Casse-têtes

The casse-tête emerged as a favoured weapon among colonial officers in Canada, particularly in the guerilla warfare that defined the frontier conflicts. In a letter to his father, colonial officer Monsieur De Beaujeu de Villemonde related his account of the battle of Grand-Pré (present-day Nova Scotia) in the winter of 1747, in which he killed a man with a 'blow of my casse-tête.'[28] A few months later, Monsieur Rigaud de Vaudreuil dispatched *enseigne* La Corne Saint-Luc of the colonial troops with some 200 men to Fort Saratoga, an British military fortification. As part of Rigaud de Vaudreuil's journal detailing this expedition, it is said that Monsieur de Saint-Luc '... charged them [the enemy] the casse-tête in hand and challenged most of them.'[29]

Daniel-Marie Chabert de Joncaire, an *enseigne* in the colonial troops, provided testimony during the Affaire du Canada (the trials that followed the loss of New France), highlighting the popularity of casse-têtes among officers in Native affairs. During a council, four Native American men allied with the British attacked him, prompting de Joncaire to recount, '...I instantly discharged a great blow from my hache d'arme.' The term hache d'arme was likely used in place of casse-tête to ensure clarity for officials in France unfamiliar with the colonial terminology.[30] During his 1749 expedition through the Ohio Valley to assert French claims to the region, Pierre-Joseph Céloron de Blainville, an officer in the regular colonial troops, had his casse-tête 'racéré' (resteeled) by blacksmiths Lecompte and Barte during a brief stop at Fort des Miamis. This repair suggests that he likely carried the weapon throughout his travels in the Ohio Valley.[31]

In 1757, two eyewitness accounts of the colonial officer Philippe Dagneau de La Saussaye, who was attacked by Cherokees allied with the British, provide further evidence that colonial officers carried casse-têtes on small war parties. A Montréal voyageur stated he recognized '... the Sieur de La Saussaye by... his casse-tête that he perfectly recognized to belong to the Sieur De La Saussaye and which he seen take from this said place.' A drummer from the Compagnie de Dubuisson reported seeing De la Saussaye dead and removing 'a casse-tête from his head with which the Native Americans had finished him', later returning it to Fort Duquesne.[32] This suggests the officer's own tomahawk, identifiable by distinguishable features, style, or type, was used to kill him and left behind. Lastly, a 1753 letter from the Marquis Duquesne de Menneville, Governor General of New France, to colonial officer Jacques Legardeur de Saint-Pierre highlights the strong connotations of bravery, honour, and heroism associated with the casse-tête. In the letter, he remarked, 'You, Monsieur, were born with a casse-tête in hand and a flour bag as a shoulder belt.'[33]

Probate records of colonial officers suggest that while a few owned personal casse-têtes, most listed in their after-death inventories

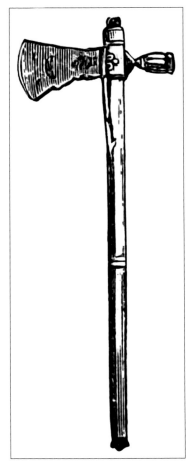

Detail of an illustration in Watterville's Le Tabac, 1891 identified as 'Pipe tomahawk given by King Louis XV, in 1763, to Native Chiefs allied to France. (Versailles)

were part of the stock in their private warehouses used as trade goods. For example, an inventory of Louis Bertin D'Amours de Louvières' possessions included four casse-têtes located in the magasin of his residence, indicating they were likely trade items rather than personal weapons.[34] By the same token, Louis de La Corne, who perished in the sinking of the *Auguste* in 1761, owned several casse-têtes listed alongside other trade goods. These included two valued at 2 livres each while five others, priced together at 1 livre 5 sols, suggest lower-quality weapons.[35]

---

28   Joseph Gagné, *Fidèle à Dieu, à la France, et au Roi » Les retraites militaires de La Chapelle et de Beaujeu vers la Louisiane après la perte du Canada 1760-1762* (Mémoire de maitrise, Université Laval, 2014), p.43.

29   LAC, F3, vol.13, Collection Moreau de Saint-Méry, p.2, p.400.

30   LAC, MG 18, G8 (6), Bigot, François (Québec literary and Historical Society Transcripts). 'L'affaire du Canada' manuscript portion of vol.IV, Mémoire pour Daniel de Jonquaire-Chabert, 1748.

31   LAC, MG1-C11A, vol.119, f.143.

32   BAnQ-M, TL4, S1, D6300, Sollicitation de Marie-Anne De Verchères pour obtenir confirmation du décès de son mari, Thomas-Philippe Dagneau de LaSaussaye, officier, 18 avril 1760.

33   ASQ, Viger-Verreau, P32/005/062.08, Lettre du marquis Ange Duquesne de Menneville à Jacques Legardeur de Saint-Pierre... , 22 juillet 1753.

34   BAnQ-M, Greffe du notaire Pierre Panet, Inventaire et vente des meubles de la communauté des biens entre feu Louis D'Amour, Sieur de Louvrière et Geneviève Catalogne, 27 février 1755.

35   BAnQ-M, Greffe du notaire Pierre Panet, Inventaire des biens de la communauté d'entre dame Marie-Anne Hubert, veuve de Sieur Chevalier de la Corne, dit Sieur De la Corne, vivant chevalier de l'ordre Royal et militaire de St-Louis, capitaine d'infanterie de sa majesté, 19 avril 1762.

In contrast, Louis-Thomas Chabert de Joncaire, a *lieutenant* in the colonial troops, owned a single casse-tête at the time of his death at Fort Niagara in 1739. It was likely a personal weapon as it was among his possessions while in garrison.[36]

Some colonial officers may have carried finer tomahawks, such as the casse-tête à calumet (pipe tomahawk) or casse-tête à dague (spear-blade pipe tomahawk), which were exchanged as diplomatic gifts and could be used as a weapon or smoked as a ceremonial pipe. The origin of this multipurpose tool, which became popular as a prestigious symbol of the Native warrior chief, is debated. According to French colonial records, the term pipe tomahawk, referred to as casse-tête à calumet in French, appeared in French colonial archival documents as early as 1747, predating the first English reference by one year. The latter was found in the journal of German Moravian bishop Johannes von Watteville who visited the Susquehanna Valley in 1748.[37] In fact, blacksmiths working out of Québec were already producing pipe tomahawks on a limited scale, and these were probably intended as presentation pieces to seal alliances with allied Native leaders during King George's War. In July of 1747, for example, a Québec blacksmith named Joseph Lépine supplied the King's storehouses with two types of pipe tomahawks: 10 'Cassetestes a calumet ciseler' (pipe tomahawks, chiseled) at a price of 10 livres each and seven 'Dagues a calumet' (pipe dagger tomahawks) at 12 livres each.[38]

Surprisingly, French colonists may have also used pipe tomahawks as a smoking tool. For instance, the 1758-dated post-mortem inventory of Pierre Clocher dit Saint-Pierre, a mason in Montréal, included a calumet à hache (a pipe-axe).[39]

In the late 1750s, numerous French pipe tomahawks were offered as gifts to Native American tribes living in the southeastern region of North America. This gesture, far from being trivial, demonstrated the importance of maintaining alliances with the Native American nations living around the Mississippi during the Seven Years War, if only to ensure their loyalty to the King of France in the eventuality they were called to fight. However, it is likely that the tomahawks sent up the Mississippi were copies following early models designed by Canadian blacksmiths. A document listing presents made to the Choctaw between 1757

Canadian voyageur, c. 1730. Note how he carries what is likely a casse-tête through his sash at the back of his waist. This unobtrusive method of carrying a hatchet provided convenient access when needed. This particular depiction of the casse-tête is probably the most historically accurate among known French images of the period, reflecting its original shape, profile, and size. (Habillemens des Coureurs de Bois Canadiens, no. 2, Anonymous, c. 1730, Beinecke Rare Book and Manuscript Library, Yale University Library, New Haven, CT, USA, WA MSS S-2412)

and 1763 reveals that 14 cassetête à calumet were provided to the Natives of that tribe in 1760, while another 12 were distributed in 1763.[40] Curiously enough, the 1891 edition of le tabac by Blondel discusses a pipe tomahawk that belonged to a certain de Watteville and had been made at Versailles and given to Native American chiefs:

36   BAnQ-M, Greffe du notaire C.-C.-J. Porlier, Inventaire des biens de feu Nicolas-Thomas de Joncaire, lieutenant d'une compagnie du détachement de la Marine et interprète pour le Roi des langues iroquoises, décédé ce jourd'hui vingt et neuf juin 1739..., 31 juillet 1739.

37   Timothy J. Shannon, 'Queequeg's Tomahawk: A Cultural Biography, 1750-1900,' *Ethnohistory*, Summer 2005, vol.52, no.3, pp.589–633.

38   LAC, MG1-C11A, vol.117, f.111v.

39   BAnQ-M, Greffe du notaire Gervais Hodiesne, Inventaire de feu Pierre Clocher dit Saint-Pierre, maçon, 23 novembre 1758.

40   Marc de Villiers du Terrage, *Les dernières années de la Louisiane française* (Paris: Librairie orientale & américaine, 1904), p.169.

One of the curiosities of this collection is without any doubt the historic pipe-shaped axe. In 1763, Louis XV had manufactured at Versailles one hundred tomahawks, or battle axes, that he presented to the Indians which, along with Montcalm, Bougainville and the Chevalier de Levis, had supported gloriously against the English, the French cause in Canada. These axes, which were marks of honour, were distributed to the main chiefs. Monsieur de Watteville has one of wrought iron, inlaid with silver, which came out of the arms manufactory of Versailles. It is hollow and can be used as a pipe. The wooden handle with a silver inlaid fleur-de-lis forms the pipe stem, and the spade contains the bowl. The silver-made axe, in itself, has eight silver fleurs-de-lis, including one within the royal sun. The heel is dated 1763, the year of the peace treaty when New France was ceded to England.[41]

Wearing Casse-têtes

There has been considerable debate about how colonial troops carried tomahawks, with some suggesting that, since swords were often left behind during campaigns or expeditions, the casse-tête may have been placed in the frog originally intended for the sword. However, this arrangement was likely impractical, as the weight of the tomahawk's head could cause it to bounce while marching, its exposed cutting edge posed safety risks, and, like the sword, it could catch on branches or other obstacles in dense terrain. Officer Paul Marin de La Malgue, who campaigned in Saratoga in 1745, wrote in his journal that 'at the second halt, we had two Frenchmen injured by their small axes which they were improperly carrying and a Gauyaukouis [sic] who pierced his thigh with his spike tomahawk as he fell.'[42]

Period illustrations and records indicate that the most common way to carry a tomahawk was tucked into a sash or waistbelt at the back. Joseph-Charles Bonin, a soldier during the Seven Years War, described the casse-tête as a 'small axe that is worn in the sash when traveling'.[43] Even the British seem to have adopted this method, as Anglo-American officer Henry Timberlake described in 1765, recounting that during his journey to the Cherokee, 'We resolved to surround the enemy's camp, giving the first fire, and, without charging again, run on them with our tommahawkes, which we had tucked in our belts for that purpose, should there be occasion.'[44]

Types or Models

Initially crafted in France and exported to New France, tomahawks became widely mass-produced in the eighteenth century by Canadian blacksmiths to supply the fur trade and equip militia and colonial troops. Those issued from the King's storehouses were inexpensive as well as uniform in shape and weight. For example, officials at the King's storehouses at Québec in 1747 recorded a total of 3,481 'uniformly-made casse-têtes' (casseteste unis) which were valued at 40 sols apiece, the majority of which were likely intended to arm troops.[45] In addition, a number of these weapons were recorded has having steel cutting edges, such as the '60 casse-tête, acérés' (edged-hardened) that were purchased from Claude le Gris to restock the King's storehouses at Québec in 1747 on behalf of the war.[46] Records from a criminal trial held at Montréal in 1731 described a 'petit casse-tête' (small casse-tête) belonging to a Habitant of Montréal as 'an axe, that is a small axe, that weighs no more than 1½ livre.'[47] Based on archaeological evidence, many of the presumed casse-tête heads found at French military sites, such as Fort Ticonderoga, Fort Gaspereau, Fort Ouiatenon, and Fort Milchilimackinac exhibit similar forms, all of which were likely colonial copies of the earlier Biscayan axe.[48]

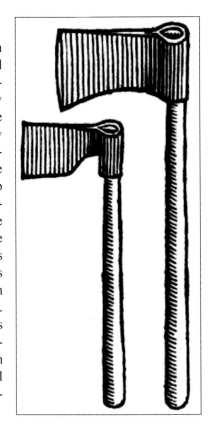

Two carpentry axes, large and small, taken from an engraving found in the 1736 edition of the *Dictionnaire de Marine*. The common casse-tête used by the colonial troops in New France may have been quite similar to a small or single-handed French Naval carpentry axe used aboard ships when one examines the construction and overall form of the smaller of these two illustrated axes.

41 Le tabac Spire Blondel, *Le livre des fumeurs et des priseurs* (Paris: Henri Laurens Éditeur, 1891), p.123.

42 LAC, MG 18, N 48, bobine M-1952, 7-05897, Journal de l'expédition de Paul Marin contre Saratoga en 1745.

43 Casgrain, *Voyage au Canada*, pp.64–65.

44 Henry Timberlake, *The Memoirs of Lieut. Henry Timberlake* (London: J. Ridley, W. Nicoll, C. Henderson, 1765), p.94.

45 LAC, MG1-C11A, vol.89, f.42v.

46 LAC, MG1-C11A, vol.117, f.106.

47 BAnQ-M, TL4, S1, D3806, Procès entre Nicolas-Antoine Coulon, sieur de Villiers, cadet dans les troupes, plaignant, et Pierre Cardinal, scieur de long, et son fils Jean-Baptiste Cardinal, journalier, accusés de voies de fait, 30 avril 1731–17 août 1731.

48 Kevin Gladysz (Gélinas) and Ken Hamilton, 'Axes in New France, Part I: The Biscayan Axe', *Journal of the Early Americas*, vol.II, Issue 4 (August/September 2012), pp.7–18.

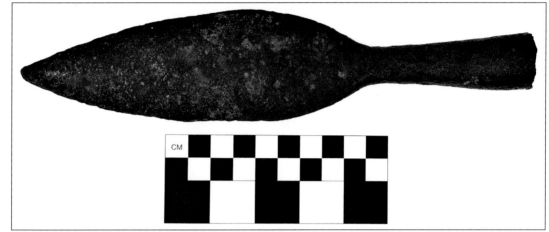

Above and right: Presumed French-made spontoon tomahawk and spear blade found at Fort St. Joseph, Michigan. (Courtesy of the Niles History Center)

Spontoon-shaped tool or weapon excavated at the Louisbourg Fortress. (Courtesy of National Historic Sites, Parks Canada. Photo Kevin Gélinas)

Many of the casse-tête heads taken from the King's storehouses may have already been hafted or provided with separate premade handles, as handles frequently appear in inventories. For example, in the mid-1740s, an account of munitions and merchandise purchased for war preparations listed 456 casse-têtes at 28 sols each, along with 450 casse-tête handles at 2 sols 6 deniers apiece.[49] These records suggest that many of the casse-têtes distributed during wartime came equipped with their own handles.

butchering, and eating, plus doubling as a weapon. Equipment lists reveal that officers and soldiers of the Compagnies franches de la Marine were generally supplied with a fixed-bladed knife termed couteau boucheron as well as one of two types of inexpensive jambette folding knives known as Flatins or Siamois knives.[50] Merchant records and markings found on archaeological artifacts confirm that the majority, if not all these knives, were made in the town of Saint-Étienne.

Fixed Blade and Folding knives (Boucherons and Siamois)

One of the most indispensable tools on the frontier was a knife, which served as an all-purpose tool for cutting,

49   LAC, MG1-C11A, vol.82, f.187v.

50   Kevin Gladysz (Gélinas) and Ken Hamilton, 'French Knives in North America, Part I: 'Flatin' and 'à la dauphine', *Journal of the Early Americas*, vol.I, Issue 4 (August 2011/September 2012), pp.7–15; Kevin Gladysz (Gélinas) and Ken Hamilton, 'French Knives in North America, Part II: Siamois and 'tin pin' knives', *Journal of the Early Americas*, vol.I, Issue 5 (October 2011/November 2011), pp.9–19.; Kevin Gladysz (Gélinas) and Ken Hamitlon, 'French Knives in North America, Part III: Boucheron Knives', *Journal of the Early Americas*, vol.I, Issue 6 (December 2011/January 2012), pp. 6–17.

Biscayen-type axe excavated at the Fortress of Louisbourg stamped with three fleur-de-lis identifying it as property of the King. (Courtesy of National Historic Sites, Parks Canada. Photo Kevin Gélinas)

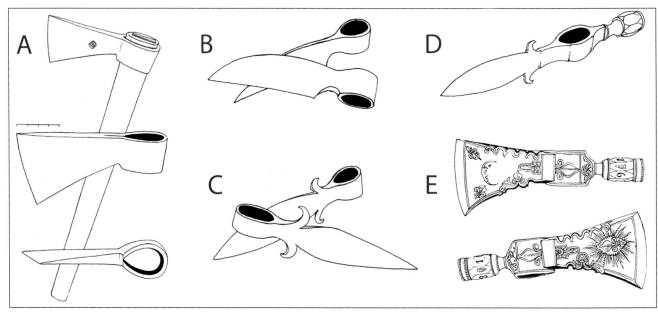

Line drawings by Michel Pétard. A) Common tomahawk (casse-tête). Based on archaeological evidence, the type of hatchet illustrated here is presumably the common one used by the colonial troops, militiamen and a number of Native allies to the French during the 1730–1760 period and possibly earlier. Artist's interpretation based on an excavated example found at Fort Ticonderoga. B) Dagger tomahawk (casse-tête à dague). Hatchets with a blade shaped in the form of a dagger were very popular amongst Natives, these were also at times used by the French colonist, such as the one made for the Canadian named Limbé by the blacksmith named Baillargeon at Fort St-Joseph in 1739. This example was rendered using ones found at the Trudeau native site (LA) c.1731–1764, the Fletcher site (Michigan) c.1740–1770, as well as at Fort St-Joseph, 1700–1781, (Michigan). C) Spontoon tomahawk (casse-tête à fleur de lys) These types of casse-têtes, mostly employed by the Native nations allied to the French, had a blade in the shape of a fleur-de-lys, which may denote a symbolic connotation as it is the symbol of French royalty. For example, one such casse-tête was described as a 'hatchet made in the shape of a Flower de Lue (fleur-de-lis)' found stuck in a door following a Native raid in Berks country in 1756. Excavated examples were found at the Trudeau Native Site (LA) c.1731–1764, the Fletcher site (Michigan) c.1740–1770, as well as at Fort St-Joseph 1700–1781, (Michigan). Artists' interpretation based on archaeological examples found at these sites. D) Spear-blade pipe tomahawk (dague à calumet) Interpretation of a spear blade pipe tomahawk or dague à calumet (pipe dagger) in French. This type of casse-tête represents a combination of the spontoon tomahawk and pipe tomahawk. Colonial blacksmiths in Canada produced these types of casse-têtes in 1747 for the very expensive price of 12 livres apiece. E) Pipe tomahawk (casse-tête à pipe) Iron hatchets manufactured with an integrated pipe bowl begin to turn up in French archival documents as early as the 1740s revealing that these implements may have been initially created and made by the French and thereafter copied by the English. For example, the earliest known mention of a pipe tomahawk in North America goes back to 1747, when a blacksmith working out of Quebec was recorded as supplying several casse-têtes equipped with pipe bowls. These ornate pipe tomahawks were likely intended as presentation pieces to seal alliances with leaders of the allied Native tribes to the French from King George's War up until the end of the Seven Years War and possibly a few years later in the Louisiana and Illinois territory. Pipe tomahawk drawn from an extant example in the collection of the Musée du quai Branly, France, engraved with the letters 'A.R.' and dated 1762.

Equipment Lists

From the earliest days, the practice of providing knives to the forces taking part in expeditions in New France was well established. The 65 Canadiens who accompanied de Troyes on his expedition to Hudson Bay in 1686 were each provided with '2 knives and 2 combs.'[51] Among the equipment colonial officer Saint-Castin's deemed necessary for attacking Boston in 1702 was '1,000 boucherons [knives]' as well as '1,000 jambette knives.'[52] Knives began to turn up on official lists of supplies issued to the colonial troops in the late 1730s, such as 11 boucheron knives that were provided to one *sergent* and five soldiers garrisoned at Niagara to be detached for the war against the Chickasaw in 1739.[53] By 1746, colonial officers and cadets were typically supplied with both a boucheron and a Siamois knife, while soldiers of the colonial troops were issued only a single boucheron knife. Part of the equipment officer Louis Saint-Blain received before going on campaign in 1746 included '1 boucheron knife' and '1 Siamois knife,'[54] while 16 soldiers detached to garrison Fort Saint-Thérèse each received one boucheron knife.[55]

Throughout the Seven Years War, the number of knives issued to each soldier or officer varied from campaign to campaign, likely reflecting procurement challenges or administrative adjustments made before each operation. Prior to the Siège of Oswego, supplies sent from Fort Frontenac for the troops included 500 Siamois knives priced together at 20 livres as well as 300 couteaux sauvages (Native-style knives) priced at 10 livres, which were likely boucheron butcher knives.[56] In 1756, the equipment issued to officers as well as metropolitan and colonial soldiers during the summer months included a single boucheron knife without any references to folding knives.[57] However, an undated equipment list by French regular officer François-Charles de Bourlamaque that presumably relates to the 1757 campaign notes that officers and soldiers were to be issued one boucheron knife as part of their summer equipment, as well as two Siamois knives for the winter months.[58] Montcalm corroborates these amounts by indicating 'one boucheron knife' and 'two Siamois knives' for each man camped out at Fort Saint-Jean in the winter of 1757.[59] A detailed account from March 1757 involving

two prisoners at Fort William-Henry, one a colonial soldier, provides valuable insight into the knives carried by soldiers on campaign. The deposition noted that 'each man had three knives given him, namely, two small knives for the pocket, and one large knife in a case, to hang at their breast (to fight as he was told).' This confirms that in 1757, soldiers were issued two Siamois knives and one boucheron knife, the latter carried in a case around the neck.[60] Lastly, an equipment list published in 1763 shows that a total of '2 boucheron knives' were allegedly issued to each colonial officer and soldier for their winter equipment, omitting folding Siamois knives altogether.[61]

Boucheron Knives: Close-Quarter Combat Weapons

Colonial soldiers likely used plug bayonets as fixed-handled knives, with French Marine officials noting in 1695 that 'the troops use it [bayonet] for all purposes, which means that most of them are lacking one.'[62] The introduction of the socket bayonet in Canada during the 1720s may have led soldiers to replace the versatile plug bayonet, which had also likely served as a knife in certain situations, with the boucheron knife.

Primary sources shed light on the term couteau boucheron (boucheron knife), a colonial designation for common French butcher knives, such as a 1699 trade goods list for the Tamarois mission near present-day Cahokia, Illinois, which included 'Per gross, butcher knives (couteaux de bouché)…24 livres.'[63] Dumont de Montigny, a French colonial officer who served in Louisiana, described a 'couteau bûcheron' (boucheron) as a 'Large sheath knife, very long and very wide',[64] while a memoir attributed to Vauclain noted that Canadian militiamen were given 'butcher knives' (couteaux de boucherie) that were altered to serve as plug bayonets, unquestionably corresponding to couteaux boucherons that were generally standard issue.[65] In 1758, at Fort Carillon, Pierre-Joseph Carrefour de La Pelouze, *aide-major* of the Régiment de Berry, noted that Native Americans

51   LAC, MG1-C11A, vol.8, f.279v.
52   *Collection de manuscrits contenant lettres, mémoires, et autres documents historiques relatifs à la Nouvelle-France: recueillis aux archives de la province de Québec, ou copiés à l'étranger* (Québec: Imprimerie A. Côté et Cie: 1884), vol.2, p.399.
53   LAC, MG1-C11A, vol.71, f.169–169v.
54   LAC, MG1-C11A, vol.86, f.191.
55   LAC, MG1-C11A, vol.117, f.206.
56   RAPQ, 1931–1932, p.28.
57   Centre d'histoire La Presqu'île, P03/T.089, Fonds De Beaujeu, 28 novembre 1756.
58   LAC, MG18, K9, vol.6, f.469–472.
59   Louis-Joseph marquis de Montcalm de Saint-Véran, *Journal du marquis de Montcalm durant ses campagnes en Canada de*

1756 à 1759 (Québec: Imprimerie de L.-J. Demers & frère, 1895), pp.156–157.
60   LOC, Colonial Office 5 folio 47, E. of Loudoun's Letter of April 25th. 1757, Declaration of two Prisoners taken the 23.d March 1757 at Fort Wm. Henry, Information of John Victor and Guillaume Chasse, two French Prisoners, Fort William Henry March 25th.
61   Bigot, *Mémoire Pour Messire François Bigot*, p.39.
62   AM, Série G, 2036 B.
63   ASQ, Missions no.107, Mémoire des effets à envoyer aux Tamarois et commentaire de l'abbé Amédée Gosselin, 1699.
64   Jean-Baptiste Le Mascrier, *Mémoires historiques sur la Louisiane… composés sur les mémoires de M. Dumont* (Paris: Chez Cl. J.B. Bauche, 1953), p. 88.
65   *Mémoires sur le Canada depuis 1749 jusqu'à 1760, en trois parties, avec cartes et plans lithographiés, publiés sous la direction de la Société littéraire et historique de Québec* (Québec: Imprimerie de T. Cary & Cie., 1838), p.180.

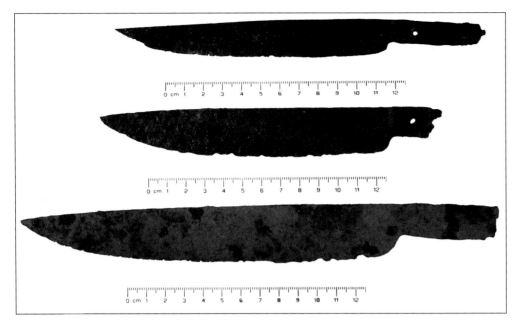

Three nearly complete excavated knife blades presumed to be of the boucheron type due to the blade's rounded shape, heel and overall profile. The top example shows its complete tang with a remaining pin at the back pinhole. (Collection of the Fort Ticonderoga Museum, New York). The inventory list of the King's storehouses at Fort Carillon (Fort Ticonderoga) in 1757 included 55 dozen boucheron knives. (LAC, MG18-K9, vol.6, f. 458)

A rare leather sheath, which may have been similar to what would have been used with a boucheron knife in New France, was excavated from the Le Machault shipwreck in present-day New Brunswick. This sheath was fashioned with a back-seam and measured 16.5 cm in length. (Courtesy of National Historic Sites, Parks Canada. Photo Kevin Gélinas)

carried butcher knives (couteaux de boucher), presumably boucheron knives, on their waist belts or sashes. He described their war gear as: 'A fusil, an ox's [powder] horn at the neck, a small bullet bag, often a spear, and always at the waist a small sharp axe and a well-sharpened butcher's knife.'[66] Furthermore, an invoice of merchandise sent to Québec in 1758 aboard the ship Saint-Pierre clearly mentions '520 dozen butcher knives (couteaux à boucher)' as well as '219 dozen jambettes' (common folding knives) which can only refer to boucheron knives since large amounts of these knives were shipped annually to New France.[67] Lastly, a 1760 probate record relating to Antoine Toupin at Château-Richer indicates that the term 'boucheron' was synonymous with 'butcher' in Canada. The notary recorded 'one sheath containing 3 knives and a fusil à boucheron', translated as 'butcher honing steel,' confirming the connection between boucheron and butcher knives.[68]

Fixed-handled knives from Saint-Étienne, France, came in three standard sizes (small, medium, large) with two distinct handle configurations. A 1743 invoice to merchant Dugard listed 'small and medium boucheron knives with the tang [extending] to the base of the handle' (la lame jusqu'au bout du manche) and 'medium boucheron knives with common blades' (lame à l'ordinaire).[69] Extant and archaeological examples suggest the common type had a half tang handle attachment with a sawn slot in the handle, whereas the former blade type had a longer tang with a two-piece handle configuration.

While butcher knives were used by colonial soldiers on detachments or raids, primary sources show they served other purposes. In 1752, Joseph Jaure dit Lafeuillade, a soldier at Fort Ouiatenon, testified after stabbing a militiaman that he held a boucheron knife 'usually used to kill bœufs' (oxen), possibly referring to bison (bœufs sauvages).[70] Seven years later, a soldier at Fort Carillon escaped

66 Pierre-Joseph Carrefour de La Pelouze, *Voyage et campagnes au Canada*: manuscript, 1757–1760. MS Can 8. Houghton Library, Harvard University, Cambridge, Mass, p.38.

67 TNA, HCA 32/234, Le Saint-Pierre, 1758.

68 BAnQ-Q, Greffe du notaire Antoine Crespin, …pour les héritiers de défunt Antoine Toupin et Françoise Lefebvre, vivant habitant de la paroisse de Château-Richer…, Québec, 17 avril 1760.

69 Centre des archives du monde du travail, Fonds Dugard, Série AQ, 62 AQ 483, Facture de Paul Roy à Orléans, 4 mai 1743; Centre des archives du monde du travail, Fonds Dugard, Série AQ, 62 AQ 198, Thiolière Le Jeune…à l'adresse de M. Paul Roy, Orléans, 24 avril, 1742.

70 BAnQ-M, TL4, S1, D5681, Procès devant le Conseil de guerre contre Joseph Jaure dit Lafeuillade, soldat de la Compagnie de

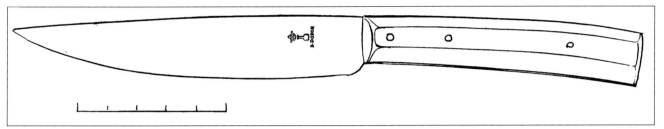

Three-pin Boucheron knife, illustrated by Michel Pétard.

prison by using a knife to dig through mortar, described as: 'A brand-new looking medium-sized boucheron knife, wooden handle, with a broken tip and the blade forced into the handle, and at one *pouce* or so from the point the edge of which is broken off a width of 3 or 4 *lignes* or about, which fractures appears to have been made by digging into the mortar...'[71]

Boucheron Knife Sheaths

Period records reveal that the practice of wearing sheath knives around one's neck, influenced by Native customs and later adopted by Canadian militiamen and colonial soldiers, was widespread throughout much of New France. For instance, soldiers captured at Fort William-Henry were described as wearing '...one large knife in a case, to hang at their breast...'[72] This practical method, convenient for combat, was recorded as early as 1673 when Sébastien Moreau testified that '... he obtained the knife and the sheath, that he showed us hanging around his neck, from Monsieur de Contrecoeur (officer in the Carignan-Salières regiment).'[73] At Fort Duquesne, colonial soldier J.C.B. noted that '...when the

Detail from a c. 1745 engraving showing a French officer on a halt holding a knife in one hand and what appears to be a piece of bread or ham to his mouth in the other. (Gravé par Ravenet, À Paris, chez Roguié, rue S. Jacques au Boisseau d'Or)

Natives go to war, they are armed with their guns, hatchets and knives. They usually have three knives: one hung at the collar around one's neck, one through the sash and the third alongside the leg on the outside of the garter. The Canadians do the same, all of this by precaution or security measures.'[74] Similarly, colonial officer Jean-Bernard Bossu described a *caporal* from the Halwyl regiment travelling

Sabrevois, originaire de Grenoble, accusé du meurtre de Pierre Labelle, soldat milicien, natif de Rivière-des-Prairies, 21 février 1752–1 février 1753.

71 BAnQ-M, TL4, S1, D6241, Procès contre Jean-Baptiste Gadoux dit Sansfaçon, soldat de la Compagnie de Vassal, au camp Carillon, et Armand Janot dit Laréole, demeurant au fort Carillon, accusés de vol de porcelaines, 18 novembre 1758–20 janvier 1759.

72 LOC, Colonial Office 5 folio 47, E. of Loudoun's Letter of April 25th. 1757, Declaration of two Prisoners taken the 23.d March 1757 at Fort Wm. Henry, Information of John Victor and Guillaume Chasse, two French Prisoners, Fort William Henry March 25th.

73 BAnQ-M, Fonds Bailliage de Montréal, Interrogatoires des prisonniers Pierre Nepveu dit Laverdure Raptrau, de Sébastien Moreau, d'André Morigny dit L'Eveillé, de Mathurin Banlie dit

Laperle , arrêtés pour rébellion contre les officiers de justice, 13 juin 1673.

74 Casgrain, *Voyage au Canada*, p.233.

through Louisiana in the 1750s wearing a knife around his neck 'in the manner of the Natives.'[75]

Interestingly, Philippe Aubert de Gaspé describes a supper at the house of a seigneur canadien: 'if it was a spring-knife, it was carried in the pocket; if, on the contrary, it was a dagger-knife (couteau-poignard), it was hung around the neck in a sheath of Moroccan leather, silk, or even birch bark, artistically crafted and adorned by the Native people.' De Gaspé also notes that '...an old Canadian gentleman, dining one day at the Château Saint-Louis after the conquest, used a fine case knife at the table, which he wore hanging around his neck', highlighting the established custom among French Canadians, including nobleman and officers, of wearing sheath knives around their necks rather than carrying them on their waist belts or garters.[76]

Most boucheron knives were shipped from France without sheaths, suggesting that the sheaths were likely made locally in the colony, probably from boiled or plain leather. While no specific records currently describe the sheaths of boucheron knives, most period documents list them without sheaths. Exceptionally, a 1738 inventory of Fort Niagara noted '6 gross of Boucheron knives with their sheaths at 45 livres per gross.'[77] This suggests that some sheaths may have been crafted in the St Lawrence Valley before being sent into the interior. A 1744 probate record detailing the possessions of a ship carpenter in Québec mentions 'four knives, chipped, with their sheaths of boiled leather', offers insights into the common types of sheaths used for fixed-handled knives.[78]

Siamois Knives: Versatile Tools on the Frontier

Colonial troops began using a folding knife known as a Flatin knife in the late seventeenth century. This term, common in New France, referred to a type of jambette knife made in Saint-Étienne, France, and named after its inventor, Denis Flatin. In 1699, '2 gross of Flatin knives' were shipped from France to Québec, likely finding their way into the hands of some colonial soldiers.[79] Archival records show that the Siamois knife gradually replaced the Flatin. Known as couteaux Siamois (Siamese knives), these were a type of jambette, mass-produced in France

A selection of maker's marks stamped on excavated boucheron knife blades from North American sites. All of the currently known marks have been traced back to the town of Saint-Étienne, a connection I made through my research in 2006 when I discovered a lead cutler's guild tablet dating to 1737, bearing the same markings found on most folding and fixed-blade knives from French context sites in North America. (Line drawing by Kevin Gélinas)

and shipped in large quantities to North America starting in the 1720s.[80] The name Siamois likely derives from the blade's resemblance to the long knives or sabres used by the Siamese, popularised after the ambassadors from Siam (modern-day Thailand) visited Versailles in 1686.

Issued to colonial officers by the 1740s and supplied to soldiers during the Seven Years War, these popular knives served as versatile tools that conveniently fitted in one's pocket such as was the custom in New France. While travelling through Montréal in 1749, the Swedish botanist Pehr Kalm commented with regards to French meals where '...each one, on the other hand, has to use his own knife. Each person, as soon as he is sitting at the table, pulls out his knife from his breech or skirt pocket.'[81] Produced in the town of Saint-Étienne, these folding knives came in three sizes (small, medium, and large) with either round or pointed blade tips, and were recorded in primary sources under various grades and types, including Bizaillon, à tête de chien (dog head), and the common Siamois variety.

Siamois Knives Used by Colonial Soldiers

Few descriptions exist of the specific varieties of Siamois pocket knives issued to or owned by colonial troops. However, a 1754 trial involving colonial soldiers accused of robberies at Fort Saint-Frédéric reveals that at least two types of presumed Siamois knives were in their possession, based on testimony and evidence. One knife was described

75 Jean Bernard Bossu, *Nouveaux voyages aux Indes Occidentales: contenant une relation des differens peuples qui habitent les environs du grand fleuve Saint-Louis, appellé vulgairement le Mississipi; leur religion; leur gouvernement; leurs mœurs; leurs guerres & leur commerce* (Paris: Le Jay, 1768), vol.2, p.124.
76 Philippe Aubert de Gaspé, *Les Anciens Canadiens* (Québec: Imprimerie Augustin Côté et Cie, 1877), vol.1, p.97.
77 LAC, MG1-C11A, vol.69, f.272.
78 BAnQ-Q, Greffe du notaire Christophe-Hilarion Dulaurent, Inventaire des biens de la communauté de défunt Jean Baptiste Lefebvre, charpentier de navire en cette ville..., Québec, 14 décembre 1744.
79 LAC, MG1-C11A, vol.113, f.65–67.

80 Gladysz (Gélinas) and Hamilton, 'French Knives in North America, Part II, pp.9–19.
81 Kalm et al, *Voyage de Pehr Kalm*, p.187–188.

Four examples of Saint-Étienne-marked 'one pin' folding knife blades excavated from the King's storehouses site (Palais de l'Intendant) in Québec City. Most of the blades feature an abrupt drop at the tip, characteristic of those used on *jambette* knives referred to as *Flatin*, likely the first type of folding knives issued to colonial soldiers serving in Canada during the late seventeenth century. An undated memoir by l'abbé Henri Roulleaux, a missionary in Illinois, highlights their popularity among the Natives of New France and the distinct hexagonal shape of their horn handles: 'We only need one type [of knife] which are the most common in France, namely, those commonly known as Jambettes, that have somewhat hexagonal horn-handles, the largest and the mid-size of this kind are the best.' (ASQ, SME2.1- La correspondance précieuse, Lettres R, no 78.). (Collection archéologique de la Ville de Québec. Photo Ville de Québec)

as 'a small knife with a black horn handle vulgarly called à chien [dog]', likely a couteau Siamois à manche de corne à tête de chien, a popular type featuring a decorative dog head ornament on the handle's tip, likely formed in moulds at the factory. The second knife, presented as material evidence, was described as 'a small knife with a yellow handle...whose base [of the handle] is burnt', this was likely a common *Siamois* knife with a boxwood handle, with the burnt tip suggesting it may have been used as a pipe tamper.[82] It is worth mentioning that an inventory list drawn up at Fort Niagara in 1738 describes a number of these knives as tête de chien knives (dog head knives) while another lot apparently was listed as tête de lion knives, which may denote the heads of sea lions.[83]

Furthermore, items found in the breech pockets of Laviolette, a deceased colonial soldier from the De Gannes' company in 1722, included: '...three playing dice, one knife, one pipe with its case, a Job's tear rosary, a pack of playing cards...' suggesting the pocket knife may also have served as a pipe tool.[84] In 1755, a drummer of the Dumas company who was accused of striking a man with his knife declared that '... he held his calumet (Native-style pipe) with one hand and his knife with the other... ' before getting ready to place them back in his pocket. The knife, likely of the common Siamois variety, was described as '...a knife with a boxwood handle, the pointed-tip blade chipped, and the handle burned at the tip,' suggesting that the handle's head was charred after repeatedly tampering smouldering tobacco in his calumet-pipe.[85] Pewter inlay may have been added to the tips of wooden or horn handles on pocket knives to prevent deterioration from use as pipe tampers, as historical records often describe folding knives with leaded (plombé) tips. Philippe Aubert de Gaspé notes in *Les anciens Canadiens* that 'The Habitants [of Canada] always used, fifty years ago, their little pocket knife for the meals; the men, their leaded knives. The blacksmiths would forge the blades; the wood handles were decorated with pewter inlay... '[86]

82   BAnQ-M, TL4, S1, D5921, Procès contre Menin Pouteau dit Parisien, sculpteur, soldat d'Herbin, Michel Dufeu dit Flame, soldat de la Compagnie de Villemonde, et Guillaume Goursol dit Lagiroflée, soldat de la Compagnie Debonne, accusés de vols dans la chambre de distribution du fort Saint-Frédéric, Montréal, 9 septembre 1754–26 février 1755.

83   LAC, MG1-C11A, vol.69, f.272.

84   BAnQ-M, TL4, S1, D2729, Procès contre Provençal, soldat de la Compagnie Deschaillons, et Laviolette, soldat de la Compagnie de Gannes, accusés de duel à l'épée, Montréal, 22 mai 1722–31 août 1722.

85   BAnQ-Q, TL5, D1795, Information contre Benoît LeRoy dit Lyonnais, tambour de la compagnie de Dumas, environ 19 ans, accusé d'avoir frappé à coups de couteau le nommé Blondin, 26 novembre–12 décembre 1755.

86   Philippe Aubert de Gaspé, *Les Anciens Canadiens, tome 1* (Québec : Imprimerie Augustin Côté et Cie, 1877), p.97

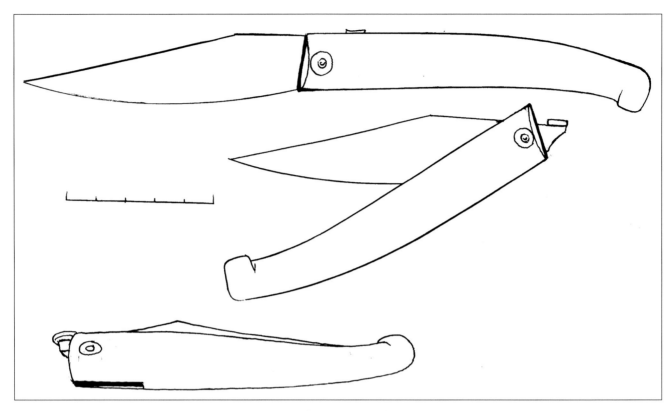

Line drawing by Michel Pétard showing a complete Siamois knife in its open, half-closed and closed position.

Three excavated Siamois knife blades found at Fort Ticonderoga showing the three common sizes (small, medium, large). (Collection of the Fort Ticonderoga Museum, New York. Photo Kevin Gélinas)

Siamois blade with its surviving pewter or lead cap and adjoining decorative strips from Michilimackinac. This end cap, being one of three found at this site, uncommon on these knives, shows the original shape of the handle's tip, which was likely inlaid in a wood handle. This pewter tip likely doubled as a pipe tamper. (Mackinac State Historical Parks Collection. Photo Kevin Gélinas)

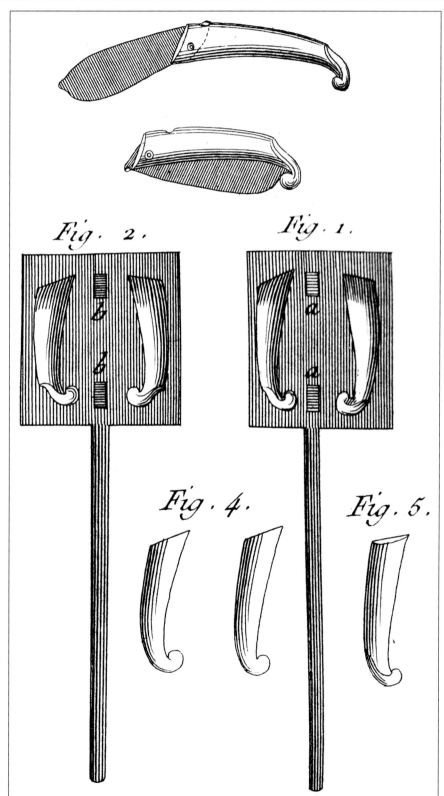

Details from illustrations by Fougeroux de Bondaroy depict iron moulds for shaping horn and wood handles, some with ornamental designs. Above them, Bondaroy shows a 'one-pin knife' and notes that the lentil on the blade's butt can 'often flay, tear clothes, and thus offers a few drawbacks.' (L'Art du Coutelier en Ouvrages Communs, 1772)

Fire Steels and Smoking Pipes

Fire steels, an essential part of the equipment issued to colonial officers and soldiers, were indispensable for fire-making, as they were struck against a gunflint or hard stone to produce sparks for various purposes, such as lighting a pipe or making a campfire. French colonial records reveal that during the early eighteenth century, these fire steels were originally oval or round in shape and mostly imported from Holland.[87] As late as 1742, the merchant Dugard of Rouen, purchased '30 dozen fire steels, oval, polished', from Monsieur DHaristog of Hoorn (Holland) for Canada.[88] By the 1740s, the bulk of these fire steels were now purchased from the town of Saint-Étienne, France, and shipped over by the thousands.[89] These French-made fire steels apparently came in three sizes, which were identified in invoices as No.10 (the small size), No.8 (the medium size) as well as No.6 (the large size) and described as oval in shape.[90] A colonial merchant's inventory written up in 1742 indicated that these round steels corresponded to the closed oval pattern since 32 dozen of these fire steels were described as 'two-face' or 'two-sided'.[91] These fire steels appear to have been available in two quality grades or finishes, as records from 1738 show a merchant offering the more expensive 'polished' or 'bright' steel variety (acier poli) priced at 1 livre 5 sols each, alongside the cheaper 'raw steel' (acier brut) type priced at 10 sols apiece.[92]

Equipment Lists

As part of their expedition and campaign supplies, colonial officers and soldiers were provided with fire steels, which were likely also distributed to those stationed at interior posts and forts from the King's storehouses. At Fort Frontenac in 1702, '5½ dozen fire steels, oval' were stockpiled in onsite supply depots for garrisoned soldiers and personnel of the fort,[93] while in 1734, 56 colonial

Engraving showing soldiers drinking wine in a cabaret in Paris. Take note of what is clearly an oval flint striker next to the pipe on the table in front of these men. (Rendez-vous Bacchique chez Ramponneau, 1759. Private collection)

soldiers under de Noyelles, heading to war against the Fox, were each issued a batte-feu (fire steel).[94] Five years later, officer De Sabrevois, acting as second in command, oversaw a group of 112 soldiers and militiamen who were each supplied with '1 fire steel' for an expedition against the Chickasaw.[95] Twenty colonial officers received '20 fire steels' during a war party in 1746, indicating one per officer,[96] and the following year, 16 soldiers at Fort Sainte-Thérèse were also issued a batte-feu.[97] In 1746 and 1747, private merchants supplied 480 'common fire steels' to replenish the King's storehouses in Québec for the war efforts, suggesting that the fire steels issued to the armed forces were primarily the standard oval type.[98] During a 1752 theft trial in Québec, a caporal in the colonial troops was found to possess items including a soldier's vest, a pewter goblet, six forks, and a fire steel, which may have been his standard-issue steel.[99] Similarly, at Fort Saint-Frédéric two years later, a cloth bag belonging to one of three colonial soldiers was discovered to contain a gun worm, a fire steel, gunflints, and two lead balls.[100]

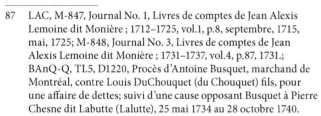

87   LAC, M-847, Journal No. 1, Livres de comptes de Jean Alexis Lemoine dit Monière ; 1712–1725, vol.1, p.8, septembre, 1715, mai, 1725; M-848, Journal No. 3, Livres de comptes de Jean Alexis Lemoine dit Monière ; 1731–1737, vol.4, p.87, 1731.; BAnQ-Q, TL5, D1220, Procès d'Antoine Busquet, marchand de Montréal, contre Louis DuChouquet (du Chouquet) fils, pour une affaire de dettes; suivi d'une cause opposant Busquet à Pierre Chesne dit Labutte (Lalutte), 25 mai 1734 au 28 octobre 1740.

88   ANMT, Fonds Dugard, Série AQ, 62 AQ 41, Facture de diverses marchandises… , 5 mai 1742.

89   LAC, MG1-B, F-287, f.224v.; MG 18, H63, Fonds famille Gradis, F-1599, M. Antoine Robert, St Etienne, 7 août 1756.

90   LAC, MG 18, H63, Fonds famille Gradis, F-1599, M. Antoine Robert, St Etienne, 7 août 1756.; BAnQ-Q, P1000,S3,D465, Inventaire des biens de François-Étienne Cugnet, 28 août 1751.

91   LAC, MG1-C11A, vol.114, f.154.

92   Archives du Séminaire de Trois-Rivières, Collection Montarville Boucher de la Bruère, Facture des marchandises livrées à Monsieur de La Verandrie…, 25 avril 1738.

93   LAC, MG1-C11A, vol.20, f.244v.

94   LAC, MG1-C11A, vol.62, f.150.

95   LAC, MG1-C11A, vol.71, f.158.

96   LAC, MG1-C11A, vol.115, f.254–254v.

97   LAC, MG1-C11A, vol.117, f.205v-206.

98   LAC, MG1-C11A, vol.117, f.104.

99   BAnQ-Q, TL5, D1667, Procès criminel contre Louis Bonin, caporal de la compagnie de Lanaudière et soldat congédié; et Denis Lemoine dit Parisien, 14 ans, soldat de la compagnie de Lanaudière en garnison à Québec, logé à la caserne Dauphine, et complices, accusés de vol, Québec, 17 février 1752–6 août 1752.

100   BAnQ-M, TL4, S1, D5921, Procès contre Menin Pouteau dit Parisien, sculpteur, soldat d'Herbin, Michel Dufeu dit Flame,

Early closed round pattern fire steel excavated at Fort Michilimackinac and likely of a Dutch origin. (Mackinac State Historic Parks collection, Michigan. Photo Kevin Gélinas)

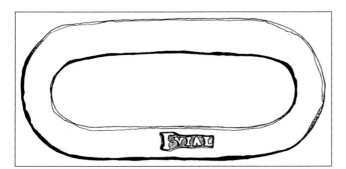

Line drawing from Michel Pétard showing a closed oval French-type fire steel found in Barron County, Wisconsin, bearing the maker's mark 'F.VIAL'. The name Vial was found to be the name of an important cutler and gunsmith family working out of Saint-Étienne, France. (Private collection)

A bundle of fire steels found at the bottom of the French River French, Ontario, among many other presumed French trade goods from over-turned canoes on their way to the Upper countries. This bundle shows how these tools were originally packaged in stacks and also reveals that trade fire steels were likely identical to those issued to the colonial troops and militia. (With permission of the Royal Ontario Museum © ROM.)

Presumed Saint-Étienne-made batte-feu found at Fort Ouiatenon bearing an undecipherable maker's mark. (Tippecanoe County Historical Association collection, Lafayette, Indiana. Photo Kevin Gélinas)

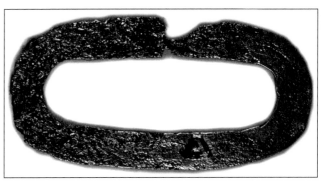

Closed oval pattern batte-feu found at Fort Michilimackinac on which is stamped a large letter 'A', possibly the mark of a Saint-Étienne maker. (Mackinac State Historic Parks collection, Michigan. Photo Kevin Gélinas)

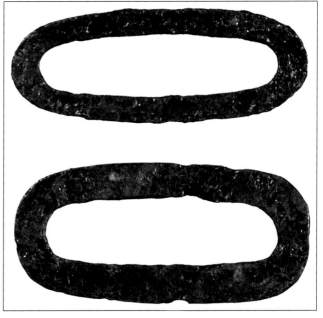

Two fire steels of the closed oval pattern found at Fort Ticonderoga. The bottom specimen, thinner but with wider edges, likely corresponds to common types produced at Saint-Étienne, while the thicker top example may have been purchased in Holland. An invoice from 1747 lists 'common fire steels' at 16 livres per gross and 'fire steels from Holland, thick' at 21 livres per gross.* Archaeological finds show that the most common fire steel at French forts from 1740-1760 was the thin, wide-edged type, likely issued to colonial troops. (Collection of the Fort Ticonderoga Museum, New York. Photo Kevin Gélinas)
* LAC, MG1-C11A, vol. 117, f.104.

The practice of distributing such items continued throughout the Seven Years War and in 1756, one batte-feu was included in the summer campaign equipment list for both officers and soldiers of the colonial and regular troops.[101] The following year, a colonial soldier taken prisoner at Fort William-Henry reported that each French soldier was provided with 'a steel and flint' as part of their standard issue campaign equipment.[102] A tobacco bag (sac à pétun) containing a fire steel and a gunflint, found on the body of colonial officer Thomas-Philippe Dagneau de La Saussaye near Saratoga in 1757, provides further evidence that these tools were carried by officers as part of their wilderness campaign gear.[103] The colonial officer Saint-Luc de La Corne, one of the few survivors of the wreck of *l'Auguste* in 1761, noted that he had kept his fire steel: 'I handed over my powder horn, fire steel and gunflint that I had fortunately kept'.[104]

In situations when colonial soldiers lacked a fire steel, a flintlock musket and gunpowder could serve as an alternative. For instance, a colonial soldier named Jolicoeur, accused of desertion near Fort de La Pointe à la Chevelure in 1735, '...made a fire with a little powder, which he placed in the pan of his flintlock musket, after having fired into the air...'[105]

Smoking Pipes (Petit Calumet)

Pipe smoking was likely common among colonial troops, as many soldiers and officers received a *livre* of tobacco monthly during summer and winter campaigns. Period records frequently describe soldiers carrying a calumet (stone pipe), likely referring to a petit calumet, a colonial term used to denote a personal stone pipe of Native American design. In 1746, two colonial soldiers in

French soldiers in 1759 around a camp in which one is smoking a pipe. Instructions given by Bourlamaque at the camp du portage near Fort Carillon in 1758 indicated that the commanding officer responsible for night scouting was to '...observe the utmost silence of his soldiers, preventing them from striking the steel and smoking.' (Représentation du feu d'artifice tiré devant l'Hotel de ville de Paris, le 1er May 1759. Courtesy of the Bibliothèque de l'Institut National d'Histoire de l'Art.)
* LAC, MG18, K9, vol.6, f.146.

Montréal were caught duelling over a calumet in one man's possession, which reportedly belonged to the other.[106] Six years later, a soldier accused of causing the Lower Town fire in Trois-Rivières was found with a 'calumet of red stone,' likely made of catlinite.[107] That same year, a soldier of the Boucherville company traded his 'pipe of red stone with a double steel wire chain,' likely connecting the pipe's base to its wooden stem.[108] At Fort Saint-Frédéric in 1754, a small chest belonging to a soldier accused of theft contained seven calumets of black stone (pierre noir), suggesting their widespread use among colonial troops.[109]

soldat de la Compagnie de Villemonde, et Guillaume Goursol dit Lagiroflée, soldat de la Compagnie Debonne, accusés de vols dans la chambre de distribution du fort Saint-Frédéric, 9 septembre 1754–26 février 1755.

101 SHAT, Dossier A1, 3417, Pièce 144.

102 LOC, Colonial Office 5 folio 47, E. of Loudoun's Letter of April 25th. 1757, Declaration of two Prisoners taken the 23.d March 1757 at Fort Wm. Henry, Information of John Victor and Guillaume Chasse, two French Prisoners, Fort William Henry March 25th.

103 BAnQ-M, TL4, S1, D6300, Sollicitation de Marie-Anne De Verchères pour obtenir confirmation du décès de son mari, Thomas-Philippe Dagneau de LaSaussaye, officier, Montréal, 18 avril 1760.

104 Saint-Luc de La Corne, *Journal du voyage de M. Saint-Luc de La Corne, ecuyer, dans le navire l'Auguste, en l'an 1761* (Montréal: Chez Fleury Mesplet, imprimeur & libraire, 1778), p.18.

105 BAnQ-M, TL4, S1, D4202, Procès devant le Conseil de guerre contre Pierre Coulo dit Jolicoeur, natif du Périgord, soldat de la Compagnie LaFresnière, accusé de désertion, 4 janvier–7 mai 1735.

106 BAnQ-M, TL4, S1, D5223, Procès contre François Chartron dit Lasonde, soldat de la Compagnie de Linctot, et François Legal dit St-Brieux, soldat de la Compagnie de Lacorne, accusés de duel, 20 avril–18 août 1746

107 BAnQ-Q, TP1, S777, D174, Procès de Pierre Beaudouin (Baudouin) dit Cumberland, Joseph Ceilier dit Beausoleil, Ponsian Allé dit Sansoucy, François-Xavier Guernoté dit Latulippe et Joseph Gamin (Jamin) dit Saint-Louis, soldats, prisonniers, accusés d'avoir provoqué l'incendie de la Basse-Ville de Trois-Rivières, d'avoir commis plusieurs vols dans les maisons incendiées, et d'avoir blasphémé le Saint Nom de Dieu. Québec, 21 mai 1752–28 août 1752.

108 BAnQ-M, TP1, TL4, S1, D5668, Procès contre Joseph François Cardon, soldat de la Compagnie de Boucherville, François Froment dit Labonté, soldat de la Compagnie de Lacorne, Antoine Didier dit Tranquille, surnommé Provençal, soldat, et François Bleau dit Prêtaboire, surnommé Flamand, cordonnier, soldat en garnison au Sault, accusés de fabrication et de distribution de fausses ordonnances. Montréal, 21 janvier–2 mars 1752.

109 BAnQ-M, S1, D5921.TL4, Procès contre Menin Pouteau dit Parisien, sculpteur, soldat d'Herbin, Michel Dufeu dit Flame, soldat de la Compagnie de Villemonde, et Guillaume Goursol dit Lagiroflée, soldat de la Compagnie Debonne, accusés de vols dans la chambre de distribution du fort Saint-Frédéric. Montréal, 9 septembre 1754–26 février 1755.

Black stone pipe with geometrical engravings on the bowl and marked with a cross on the base, possibly added by its original owner as to represent a catholic symbol. Excavated at Fort Senneville (1696–1776), Senneville, Quebec. (With permission of the Royal Ontario Museum © ROM)

Clay pipe found at the LeBer-LeMoyne site at Lachine near Montréal (1633–1706) showing the profile of a man. Similarities in craftsmanship between this pipe and two others found on the same site suggest that the same person may have made them. Their decoration is intriguing: the presence of a fleur-de-lis, a stylised plant (perhaps a tobacco plant) as well as their inscription: 'TREILLE CONT GA' and 'LATRE_LL'. This name, or portion of the name La Treille, could be associated with Jean Marin dit La Treille, a soldier assigned to the Lachine garrison in the seventeenth century. His name is inscribed on two pipes discovered during archaeological excavations at the heritage site of Le Ber-Le Moyne. (© Musée de Lachine / photo Richard-Max Tremblay)

Red catlinite stone petit calumet pipe with broken bowl and the letters 'IHS' engraved at the front of the base. (Mackinac State Historic Parks collection, Michigan. Photo Kevin Gélinas)

Pipe engraved with the name 'Treille' excavated at the Le Ber-Le Moyne site. (Collection du Musée de Lachine (Ville de Montréal) Photo: Richard-Max Tremblay)

Awls

An important yet often overlooked piece of equipment issued to colonial soldiers and officers during campaigns and expeditions was the iron awl or stitching awl. This slender metal tool, with its pointed ends, was primarily used for piercing holes in leather to make winter or summer moccasins (souliers sauvages). However, its utility extended beyond this primary function; it could also be used for clearing clogged pipes or as a vent pick for muskets. The awl was typically fitted with a wooden, bone, or antler handle by the user, enhancing its versatility and ease of use.

As early as the seventeenth century, colonial soldiers were equipped with awls for expeditions, including in 1696, when 72 awls, priced at 30 sols each, were issued to soldiers under Villieu's command for an attack on Fort Pemaquid.[110] In 1702, a memoir by colonial officer Saint-Castin listed '1,000 awls with squared tips' as necessary supplies for an expedition from Québec involving colonial soldiers, Canadians, and allied Native American warriors against New England.[111] About 30 years later, 56 colonial soldiers were each issued an awl for their campaign against the Fox tribes,[112] a practice echoed during the 1739 Chickasaw campaign, where officers received two awls each and soldiers one.[113]

By the time of King George's War, large quantities of predominantly straight awls were purchased from colonial merchants for the war effort. In 1745, for instance, 1,728 straight awls were acquired.[114] Two years later, another batch of 1,728 straight awls, along with 864 crooked awls, was collected to replenish the King's storehouses.[115] A portion of these pointed tools were likely supplied to a war party sent to Acadia under Sieur Marin in 1745 which included 567 'straight awls'.[116] In 1746, officers serving in a party under de Rigaud de Vaudreuil, *major* of Trois-Rivières, each received two awls,[117] while three officers assigned to diplomatic missions into the interior were provided with four awls each.[118] That same year, each of the 16 colonial soldiers stationed at Fort Sainte-Thérèse was issued one awl.[119]

Detail from a plate titled Bourrelier et Bourrelier-Bastier (Harness maker) in Diderot's *Encyclopédie*, showing a worker using an awl to punch holes in a piece of leather.

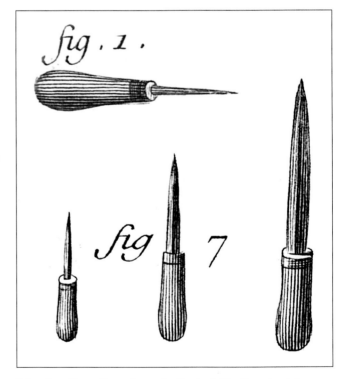

Taken from Bourrelier et Bourrelier-Bastier in The Encyclopédie, illustrating tools used to punch holes in leather before stitching. Figure 1 shows a 'Sewing awl,' and Figure 7 depicts three straight awls of varying sizes mounted in their respective handles.

---

110   LAC, MG1-C11A, vol.2, f.97.
111   *Collection de manuscrits contenant lettres, mémoires, et autres documents historiques relatifs à la Nouvelle-France: recueillis aux archives de la province de Québec, ou copiés à l'étranger. vol.II* (Québec: Imprimerie A. Côté et Cie: 1884), p.399.
112   LAC, MG1-C11A, vol.62, f.150v.
113   LAC, MG1-C11A, vol.71, f.156–159, 161.
114   LAC, MG1-C11A, vol.84, f.123, 125v, 127v.
115   LAC, MG1-C11A, vol.117, f.95, 111.
116   LAC, MG1-C11A, vol.84, f.148.
117   LAC, MG1-C11A, vol.115, f.254.
118   LAC, MG1-C11A, vol.117, f.177.
119   LAC, MG1-C11A, vol.117, f.206.

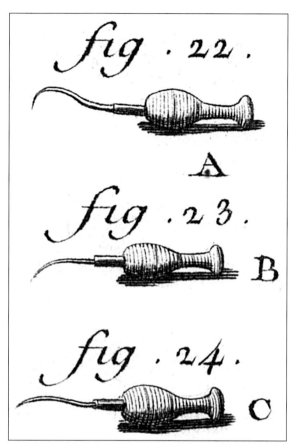

From left to right: A crooked awl having a zigzag or crooked shape with a cross-section. Although more expensive to manufacture, these awls were likely first introduced to overcome a problem with the handles, where the wood or bone handles of straight awls tended to split under pressure. The offset design in the example presented above anchors the awl firmly in its handle. (Private collection)

A cobbler's awl (alêne de cordonnier) found at Fort Ticonderoga. (Fort Ticonderoga Museum collection, New York. Photo Kevin Gélinas)

Detail taken from Diderot's plate labelled Cordonnier et Bottier (Cobbler and Bootmaker) showing various English-style awls (alênes à l'anglaise) each having a pronounced curved point similar to the specimen.

Cobbler's awl mounted in an octagonal shaped bone handle excavated at Fort Michilimackinac. (Mackinac State Historic Parks collection, Michigan. Photo Kevin Gélinas)

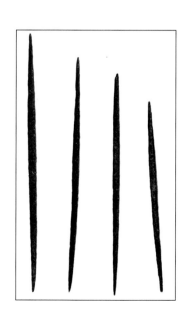

Four awls that are straight and square in cross-section which were found at Fort Ticonderoga. These are presumably the common straight awls manufactured at Saint-Étienne, France, which served as much as a trade item then as part of the gear each colonial soldier and officer received prior to an expedition or campaign. (Fort Ticonderoga Museum collection, New York)

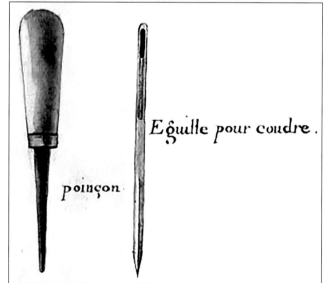

A poinçon and a sewing needle as shown in an inventory of what was on-hand at the Brest seaport arsenal in 1737. (SHD-Brest, bibliothèque R3415. Photo Christian Lemasson.)

The allocation of awls to colonial officers and soldiers during the Seven Years War appears to have varied. For example, during the 1755 campaign under Dieskau, each officer, soldier, or Canadian was issued one awl for the summer months.[120] However, by November 1756, an equipment list specified that colonial soldiers were to receive five awls each for the summer campaign.[121] The following year, according to Bourlamaque, colonial officers were provided with six awls for summer campaigns, while soldiers were given only one.[122] In February 1757, an equipment list prepared by Louis-Antoine de Bougainville indicated that each soldier participating in a winter campaign received one awl.[123]

Additionally, two French soldiers captured at Fort William-Henry in 1757 reported that each colonial and regular soldier carried, among other items, 'one shoe awl, six needles, and a quantity of thread'.[124] The awls distributed to the troops at this time were likely of the straight variety, as confirmed by the inventory at Fort Carillon in 1757, which listed '10 gross, 3 dozen and 4 straight awls' without any mention of crooked ones.[125] Finally, an invoice for military supplies sent from Trois-Rivières to Montréal in late spring 1760 included '1,584 trade awls', usually described as straight in other records, suggesting that straight awls remained the most common type in use by French troops.[126]

By the 1730s, records indicate that two types of awls, 'straight' and 'crooked', were imported from France to New France, based on a shipment sent to Louisiana in 1733.[127] A 1758 post-mortem inventory from a Québec-based merchant further reveals that three types of awls were available in the colony: crooked awls, straight awls, and cobbler's awls.[128]

Straight Awls (Alênes Droites)

Throughout the eighteenth century, most awls imported from France were described as 'straight' and primarily intended for the fur trade,[129] with large shipments produced in Saint-Étienne arriving in New France by the 1740s.[130] A 1742 merchant record specified these awls as 'square,' likely referring to a square cross-section,[131] and in 1746 and 1747, substantial quantities were purchased from Québec merchants to stock the King's storehouses for wartime distribution to colonial troops. In the final years of the French regime, Bordeaux merchants Gradis supplied vast numbers of awls, including '2,160 square awls', '8,640 straight awls', and '14,400 straight awls' from Antoine Robert of Saint-Étienne in 1756.[132] The following year, Gradis acquired '43,200 straight awls' from the Thiolière brothers, also of Saint-Étienne.[133] Thus, straight awls remained the most common type available in the colonial market until the conquest of New France.

Crooked Awls (Alênes Courbées)

The second type of awl, described as courbée (crooked), likely referred to an offset centre design. The unique shape, with its offset portion, rested on the handle, providing leverage. This allowed the user to apply more force with less effort, which was essential for punching through thicker materials like deerskin when making moccasins, while also preventing the awl from causing the handle to split under pressure. In 1747, the merchant Goguet supplied 864 crooked awls to replenish the Québec storehouses in preparation for war.[134] By 1756, the ship La Marguerite, en route to Louisiana, was captured at sea, revealing in its cargo 10 gross of trade awls (alênes de traite) priced at 33 sols per gross and nine gross of awls 'bent in the middle' (courbées par le milieu) priced at 61 sols 9 deniers per gross.[135] This significant price difference suggests that crooked awls were nearly twice as expensive as trade awls, which were likely of the straight variety.

Cobbler's Awls (Alênes à Cordonnier)

Cobbler's awls, though uncommon, are mentioned in period documents, such as a 1752 merchant's invoice from Québec listing 2,000 polished cobbler's awls, described as assorted and bearing a 'grapes' maker's mark, with a

120 Société historique de Montréal, Campagne de 1755 (Montréal, Québec: C.A. Marchand, 1899), p.34.

121 Centre d'histoire La Presqu'ile, P03/F.089, Fonds De Beaujeu, 28 novembre 1756.

122 LAC, MG18, K9, vol.6, f.469–472.

123 De Bougainville, Écrits sur le Canada, p.168.

124 LOC, Colonial Office 5 folio 47, E. of Loudoun's Letter of April 25th. 1757, Declaration of two Prisoners taken the 23.d March 1757 at Fort Wm. Henry, Information of John Victor and Guillaume Chasse, two French Prisoners, Fort William Henry March 25th.

125 LAC, MG18, K9, vol.6, f.457–463.

126 BAnQ-Q, Greffe du notaire Jean-Claude Panet, Facture des marchandises et munitions qui ont été tirées des magasins du Roi aux Trois-Rivières et chargées sur le bateau le St-Henry, capitaine Laparre pour porter et remettre à Monsieur Fayolle, garde des dits magasins à Montréal... 25 août 1764.

127 Marie Gérin-Lajoie, Montreal Merchant's Records Project, (microfilm copy of M496 Montreal Merchants Records Project, Research Files, 1971–1975, 1 roll — St. Paul: Minnesota Historical Society Library Copy Services), Archives des Colonies, F1A, 1732–3, Awls.

128 BAnQ-Q, Greffe du notaire Claude Barolet, Inventaire des biens de la communauté d'entre le feu Joseph Roussel (vivant bourgeois en cette ville) et Marie-Madeleine Gauvreau, 21 février 1758.

129 ASQ, Missions no.107. Mémoire des effets à envoyer aux Tamarois et commentaire de l'abbé Amédée Gosselin, 1699, 25 août, 1699.

130 LAC, MG1-B, vol.84, f.172.

131 LAC, MG1-C11A, vol.114, f.154.

132 LAC, MG 18, H63, Fonds famille Gradis, F-1599, M. Antoine Robert, St Etienne, 7 août 1756.

133 LAC, MG 18, H63, Fonds famille Gradis, F-1600, M. Thiolière frères, St-Etienne, 11 octobre 1757.

134 LAC, MG1-C11A, vol.117, f.111.

135 TNA, HCA, 32, vol.22, La Marguerite de Bordeaux, 1758.

note stating: 'These are for the Natives'.[136] Four years later, an inventory from two merchants in Montréal included 26 straight awls, seven cobbler's awls, and 19 hafted awls, suggesting their presence, albeit in smaller quantities, alongside other types.[137] We can suppose that the more expensive curved cobbler's awl was likely used for thicker types of leather, such as tanned leather, while the more affordable straight or offset awls were probably suited for piercing softer leather, like the deerskin used for winter moccasins. The curve of the cobbler's awl allows the tip to enter the leather at an angle, reducing resistance when working with denser, thicker, tanned leather, such as that used for oxhide shoes, European-style footwear, belts, straps, and similar items.

The cobbler's awls imported into New France were likely intended for shoemakers making European-style shoes in the colony or those mass-producing oxhide moccasins for the troops. These may also have been adopted by certain Native nations to work on complex or detailed leather designs, as they could benefit from the precision and efficiency the tools offered.

Sewing Needles and Thread

Needles for hand sewing (aiguilles à coudre) were an important tool for any soldier stationed in New France since they could repair clothes themselves, resulting in clothing lasting longer, which would greatly reduce expense. These slender tools would have been quite convenient for general hand sewing, such as mending tears in clothing, sewing a button back on or stitching together souliers sauvages (moccasins) once the guide holes were punched in the leather using an awl. This little but rather important item was part of the standard equipment that was issued to each colonial soldier and officer before a campaign or expedition.

Sewing needles were a standard part of the Petit habillement issued to colonial soldiers in New France. In 1732, 1,440 sewing needles were requested from France for the

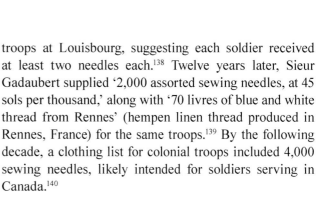

Above: Taken from Diderot's *Tailleur d'habits et tailleur de corps* showing sewing needles of various sizes as part of the tools used by tailors of suits. Figures 5. 6. and 7; Needles of different sizes. AAA; the heads. BBB; the points. This form of sewing needle would have been nearly identical to those used by colonial soldiers serving in Canada.

Right: Two sizes of 'common' pointed needles excavated at Fort Michilimackinac. These exhibit diamond-shaped points, otherwise having a four-sided diamond-shaped cross-section with the remaining shaft being round. (Mackinac State Historic Parks collection, Michigan. Photo Kevin Gélinas)

troops at Louisbourg, suggesting each soldier received at least two needles each.[138] Twelve years later, Sieur Gadaubert supplied '2,000 assorted sewing needles, at 45 sols per thousand,' along with '70 livres of blue and white thread from Rennes' (hempen linen thread produced in Rennes, France) for the same troops.[139] By the following decade, a clothing list for colonial troops included 4,000 sewing needles, likely intended for soldiers serving in Canada.[140]

136 BAnQ-Q, P908, P9, Mémoire à accomplir par les frères Rouffio et Romagnac pour l'année 1753 relativement aux commandes de marchandises auprès de négociants de France et de Hollande, destinées à être envoyées au Québec… , 1752.

137 BAnQ-M, Greffe du notaire C. Monmerque dit Dubreuil, Inventaire des marchandises invendues appartenant à la société de Messieurs Courthiau et Greenhil fait en 1756, 10 octobre 1756.

138 LAC, MG1-C11B, vol.13, f.44v,

139 LAC, F1, MG1 16, vol.25, 1744.

140 LAC, MG1-B, vol.96, f.172.

Throughout the 1730s and 1740s, administrative military equipment lists for various expeditions and campaigns routinely included sewing needles and thread from Rennes. For example, in 1747, '1,000 sewing needles' along with '6 *livres* of Rennes thread' were delivered to Monsieur de Lavaltry, commandant at Sault Saint-Louis, for the service of the guard house,[141] while another 500 needles were supplied to Monsieur de Vassant at Saint-Thérèse.[142] Colonial officers were also equipped with these tools prior to detachments or military operations. In 1734, officers under de Noyelles, preparing for war against the Fox, were issued 1 *livre* of Rennes thread along with 1,000 sewing needles for their troops,[143] whereas officers de La Corne, Dubreuil, and Bellestre, who were dispatched to the interior to muster allied Native American nations in 1747, received a total of 60 sewing needles and ¾ *livre* of Rennes thread.[144]

During the Seven Years War, each colonial soldier was typically issued six sewing needles and two skeins of thread for a summer campaign,[145] a standard reflected in officer Bourlamaque's 1757 report that both officers and soldiers received these supplies.[146] This practice is further confirmed by the testimony of a French colonial soldier and a member of the Régiment du Languedoc captured at Fort William-Henry, who stated that each man serving under the King of France was provided '...six needles and a quantity of thread.'[147]

A 1752 merchant's invoice shows that sewing needles were available in three sizes, No. 3, No. 4, and No. 5, and were typically sourced from merchants in Rouen, France.[148] Between 1755 and 1757, Bordeaux merchants Gradis secured large quantities of these needles for Canada, ordering hundreds of thousands in assorted sizes or primarily the popular large size from dealers Horutener and Le Moyne in Rouen.[149] Some of these needles may have been manufactured in Paris, as indicated by a 1758 invoice

listing '4,750 sewing needles from Paris' included in goods sent to Detroit.[150] According to Savary, most needles were produced in Paris, Rouen, Évreux, and Germany.[151] Soldiers and officers likely stored their needles in étuis, small cases made from wood, tin, or leather. Probate records of colonial merchants suggest many of these cases were crafted from boiled leather or wood.

Combs

Another trivial article issued as part of the colonial troops' standard equipment was a comb, or *peigne* in French, typically made from horn or boxwood. Savary describes a *peigne* as an '... instrument used to untangle and clean the hair,' noting that they were crafted from various materials such as boxwood, ivory, horn, and tortoise shell.[152] Given the close quarters and often unsanitary conditions in which colonial troops lived, combs were not only useful for grooming but also crucial for addressing the pervasive issue of lice. Philippe Aubert de Gaspé mentioned that fine combs from the French era were particularly effective against lice: 'Would you have, M. Verrault, some of those good fine combs, such as back in the French days, that could kill fifty, sixty, eighty, one hundred scoundrels (lice) with one rake?'[153]

The soldier's comb remained a standard-issue item throughout this period, supplied to every newly recruited colonial soldier and included in the campaign equipment for all soldiers serving in Canada during the Seven Years War. A 1732 letter from Governor Beauharnois to Minister Maurepas confirms the practice of issuing a comb to each new recruit sent to the colonies: 'It has always been customary to give to each of the new-recruited soldiers who embark for the colonies, 2 shirts, a smock-frock, a pair of breeches, a pair of stockings, a pair of shoes, a woollen cap, and a comb.'[154]

As early as the 1680s, combs were issued annually or biannually to colonial troops in the French colonies of North America. In 1687, a merchant named Mênier from Rochefort supplied combs for 800 soldiers traveling to

141 LAC, MG1-C11A, vol.117, f.208v.
142 LAC, MG1-C11A, vol.117, f.210.
143 LAC, MG1-C11A, vol.62, f.150.
144 LAC, MG1-C11A, vol.117, f.177.
145 Centre d'histoire La Presqu'île, P03/F.089, Fonds De Beaujeu, 28 novembre 1756.
146 LAC, MG18, K9, vol.6, f.469, 470.
147 LOC, Colonial Office 5 folio 47, E. of Loudoun's Letter of April 25th. 1757, Declaration of two Prisoners taken the 23.d March 1757 at Fort Wm. Henry, Information of John Victor and Guillaume Chasse, two French Prisoners, Fort William Henry March 25th.
148 BAnQ-Q, P908, P9, Mémoire à accomplir par les frères Rouffio et Romagnac pour l'année 1753 relativement aux commandes de marchandises auprès de négociants de France et de Hollande, destinées à être envoyées au Québec... , 1752.
149 LAC, MG 18, H63, Fonds famille Gradis, F-1598, MM. Horutener et compagnie, Rouen, 18 octobre 1755.; LAC, MG 18, H63, Fonds famille Gradis, F-1599, M. Horutener et compagnie, Rouen, 7 août 1756.; LAC, MG 18, H63, Fonds famille Gradis, F-1600, M. Le Moyne, Rouen, 11 octobre 1757.; LAC, MG 18,

H63, Fonds famille Gradis, F-1600, M. Horutener et compagnie, Rouen, 10 octobre 1757.
150 LAC, Monière, M-850, Doit Monsieur Jean Chapron, voyageur, pour marchandises remise pour l'exploitation d'un congé à lui accordé en mai 1758 pour le Détroit, 4 avril, 1759.
151 Jacques Savary des Bruslons, Philémon Louis Savary, *Dictionnaire universel de commerce* (Amsterdam: Chez François l'Honoré & Fils, 1741), vol.1, pp.52–56.
152 Jacques Savary des Bruslons, Philémon Louis Savary, *Dictionnaire universel de commerce: P-Z* (Genève: Freres Cramer & C. Philibert, 1750), p.104.
153 Philippe Aubert de Gaspé, *Mémoires* (Montréal, Québec: Fides, 1971), p.63.
154 AR, 1E, 361, pièce 219, Beaucharnois à Maurepas, Rochefort, 4 octobre 1732.

Detail taken from a c. 1635 engraving entitled 'Un homme se faisant peigner et habiller par des femmes' showing two women grooming a man using a double-edged comb. (Private collection)

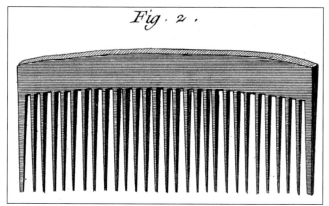

Taken from Diderot's plate labelled Tabletier-Cornetier illustrating comb fashion from horn used to untangle hair having a single row of teeth and an arched top.

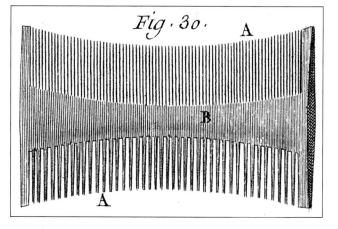

Detail from a plate entitled Perruquier-Barbier taken from the *Encyclopédie* showing a comb described as an 'Ivory comb to untangle (hair) with two sets of teeth...' which may represent, based on archaeological examples, one of the most common forms of European combs of the period which has one row of fine teeth for cleaning and removing lice and their nits, the other row wider-spaced teeth, or coarse teeth, for grooming. Traditionally associated with comb making, boxwood was often used because the wood is hard with a dense, smooth grain. This type of double-sided wooden comb changed very little from the Roman period onwards.

Canada,[155] while troops in Acadia and Plaisance each received two combs.[156] Over the decades, boxwood combs became a standard request for troops stationed abroad.[157] In 1721, recruits heading to Canada received '100 boxwood

---

155 LAC, F1, MG1–16, vol.3, État de la dépense qui a été faite… pour la levée et habillement de 800 soldats pour le Canada, 1687.

156 LAC, MG1-C11A, vol.3, f.123.

157 AR, IE, 87, fol. 167.

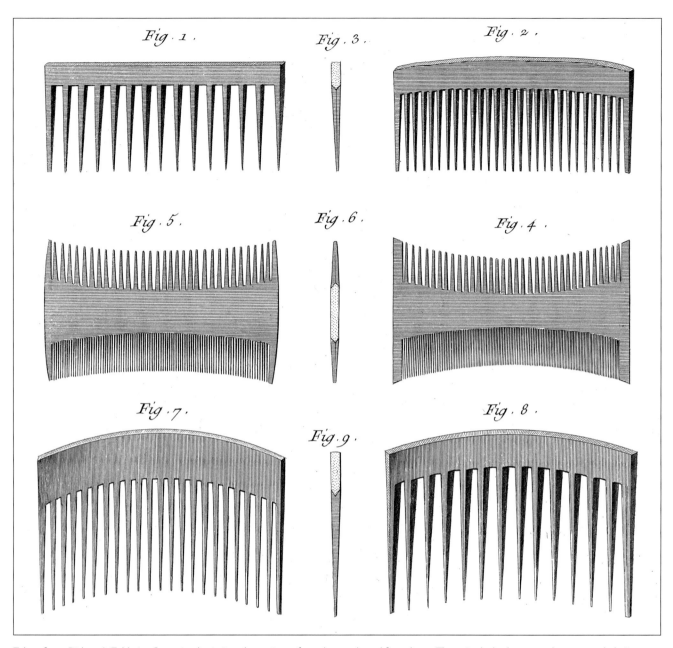

Taken from Diderot's *Tabletier-Cornetier* depicting the variety of combs produced from horn. These include those used to untangle hair having a single row of teeth with a straight or arched back (Fig. 1–3), double-edged combs having a straight or curved row of teeth (Fig. 4–6) as well as the curved combs termed Chignon combs.

combs at 5 sols each',[158] and in 1727, '720 boxwood combs' were sent to Louisbourg as part of the Petit habillement.[159] Additional large quantities were supplied to this fortress in 1732,[160] 1733,[161] and 1734.[162] By 1744, specific measurements were introduced: each soldier at Louisbourg was issued two boxwood combs annually, measuring 'four to five pouces' in length.[163]

Although specific information on the combs issued to colonial soldiers in Canada is scarce, it is probable that these were the same models used in the fur trade, likely managed jointly for administrative convenience. In 1750, it was requested that each soldier in the Canonniers-Bombardier company in Canada receive two boxwood combs as part of their standard equipment, indicating that such combs were likely also issued to troops stationed across the St Lawrence Valley and in the interior.[164]

By the early 1750s, combs made of boxwood or horn were being supplied to troops in New France as shown by a 1752 transportation permit for colonial soldiers listing

158 AR, C3, 8, État des hardes nécessaires pour les soldats de nouvelle levée qui doivent passer à Québec sur la flûte Le Chameau, Rochefort, 7 juin 1721.
159 LAC, MG1-C11B, vol.10, f.120-121.
160 LAC, MG1-C11B, vol.13, f.44–45v.
161 LAC, MG1-C11B, vol.13, f.95–98v.
162 LAC, MG1-C11B, vol.14, f.222–224.
163 LAC, F1A, vol.35, f.10-11.

164 LAC, MG1-B, vol.91, f.240v.

'3,000 boxwood or horn combs'.[165] In 1755, '3,522 boxwood combs' were taken from the King's storehouses in Québec as part of the necessary military supplies required for the battalion of the regular troops sent to Canada, indicating that most combs issued were of the standard wooden type.[166] During the 1756 campaign, a comb was included in the summer equipment for soldiers,[167] and the following year, they were also part of the summer gear for officers, soldiers, and militia.[168]

Bougainville noted in 1757 that 'one comb' was included in the winter equipment issued to the regulars,[169] and a colonial soldier captured at Fort William-Henry declared that each French soldier serving in the present campaign had 'a Comb'.[170] Combs, likely primarily boxwood, were provided to colonial soldiers and officers for both summer and winter campaigns, as confirmed by fort inventories.[171] For example, 262 boxwood combs were listed in the 1757 inventory of Fort Carillon (Fort Ticonderoga),[172] and 10 years later, '72 boxwood combs' were recorded in an inventory of goods moved from Fort de Chartres to St Louis.[173]

Records of combs owned by colonial soldiers often describe them as being made of horn or unspecified materials, such as boxwood or ivory. In 1716, the post-mortem inventory of colonial *sergent* Jacques Bonin dit Laforest listed 'one sealskin wallet containing a horn comb.'[174] Similarly, in 1752, during an investigation in Trois-Rivières, soldiers Cumberland, Beausoleil, and Sanssoucy, accused of causing a fire, were found with 'one wallet made from a piece of old white garb in which [was found] three new combs to untangle, all made of horn' and 'an old wallet in which was found two old combs.'[175] Officers

also owned combs, as established by colonial officer Girard, stationed in the Illinois country in 1723, who had a boxwood comb,[176] and *capitaine* d'Arrazola, *aide-major* at New Orleans in 1755, who owned two combs made of coconut wood.[177]

Under the article labelled peigne (comb), Savary's *Dictionnaire universel de commerce* notes that most combs of the period were produced in Paris and Rouen and sorted by a classification system. Boxwood combs were labelled with letters (A, B, C, D, and O) for smaller sizes and numbers (1 to 12) for larger ones, with size A measuring 2 *pouces* and each subsequent size increasing by 6 *lignes* up to 12 *pouces* for size 12. Horn combs were typically longer, starting at size size 4 and extending to size 15. Colonial merchants such as Martel, Monière, Cugnet, Hervieux, and Rouffio used this classification in their inventories. Savary also describes styles like two-row combs (à deux côtés), single-arched combs (à dos), Indian-style combs (à l'indienne), and oval combs (à macaron).

Blankets of the Colonial Troops

Although not a standard issue item for soldiers in France, wool blankets, known as couvertes or couvertures in French records, were commonly carried by each man serving in Canada during both winter and summer campaigns. These were used to keep warm while lying down or sleeping and served as makeshift beds when setting up camp. A memoir from around 1705 notes that Canadians wrapped themselves in their blankets during winter travel, '…which serves them as bedding at night…'[178] Colonial officer Jean Bernard Bossu, who explored the Mississippi region, emphasised the importance of a blanket when travelling in New France: 'When I was required to travel to uninhabited lands, I carried my house and my bed, that is to say, I brought along a wool blanket or a skin.'[179]

Manufactured from sheep's wool and imported from France, various types and grades of blankets were provided to the colonial troops throughout this period. Initially, records indicate that soldiers engaged in wilderness campaigns or stationed in towns across Canada were supplied with blankets from Bordeaux, although by the

165 LAC, MG1-B, vol.96, f.172.

166 LAC, MG1-C11A, vol.100, f.264v-265v.

167 SHD, Archives de la guerre, A1, vol.3417, pièce 144.

168 LAC, MG18, K9, vol.6, f.469–472.

169 De Bougainville, *Écrits sur le Canada*, p.168.

170 LOC, Colonial Office 5 folio 47, E. of Loudoun's Letter of April 25th. 1757, Declaration of two Prisoners taken the 23.d March 1757 at Fort Wm. Henry, Information of John Victor and Guillaume Chasse, two French Prisoners, Fort William Henry March 25th.

171 SHD, Archives de la guerre, A1, vol.3417, pièce 144.; LAC, MG18, K9, vol.6, f.469–472.

172 LAC, MG18, K9, vol.6, f.457–463.

173 Frederic L. Billon, *Annals of St Louis in its Early Days under the French and Spanish domination* (St Louis: Press of Nixon-Jones Printing Co., 1886), p.49.

174 BAnQ-M, TL4, S1, D1864, Procès contre Jacques Bonin dit Laforet, sergent de la compagnie d'Esgly, accusé de vol d'argent chez le trésorier de la marine à Québec, 19 février–19 mai 1716.

175 BAnQ-Q, TP1, S777, D174, Procès de Pierre Beaudouin (Baudouin) dit Cumberland, Joseph Ceilier dit Beausoleil, Ponsian Allé dit Sansoucy, François-Xavier Guernoté dit Latulippe et Joseph Gamin (Jamin) dit Saint-Louis, soldats, prisonniers, accusés d'avoir provoqué l'incendie de la Basse-Ville de Trois-Rivières, d'avoir commis plusieurs vols dans les maisons incendiées, et d'avoir blasphémé le Saint Nom de Dieu, 21 mai–28 août 1752.

176 Kaskaskia Manuscripts, Randolph County Courthouse, Chester, Illinois, Vente après inventaire (Girard, officier des troupes à Kaskaskia), 23 juillet 1723.

177 LAC, MG1-E, vol.9, 19 avril 1755.

178 LAC, MG1-C11A, vol.122, f.155–155v.

179 Jean Bernard Bossu, *Nouveaux voyages dans l'Amérique Septentrionale: contenant une collection de lettres écrites sur les lieux, par l'auteur; à son ami, M. Douin … ci-devant son camarade dans le Nouveau Monde* (Amsterdam: Chez la Veuve Duchesne, 1778), p.236.

second quarter of the eighteenth century, most woollen blankets issued during campaigns were couvertes à points (point blankets) produced in Darnétal near Rouen.

Bordeaux Blankets (Couvertes de Bordeaux)

Period records indicate that colonial troops were initially supplied with couvertes de Bordeaux (Bordeaux blankets) for wilderness campaigns, a practice already in place when these troops first arrived in 1683. That year, Governor La Barre requested 'a wool blanket for each soldier' participating in a wilderness assault.[180] By 1687, new army recruits who were to join Denonville's expedition against the Iroquois were required to have 'a good blanket from Bordeaux', alongside an order for 'Five hundred blankets from Bordeaux for the said soldiers in the country, which are indispensable, especially when waging war and when stationed in the posts which we will have to occupy'.[181]

In 1692, '40 blankets from Bordeaux' were to be sent to Acadia to outfit the colonial soldiers returning from Boston Prison, indicating their widespread use among colonial troops at that time.[182] In some cases, these blankets were also referred to as couvertes de munition (munition blankets). For example, during a criminal trial in Montréal, the wife of an innkeeper was reported to have bought one of these blankets from a soldier: 'She had purchased from the soldier Lionnais … a munition blanket.'[183] In 1697, '300 blankets from Bordeaux with red stripes' were slated for shipment to Canada,[184] likely for colonial soldiers, as demonstrated by a subsequent request in 1701 for '60 Bordeaux blankets for the soldiers' at Port Royal in Acadia.[185]

By the 1710s, it was standard practice to issue 'one blanket from Bazas' to new recruits heading to the colonies. Bazas, a town near Bordeaux in southwestern France, was known for its blanket production. In 1716, military records noted that '…it was customary to give recruits…a blanket from Bazas… [valued at] 4 livres.'[186] Similarly, in 1721, recruits crossing to Québec were to receive '60 woollen blankets from Bazas at 5 livres apiece.'[187] According to the *Dictionnaire universel de la géographie commerçante*, manufactories near Bazas supplied '…coarse blankets' to Canada,[188] and Savary Des Bruslons described the Bazas

blanket factory as significant but producing blankets that were '…not extremely fine and they sell only 24 to 25 livres a dozen.'[189]

After the fire of 1734 in Montréal, which destroyed many buildings, 48 soldiers of the town's garrison were compensated for lost equipment, including '16 blankets from Bordeaux.'[190] This indicates that Bordeaux blankets were likely standard issue for soldiers garrisoned throughout Montréal at the time. That same year, a Bordeaux blanket priced at 4 livres 10 sols was sent from Montréal to Fort de la Pointe-à-la-Chevelure for the use of the fort, voyages for the service of the King and changes of garrison.[191] During the Chickasaw campaign of 1739, two Bordeaux blankets were provided to five cadets and two soldiers to share, '… to help them make the journey,'[192] while in 1748, 20 of these blankets were kept in reserve at Fort Saint-Frédéric, emphasizing their importance as indispensable supplies for frontier operations.[193]

Blankets manufactured in Bordeaux featured a double weave and were generally produced in a single size, shipped in double widths that were later cut down the centre and separated for sale. They were typically white with narrow red or multicoloured stripes, which varied by manufacturer. In a 1751 inventory of a deceased colonist's belongings in Québec, a single 'large white wool blanket from Bordeaux having 11 stripes, new' was recorded, valued at 30 livres.[194] Also, the 1748 import duty roster for goods shipped from France to Canada listed certain Bordeaux blankets as de ville (town blankets) or poil de chien (dog hair blankets).[195] Savary notes that some bed covers were made with dog hair, while wool cloths were sometimes edged or hemmed with white or black dog hair imported from Denmark.[196]

Toulouse and Mont-de-Marsen Blankets (Couvertes de Toulouse)

In army barracks, soldiers would have typically sleep two to a bed, sharing an oversized wool blanket. According to the October 25, 1716 ordonnance on the quartering of men of war, the blankets provided to infantry soldiers in barracks were described as follows: 'The blankets shall be of white

180 LAC, MG1-C11A, vol.6, f.143v.
181 LAC, MG1-C11A, vol.9, f.169v.
182 LAC, MG1-B. vol.16, f.74.
183 BAnQ-M, Fonds Bailliage de Montréal, 3306, 11576, 22, 19 avril 1692.
184 LAC, MG1-B, vol.19, f.117.
185 LAC, F1A, vol.10, f.180.
186 AR, IE, 87, fol. 167.
187 AR, C3, p.8, 7 juin 1721.
188 Jacques Peuchet, *Dictionnaire universel de la géographie commerçante, contenant tout ce qui a raport à la situation et à l'étendue de chaque Etat commerçant…* (Paris: Chez Blanchon, 1798), vol.2, p.743.

189 Jacques Savary des Bruslons, *Dictionnaire universal du commerce…* (Paris: Chez la veuve Estienne, 1741), vol.1, pp.37–38.
190 LAC, MG1-C11A, vol.61, f.141.
191 LAC, MG1-C11A, vol.66, f.56.
192 LAC, MG1-C11A, vol.71, f.162v.
193 LAC, MG1-C11A, vol.98, f.33v.
194 BAnQ-Q, Greffe du notaire Claude Barolet, Inventaire des biens de la communauté d'entre Jean Godin (habitant de la Seigneurie de Bélair paroisse de St-Jean-Baptiste, veuf) avec feue Marie-Anne Auger, sa seconde femme, 12 janvier 1751.
195 LAC, MG1-C11A, vol.121, f.188v.
196 Des Bruslons, *Dictionnaire universel de commerce*, vol.1, pp.753, 1596.

wool, 8 pieds 6 pouces long, 7 pieds 4 pouces wide.'[197] In 1749, France requested '200 blankets from Toulouse, green and blue, large, to cover two men' for the barracks at Québec, which would have adhered to the dimensions specified in the 1716 ordonnance.[198] Blankets manufactured in Toulouse, France, were typically described as black, dark blue, green, or white and were primarily used for bedding. The 1748 tarif listed sheep wool blankets from Toulouse in two colours: the solid white variety, valued between 9 livres and 9 livres 10 sols, and the solid green variety, estimated at 10 livres to 10 livres 10 sols.[199] In 1757, for example, Antoine Simon dit Simon, a *sergent* in the Canonniers-Bombardiers at Québec, owned 'two wool blankets, a white one from Rouen of 9-points and another white one from Toulouse',[200] while that same year, an inventory list from Fort Carillon included 'one blanket from Toulouse, damaged.'[201]

Woollen blankets provided to colonial soldiers in the barracks at Louisbourg were manufactured in Mont-de-Marsan, France, and featured a distinctive fleur-de-lis design at their centre. In 1744, '50 white woollen blankets from Mont-de-Marsan with fleur-de-lis embroidered in the middle' were requested from France for the soldiers' barracks at Louisbourg[202] Twelve years later, the blankets needed for the soldiers' sleeping quarters were described as: '500 large blankets of white wool from Mont-de-Marsan, marked with a fleur-de-lis, for the replacement of the soldiers' beds.'[203] It is worth noting that these blankets were likely specific to Louisbourg, as no documentation suggests they were supplied to soldiers serving in other regions of New France.

Point Blankets (Couvertes à points)

For over two centuries, the point blanket has been an iconic woollen blanket in Canada and beyond, originally traded for furs and made famous by the Hudson's Bay Company. As one of the most popular and sought-after items in the fur trade, French-made point blankets were also widely used in military campaigns in New France. The 'points', short bars stitched or woven into the fabric

near one end with blue wool, indicated the size and weight of the blanket, serving as a kind of early barcode.[204]

The French verb 'empointer', which means 'to stitch' on woollen cloth, may explain why the term couverte à points refers to a stitched blanket. The 1723 edition of the *Dictionnaire universel de commerce* defines empointer as: 'Empointer, appointer, or pointer a piece of wool cloth. This means to make a few stitches using silk, thread, or string... '.[205]

According to French primary sources, the Hudson's Bay Company, founded in 1670, was not the originator of the point blanket, as references to couvertures à points in France date back to 1653.[206] Point blankets, often referred to as couvertes à points, couvertes de Rouen, Canadas, or Catalognes in various French records, were exclusively manufactured in Darnétal, a town in the Seine-Maritime department of Normandy, just a few miles east of Rouen. Once completed, these blankets were sold to traders at the Halle des Draps in Rouen, who then exported them abroad. This is why they were often referred to as 'couvertes de Rouen' (blankets from Rouen) in historical documents, concealing their true manufacturing origin in Darnétal.

Point blankets were likely introduced to New France around 1690, and a memoir from 1699 highlights their popularity in the fur trade, especially those having two or three points.[207] French merchants commonly called them Canadas, reflecting their frequent shipment to Canada and widespread use in the fur trade. An account from Nicolas Cauchois of Darnétal in May 1747 to the merchant Dugard of Rouen included '100 Canadas of 2½ points at 7 livres 2 sols 6 deniers,'[208] and an essay published in the late 1700s explains their designation:

> Darnétal mostly produced woollen blankets, called Canadas, after the name of the northern part of America where they used them the most. Twenty manufactures scarcely sufficed for their production, but the loss of that distant region taken from France led to the downfall of the manufactories which never recovered their glory.[209]

197 Pierre de Briquet, *Code militaire, ou, Compilation des ordonnances des roys de France ...* (Paris: Imprimerie Royale, 1728), vol.1, pp.69–70.
198 LAC, MG1-C11A, vol.93, f.343.
199 LAC, MG1-C11A, vol.121, f.188v.
200 BAnQ-Q, Greffe du notaire Claude Barolet, Inventaire des biens de la communauté de Sieur Antoine Simon dit St-Simon (sergent des canonniers-bombardiers en ce pays y demeurant rue des Grisons, veuf) avec feue Marie-Louise Levasseur, 7 novembre 1757.
201 LAC, MG18, K9, vol.6, f.457–463.
202 LAC, MG-1-C11B, vol.35, f.10.
203 LAC, MG1-C11B, vol.37, f.213.

204 Personnal communication with Francis Back, November 2013.
205 Des Brûlons, *Dictionnaire universel de commerce*, vol.1, p.1809.
206 *Inventaire de tous les meubles du Cardinal Mazarin: Dressé en 1653, et. pub. d'après l'original, conservé dans les archives de Condé* (Londres: Imprimerie de Whittingham et Wilkins, 1861), p.220.
207 LAC, MG18-G6, vol.1, p.219–220.
208 Centre des archives du monde du travail, Fonds Dugard, Série AQ, 62 AQ 41, 0863, No 69, 31 mai 1747. Mémoire de marchandises. Signé Nicolas Cauchois.
209 Simon Barthélemy Joseph Noël, *Premier [et deuxième] essai sur le département de la Seine-Inférieure, contenant les districts de Gournay, Neufchâtel, Dieppe et Cany...* (Rouen: De l'imprimerie des arts, 1795), p.193.

Equipment Lists

During the last two decades of the French regime, the colonial term *couvertes à points*, otherwise referred to as point blankets, were frequently distributed to officers, cadets and soldiers of the colonial troops serving in Canada and stockpiled in great numbers in the King's storehouses as part of the war efforts. Throughout King George's War, colonial records show that officers and cadets typically received a single 3-point blanket. During 1746, the Canadian officer named Mézière was given a 3-point blanket as a replacement to the one '…he had burned in the last campaign in which he had taken part on the coast of New England'[210] whereas a single 3-point blanket was supplied to a cadet named Mézière de Lepervanche in replacement to the one he had lost in a war party.[211]

The following year, officers La Corne, Dubreuil, and Bellestre each received 'three 3-point blankets' before heading to the Upper Countries,[212] while *Cadet* Mouaitte, heading to war with Native Americans of the Lac des Deux Montagnes, was given '1 spoiled 3-point blanket'.[213] Officer De la Chauvignery was also issued a 3-point blanket for a 1747 diplomatic mission among the Onondaga nation.[214] However, in October of 1746, Saint-Blain (Saint-Blin), a colonial officer who was to join up with the war party commanded by Langy, was provided with a smaller size 2-point blanket as opposed to the larger 3-point blanket.[215]

Several of these blankets were also provided for the military personnel stationed at outlying posts. At Sault Saint-Louis, Commandant Lavaltry was given a dozen 2½-point blankets intended '…as much for the use of the guardroom as for the needs of the [military] service',[216] while another 12 were sent to the guardroom (corps de garde) at the Lac des Deux Montagnes fort.[217] An undated dispatch from the Paul Marin de La Malgue papers, likely from the early 1750s, reported a shortage of merchandise at many posts, including white blankets carried off by Native Americans, likely referring to point blankets: 'I beg you, my dear friend, to put everything in place to obtain many large, medium, and small white blankets and kettles to replenish the posts and especially for our Habitants and soldiers who do not have any.'[218]

Throughout the Seven Years War, blankets were issued to the officers and soldiers of the regular and colonial troops campaigning in Canada. One of these blankets was listed among the supplies provided to soldiers for the summer campaign of 1756,[219] while an undated inventory by Bourlamaque specifies that both soldiers and officers received blankets for the summer months, with those issued to officers valued at 9 livres.[220] Montcalm likewise noted that each man posted at Fort Saint-Jean in February 1757 was given one blanket estimated at 9 livres,[221] which was echoed by Bougainville in a separate report.[222]

When blankets were described in military-related records, they were regularly referred to as point blankets of the 2½-, 3-, 3½-, or 4-point sizes. In 1756, officers of the Régiment de Guyenne posted at Niagara were provided with a 3-point blanket valued at 12 livres, as well as those given to their domestiques esteemed at 8 livres, indicating that these high-ranking military men likely received point blankets of finer wool.[223] That same year, a testimony as part of a criminal trial held in Montréal revealed that a '2½-point blanket' as well as a 'small English tin canteen' was allegedly stolen from Charles Dagneau, a cadet in the colonial troops.[224] Lastly, a memoir published by Intendant Bigot, which contained a supply list of items issued to colonial officers, listed a '4-point wool blanket,' which was also said to have been provided to common soldiers, militiamen, and allied Native American warriors.[225]

Point blankets were also the most predominant type of blankets stockpiled at forts and frontier outposts in New France. At Fort Frontenac, two 4-point blankets valued at 10 livres apiece were set aside for the needs of the personnel and its garrison in 1702,[226] while at Fort Saint-Frédéric in 1739, ten 2-point blankets valued at 8 livres each were recorded for the fort's maintenance and personnel's needs.[227] The following year in Montréal, hundreds of point blankets of the 3-point and 4-point varieties were included on a statement of expenditures pertaining to the Chickasaw campaign.[228] At the dawn of King George's War, the following blankets were purchased from the King's storehouses in preparation for the conflict:

210 LAC, MG1-C11A, vol.86, f.211.
211 LAC, MG1-C11A, vol.86, f.225v.
212 LAC, MG1-C11A, vol.117, f.176v.
213 LAC, MG1-C11A, vol.117, f.202.
214 LAC, MG1-C11A, vol.117, f.196v.
215 LAC, MG1-C11A, vol.86, f.205v.
216 LAC, MG1-C11A, vol.117, f.208v.
217 LAC, MG1-C11A, vol.117, f.212.
218 ASQ, Viger-Verreau, P32/005/060.11, Papiers Paul Marin de la Malgue.

219 Centre d'histoire La Presqu'île, P03/F.089, Fonds De Beaujeu, 28 novembre 1756.
220 LAC, MG18, K9, vol.6, f.469–472.
221 Casgrain, *Collection des manuscrits du maréchal de Lévis*, pp.156–157.
222 De Bougainville, *Écrits sur le Canada*, p.168.
223 RAPQ, 1933–1934, pp.72, 77.
224 BAnQ-Q, TL5, D1858, Procès criminel contre Marie-Anne, sauvagesse montagnaise, pour vol, 9 septembre 1756–19 novembre 1756.
225 Bigot, *Mémoire Pour Messire François Bigo*, p.39.
226 LAC, MG1-C11A, f.260v.
227 LAC, MG1-C11A, vol.73, f.157.
228 LAC, MG1-C11A, vol.72, f.216v.

11 × 4-point blankets
16 × 3-point blankets
135 × 2½-point blankets
100 × 2-point blankets
174 × 2-point blankets[229]

A few years later, indispensable supplies needed for Fort Duquesne in 1755 included '3-point blankets' as well as '2½-point blankets,' the latter marked down as 'essential'[230] whereas at Fort Carillon two years later, a quantity of '229 2½-point blankets' were accounted for in the storehouses.[231]

Probate Records

Probate records relating to colonial officers reveal that these men personally owned a wide variety of blankets which may have been either bedroom-related items or intended for military service. For instance, an auction following the probate inventory of the officer Girard at Kaskaskia included a 'couverte poil de chien',[232] whereas the 1737 post-mortem inventory of the goods owned by Joseph Dejordy de Cabanac contained '1 white wool blanket and another of green wool'.[233]

By the 1740s, records show that point blankets were predominant among the personal goods owned by colonial officers serving in New France. In 1741, 'one 4-point blanket' belonging to *sergent* Charles Henry at Kaskaskia was handed over to Madame St-Ange for safekeeping,[234] while at Montréal, 'three 2-point blankets at 21 livres', 'two of 2-points at 12 livres' along with 'one fine 3-point blanket at 30 livres' were part of the personal possessions of Claude Michel Bégon, officer in the colonial troops.[235] The following year, the personal effects left behind after the death of Pierre Gaultier de La Vérendrye, *capitaine*, explorer and fur trader, included 'two 2½-point blankets'.[236] Paul Marin de La Malgue, Knight of the order of Saint-Louis and infantry *capitaine* in the colonial troops, however, owned a wide range of

blankets among which was 'one green Toulouse blanket, two blankets de ville and one said 2-point, all of which are very old…10 livres'.[237] Charles Decombre, a detached officer of the colonial troops, had left 'two white blankets, one of 4-point and the other from Toulouse', in addition to various belongings, with a widow named Marie Couture prior to his departure for Montréal in May of 1757.[238]

The Point System

The enduring misconception that the points signified the blanket's cost in beaver pelts is not supported by evidence. In fact, the point system was both a size and weight unit, ensuring that, notwithstanding the dimension of a blanket, this one would preserve the same wool density, in other words, its thermal insulation or warmth value. Although the blanket makers at Darnétal kept their regulations and weaving techniques highly confidential to protect their interests, clues to understanding the point system are revealed through the writings of an Italian industrial spy named Gian-Battista Moccafy, who visited Darnétal in the late 1760s:

> In Darnétal, there is also an infinite number of manufactories producing blankets called catalogne. These blankets are woven with very large yarns spun with wool as open as possible and strung in the same way as sheets. They are made of three qualities called fine, semi-fine and common. The widths are of five [points] and are marked with blue stripes. Each manufacturer establishes their own standard, which they submit to the inspector. Manufacturers have the freedom to start with any numbering system they choose. For example, whoever wants to identify the smallest with the number 1 in proportion is required to reach 5 without reducing the width intended for the first quality until the fifth. Supposing that the smallest coverage is given as number 1, the covers should be of the following [widths and lengths]:[239]

229 LAC, MG1-C11A, vol.117, f.83.

230 ASQ, Viger-Verreau, P32/002/164a, Papiers Contrecoeur.

231 LAC, MG18, K9, vol.6, f.459.

232 Kaskaskia Manuscripts, Randolph County Courthouse, Chester, Illinois, Vente après inventaire (Girard, officier des troupes à Kaskaskia), 23 juillet 1723.

233 BAnQ-Q, Greffe du notaire Charles René Gauchon de Chevremont, Inventaire des biens de feu Sieur Joseph Dejourdy de Cabanac, lieutenant d'une compagnie des troupes de ce pays, Montréal, 27 mars 1737.

234 Kaskaskia Manuscripts, Randolph County Courthouse, Chester, Illinois, État des hardes entres les mains Mme Saint-Ange, fort de Chartres, 4 mars 1741.

235 BAnQ-M, Greffe du notaire Danré de Blanzy, Inventaire de Claude Michel Bégon, gouverneur de Trois-Rivières, demeurant à Montréal… officier dans les troupes de la Marine, 19 août 1748.

236 BAnQ-M, TL4, S1, D5475, Apposition et levée des scellés sur les effets de feu Pierre Gauthier, sieur de LaVérandrye, capitaine, 7 décembre 1749–28 février 1750.

237 BAnQ-M, Greffe du notaire Danré de Blanzy, Feu Paul Lamarque (Lamalgue), Sieur Marin, chevalier de l'ordre militaire de Saint-Louis, capitaine d'infanterie, 2 janvier 1754.

238 BAnQ-Q, TL5, D1944. TL5, Procès de Charles Decombre (Porcheron dit Decombre), officier détaché des troupes de la Marine, contre Marie Couture, veuve de Simon Massy, 26 février 1758–28 mars 1759.

239 Corine Maitte, 'Les yeux dans la laine : la Normandie sous le regard italien Le voyage de Gian Batta Xaverio Moccafy'. La draperie en Normandie du XIIIe siècle au XXe siècle, édité par Alain Becchia, Presses universitaires de Rouen et du Havre, 2003, <https://doi.org/10.4000/books.purh.7238>.

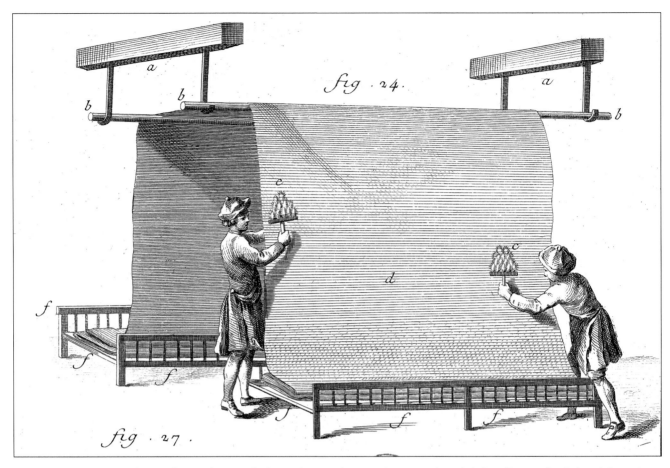

Two men working in a cloth manufacture showing the 'lainage' step in the manufacturing of wool cloth as illustrated in Diderot's Draperie.

Table 6. Blanket measurements.

No	Width	Length
1 point	1¾ *aune*	1¼ *aune*
2 points	2 *aunes*	1½ *aune*
3 points	2¼ *aunes*	1¾ *aune*
4 points	2½ *aunes*	2 *aunes*
5 points	2¾ *aunes*	2¼ *aunes*

Fundamentally, Moccafy revealed that a basic 1-point blanket measured 1¾ *aune* in width and 1¼ *aune* in length.. To add a point, one had to weave them a quarter of an *aune* on both sides of the blanket up to a maximum of 12 points.

Quality Grading

Besides the size and weight, they also came in three different grades of quality which played an important role in establishing their value: Fine, made from the best Spanish lamb's wool. They were lighter, softer and warmer and were called Catalogne, a term still in use today in Québec; Semi-fine, made from a mix of Normandy and Spanish wool; Common, made mainly of local wool.

The highest quality point blankets were known as Catalogne, named after Catalonia, a region in northeastern Spain, as they were made from carefully selected Spanish lamb's wool. Technically, they were woven (warp and weft) entirely of wool but had a serge weaving structure. Fine point blankets were occasionally requested for New France, with records showing that in 1753, Québecbased merchants purchased '100 fine 2½ [point] blankets' from their supplier in Rouen.[240] Some five years later, an invoice for goods loaded aboard a ship headed for Québec listed '100 3½-point blankets, fine and large, of the first quality of this type, at 9 livres apiece'.[241]

Blue or Black Stripes

Point blankets made at Darnétal were white and typically featured a three- to four-finger-wide light blue stripe, sometimes black, at both ends. The blue stripes were positioned widthwise, six to eight fingers from the edges. A memoir written by the Rouffio brothers of Québec in 1753 requested 500 2½-point blankets from Rouen from their suppliers in France while observing that '…the stripe

240 BAnQ-Q, P908, P9, Mémoire à accomplir par les frères Rouffio et Romagnac pour l'année 1753 relativement aux commandes de marchandises auprès de négociants de France et de Hollande, destinées à être envoyées au Québec… , 1752.
241 TNA, HCA, 32, vol.234, Le Saint-Pierre, 1758, Facture des marchandises ci-après chargée d'ordre et pour compte de Monsieur Goossens de Paris.

of these be of a very dark blue',[242] while 100 point blankets sent over to Canada aboard the ship Saint-Pierre on account of a man named Goossens of Paris in 1758 were described as '2½-point blankets with blue stripes'.[243] Two decades earlier, the merchandise required at the Tadoussac post in 1735 included 'Blankets from Rouen, one hundred 2-point blankets, with black stripes'.[244] indicating that these blankets also came with black stripes.

By the early 1760s, the popularity of Darnétal-made blankets was so significant that British traders offered them at frontier trading posts in the interior. In 1762, for instance, the Detroit trader James Sterling had specified a few of the trademark features found on a French point blanket to James Syme, victualling agent at Albany, which consisted of the width and colour of the stripes as well as a series of letters representing what was likely the blanket maker's markings along the inside of the stripe: 'The French Blankets which are very good and only want a row of capital letters ranging close along the inside of one of the stripes of each blanket, the stripes are also more commonly blue then Black but never ought to exceed a full inch or an inch and half in breadth.'[245]

A few years earlier, William Johnson, the British Indian commissioner who had very close ties to the Iroquois, had probably referenced French-made point blankets, which were said to be lettered as per those traded with the Natives in Canada: 'Pray let me know if there be a possibility of Sending me parcel of French Blankets, Kersey whale [wool] & lettered, such as the Send to Canada for the use of the Indians, also purple & white ratteen for Stocking Stuff ; all wh. they have better than ours — & also French Guns.'[246] One might wonder if a blanket, listed among items captured by British forces after the Battle of Lake George in 1755, could have been a lettered French point blanket: 'Capt. Burt hath a French gun, a blue great coat a blanket marked B. R. 3 shirts, 2 bags, 1 cutlass'.[247]

242 BAnQ-Q, P908, P9, Mémoire à accomplir par les frères Rouffio et Romagnac pour l'année 1753 relativement aux commandes de marchandises auprès de négociants de France et de Hollande, destinées à être envoyées au Québec... , 1752.
243 TNA, HCA, 32, vol.234, Le Saint-Pierre, 1758.
244 AR, 1E, 122, Mémoire des marchandises nécessaires pour l'exploitation de la traite de Tadoussac.
245 William L. Clements Library, The University of Michigan, James Sterling Letter Book – 1761–1765, p.61.
246 James Sullivan et al (eds), *The Papers of Sir William Johnson* (Albany, NY: The University of the State of New York, 1921), vol.1, pp.376-377.
247 James Russell Trumbull, *History of Northampton, Massachusetts, from Its Settlement in 1654* (Press of Gazette printing Company, 1902), vol.2, p.279.

Left An infantry soldier carries a campaign axe secured in a frog attached to a red leather carrying bag. This broad-axe, part of a set of tools used for fortification works, was among the essential equipment brought along by soldiers. The 5 October 1685 edicts applying to the five infantry companies at Montreal required that 10 campaign axes be present in each company versus the casse-tête, which was a personal weapon issued to each colonial soldier. (Courtesy Musée de la Marine, Paris. Joseph Vernet, La rade d'Antibes, Photo Kevin Gélinas)

Centre: Portrait of Pierre-François de Rigaud de Vaudreuil, a colonial officer and administrator whom Canadians called 'Monsieur de Rigaud.' In 1747, this officer detached La Corne Saint-Luc, *enseigne* in the colonial troops at the time, with about 200 men to Fort Saratoga, and as part of Rigaud de Vaudreuil's journal detailing the expedition, it is said that Monsieur de Saint-Luc '...charged them [the enemy] casse-tête in hand and challenged most of them.' (Portrait of François-Pierre de Rigaud de Vaudreuil. Between 1700 and 1800. Anonymous. Collection du Musée national des beaux-arts du Québec)

Right: Detail from a painting representing a camp of the Régiment royal du Roussillon during the War of Austrian Succession showing what appears to be a soldier holding a fixed-bladed knife in his hand. This regiment was present during the 1758 battle of Fort Carillon and was commanded by the Marquis de Montcalm. Metropolitan as well as colonial soldiers and officers alike would have been issued a fixed-blade boucheron knife and two Siamois folding knives as part of their standard campaign equipment. De Jambert, a *lieutenant* of the Régiment de Béarn stationed at Fort Carillon was recorded as having 'one boucheron knife' as part of his personal possessions in 1758. (Fort Ticonderoga Museum collection, New York)

Well preserved knife found as part of a quantity of 76 facetted and rounded boxwood knife-handle-halves, bearing two pins at the front and one at the back, corresponding to those of the boucheron type. These were recovered at the bottom of the French River in Ontario in the 1960s and are presumed to be French goods from overturned canoes. This type of knife would be identical to what would have been issued to colonial soldiers. (With permission of the Royal Ontario Museum © ROM)

Presumed Boucheron knife found at the Place Royale in Quebec City, bearing the mark 'ANTOINE/DVCHON' a cutler at Saint-Étienne, France. (Courtesy of the Ministère de la Culture, des Communications et de la Condition féminine du Québec, Laboratoire et Réserve d'archéologie du Québec. Photo Kevin Gélinas)

Presumed French Boucheron knife with a largely intact wooden handle, found at the Parade Ground in front of the East Barracks at Fort Ticonderoga. (Collection of the Fort Ticonderoga Museum, New York)

One-pin folding knife found at Fort Beauséjour in present day New Brunswick, Canada. This rare, excavated knife found in a 1750–1751 context, retains its handle (with a missing tip) and blade fragments (Courtesy of National Historic Sites, Parks Canada. Photo Phil Dunning)

Eighteenth century French jambette with a boxwood handle bearing the mark of Eustache Dubois stamped 'EUSTACHE.DUBOIS' on one side and 'VERITABLE' (Genuine) on the other. Deceased in 1721 at Saint-Étienne, his son continued to use his father's trademark. Even today, this cutler's name is still synonymous in France with common folding knives. In 1754, Jean-Louis Fremont, a reseller at Québec, had 'six 2-pin Eustache Dubois knives' valued at 2 livres 12 sols.* (Musé national du Moyen Âge – Thermes de Cluny, Paris, France. Photo: René-Gabriel Ojéda. @RMN-Grand Palais/Art Resource, NY)
* BAnQ-Q, Greffe du notaire Claude Barolet, Inventaire des biens de la communauté du Sieur Jean-Louis Fremont, 29 novembre, 1754.

An excavated knife with an intact handle found at Fort Ticonderoga, likely representing a rare Siamois knife with a pointed blade. The handle bears the stamp of ANDRE BRENON, a cutler from Saint-Étienne, France. The Bizallion variety of these knives, popular among colonists and voyageurs, was of higher quality and often stamped 'VÉRITABLE BIZALLION' to distinguish it from imitations. Merchant invoices from 1740 describe Siamois knives with yellow handles (boxwood) as either 'genuine' or 'in the style of Bizallion,' indicating that imitations were common. This knife may be one such imitation. (Collection of the Fort Ticonderoga Museum, New York)

Left and above: Rare surviving c.1720–1750 'Dog Head' siamois knife with its original horn handle (couteau Siamois à tête de chien). These knives, recorded with horn handles, had a dog head decorative ornament on the handle's tip which was likely created by a design located in the cavity of certain knife handle presses at the factory in Saint-Étienne, France. The detail on the left displays the tip of this handle where one can see the head of what appears to be a dog, the nose of which may have been broken or altered at some point in its lifetime. (Private collection)

Leather pouch containing two well-preserved wood combs excavated from the wreckage of the La Belle, one of four ships in a 1684 expedition led by the French explorer Robert Cavelier, Sieur de La Salle, that sank off the coast of Texas in 1686. (James E. Bruseth, Amy A. Borgens, Bradfort M. Jones, Eric D. Ray, *La Belle: The Archaeology of a Seventeenth-Century Ship of New World Colonization*, Texas A&M University Press). (Photo by the Conservation Research Laboratory, Texas A&M University)

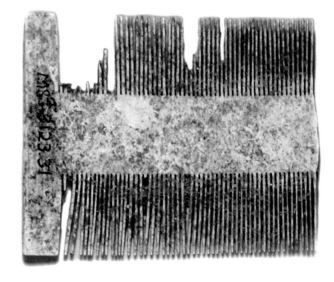

Petit calumet made of black stone found at Fort Ticonderoga, similar to the one found at Fort Senneville. It is possible that this style of pipe is attributed to Étienne Gibeau. According to Marie Gérin-Lajoie, the Montreal merchant Monière frequently sold, or at least supplied the wooden stems for petits calumets, as recorded in his invoices. He equipped many voyageurs with calumets 'made by Gibeau.' Étienne Gibeau, a woodworker whom Monière sometimes referred to as a 'sculpteur,' likely carved both the stems and bowls of these pipes. (Fort Ticonderoga Museum collection, New York)

Fragment of a bone or boxwood comb excavated at Fort Michilimackinac and of the à deux côtés (two sided) type as per Savary. (Mackinac State Historic Parks collection, Michigan. Photo Kevin Gélinas)

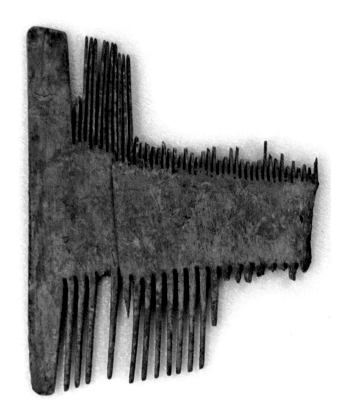

Comb fragment of the two-sided type unearthed at Fort de Chartres. (Courtesy of the Illinois Historic Preservation Division. Photo Kevin Gélinas)

Noël Hallé's Une savoyarde (1757) showing at the rear what could be a French point blanket depicted with a light blue end stripe. Take note of the artists signature 'HALEE' in large capital letters alongside '1757' placed along the stripe, which may have simulated Darnétal's blanket maker's markings found on the legitimate point-blankets. (Creative Commons)

Left: Horn comb found on the wreck of the ship Le Machault sunk in 1760 near the Restigouche River. (Courtesy of National Historic Sites, Parks Canada. Photo Kevin Gélinas)

Detail from Vue du port de Rochefort, prise du Magasin des Colonies by Joseph Vernet (1762) showing several men on the docks of the port of Rochefort inspecting blankets which have a set of blue end-stripes. (Musée national de la Marine, Paris. Photo Kevin Gélinas)

La Piété filiale by Jean-Baptiste Greuze, 1763. This particular scene shows an aged man surrounded and cared for by his family. The blanket laid out at his feet displays a single end stripe with what appears to be lettering on the inside of the end-stripe near the child's shoe. (Creative Commons)

Detail of a Native child wearing a white wool trade blanket with a blue stripe. (A Plan of the Inhabited Part of the Province of Quebec, James Peachey, 1785. (Creative Commons)

3

Winter Campaign Equipment of the Colonial Troops

Colonial troops in Canada quickly adopted Indigenous methods of warfare during winter campaigns, incorporating elements of Native American dress and mobility, such as snowshoes and toboggans. By mastering the use of snowshoes, French colonists and soldiers gained the ability to launch winter offensives against their enemies, recognising, as Antoine-Denis Raudot noted around 1710, that 'it was necessary to adopt the ways of the Natives to be able to fight alongside them and subdue them, in order to live peacefully. War here is different from in Europe… If these [war] parties take place in winter, we must wear moccasins and snowshoes to walk on the snow.'[1]

The equipment required to undertake such tactical winter expeditions was quite different from what was issued during summer campaigns and usually consisted of several specialised items. Malartic, an officer in the regular troops, meticulously documented the specific supplies allocated to each officer and soldier during the winter campaigns in Canada during the Seven Years War:

> We have for winter equipment, above what we receive during summer, two pairs of wool slippers, a pair of mittens, a vest, nippes [pieces of woollen cloth to place in the shoes], a deerskin to make shoes, a tumpline for pulling, a toboggan on which each man places his provisions, his luggage, a pair of snowshoes, and a sealskin to cover everything.[2]

Bougainville, Montcalm's aide-de-camp, had noted that this equipment was termed Apichimon by the colonists living in Canada, 'Apichimon, a Native term used in the French language among Canadians to designate winter equipment, where we additionally have a bear skin, a sealskin, snowshoes, a toboggan, a tumpline, mittens, etc.'[3]

This winter gear was generally stockpiled in the King's storehouses at Montréal and Québec, whereas various items were purchased directly from domiciled Native American nations living in the St Lawrence Valley. Jean-Victor Varin de La Marre, commissary and controller of the Marine at Québec who had published a memoir as part of his defence in the 'Affaire du Canada', remarked that the equipment provided to the soldiers were 'snowshoes, toboggans and tumplines and other things of this kind, that one purchases from the Natives.'[4]

Winter Campaign Equipment

By adopting articles of Native origin such as snowshoes and toboggans, the French colonists and soldiers widened their range of action during the winter season, going as far as carrying out winter assaults against distant enemies. This type of approach was first employed by the French in January of 1666 when Governor Courcelle set off with some 1,300 men who marched on snowshoes to invade the Mohawk country in midwinter. The Canadian Rene-Louis Chartier de Lotbiniere, who had left a burlesque poem recounting this expedition, remarked that the men used both toboggans and snowshoes: 'On toboggans everyone is fastened… But not without putting on a snowshoe.'[5] Some 20 years later, '50 dog-pulled toboggans' as well as '50 pairs of snowshoes to walk on the snow' were provided to the colonial soldiers and Canadians who accompanied Pierre de Troyes on an overland expedition from Montréal to James Bay.[6]

Following the Lachine massacre in 1689 and the siege of Québec in 1690, Governor Frontenac increased the number of winter raids and in a very short time formed three winter expeditions against Salmon Falls, Casco and then against Schenectady. A war party composed of 600 raiders, which included a contingent of colonial soldiers under the command of Mantet, Courtemanche and La

1   LAC, MG1-C11A, vol.122, f.154–158.
2   Anne-Joseph-Hippolyte de Maurès comte de Malartic, *Journal des campagnes au Canada de 1755 à 1760* (Dijon: L. Damidot, 1890), p.95.
3   De Bougainville, *Écrits sur le Canad*, pp.92–93.

4   Anon., *À Monseigneur de Sartine*, pp.17–18.
5   BAnQ-Q, P1000, S3, D2730, Photostat au sujet du voyage de M. de Courcelles (1666). 'Vers burlesques sur la Campagne du gouverneur de Courcelles contre les Iroquois' en 1666. p.4.
6   LAC, MG1-C11A, vol.8, f.274.

Winter raiding party composed of three colonial soldiers led by an officer. (Francis Back © Raphaëlle et Félix Back)

Noue, left La Prairie near Montréal to attack a Mohawk village in January of 1693. Bacqueville de La Potherie details the methods of winter warfare at this time, notably mentioning the arduous journey through forests, the use of snowshoes, and sleeping on the snow: 'Our French cut across the land to Lake Chambly while the Native Americans hunted along the way, as it is customary to do so when going to war. We had to travel through forests, using snowshoes, sleeping on the snow, each carrying his war ammunition and rations.'[7] A few years later, in

the winter of 1696, the colonial officer Jacques Testard de Montigny and a group of Canadians crafted snowshoes in preparation for their attack on the English coastal area of Newfoundland, where, as Father Beaudoin observed, '… nobody comes out on this island [Newfoundland] without using snowshoes.'[8]

The use of snowshoes often gave French forces a significant military advantage, as many English colonists and some Native nations were unfamiliar with them, allowing the French to adopt Native methods of warfare

---

7   Claude Charles Le Roy Bacqueville de la Potherie, *Histoire de l'Amerique Septentrionale* (Paris: Chez Nyon fils, 1753), vol.1, p.320.

8   Jean Beaudoin, *Journal de l'expédition de d'Iberville en Acadie et à Terre-Neuve…* (Évreux : Imprimerie de l'Eure, 1900), p.39.

Drawing by Jesuit Claude Chauchetière in 1682 depicting the Saint-François-Xavier Mission at the Sault St Louis, near Montreal. Entitled 'The six first Natives from La Prairie come from d'Onneiout on the snow and ice', the illustration shows the teardrop-shaped snowshoes and their attachment method. The Native at the centre carries a bedroll using a tumpline decorated with zigzag motifs. (Les Archives de la Gironde, France)

on snow-covered ground, surprise the enemy, and retreat before a counterattack. In February 1704, following the attack on the town of Deerfield (Massachusetts) led by Canadian officer Hertel de Rouville and his men, who had travelled on snowshoes from Montréal, the New England militia from nearby villages attempted to pursue the assailants but failed due to their lack of snowshoes. According to Samuel Patridge, a lieutenant colonel in the militia, 'the snow being at least 3 feet deep and impassible without snowshoes (which we had no supply of)'.[9]

In the winter of 1732, snowshoes provided a significant advantage in winter warfare for a group of Hurons and Iroquois led by colonial officer Paul-Joseph Lemoyne de Longueuil during their attack on the Fox nation: '…it was easier to destroy them because the latter [Fox] were not accustomed to using snowshoes, nor were they as skilled in using them as the Hurons and the Iroquois. Our warriors had a considerable advantage over them'.[10]

Throughout King George's War, pelts, snowshoes, tumplines and toboggans were generally issued to soldiers, cadets and officers alike as part of winter expeditions or detachments. In 1745, a statement of supplies distributed to a war party sent out from Québec to Louisbourg under the command of the officer Marin de La Malgue included '62 tumplines for toboggans', '195 pairs of snowshoes', '360 sealskins', '32 bearskins' as well as '150 toboggans' as well as '4 dogs, for toboggans'.[11] Two years later, the Chevalier de Niverville and three cadets, taking part in a war party set out to attack New England, were each supplied with the usual winter campaign gear which included a tumpline, a bearskin, snowshoes and a toboggan.[12]

Colonial officers and soldiers detached to a fort or outpost in the winter months were generally issued the whole or a portion of this equipment. The colonial officer Le Mercier, detached to garrison at Fort Saint-Frédéric in January of 1747, was issued a complete winter outfit consisting of a bearskin, a sealskin, a pair of snowshoes, a toboggan and a tumpline amongst other articles,[13] while the same year, a number of soldiers detached to quarters at Saint-Thérèse and Fort Châteauguay, were each provided with a bearskin and a tumpline.[14] The following month, a detachment consisting of three officers who were to leave for the upper countries were issued a total of '6 tumplines', '3 wood splint toboggans', as well as '4 pairs of snowshoes, including 2 pairs for M. de La Corne' indicating that the

This engraving by Bacqueville de La Potherie represents a Canadian militiaman or soldier heading off to war with snowshoes. Despite its naive style, the illustration highlights the crucial role snowshoes played during winter campaigns. (Claude-Charles Le Roy Bacqueville de La Potherie, *Histoire de l'Amérique Septentrionale*, 1722. Canadiens en raquette allant en guerre sur la neige, Creative commons)

commanding officer was allocated an additional pair of snowshoes.[15]

By the Seven Years War, snowshoes, toboggans, and tumplines were standard issue for every colonial and regular officer and soldier, appearing in official equipment lists compiled by French officers. In 1757, Bougainville takes note that for winter war parties, soldiers were issued two tumplines, one pair of snowshoes and one toboggan,[16] while other supply lists prior to 1757 reference but one tumpline per soldier or officer. A declaration by two French prisoners taken in March 1757 at Fort William-Henry offers solid evidence of the winter equipment issued to every soldier, which reportedly included: '…one fine blanket, and every man in the army had a bear skin … one pair of Snow Shoes, a pair of Iron Creepers to walk on the Ice… Each man was provided with a hand sleys [toboggan] and a strong rope [tumpline] to draw by it.'[17]

9   Evan Haefeli, Kevin Sweeney, *Captive Histories: English, French, and Native Narratives of the 1704 Deerfield Raid* (Amherst and Boston: University of Massachusetts Press, 2006), p.66.
10   LAC, MG1-C11A, vol.57, f.321.
11   LAC, MG1-C11A, vol.84, f.148–150.
12   LAC, MG1-C11A, vol.117, f.192–192v.
13   LAC, MG1-C11A, vol.88, f.214–214v.
14   LAC, MG1-C11A, vol.117, f.205v, 206v.

15   LAC, MG1-C11A, vol.117, f.176v-177.
16   De Bougainville, *Écrits sur le Canada*, p.168.
17   LOC, Colonial Office 5 folio 47, E. of Loudoun's Letter of April 25th. 1757, Declaration of two Prisoners taken the 23.d March

The use of snowshoes and toboggans was undeniably essential for large-scale wilderness winter campaigns. For example, the March 1756 expedition against Fort Bull, led by colonial officer Chaussegros de Léry and comprising forces from colonial and regular troops, Canadian militia, and Native allies, required numerous toboggans to transport vital supplies. Some of these hand-pulled sleds were large enough to carry a birchbark canoe, as noted in a letter to Léry in which Montcalm mentioned sending him a few Canadians 'armed with traînes d'éclisses (wood splint toboggans), to pull the boats and the provisions on the ice.'[18]

In January of the following year, a small contingent led by M. de Rouilly, using toboggans to retrieve supplies at Fort Saint-Frédéric, was ambushed by British forces, resulting in seven Frenchmen being captured, prompting a detachment of 100 soldiers, Canadians, and Native Americans to pursue the British retreat and rescue the prisoners, with Malartic remarking, 'they would have not been able to save a single one had it not been for our soldiers that had snowshoes which would have prevented them from sinking in the snow'.[19] A few weeks later, a winter expedition sent out to weaken British Fort William Henry consisting of grenadiers, Canadians, Native Americans and colonial soldiers, was said to be equipped with snowshoes, toboggans and dogs: 'This detachment has sixty lieues to cover with snowshoes on their feet, with provisions on toboggans that we can, on good trails, have them pulled by dogs, sleeping in the middle of the snow, on bearskins, with a simple sail that serves as shelter against the wind.'[20]

While preparing to reclaim Québec in the winter of 1760, an anonymous letter outlined the logistical requirements for a potential retreat in winter conditions: 'About fifty toboggans arranged to retreat promptly by placing them side by side; enough snowshoes to be able to distribute at least ten pairs to each picket of troops, a greater number to the Canadiens and a pair to each Native'.[21] During this campaign, officer Jean-Baptiste d'Aleyrac noted the harsh conditions, remarking that he had to keep his snowshoes on even while at camp: 'I had to spend every night in the bivouac shelter in the snow with snowshoes strapped to my feet...'[22]

Snowshoes (Raquettes)

Native snowshoes, paired with deerskin moccasins, were a crucial part of Canadian winter campaign gear, enabling wearers to traverse deep snow without sinking, a necessity highlighted by an officer of the Régiment de la Sarre stationed in Canada, 'for the snow, a pair of snowshoes that are tied to our feet so as not to sink.'[23] A number of European accounts (for example, Jacques Cartier, Frère André Thevet, or Samuel de Champlain) stretching back to the sixteenth century up to the Seven Years War, go into great detail as far as describing the distinctive traditional snowshoe models in use by the Native Americans living North America.

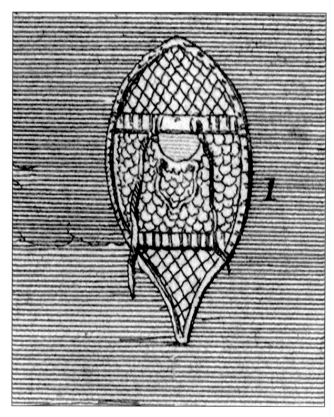

Teardrop-shaped snowshoe with a short tail, illustrated in Joseph-François Lafitau's 1724 edition of *Moeurs des sauvages Ameriquains*. According to Lafitau, 'In the snow where there is no cleared path, Natives are required to use snowshoes; otherwise, all travel, whether for war or hunting, would be impossible. The longer ones measure 2½ *pieds* in length and 1½ *pied* wide. The frame is composed of fire-hardened wood and pierced around its circumference, resembling the rackets of our game of paulme.'

By 1626, the *Relations des Jésuites* mentioned that Frenchmen had by now adopted the use of snowshoes, 'even our French told me, that they had dragged a tree on the snow ... using snowshoes; for it is the custom in this country to walk on snowshoes during winter for fear of

1757 at Fort Wm. Henry, Information of John Victor and Guillaume Chasse, two French Prisoners, Fort William Henry March 25th.

18   RAPQ,1926–1927, pp.374–375.

19   De Malartic, *Journal des campagnes au Canada de 1755 à 1760*, pp.93–94.

20   Casgrain, *Collection des manuscrits du maréchal de Lévis, Relations et journaux de différentes expéditions faites durant les années 1755–56–57–58–59–60* (Québec: Imprimerie de L.-J. Demers & Frère, 1895), vol.9, p.74.

21   Casgrain, *Collection des manuscrits du maréchal de Lévis*, pp.188–189.

22   BAnQ-M, ZF8, Fonds Jean Baptiste d'Aleyrac.

23   R. Douville, 'Le Canada 1756–1758, vu par un officier du régiment de La Sarre', *Les Cahiers des Dix*, 24 (1959), p.116.

Detail from a plate by Lafitau showing snow travel. Three Natives at the front pull their supplies on toboggans, while those at the rear carry bundles using tumplines. This image is fantasy-based in the way the natives are dressed, reflecting a stylized or imaginative representation of Indigenous peoples as seen by European illustrators, particularly in their clothing and snowshoes.

sinking in the snow, in imitation of the Natives who do not otherwise go moose hunting without them.'[24] Eighteen years later, Marie de l'Incarnation noted that French colonists living in the St Lawrence Valley used snowshoes and moose-hide moccasins for winter travel: 'The French do not wear others [shoes] in winter, because one cannot go out to walk on the snow without snowshoes, and for that reason we cannot use French shoes.'[25] Snowshoes intended for military use are documented as early as the 1660s in Canada, with René-Louis Chartier de Lotbinière, who participated in the Carignan-Salières regiment's expedition into Iroquois territory in January 1666, describes the snowshoes worn by the men, 'which is a shoe that the French as well as the Natives use to walk on the snow. They are made like string rackets to play paulme (tennis). We must have moccasins, made like skin slippers on our feet, to attach them. They are not made of string, but small strips of moose leather.'[26]

A report on the 1704 raid on Deerfield, published in the 1705 edition of le Mercure Galant, notes that snowshoes used in Canada came in various sizes, suggesting either regional differences or variations in length tailored to the user's proportions: 'There are many sizes in Canada, and according to the people, they are commonly 2 *pieds* long and 1 *pied* wide. The wood frame that holds the webbing is quite thick having one or 2 *pouces*, depending on the size of the snowshoes. The webbing is in a triangular figure, made of strips of moose skins, but cut very gently. The Natives quite often paint these snowshoes in red or green.'[27]

On the other hand, an anonymous letter written around 1720, highlighting the bravery and endurance of Canadians as well as the way in which winter war parties were conducted, reveals that snowshoes in Canada could be quite lengthy: 'The snowshoes are about 3 and a half *pieds* long and 15 to 16 *pouces* wide. They decrease by the two extremities of which one is round and the other ending in a point. They have a wood frame all around, in which there are two bars at about four *pouces* from each end and are tied around using small strips of hide about two *lignes* wide. They are tied to his feet with strips of hide.'[28] The French Jesuit priest, Pierre François Xavier de Charlevoix corroborates that raquettes could be as long as 3 *pieds* as he notes that these '…measure about 3 *pieds* long and 15 or 16 *pouces* in their greatest width. They are oval in shape, except that the back-end finishes in a point.'[29]

24 *Relations des Jésuites contenant ce qui s'est passé de plus remarquable dans les missions des pères de la Compagnie de Jésus dans la Nouvelle-France* (Québec: Augustin Coté, 1858), vol.1, p.2.

25 L'Abbé Léon Chapot, *Histoire de la vénérable mère Marie de l'incarnation: première supérieure du Monastère des Ursulines de Québec d'après Dom Claude Martin ; ouvrage entièrement remanié, complété a l'aide de plusieurs autres historiens et documents et précédé d'une introduction générale par L'Abbé Léon Chapot* (Paris: Librairie Ch. Poussielgue, 1892), vol.1, p.409.

26 BAnQ-Q, P1000, S3, D2730, Photostat au sujet du voyage de M. de Courcelles (1666). 'Vers burlesques sur la Campagne du gouverneur de Courcelles contre les Iroquois' en 1666, p.1.

27 *Le Mercure Galant* (Paris: Chez Michel Brunet, 1705), pp.20–21.

28 LAC, MG1-C11A, vol.22, f.157–157v.

29 Pierre-François-Xavier de Charlevoix, *Histoire et description generale de la Nouvelle France: avec le Journal historique d'un voyage fait par ordre du roi dans l'Amérique Septentrionnale* (Paris: Chez Pierre-François Giffart, 1744), vol.5, p.326.

An ice skate blade found at Fort Ticonderoga. Colonial accounts highlight the importance of skating during winter campaigns. Storekeeper Joseph-Charles Bonin noted that skilled skaters could pull up to eight toboggans carrying men across frozen Lake Ontario. Officer D'Aleyrac also attempted skating near Fort Carillon in the winter of 1755–1756 but abandoned it after a near-fatal fall through the ice on the Carillon River. (Collection of the Fort Ticonderoga Museum, New York)

By the 1750s, journals and accounts by military officials in Canada often described snowshoes worn by certain Native nations, which may have been similar to those issued to troops on winter expeditions. Joseph-Charles Bonin dit Jolicoeur, a soldier in the Canonniers-Bombardiers in Canada and later a storekeeper at Fort Duquesne, also provided physical descriptions, 'snowshoes are made in the way of flattened pears…18 to 20 *pouces* in length, about 15 in breadth. They are tied to the feet using straps like skates.'[30] *Capitaine* Pierre Pouchot, stationed at Fort Niagara from 1755 to 1760, references much longer snowshoes worn by the Native Americans of Canada which are said to be, '…4 to 5 *pieds* long, and about 2 *pieds* in their widest section'.[31]

Snowshoes for Compacting Trails

Various accounts reveal the usefulness of snowshoes to hard-pack snow trails therefore allowing the men at the rear of a column to walk on the hard-packed trails using only common shoes. An early eighteenth-century primary source account entitled 'The way war is waged during the winter against the enemy nations', explains the manner in which this practice was carried out:

> We acquired the usage of snowshoes, and the moccasins, from the peoples of this continent and there are sufficient good 'snowshoers' to cover in one day 15 and 20 *lieues* in these crews, and packing the snow so strongly that it becomes so hard in places where many pass that when the party is made up of more than 40 men, the others need not use snowshoes and simply walk along in their moccasins.[32]

In January of 1760, a report relating to the offensives planned against British posts in front of Québec included snow-packing manoeuvres performed by soldiers on snowshoes placed at the head of the columns highlighting the need to adapt traditional European war tactics to the challenges of snow-covered battlefields in New France : 'The ground, covered with three or four *pieds* of snow, prevents us from marching in battle formation; it is maybe only by marching in a column, the soldiers at the head of the columns having snowshoes to pack and consolidate the snow'.[33]

Snowshoes: A Multipurpose Implement

Snowshoes also served as a versatile tool, occasionally doubling as a snow shovel when setting up camp on snow-covered ground. As early as 1633, the Jesuit Paul Lejeune observed that, when setting up camp, 'everyone undoes their snowshoes which they use as a shovel to clear the snow from the area where they want to sleep',[34] while another period account of a winter expedition describes the process similarly: 'We first camp at dusk after having chosen a site, some by removing the snow or using their snowshoes like a shovel'.[35]

Desertions

Following an expedition, snowshoes were at times required to be returned to the King's depots to circumvent desertions. An unsigned letter addressed to Lévis in January of 1759 raises the issue of French soldiers deserting in winter by means of snowshoes while requiring that strict control be exerted as to the distribution and obtainability of this type of footwear: 'Please recommend to d'Hébécourt that, if he sends soldiers from his garrison on war parties with snowshoes, that he should return them in the storehouses, let it be seen that the Natives do not give nor sell them any; this can facilitate desertion.'[36]

30   Henri Raymond Casgrain, *Voyage au Canada: dans le nord de l'Amérique septentrionale: fait depuis l'an 1751 à 1761 / par J. C. B.* (Québec: Imprimerie Léger Brousseau, 1887), pp.76–77.
31   Pouchot, *Mémoires sur la dernière guerre de l'Amérique septentrionale*, p.280.
32   LAC, MG1-C11A, vol.122, f.155–155v.

33   Casgrain, *Collection des manuscrits du maréchal de Lévis*, p.199.
34   *Relations des Jésuites: contenant ce qui s'est passé de plus remarquable dans les missions des pères de la Compagnie de Jésus dans la Nouvelle-France* (Québec: Augustin Coté, éditeur-imprimeur,1858), p.130.
35   LAC, MG1-C11A, vol.122, f.156.
36   Henri-Raymond Casgrain, *Collection des manuscrits du maréchal de Lévis, Lettres du marquis de Montcalm au chevalier de Lévis* (Québec: Imprimerie de L.-J. Demers & Frère, 1894), p.145.

Manufacturing Source of Snowshoes

In the early years, private merchants appear to have acted as intermediaries in supplying snowshoes for expeditions. For instance, the expenses incurred for the 'war against the Iroquois' in 1688 included snowshoes, deerskin moccasins and other merchandise supplied by François Hazeur, a prominent Québec merchant and entrepreneur,[37] which probably meant that these snowshoes would have been purchased from Native villages in proximity to Québec such as the Hurons or Innus.[38] These snowshoes were likely sourced from nearby Native villages, such as those of the Hurons or Innus, given their proximity to Québec.

By King George's War, snowshoes were purchased in sizeable quantities and stocked up in the King's storehouses in the event of an enemy attack or to outfit a winter expedition. This practice was well documented according to Jean-Baptiste Martel, écuyer, storekeeper, and inspector of the King's storehouses at Montréal, who outlined the practice of price fixing for snowshoes based on supply and demand, 'when suddenly there is a proposed plan to send a detachment of 3,000 or 4,000 men, and hold Sieur Lemoine [storekeeper at Montréal] or any other responsible to have 4,000 pairs of snowshoes made and to have them ready in three months, the time which is set for the departure of the troops'.[39] In preparation for war, 565 pairs of snowshoes priced at 4 livres 14 sols each were purchased from private merchants at Québec in 1744,[40] with an additional 600 pairs acquired at Montréal.[41] Some three years later, 1,143 pairs of snowshoes valued at 8 livres were stocked up in the King's storehouses at Montréal,[42] in addition to another 586 pairs that were on hand in the storehouses at Québec.[43] Evidently, these numbers, and their prices, fluctuated over the years while many were redistributed to frontier forts or outposts. For example, five pairs of snowshoes were itemised at Fort Frontenac in 1702,[44] while in 1748, '159 pairs of snowshoes, where 96 are unserviceable' were inventoried at Fort Saint-Frédéric.[45] Nine years later, '84 pairs of snowshoes, a portion unserviceable' were stored away in the storehouses at Fort Carillon.[46]

According to official government records, snowshoes supplied to French forces during the final two decades of the French regime were primarily sourced from the Hurons at the mission village of Lorette near Québec, the Iroquois of the Sault Saint-Louis mission near Montréal, or the Native nations at the Lac-des-Deux-Montagnes mission, a village predominantly inhabited by Iroquois, Algonquins, and Nipissings. Therefore, snowshoe styles may have varied from one mission or village to another, reflecting regional preferences and techniques in their construction. For instance, the post-mortem inventory of the personal belongings of Étienne Banchaud at Montréal in 1669 listed '6 pairs of snowshoes, knowingly, 4 pairs à l'Algonquienne' (in the Algonquin style) and the others 'à l'Iroquoise' (in the Iroquois style), highlighting that snowshoes crafted by different Native Nations exhibited distinct physical characteristics, such as variations in webbing style, frame profile, length, construction methods, and materials used. The Hurons of Lorette were the main suppliers of snowshoes in Québec, as shown in a 1747 war supply invoice detailing 245 pairs purchased directly from des Sauvages Hurons de Lorette (Huron Natives from Lorette) at a price of 8 livres per pair. These included snowshoes supplied or made by the Hurons named Thomas Sauvage and André Sauvage.[47] Those generally purchased near Montréal came from the Sault Saint-Louis or Lac-des-Deux-Montagnes missions. Storekeeper Martel, for instance, took note that the Natives of the Sault Saint-Louis village had made a large number of snowshoes for the King's storehouses at Montréal, 'I am a witness that Sieur Lemoine had snowshoes made by the Sault Saint-Louis Natives which came to 9 livres a pair, although he supplies them with cow and deerskin hides, and yet these snowshoes were only paid 9 livres 10 sols.[48] In 1744, the Jesuit Jean-Baptiste Tournois, superior of the Sault Saint-Louis mission, was paid 6 livres 13 sols 7 denier per pair of snowshoes for a total of 312 pairs which he supplied to the King,[49] while that same year, l'Abbé Piquet, a Sulpician priest who served from 1739 to 1749 at the Lac-des-Deux-Montagnes mission, had supplied another 196 pairs priced at 7 livres 8 sols apiece.[50] Storekeeper certificates from the late 1750s reveal that snowshoes in Acadia, generally priced at 20 livres each, were sourced from both colonists and Native Americans, such as Michel Lanoux, who earned 80 livres for four pairs, and Pabrouette Sauvage of Miramichi, who received 20 livres for a single pair of raquettes.[51]

37   LAC, MG1-C11A, vol.10, f.130v, État de la dépense faite en l'année 1688 jusqu'au premier novembre au sujet de la guerre contre les Iroquois, 1 November 1688.

38   LAC, MG1-C11A, vol.10, f.130v.

39   Martel, *Mémoire pour Jean-Baptiste Martel*, pp.14–15.

40   LAC, MG1-C11A, vol.82, f.187–187v.

41   LAC, MG1-C11A, vol.82, f.186–186v.

42   LAC, MG1-C11A, vol.89, f.37.

43   LAC, MG1-C11A, vol.89, f.45v.

44   LAC, MG1-C11A, vol.20, f.262.

45   LAC, MG1-C11A, vol.92, f.38.

46   LAC, MG18, K9, vol.6, f.461.

47   LAC, MG1-C11A, vol.117, f.96, 96v, 101v, 102, 103v.

48   Martel, *Mémoire pour Jean-Baptiste Martel*, pp.14–15.

49   LAC, MG1-C11A, vol.115, f.181v.

50   LAC, MG1-C11A, vol.115, f.181v.

51   LAC, Archives de la marine, G.239, Colonies, Arrêts relatifs à la liquidation des dettes du Canada, 1767, Pièces numéro 8, 20 et 49.

Two members of the Chevalier De Troyes expedition of 1686 dressed 'à la canadienne'. The soldier in the foreground is distinguished by his waist belt, powder flask, and ammunition pouch. (Drawing by Francis Back. © Raphaëlle & Félix Back)

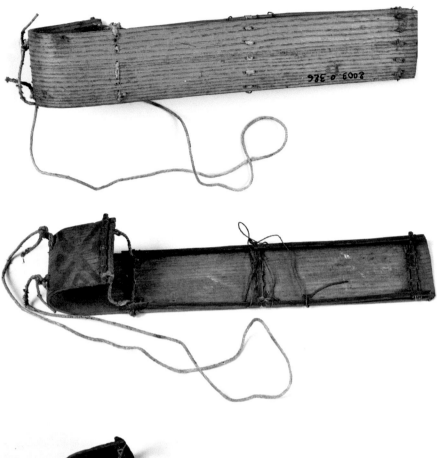

Detail from a c. 1780 watercolour by an unknown German artist, showing a Canadian wearing snowshoes in winter. French colonists in the Saint-Lawrence Valley had already adopted the use of snowshoes by the 1640s. (With permission of the Royal Ontario Museum © ROM)

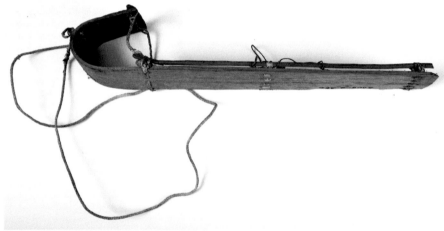

A miniature toboggan c. 1750–1800, shown from top, bottom, and side views. This rare surviving example of an early Huron toboggan provides detailed insights into its construction and design. (Courtesy of the Musée des beaux-arts de Chartres)

This Kanienkehaka (Mohawk) prisoner halter, circa 1746, closely resembles a tumpline, with its woven strap and decorative design. Discovered after the Bars Fight in Deerfield, Massachusetts, during King George's War, it was likely used to restrain prisoners by tying it around their necks, with individuals holding each end. (Courtesy Pocumtuck Valley Memorial Association's Memorial Hall Museum, Deerfield, MA)

Toboggans (Traînes Sauvages or Traînes de Clisses)

The toboggan, termed traîne sauvage (Native sled) or traîne d'éclisses (splint sled) in French, corresponded to a simple wood sled made of bound, parallel wood slats, bent up at the front, which was a traditional form of transport used by the Native Americans nations of Canada. This ingenious vehicle was used for dragging people, provisions, or heavier pieces of gear over snow and ice and was drawn by people or dogs. An early eighteenth-century account offers valuable insight into how toboggans were utilised in winter warfare against enemy Native nations and is worth citing here:

> The rations that one carries in these trips consists of grounded corn (it is the one that we call blé de Turquie in France) and which is the main food, a little fat or lard with a small bottle of eau-de-vie in his pocket. In addition, you must carry your fusil, a small axe, a blanket to wrap oneself during the night, and a little kettle; those who do not want to carry everything, place all of these things on a toboggan which they pull. It is made of wooden splints so that it glides easier on the snow, measuring approximately 1 *pied* in width, 3 to 4 *pieds* in length and raised on the side where it is drawn. We have these sleds drawn by a dog when we can purchase trained ones for these exercises. These are rare and expensive, and it is a resource for the one who can afford them. When he runs out of food, he eats his dog.[52]

According to several period descriptions, the length of these toboggans appears to vary from 3 *pieds* to 12 *pieds* in length, indicating that these came in a variety of sizes. For instance, the toboggans used as part of Courcelle's winter campaign of 1666 were described as '…traîne, it is an assembly of thin planks having 8 to 10 *pieds* and 2 or 2½ *pouces* in width, the thickness of the planks having half of a finger's thickness'.[53] By the 1750s, the soldier and storekeeper Joseph-Charles Bonin described in detail what were likely toboggans similar to the ones used by the colonial troops during winter travels: 'The toboggan is a thin plank of 6 to 9 *pieds* long, 12 to 15 *pouces* wide, curved with a semi-circular end called a chaperon … The toboggan has, lengthwise and on the edges, animal hide thongs in which a cord is passed in a manner of laces to fasten the supplies of which the toboggan is loaded.'[54]

Capitaine Pouchot, however, goes on to describe toboggans that were probably in use by the Native Americans nations living around Lake Ontario:

> They also make toboggans, to carry their equipment, which are very convenient. They are made of two planks of a hard and more flexible wood, from 10 to 12 *pieds* long. They are used to build a type of toboggan, from 1 pied to 1½ *pieds* wide, with a bottom made from birchbark or elm wood, and the front raised in a semicircle to overcome the snow. They secure their equipment overtop. With their tumplines resting against both shoulders, they drag it themselves, or have it drawn by a dog. This type of toboggan can carry 80 livres.[55]

Dog-Pulled Toboggans

Occasionally, officers were provided with dogs to pull their toboggans during winter expeditions, a practice dating back to at least 1683. That year, a domestique accompanying officers Charles le Moyne, Paul le Moyne de Maricourt, and Louis le Ber de St-Paul stopped at Trois-Rivières to greet Governor De Varennes while returning to Montréal from Québec, 'took the toboggans, shoes, snowshoes, mittens, blankets and other things that they badly needed in the said trip, even the dogs who were pulling [the toboggans].'[56] At the very end of King George's War, expense records compiled at Québec show that dogs used to pull toboggans were sold for anywhere from 30 to 45 livres each.[57] By the 1750s, officers serving in Canada were apparently supplied with a dog when taking part in winter expeditions or campaigns, as listed in a 1756 supply list for officers of the regular and colonial troops, which included 'large dogs who pull the officer's toboggans'.[58] At times, soldiers were recorded as using dogs to draw their traîne sauvage such as Joseph-Charles Bonin, who was apparently using a dog he had purchased to pull his toboggan: 'This dog, that I have had for the last two years and that cost me 300 francs, had earned me, by his labour and diligence, already 200 francs. Without counting the other services which he had rendered while pulling me on my toboggan over snow and ice.'[59]

---

52 LAC, MG1-C11A, vol.122, f.154–158.

53 BAnQ-Q, P1000, S3, D2730, Photostat au sujet du voyage de M. de Courcelles (1666). 'Vers burlesques sur la Campagne du gouverneur de Courcelles contre les Iroquois' en 1666. p.4.

54 Henri-Raymond Casgrain, *Voyage au Canada: dans le nord de l'Amérique septentrionale : fait depuis l'an 1751 à 1761 / par J. C. B.* (Québec: Imprimerie Léger Brousseau, 1887), p.76.

55 Pouchot, *Mémoires sur la dernière guerre de l'Amérique septentrionale*, pp.279–280.

56 BAnQ-M, Baillage de Montréal, 11584, 379, Plainte des Sieurs Charles le Moyne de Longueuil, Louis LeBer de St-Paul et Paul Lemoyne de Maricourt contre un nommé Jean Patenoste, serviteur, 4 mars 1683.

57 LAC, MG1-C11A, vol.116, f.107, 107v.

58 SHAT, Dossier A1, 3417, Pièce 144.

59 Henri-Raymond Casgrain, *Voyage au Canada: dans le nord de l'Amérique septentrionale: fait depuis l'an 1751 à 1761 / par J. C. B.* (Québec: Imprimerie Léger Brousseau, 1887), p.97.

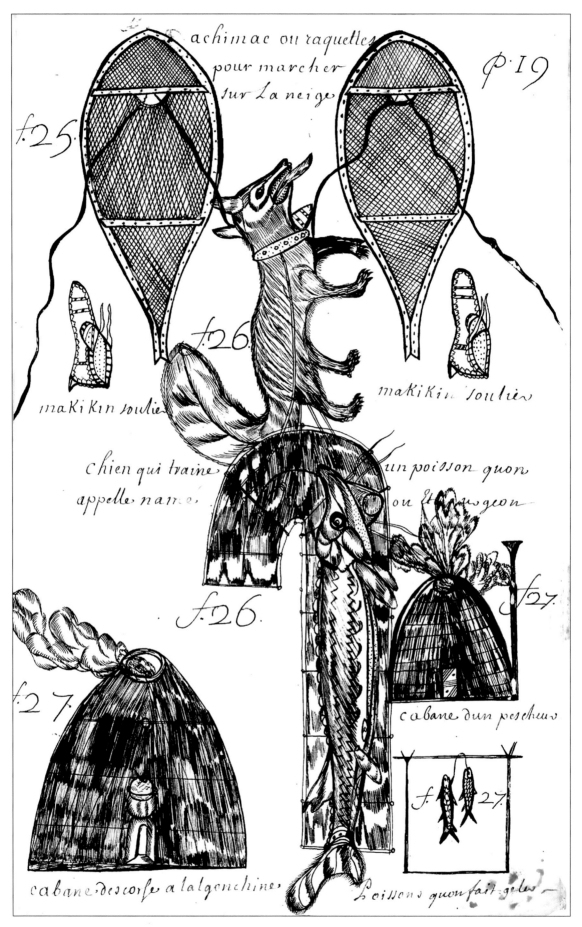

Illustration from the *Codex canadensis* c. 1675, showing a short toboggan pulled by a dog, a pair of snowshoes called achimac, and Native shoes known as makikin. (Creative commons)

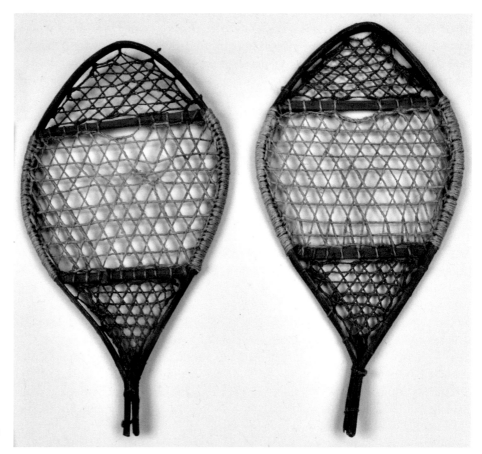

Miniature models of Huron snowshoes c. 1750–1800, currently in the Trésor de la Cathédrale de Chartres collection, France. These snowshoes feature a frame and short tail similar to the Montaignais or Innu design identified by modern researchers. Snowshoes made by the Hurons at Lorette for colonial troops and Canadian militia would have been similar to these. (Courtesy of the Musée des beaux-arts de Chartres)

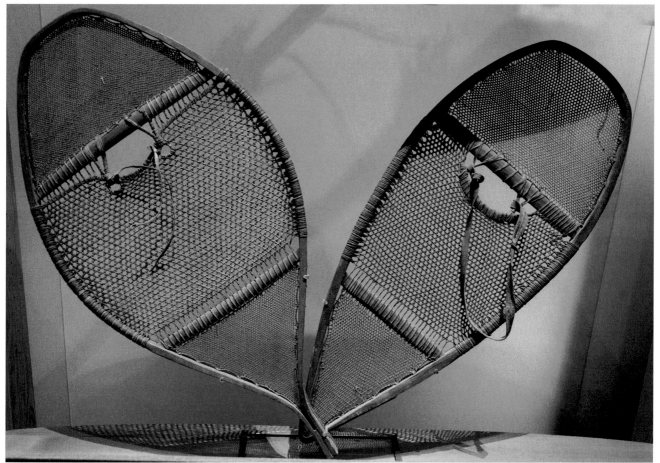

Two eighteenth-century snowshoes from the Cabinet of Curiosities at the Bibliothèque Sainte-Geneviève, France, originating from Canada. (Creative commons)

Manufacturing Sources of Toboggans

Prior to King George's War, primary source records indicate that only small quantities of toboggans were held in reserve in the King's storehouses in Canada, with eight toboggans stockpiled at both Montréal and Québec in 1740.[60] After the outbreak of the war, hundreds of toboggans were purchased by the King for his forces, including 708 procured in Montréal in 1746,[61] and 1,122, valued at 4 livres each, recorded in the same town the following year.[62]

As with snowshoes, toboggans were generally subcontracted to domiciled Native Americans living around Québec or Montréal and stockpiled in the King's depots. For example, a quantity of 348 of these sleds, each valued at 3 livres 11 sols, were supplied by the Jesuit Jean-Baptiste Tournois of the Sault Saint-Louis mission in 1744, whereas the Sulpician François Piquet serving at Lac-des-Deux-Montagnes mission had provided another 207 toboggans at the same price.[63] Three years later, 343 toboggans at 4 livres 10 sols each, supplied by the Hurons of Lorette near Québec, were listed in a statement of munitions provided by private individuals for the King's storehouse at Québec, including contributions from Hurons André Sauvage and Jacques Sauvage.[64] In 1748 at Montréal, a man named Gayentagarouche Sauvage was paid 33 livres 15 sols for providing nine toboggans.[65] A few years later in Acadia, several toboggans were supplied by local Native Americans and French colonists, including Simon Larozette, who received 50 livres for five traînes sauvages, as well as Étienne Sauvage and Pierre Chise Sauvage, who each supplied one of these types of sleds.[66]

Tumplines (Colliers de Portage)

Issued as part of both winter and summer campaign equipment, colliers de portage, often shortened to collier and also known as carrying straps, tumplines, or burden straps, were used for pulling toboggans or carrying loads over portages to the next landing. Typically worn around the forehead or across the shoulders, these straps proved invaluable to colonial soldiers tasked with transporting supplies over long distances. The Jesuit missionary Lafitau observed that when portaging, bales were attached to 'straps, or lanyards, made from basswood fibre, braided in a band',[67] whereas a memoir published in 1763 by storekeeper Jean-Baptiste Martel, describes a collier de portage as 'a kind of trinket made from tree bark that serves to load bales of goods on one's back.'[68]

In 1734, 78 tumplines were provided to 56 colonial soldiers as well as 22 Canadians who accompanied M. de Noyelles to attack the Fox nation,[69] while five years later, 112 tumplines were issued to both colonial soldiers, cadets and Canadians traveling in 16 canoes, indicating that these were used for portaging.[70] On winter expeditions, the Canonnier-Bombardier Bonin remarked that tumplines are attached to the front end of toboggans when pulling them and that this strap is 'made of birch fibre cord approximately three brasses in length, the centre of which is about 3 to 4 *pouces* wide over a span of 16 to 18 *pouces*. This strap is used yet again to carry a load and its centre width rests on the forehead or across the chest and shoulders while at times in a sling.'[71]

Sources of Production

When, in 1744, King George's War officially broke out in North America, colonial authorities had begun stockpiling munitions, including portage collars, with 1,000 of these straps priced at 15 sols purchased at Montréal.[72] Two years later, another 3,286 were purchased in this same town 'for the war',[73] and by 1747, a total of 4,414 tumplines costing 25 sols each were amassed in these depots.[74] According to the storekeeper Martel at Montréal, there was such an overabundance of these straps in the storehouses that they could have been dispensed with: "'…tumplines, oars for boats, birchbark canoes, tobacco, and other utensils or commodities which were abundant in the King's storehouses, but that Sir Varin himself supplied and had some provided by his domestiques. What! Sir," I said to him one day, "Do you want to put all the King's money into tumplines?"'[75] Many of these collars were sent to forts and outposts, with 178 tumplines inventoried at Fort Saint-Frédéric in 1748,[76] and, nine years later, 22 quarts of tumplines were stored in two barrels at Fort Carillon.[77]

Guillaume Estèbe, storekeeper at Québec, explained that the prices of tumplines paid to Iroquois Natives of

60 LAC, MG1-C11A, vol.73, f.362, f.349v.
61 LAC, MG1-C11A, vol.117, f.84v.
62 LAC, MG1-C11A, vol.89, f.37v.
63 LAC, MG1-C11A, vol.115, f.181v.
64 LAC, MG1-C11A, vol.117, f.96, 100v, 101v, 102.
65 LAC, MG1-C11A, vol.116, f.107v.
66 LAC, Archives de la marine, G.239, Colonies, Arrêts relatifs à la liquidation des dettes du Canada, 1767, Pièces numéro 14, 26.

67 Joseph-François Lafitau, *Moeurs des Sauvages Amériquains* (Paris: chez Saugrain, 1724), vol.3, p.219.
68 Martel, *Mémoire pour Jean-Baptiste Martel*, pp.16–17.
69 LAC, MG1-C11A, vol.62, f.150v.
70 LAC, MG1-C11A, vol.71, f.161.
71 Henri-Raymond Casgrain, *Voyage au Canada: dans le nord de l'Amérique septentrionale: fait depuis l'an 1751 à 1761 / par J. C. B.* (Québec: Imprimerie Léger Brousseau, 1887), pp.76–77.
72 LAC, MG1-C11A, vol.82, f.186–186v.
73 LAC, MG1-C11A, vol.117, f.83v.
74 LAC, MG1-C11A, vol.117, f.165v.
75 Martel, *Mémoire pour Jean-Baptiste Martel*, pp.16–17.
76 LAC, MG1-C11A, vol.92, f.34.
77 LAC, MG18, K9, vol.6, f.458.

the Sault St-Louis (present-day Kanahwake) varied from year to year, ranging anywhere from 20 to 40 sols each, while some years the prices of these straps increased to appease them for various reasons including when the French 'prevented them from hunting'.[78] According to colonial records, tumplines, which would have been distributed from the King's storehouses to the colonial troops dispersed throughout Canada, were at times manufactured and sold by colonists, such as cobblers (cordonniers), while in most cases domiciled Natives living near Montréal or Québec supplied the bulk of these straps which are often referenced as being made by Native women. Alexis Charlan, a cobbler from Québec, was paid 6 sols for each of the 182 tumplines he had supplied for the King's storehouses in 1744,[79] while that same year l'Abbé Piquet of the Lac-des-Deux-Montagnes mission had supplied a few hundred tumplines.[80] Père Tournois from the mission at Sault Saint-Louis sold an additional 853 tumplines at a rate of 15 sols and 6 deniers each,[81] while in 1747, a smaller quantity of tumplines was supplied by the Hurons of Québec.[82] A woman referred to as Marie Sauvagesse, living near Montréal, who was often identified as a maker of tumplines, was compensated for 'having made 30 tumplines' in 1748.[83]

Tumplines used by the French in Canada were commonly crafted from leather, bark fibre, or nettle fibre. In 1753, Pierre Biguez supplied 30 leather tumplines to Monière, a Montréal-based merchant outfitter in the fur trade, at 30 sols each.[84] A few years earlier, Abbé Piquet provided the King's storehouses in Montréal with 385 tumplines made of ortie (nettle), priced at 20 sols 6 deniers each.[85] This suggests that the Native inhabitants of the Lac-des-Deux-Montagnes mission braided these straps using nettle fibres. Further evidence of their use comes from the post-mortem inventory of colonial officer Joseph Langy, who resided aux Outaouais; his belongings included 'an old tumpline of ortie', valued at 1 livre.[86]

However, several records concerning tumplines in the Québec region, which were presumably made by Huron

Dog collar belonging to Emmanuel de Rohan, Grand maitre de l'ordre souverain de Malte, eighteenth century. (Musée de la chasse et Nature, Paris. Photo Kevin Gélinas)

hands, include the description colliers de portage de racine, which can be translated to 'tumplines made from roots', which probably designate a vegetable fibre. In 1747, 2 colliers de racine priced at 30 sols each were supplied by Hurons of Lorette at Québec while two years later, 50 tumplines made from racine were sent from the King's storehouses at Québec to Shediac, a portion of which were used by the colonial officers and soldiers under the command of *capitaine* De La Corne.[87] The 1752 inventory of the King's storehouses at Québec recorded '812 tumplines of racine for portaging', making it logical to conclude that these tumplines were probably supplied by the Hurons.[88]

Numerous period accounts also point to bark fibre as the most common material used to braid or weave tumplines. As previously cited, Lafitau, on the one hand, mentions tumplines made from basswood fibre while Bonin references birch fibre cord as the material used to braid theses straps. Certain tumplines may also have had geometric designs in the weaving. In 1740, for instance, 54 colliers à fleches' (tumplines having arrows) valued at 35 sols each, were purchased, along with numerous other trade goods, from the merchant outfitter Alexis Lemoyne-Monière of Montréal by a trader named Giasson.[89] An Iroquois tumpline from 1710, housed at The British Museum (Registration number Am,SLMisc.574), is one of the earliest known examples, likely similar to those used by

78 Anon., *À Monseigneur de Sartine*, p.17.
79 LAC, MG1-C11A, vol.115, f.74.
80 LAC, MG1-C11A, vol.115, f.181v.
81 LAC, MG1-C11A, vol.115, f.181v.
82 LAC, MG1-C11A, vol.117, f.106.
83 LAC, MG1-C11A, vol.116, f.110v.
84 Marie Gérin-Lajoie, Montreal Merchant's Records Project, (microfilm copy of M496 Montreal Merchants Records Project, Research Files, 1971–1975, 1 roll —St. Paul: Minnesota Historical Society Library Copy Services), Monière, Microfilm M-850, Livre des Engagés, No. 1, 1753–63, vol.15, f.13, 15 juin 1753.
85 LAC, MG1-C11A, vol.115, f.181v.
86 BAnQ-M, Greffe du notaire Louis-Claude Danré de Blanzy, Inventaire de Catherine d'Ailleboust du Manthet et de Jean-Baptiste Levreau écuyer Sieur de Langy, officier demeurant aux Outaouais, 26 avril 1760.

87 LAC, MG1-C11A, vol.119, f.4.
88 LAC, MG1-C11A, vol.98, f.239v.
89 BAnQ, Lemoine-Moniere, Jean-Alexis, 06, M-P 218. Film No M614.1. Livres de comptes du 27 juin 1739 au 8 janvier 1751. Doit à Monsieur Giasson… , 12 juin 1740.

Detail from a circa 1730 watercolour depicting a Native carrying a bale of furs using a tumpline, alongside a coureur des bois holding a paddle. The tumpline's strap rests on the forehead to support the load. (Vignette pour la Pesche des Castors..., Anonymous, c. 1730, Beinecke Rare Book and Manuscript Library, Yale University Library, New Haven, CT, USA, WA MSS S-2412)

colonial soldiers and Canadian voyageurs to carry heavy loads. It is made of hemp and measures 540 cm in length.

Ice Creepers

Although not a standard-issue item for campaigns, ice creepers or cleats were likely provided to colonial soldiers assigned to winter expeditions or tasked with duties in the harsh winter conditions of New France. Referred to as grappins à souliers in French colonial records, these metal cleats were tied or strapped to the instep of shoes to improve traction on slippery surfaces, such as frozen rivers, icy ground, or hard-packed snow.

The practice of using ice creepers in certain regions of France, commonly termed 'grappes d'acier', 'grappin' or 'crampons à glace', extends back many centuries. Peasants from the Savoie region were using grappes d'acier as early as the sixteenth century to travel through the Alps,[90] while Louis XIV equipped 12,000 of his men with crampons de fer (steel cleats) when marching on ice toward La

---

90 *Nouveau théâtre du monde contenant les estats, empires,*
    royaumes et principautez... (Paris: Pierre Rocolet, 1644), p.510.

Haye in 1672.[91] Colonial records suggest that the use of ice creepers by soldiers in Canada dates back to at least the 1660s, as noted by a commanding officer of the Carignan-Salières regiment, who reported that the men were poorly equipped, stating, 'the soldiers having no snowshoes, very few axes, one blanket per three, no cleats, having only a pair of moccasins'.[92] A poem written by René-Louis Chartier de Lotbinière which recounted 'Monsieur de Courcelles' trip' into the Iroquois country in 1666, described the term grappins as: 'a [piece of] iron that goes under the shoes to prevent slipping on ice'.[93]

Additional evidence of the military use of ice creepers emerges from documents detailing munitions and supplies stored at forts and outposts. In 1702, Fort Frontenac recorded '3 pairs of ice creepers [grappins à glace]' valued at 30 sols per pair.[94] Similarly, in 1743, 28 pairs of 'ice creepers for shoes', appraised at 20 sols per pair, were sent from Montréal to Fort Saint-Frédéric as part of wartime supplies.[95] The distribution of these traction cleats was particularly notable during King George's War, with a statement of munitions purchased in 1746 listing an impressive 1,133 pairs of iron cleats supplied at Montréal for the war effort.[96]

In 1756, Governor Pierre de Rigaud de Vaudreuil de Cavagnial of New France wrote to colonial officer Chaussegros de Léry, stationed at La Présentation, to inform him that he was sending several toboggans loaded with '100 pairs of ice cleats.' This correspondence highlights the critical importance of such equipment for winter marches and expeditions during the Seven Years War.[97] Further evidence comes from an account by a captured colonial soldier at Fort William Henry, who reported that each French soldier carried 'a pair of Iron Creepers to walk on the Ice'.[98]

French colonial probate records reveal the widespread use of these devices among colonists and military

Ice creeper of French origin stamped with a fleur-de-lis, possibly indicating official use under the King of France in New France. Excavated at the Parc-de-l'Artillerie in Québec. In 1747, Canadiens participating in the winter raid on New England, led by Chevalier de Niverville, were each issued a pair of ice creepers (grappins à souliers) alongside their winter campaign gear. Many of these cleats were made by blacksmiths in Québec for the King's storehouses. The unique design of these cleats, found at several French sites, may have been developed to adapt to the harsh Canadian winter conditions. (Courtesy of National Historic Sites, Parks Canada. Artefact number: 18G39J7-3Q)

personnel in Canada and as far south as the Illinois Territory, as shown by a pair found in the personal possessions of Charles Henaux at Fort de Chartres.[99] In 1724, the Marquise de Vaudreuil, residing in Montréal, remarked on the damage caused by ice creepers to the cedar floors of Château Vaudreuil, stating, 'the planks of bad cedar, which M. Raudot knows very well cannot last here one winter, due to the ice creepers that the men wear under their shoes.'[100] It was Claude Le Beau who noted that during the winter, the inhabitants of Québec would have never been able to climb from the Lower Town to the Upper Town 'if they did not have ice creepers under their shoes.'[101] Ice creepers may also have been paired with snowshoes to improve traction on icy terrain, as suggested by the inventory of the Sieur de Saint-Agnant's domestique, which included 'a pair of snowshoes with iron cleats.'[102]

Both colonial and regular French officers were recorded as owning ice creepers, highlighting their practical importance in winter conditions. Among these were a pair belonging to *lieutenant* Milon of the colonial infantry,

91 Adrien Pascal, Nicolas Germain Brahaut, *Histoire de l'armée et de tous les régiments depuis les temps de la monarchie francaise jusqu'a nos jours* (Paris, A. Barbier: 1847), vol.2, p.100.

92 Régis Roy, Gérard Malchelosse, Benjamin Sulte, *Le régiment de Carignan: son organisation et son expédition au Canada (1665–1668), officiers et soldats qui s'établirent en Canada* (Montréal: G. Ducharme, 1925), p.55.

93 BAnQ-Q, P1000, S3, D2730, Photostat au sujet du voyage de M. de Courcelles (1666). 'Vers burlesques sur la Campagne du gouverneur de Courcelles contre les Iroquois' en 1666. p.4.

94 LAC, MG1-C11A, vol.20, f.261.

95 LAC, MG1-C11A, vol.82, f.169.

96 LAC, MG1-C11A, vol.117, fol. 84.

97 BAnQ-Q, P386, D253, Fonds Famille Chaussegros de Léry, Lettre du sieur [Pierre de Rigaud] de Vaudreuil [de Cavagnial] au sieur [Gaspard-Joseph] Chaussegros de Léry, 28 février 1756.

98 LOC, Colonial Office 5 folio 47, E. of Loudoun's Letter of April 25th. 1757, Declaration of two Prisoners taken the 23.d March 1757 at Fort Wm. Henry, Information of John Victor and Guillaume Chasse, two French Prisoners, Fort William Henry March 25th.

99 Kaskaskia Manuscripts, Randolph County Courthouse, Chester, Illinois, Inventaire de feu Charles Henaux, demeurant au Fort de Chartres… , 29 juillet 1744.

100 BAnQ-Q, P1000, S3, D2736, Documents concernant la famille Rigaud de Vaudreuil, pp.125–126.

101 Claude Le Beau, *Avantures du Sr. C. Le Beau, avocat en parlement, ou, Voyage curieux et nouveau parmi les sauvages de l'Amérique septentrionale…* (Amsterdam: Uytwerf, 1738), p.75.

102 BAnQ-TR, Greffe du notaire Nicolas Duclos, Inventaire des biens du domestique du Sieur de St-Agnant, 9 septembre 1751.

Three ice creepers found at Louisbourg showing a fleur-de-lis type marking. (Courtesy of National Historic Sites, Parks Canada. Photo Kevin Gélinas)

who died at La Baie in 1749,[103] and another pair recorded in 1756 at Fort Carillon as the property of *lieutenant* M. de Jambert of the Régiment de Béarn.[104] It is plausible that a French military engineer examining l'Île-Royale during the winter of 1757 also relied on cleats for stability on the ice, as he described the challenges of traversing 'rough and uneven ice' and noted, 'after walking for three hours, with my moccasins, we were constrained, unable to go any further by the pain we suffered on the soles of the feet, to use French shoes'.[105]

Most of these ice creepers were crafted by colonial blacksmiths in New France rather than being imported from France. In one transaction, blacksmith Joseph Legris of Québec produced 18 pairs for the King's storehouse emphasizing the local production of such essential winter gear to meet the demands of the colony.[106]

Sealskins and Bearskins

Bearskins and sealskins were traditionally supplied to the colonial officers and soldiers detached to a fort or when taking part in expeditions during colder months. Officer Malartic aptly described the harsh realities of such campaigns in 1757, writing, 'The blanket and a bear skin are the bed of a man of war in a similar expedition'.[107] Sealskins, while primarily used as waterproof coverings for supplies transported on toboggans during winter expeditions, were occasionally issued to soldiers as ground coverings for camping.

---

103 LAC, MG1-E, vol.314, p.5.

104 ASQ, Fonds Casgrain, document divers, vol.1, doc. 2, État des effets de M. de Jambert, lieutenant au Régiment de Béarn… qui y ont été vendus à Carillon, 22 septembre 1758.

105 LAC, MG 4, C 2, Ms in-folio 210f.

106 LAC, MG1-C11A, vol.117, f.96.

107 Anne-Joseph-Hippolyte de Maurès comte de Malartic, *Journal des campagnes au Canada de 1755 à 1760* (Dijon: L. Damidot, 1890), p.132.

By the time of King George's War, the distribution of bearskins to troops was a well-established practice. In January 1746, for example, the officer Le Mercier, stationed at Fort Saint-Frédéric, received a bearskin as part of his winter equipment.[108] Similarly, in April of the following year, a detachment of a *sergent* and six soldiers garrisoned at Fort de Châteauguay was issued '7 bearskins.'[109] In March of the same year, colonial officer De Niverville received a bearskin as part of the supplies provided to a large war party preparing to launch an attack on New England.[110]

Initially, bearskins were used as bedding for both officers and soldiers during campaigns. However, by the time of the Seven Years War, soldiers were occasionally issued sealskins as substitutes, likely due to a shortage of bearskins within the colony. A letter from Marquis Ange Duquesne de Menneville to Claude-Pierre Pécaudy de Contrecoeur, commandant at Fort de la Rivière au Bœuf, dated December 1753, discusses the difficulty of acquiring enough bearskins for winter detachments: 'I beg you to log the names of all those to whom they [bearskins] have been given to and you will warn them that they must be returned in the early spring to be distributed equally since it is so difficult to find some here that the winter detachments will be reduced to having only one per three men.'[111]

At the onset of the Seven Years War, Guillaume de Méritens de Pradals, an officer of the Régiment de la Sarre, noted that during winter campaigns, soldiers were issued 'one sealskin on which the soldiers sleep', while officers received 'one bearskin for us during winter.'[112] Likewise, in February 1757, at Fort Saint-Jean, Montcalm recorded that each officer was provided a bearskin in addition to the standard issue for soldiers. In the margins, he added: 'Each soldier was given a bearskin contrary to ordinary practices, which allowed us to deliver a number of bad ones', confirming that, prior to this campaign, soldiers were typically issued sealskins instead of bearskins.[113]

Malartic provides a detailed account of how colonial soldiers and Canadians skilfully set up their camp outside Fort Saint-Jean using their bearskins: 'They managed quite well by digging large holes in the snow, placing branches on the ground, and then covering these branches with the bearskins to be warm when lying down. They were protected from the rain by tarpaulins, which are given per four men.'[114] According to the officer La Pause, 'a sealskin, for as much to sleep on and another to cover the food rations' was included as part of the supplies issued for the winter season.[115] This is corroborated in a memoir written by Intendant Bigot, who states: 'The winter gear for the colonial officers consisted of the following: 1 bearskin for their bed…The soldier, the militia, the domestiques, and the Native, had the same winter gear as the officer, except that they had only a sealskin, instead of a bearskin.'[116]

Sealskin, on the other hand, offered the advantage of being a waterproof material, making it ideal for protecting supplies and gear from the elements, such as snow or rain, whether carried on a toboggan or stored in a camp. According to Malartic, one sealskin was specifically used to cover the men's food and gear,[117] while an anonymous list of supplies dated 1756, detailing provisions issued to colonial and regular troops, further noted that during winter expeditions, sealskins were used '…to cover the supplies on the toboggans.'[118]

---

108 LAC, MG1-C11A, vol.88, f.214–214v.
109 LAC, MG1-C11A, f.206v.
110 LAC, MG1-C11A, vol.117, f.191v-192.
111 ASQ, Viger-Verreau, P32/001/037, Papiers Contrecoeur, 25 décembre 1753.
112 'Lettres de Guillaume De Méritens De Pradals, officier au régiment de La Sarre écrites à son frère, pendant la campagne de 1756 à 1758, au Canada', *Cahiers des dix*, vol.24 1959, p.116.
113 Henri-Raymond Casgrain, *Collection des manuscrits du maréchal de Lévis, Journal du marquis de Montcalm durant ses campagnes en Canada de 1756 à 1759* (Québec: Imprimerie de L.-J. Demers & Frère, 1895), p.157.

114 Anne-Joseph-Hippolyte de Maurès comte de Malartic, *Journal des campagnes au Canada de 1755 à 1760* (Dijon: L. Damidot, 1890), pp.95–96.
115 RAPQ,1933–1934, p.210.
116 Bigot, *Mémoire Pour Messire François Bigot*, p.40.
117 Anne-Joseph-Hippolyte de Maurès comte de Malartic, *Journal des campagnes au Canada de 1755 à 1760* (Dijon: L. Damidot, 1890), p.96.
118 SHAT, Dossier A1, 3417, Pièce 144.

4

Campaign Cookware of the Colonial Troops

From a military standpoint, meal preparation methods and eating habits of the colonial troops stationed in New France differed little from those of Marine soldiers or infantrymen serving in France, with colonial officers likely closely following the same practices as their French counterparts. French colonial soldiers typically prepared their meals in copper or brass kettles, known as chaudières, or in marmites (cooking pots) while in military barracks. Unlike modern eating habits, they generally ate from a shared serving bowl or dish (gamelle), likely using their fingers and tablespoons, with small drinking kettles or tin cups also passed around for everyone to drink from. As table manners evolved in French society, by the Seven Years War, the fork had been introduced alongside the spoon and folding knife as a soldier's main eating utensils.

When detached on expeditions, despite their increased rations to provide extra sustenance for their heightened efforts, soldiers often travelled light, carrying only basic cooking tools. They preferred lighter copper or brass kettles to the heavier cast-iron marmite cooking pots, which served as both cooking vessels and communal serving bowls. On larger campaigns, colonial officers would traditionally carry their own personal tableware, which might include pewter plates, silver tumblers, silver cutlery, and at times, a tin cup and coffee pot. By 1755, pewter plates, small cooking pots, imitation silver spoons, and steel forks had become standard issue for French officers of the metropolitan troops in Canada. When leading small detachments, colonial officers likely travelled light but may have carried finer cutlery as a status symbol and mark of rank.

Official Military Ordinances

From a Marine perspective, the 1674 ordonnance outlined the necessary cookware as part of every ship's equipment: 'The agent will provide the utensils necessary for the distribution of provisions, such as water cans, serving bowls: His Majesty bestowing the right to supply exclusively from his stores, the marmite cooking pots, kettles,

andirons, and other utensils used to cook the meat'[1] The 1689 Marine ordonnance, which addressed the supply and administration of food aboard ships, specified that food was to be distributed in groups of seven men per dish.[2] The necessary utensils for food distribution included a bidon (water can) and a gamelle (serving bowl). The port master would supply the 'serving bowls, water cans, and baskets of the prescribed size, and the other necessary utensils for the distribution of the provisions.'[3]

On land, it is likely that the colonial troops serving in North America followed the same guidelines as those serving aboard ships. A 1738 memoir indicates that colonial troops stationed in garrisons, such as Louisbourg, were instructed to follow the same orders as ship-borne troops: '… so that it be supplied to the troops, as with the King's ships, per seven men, a serving bowl for eating soup, a water can, and two sillons [water furrows] in each room to get water. The soldier is required to eat his soup from his marmite cooking pot, to draw his beer using various inadequate bowls that are on hand, the majority of which they lose'.[4]

When stationed in barracks, outposts or forts, colonial soldiers serving in Canada would have normally prepared their meals in their respective quarters, usually in a mess of seven men,[5] likely taking turns with cooking duties. The kitchen inventory at Fort Frontenac in 1700, for example, included five pewter plates, one cooking spoon, two pewter porringers, eight gamelles, three steel marmites, and two pewter dishes.[6] At Fort Niagara in 1738, the cooking utensils for trade and garrison service consisted of '2 steel marmites, one with a lid, 6 pewter plates, 1 pewter basin, 8 steel marmites, four with lids, and 3 mid-sized brass kettles,' while in the barracks, they

1   Jean-Baptiste Torchet de Boismêlé, *Histoire générale de la marine contenant son origine chez tous les peuples du monde, ses progrès, son état actuel, et les expéditions maritimes, anciennes et modernes* (Paris : Chez Antoine Bouder, 1758), vol.3, pp.59–60.

2   De Boismêlé, *Histoire générale de la marine*, vol.3, p.273.

3   De Boismêlé, *Histoire générale de la marine*, vol.3, p.276.

4   LAC, MG1-C11B, vol.20, f.318.

5   LAC, MG1-C11A, vol.95, f.74.

6   LAC, MG1-C11A, vol.20, f.260v.

found '1 mid-sized copper kettle, 1 old frying pan, and an old cooking fork.'[7]

Many of these military men were housed with the Habitants (colonists) throughout the St Lawrence Valley, and in May of 1695 Intendant Jacques de Meulles reminded the colonists that they were not obligated to provide soldiers with more than '...a marmite cooking pot and a kettle.'[8] A few months later, another decree clarified that the Habitants '...shall be required to provide them with only a straw mattress, tableware (couvert), a marmite cooking pot or kettle, and a place at their fire', indicating that the soldiers used the same utensils as the colonists.[9] By 1757, an ordonnance from Jacques-Joseph Guiton de Monrepos, *lieutenant général* of Montréal, required citizens in the Montréal area to be ready to house troops who came to take up their winter quarters and to provide '...marmite cooking pots and pewter spoons for the soldiers.'[10]

In the regular army, however, the ordonnance of April 15, 1718, instructed all troops, whether in garrison or on foot, to carry with them '...bowls and casks.'[11] The 1753 ruling further required that each tent or chamber full of soldiers '...be provided with a marmite, bowl, and a cask or can.'[12] In the 1719 edition of *le service journalier de l'infanterie*, le Comte Henri François de Bombelles observed that before entering a campaign, *capitaines* should inspect their companies and, if needed, advance them '...an écu or two per chamber, to acquire ... a gamelle, a baril or steel bidon, or other small things.'[13] In North America, each infantry soldier arriving at Québec in 1755 was to receive: '...one knife, one spoon, and one fork, and per company, a certain quantity of water cans, serving bowls',[14] revealing that by this time, the knife, spoon, and fork had become standard issue items in French regiments of the period.

Pots and Kettles

Based on archival, iconographic and archaeological evidence, there appears to be two main categories of cooking vessels used by the colonial troops in New France. These include the marmite cooking pot and well as various copper and brass chaudières (kettles) equipped with or without lids.

The Marmite Cooking Pot

In terms of food preparation inside a French fort, at an outpost, or in barracks, historical records showed that the marmite cooking pot was the most popular vessel used by the troops. French dictionaries of the period of the period described a marmite as: '...a pot of copper, cast iron, or earthenware, in which the meat is boiled for the soup. There are large and small pots according to the amount of meat to be used.'[15] According to *L'Art du chaudronnier*, '...the copper marmite is a deep vase and covered with a lid ... The copper marmite is usually without legs and laid on its base, unlike those of iron or cast iron, which commonly have three legs.'[16] Essentially, these cooking vessels were distinguishable by their vase-shaped form, with a deep, wide base and a narrow opening. An early account of marmites used in a military context in New France provided sufficient evidence that these vessels were much narrower at the rim than at the base. For instance, in 1696, '8 iron marmites with their lids, holding 6 *pots* apiece, and narrow at the top' were sent from the port of Rochefort to Fort Naxouat.[17] A *pot*, an old French unit of capacity, represented roughly 1.9 litres.

In the following century, marmite cooking pots were frequently listed as part of the furniture and utensils for outlying forts, often described as made of iron. In 1724, an inventory of items needed for the barracks at Québec detailed the cooking utensils typically provided to soldiers, which included '40 iron marmites with their sheet metal lids and their iron handles, from 6 to 8 *pots*', '40 iron grills' and '40 frying pans'.[18] At Louisbourg in the early 1730s, the items requested for the troops included iron marmites with serving ladles, specified to hold 4 and 5 *pots* in 1732, while those requested the following year were to be of the larger 5-*pot* size.[19] Five years later, the marmites needed for this fortress appeared to be larger, as '30 iron marmites of 8 *pots* with their handles and marked with the King's emblem' were listed among the munitions required for the

7   LAC, MG1-C11A, vol.69, f.273v-274, 276.

8   Philippe Fournier, *La Nouvelle-France au fil des édits* (Sillery, Québec: Les éditions du Septentrion, 2011), p.189.

9   Fournier, *La Nouvelle-France*, p.194.

10   E.-Z. Massicotte, *Montréal sous le Régime français. Répertoire des arrêts, édits, mandements, ordonnances et réglements...* (Montréal: G. Ducharme, 1919), p.136.

11   *Dictionnaire universel françois et latin: vulgairement appelé Dictionnaire de Trévoux ... avec des remarques d'érudition et de critique; le tout tiré des plus excellens auteurs, des meilleurs lexicographes ... qui ont paru jusqu'ici en différentes langues* (Paris: Par la Compagnie des Libraires Associés, 1771), vol.4, p.398.

12   *Ordonnance du roi, portant reglement sur le service de l'infanterie en campagne: Du 17 fevrier 1753* (Paris: de L'imprimerie royale, 1753), p.5.

13   Henri-Francois Comte de Bombelles, *Le service journalier de l'infanterie* (Paris: Chez Louis-Denis Delatour, 1744), p.160.

14   Société historique de Montréal, *Campagne de 1755* (Montréal: C.A. Marchand, 1899), p.4.

15   *Dictionnaire pratique du bon ménager de campagne et de ville...* (Paris: Chez Pierre Ribou, 1715), vol.1, p.89.

16   *Encyclopédie méthodique: Arts et métiers mécaniques ... Art du chaudronnier* (Paris: Charles-Joseph Panckoucke, 1782), vol.1 pt.2, p.627.

17   LAC, MG1-B, vol, 19, f.31.

18   LAC, MG1-C11A, vol.46, f.158.

19   LAC, MG1-C11B, vol.13, f.44–45v; vol.14, f.222–224.

A French military encampment of the Compagnie des Gardes du Corps, showing a rudimentary campfire and cooking pot. A stack of food preparation equipment is visible at the bottom right. (Rue d'un camp destiné pour une Brigade des Gardes du Corps, 1742, public domain)

An excerpt from a circa 1761 hand-coloured perspective view of the interior of the Hôtel des Invalides in Paris, depicting the refectory where convalescing soldiers eat, illustrating the soldiers' dining habits and utensils of the period. (Vue perspective du réfectoire de l'Hôtel Royal des Invalides à Paris. Anon. J.G. de Groot Jamin Bequest, Amsterdam, Rijksmuseum)

An illustration from Diderot's *Encyclopédie* labelled *Chaudronnier* (boilermaker) depicting a marmite. According to *L'Art du chaudronnier*, the copper marmite is a deep vase with a lid. Unlike iron or cast-iron versions, which often had three legs, the copper marmite is legless and rests on its base.

Presumed French cast iron cooking pot fragments found at Fort Jacques-Cartier, a fort built in 1759 and surrendered to British forces in September 1760. (CeEw-1-5D4-27, Laboratoire et Réserve d'archéologie du Québec)

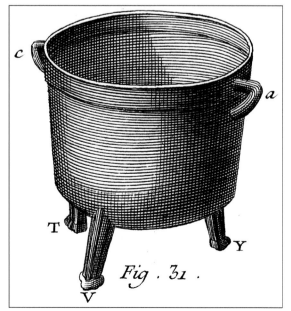

Left: A finished three-legged pot-bellied marmite, fresh out of the mould, as described in Diderot's section on *Forges ou art du fer*. Diderot illustrates the stages of loam moulding for cast iron pots.

Above: Detail from *Veuë du Camp de la Concession de Monseigneur Law*, a sketch of the settlement at Biloxi, Mississippi, in 1720. The drawing shows a camp in New France, with a tripod cooking pot, likely a marmite, hung over a fire and a jug, possibly a bidon, at its side. (The Newberry Library, Chicago. Drawn by Jean Baptiste Michel le Bouteux, 1720)

Line drawings of two cast iron pots based on excavated fragments from various French context sites, including the King's coat of arms (in the middle) found on one of the fragments. (Line drawing by Michel Pétard)

A fragment of a cast iron cooking pot found at Fort Ouiatenon, featuring a partial fleur-de-lis design. (Tippecanoe County Historical Association collection, Lafayette, Indiana. Photo Kevin Gélinas)

Cast iron cauldron fragment from Fort Senneville, displaying the French coat of arms. Such fleur-de-lis adorned cooking pots were used by colonial troops at Louisbourg. Archaeological evidence suggests that colonial troops stationed at forts or posts in Canada used heavy cast iron pots rather than copper due to their better thermal performance and lower cost, with many pots produced using sand-cast moulding. (With permission of the Royal Ontario Museum © ROM)

Right: A cast iron cooking pot with three short legs, recovered from the Fortress of Louisbourg. This durable pot would have been essential for daily meal preparation, reflecting the practical and resilient nature of cast iron cookware used by colonial soldiers in the harsh coastal environment. (Courtesy of National Historic Sites, Parks Canada. Photo Kevin Gélinas)

Far right: Fragment of a cast iron cauldron bearing a fleur-de-lis from Louisbourg. (Courtesy of National Historic Sites, Parks Canada. Photo Kevin Gélinas)

colony.[20] The King's emblem referenced in this statement likely corresponded to the royal coat of arms featuring three fleur-de-lis. By 1741, a quantity of 60 iron marmites requested for the soldier's barracks at Louisbourg they were to be marked with fleur-de-lis symbols, likely to indicate military ownership and deter theft or bartering.[21]

These cooking pots were also frequently mentioned at forts on the frontier such as '8 iron marmites' that were listed at Fort Niagara,[22] '10 marmites' at Fort Frontenac,[23] and '15 iron marmites' at Fort Saint-Frédéric.[24] In 1746, six iron marmites and two chaudrons (cooking pots), weighing a total of 175 *livres*, were delivered to the King's clerk at Fort Saint-Frédéric.[25] The following year, '4 large iron marmites' and '1 mid-size iron marmite,' weighing altogether 110 *livres*, along with five sheet iron lids, were sent to Monsieur Demuy, *commandant* at Lac-des-Deux-Montagnes, for the garrison's service.[26] A quantity of '42 iron marmites,' including six that were 'broken and mended,' were part of the utensils at Fort Saint-Frédéric in 1748,[27] while seven years later, 50 iron marmites were requested at Fort Duquesne, along with kettles made of cuivre (brass or copper)[28] and beer-making kettles.[29] In February 1757, Malartic ordered marmites for Canadians and colonial soldiers at Fort Saint-Jean '…so that they could camp and make soup in the woods, to the left of the fort.'[30]

During the 1760 campaign, cooking pots were in such short supply that military officials suggested purchasing them from nearby colonists at Fort Jacques-Cartier: 'The article which worries me most … are the soldier's marmites … they must be assembled together and see if any can be found among the Habitants; you will negotiate a deal and I would purchase them. I expect that three common ones [marmites] per company will be sufficient.'[31] The

An illustration of a small chaudière from the preparatory sketches for *Plumassier et Panachier*, intended for the *Encyclopédie*. This illustration corresponds to kettle artefacts excavated from several North American French archaeological sites. (Par Desgerantin. Planche 2. Marseille, MuCEM, Musée des Civilisations de l'Europe et de la Méditerranée)

cooking pots used by colonial soldiers in Canada were likely identical to those at in use at Louisbourg in 1744 and were described as '…iron marmites for a serving of seven men, with fleur-de-lis, fitted with an iron ring all around with their [baling] handle and serving spoon.'[32] In 1756, a request for '…50 iron marmites of 5 or 6 *pots* [capacity] with their lids and [baling] handles, each fitted with an iron ring all around for the soldier's chambers and for a serving of seven men' for the Louisbourg troops, provides insight into their size.[33] By 1759, a statement of supplies to be sent to Louisiana included 'Three hundred iron tripod kettles with [baling] handles for the use of the barracks and detachments in all of the posts of the colony', indicating that these three-legged vessels may have also been used during expeditions in the interior.[34]

Most of these cooking vessels were imported from France, such as the iron marmites supplied by Sieur Maisonneuve in 1745 for Louisbourg.[35] By the mid-1740s, however, cast-iron marmites were being produced at the Forges du Saint-Maurice near Trois-Rivières. A letter from Gilles Hocquart in 1744 noted that the moulds requested for these kettles had capacities of 25 to 60 *pots*, much too large to be issued to colonial soldiers.[36] On the other hand,

20 LAC, MG1-C11B, vol.20, f.202–202v.

21 LAC, MG1-C11B, vol.24, f.174v.

22 LAC, MG1-C11A, vol.68, f.105.

23 LAC, MG1-C11A, vol.68, f.111.

24 LAC, MG1-C11A, vol.69, f.280v.

25 LAC, MG1-C11A, vol.88, f.219.

26 LAC, MG1-C11A, vol.117, f.225.

27 LAC, MG1-C11A, vol.92, f.36v, 37v.

28 In French, the word cuivre can refer to both brass and copper, depending on the context. So, while cuivre literally means copper, it may be used more broadly in French to indicate brass, particularly when referring to objects made from the alloy. The exact meaning can usually be inferred from the context in which it is used.

29 ASQ, Viger-Verreau, P32/002/164a, Papiers Contrecoeur, État des effets demandés à Montréal pour le Fort Duquesne, 15 janvier 1755.

30 De Malartic, *Journal des campagnes au Canada de 1755 à 1760*, p.95.

31 Henri-Raymond Casgrain, *Collection des manuscrits du maréchal de Lévis, Lettres du chevalier de Lévis concernant la guerre du Canada (1756–1760)* (Montréal: C.O. Beauchemin & Fils, 1889), p.274.

32 LAC, MG1, F1A, vol.35, f.10.

33 AR, État des approvisionnements à envoyer à l'île Royale en 1756.

34 Patricia Kay Galloway, Dunbar Rowland, A.G., Sanders, *Mississippi Provincial Archives* (Louisiana University Press, Bâton Rouge and London, 1984), pp.228–229.

35 LAC, MG1-C11A, vol.27, f.86.

36 LAC, MG1-C11A, vol.112, f.245.

Detail from the plate entitled Chaudronnier Grossier as part of the Chaudronnier series, *Encyclopédie*, 1763. This workshop scene shows several craftsmen at work on different parts of the production line. The chaudronnier grossier was the maker of pots, pans and other kitchen utensils, often specialising in copper or brass.

these cast-iron vessels would have been brittle and would have broken or cracked when dropped during transport and would have also weighed considerably more than their copper or brass counterparts. Pehr Kalm, a Swedish botanist who visited Canada in 1749, noted that Native Americans much preferred copper or brass kettles as opposed to iron marmites, 'because [marmites] cannot be easily carried on their continual journeys and would not bear such falls and knocks as their kettles are subject to.'[37]

These drawbacks likely led military administrators to adopt lighter, more durable cooking vessels for lengthy campaigns. By 1755, French regular troops arriving in Québec were supplied with 300 marmites described as '... marmites of fer battu with their pan, serving as lids', likely intended for a chamber or tentful of soldiers.[38] According to the *Manuel du naturaliste*, fer battu refers to tinplate: '... Tinplate is nothing else than fer battu reduced into sheets and soaked in a molten pewter crucible.'[39]

A few years earlier, a letter published in a French periodical noted that fer battu cooking pots for military use were considered lighter, more efficient, and safer than their copper or brass counterparts. Many military officials had been purchasing these pots in Paris since the 1740s due to the '...lightness sought by military officers in the last wars. There were even several cooks following the armies, who requested them thin, because they were often short on wood and coal: the thinner the pot and cauldron, the better the food absorbs the heat, requiring less coal.' The letter also emphasised that tinplate cookware did not produce verdigris like copper or brass: 'The main object was to avoid the accidents of verdigris, both for the officers and the soldiers.'[40] By this time, the cast-iron marmite had been replaced with lighter, more portable tinplated models, as seen in 1757 when '53 new tinplate marmites, 4 per company and 5 for the grenadiers', were provided to the Régiment de Guyenne before their campaign in Canada.[41] The shift is further illustrated by seven marmites made of fer blanc (tinplate) found aboard the frigate *Saint-Pierre* bound for Québec in 1758,[42] and '15 tinplated marmites of 4 pots' aboard the ship *L'Aurore* en route to Canada in 1760.[43]

37   Kalm et al, *Voyage de Pehr Kalm*, p.272.
38   LAC, MG1-C11A, vol.100, f.284v
39   Georges-Louis Leclerc Comte de Buffon, *Manuel du naturaliste: ouvrage utile aux voyageurs ...* (Paris: de l'Imprimerie Royale, 1771), p.316.

40   *La nouvelle bigarure: contenant a qu'il y a des plus intéressant dans le Mercure de France, et de plus curieux dans les autres journaux & feuilles périodiques etc* (À la Haye: Pierre Gosse junior, 1754), vol.XI, Janvier 1754, pp.3–23.
41   RAPQ, 1933–1934, p.80.
42   TNA, HCA, 32, vol.234, Le Saint-Pierre, 1758.
43   TNA, HCA, 32, vol.165, L'Aurore, 1760.

Kettles (Chaudières)

On campaigns, detachments, or raids, historical records show that colonial soldiers were typically issued a chaudière (cooking kettle) made of cuivre (which could mean brass or copper) for groups of four to six men. These kettles were lighter and more practical than the heavier cast iron marmite. The term chaudière originated as a nautical term and was later adopted in the French colonies of North America to refer to a specific type of cooking vessel. The *Dictionnaire de Marine* defines a chaudière as '…a large copper vessel in which the meat, or other food of the crew, is cooked,'[44] while Richelet's *Dictionnaire portatif* describes it as a '…large metal vase suitable for the kitchen and for the use of several workers and craftsmen,'[45] referring to both domestic and industrial kettles.

The phrase 'faire chaudière', commonly found in colonial documents on expeditions in New France, meant 'lighting the kettle' or 'cooking for the crew',[46] 'making soup',[47] or 'camping'.[48] According to the *Mercure Galant* of 1705, however, it was a 'Canadian term which means to boil the kettle, this word or rather this way of speaking comes from the Natives.'[49] Colonial officer Dumont de Montigny, serving in Louisiana, offers a vivid account of mealtime in a military camp, '…when the chaudière (kettle) is ready, everyone eats at his dish, after which, having smoked the pipe, we go to bed. While the majority are sleeping, the weapons are at their bell-of-arms, and there is always a guard … who also makes sure to boil the kettle for the next day.'[50]

Colonial Soldier's Kettles

Cooking kettles issued to colonial soldiers on detachments date back to the late seventeenth century and were often referenced as made from brass or copper (cuivre), with capacities ranging from 3 to 6 *pots*. As early as 1683, an account of supplies needed from France for a campaign against the Iroquois included 'one chaudron (cooking pot) per four [men]',[51] and four years later, essential articles requested for a similar campaign specified kettles for the soldiers, noting that 'they have 3 to 4 *pots* each, being one chaudière per six men.'[52]

In 1696, equipment withdrawn from Rochefort for Fort Naxouat in Acadia included '…4 kettles of cuivre for the detachments, without legs, from 4 to 5 *pots* each',[53] indicating they had flat bottoms. The following year, '8 iron kettles of 3 to 4 *pots*' and '6 copper kettles pour voyage [for travels] of 3 to 4 *pots*, without legs' were listed as loaded aboard the King's ships for the soldiers, showing that the kettles described 'for travels' were intended for detachments, as with those requested in 1696.[54] The previous year, historical records show that kettles supplied to 100 colonial soldiers sent from Québec to attack the English settlement at Pemaquid (now Bristol, Maine) were included as part of the canoe's supplies: 'It is needed, for the return of the hundred soldiers at Québec in their 25 canoes, 13 kettles of 5 *pots* each with their handles.'[55] We can also assume that when these men travelled for extended periods in birchbark canoes, they used the copper or brass kettles assigned to their vessels as primary cooking pots, which likely also doubled as tools for bailing water or melting spruce gum for repairs. This practice also appears to have been common throughout much of New France: 'We will supply what shall be needed for the subsistence of 100 soldiers boarded for two and a half months' as it is customary to give them in Canada.'[56] By 1697, round-bottom kettles made of brass, rather than copper, were requested for the troops stationed in Canada: '300 round kettles à pot, suitable for the soldiers who travel from 3 *pots* up to 5 or 6 *pots* made of brass.'[57] Meanwhile, camp cooking vessels for Acadian soldiers were described as '…6 kettles of cuivre for travels of 3 to 4 *pots*, without legs, priced at 5 livres each.'[58]

Throughout the eighteenth century, equipment lists for colonial troops prior to detachments typically included kettles. In 1706, for instance, one kettle weighing 5 *livres* was supplied to four colonial soldiers, as well as to officer De Boucherville. This was part of the expenses made by Lamothe Cadillac to prevent the Miamis, Pepitakokia, and Ouiatenons from waging war against the Outaouais.[59] A decade later, large quantities of kettles were provided to troops before their campaign against the Fox nation.[60] Unlike the cast iron marmites issued to soldiers in garrison at Louisbourg or Québec, kettles requested for outposts in the interior were likely made of copper

44 Nicolas Aubin, *Dictionaire de marine: contenant les termes de la navigation et de l'architecture naval* (Amsterdam: Chez Pierre Brunel, 1702), p.199.

45 Pierre Richelet, *Dictionnaire portatif de la langue françoise, extrait du grand dictionnaire…* (Lyon: J.M. Bruyset, 1775), p.291.

46 Aubin, *Dictionaire de marine*, p.199.

47 De Malartic, *Journal des campagnes au Canada de 1755 à 1760*, pp.11–12.

48 Robert Toupin, *Les écrits de Pierre Potier* (Ottawa: Les Presses de l'Université d'Ottawa, 1996), pp.282, 420.

49 *Mercure Galant dédié à monseigneur Le Dauphin. Janvier, 1705* (Paris: Chez Michel Brunet, 1705), pp.87–88.

50 Dumont de Montigny, *Regards sur les monde atlantique 1715–1747* (Sillery, Québec: Septentrion, 2008), p.148.

51 LAC, MG1-C11A, vol.6, f.155.

52 LAC, MG1-C11A, vol.9, f.169.

53 LAC, MG1-B, vol.19, f.31.

54 LAC, MG1-C11D, vol.3, f.57.

55 LAC, MG1-C11C, vol.2, f.97v.

56 LAC, MG1-C11C, vol.2, f.97.

57 LAC, MG1-B, vol.19, f.130, 131.

58 LAC, MG1-B. vol.19, f.142v.

59 LAC, MG1-C11A, vol.24, f.290v.

60 LAC, MG1-C11A, vol.38, f.185–190v.

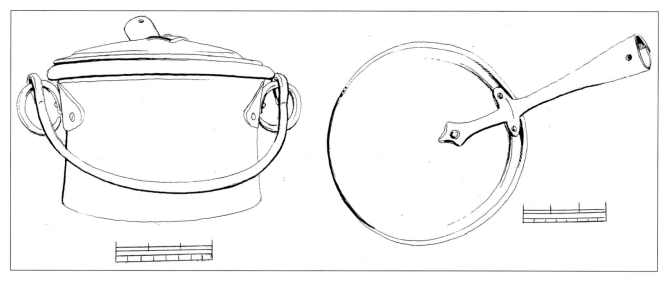

Artist's rendition of what is likely a French travelling kettle (chaudière de voyage) excavated from the Fletcher Site in Bay City, Michigan (c. 1740–1770). These cooking vessels were popular among militia and colonial officers during detachments or raids, providing a convenient way to carry both a pot and a pan, which served as a lid. Manufactured partly at Villefranche-de-Rouergue, France, in the 1750s, they were also intended for French settlers in New France. (Line drawing by Michel Pétard)

A 1757 engraving showing a *sergent* handing his pipe and fire steel to a woman in a military encampment. On the table, a cooking kettle with a cover doubling as a frying pan can be seen, likely a chaudière de voyage. (Le Testament de La Tulipe, P. Lenfant pinx., Beauvarlet Sculp., 1757)

or brass, as they were lighter and easier to transport by canoe over long distances. For example, in 1706, Lamothe Cadillac requested '…40 kettles weighing 9 *livres* [each]… indispensably necessary to place the soldiers in barracks because of the heat of the summer in these places,' suggesting these vessels may have also served as water reservoirs for drinking.[61]

During the Chickasaw wars, colonial officer Dumont de Montigny, who accompanied Bienville on a large-scale military campaign, noted that soldiers were using kettles: 'For it was necessary to abandon, to pick up the kettle, blankets, jars…A [mess] bowl is, as we know it, for five or six people'.[62] In 1734, kettles provided to 56 colonial soldiers on a campaign against the Foxes were included

---

61   LAC, MG1-C11A, vol.24, f.272.

62   *Journal de la société des américanistes* (Paris: Au siège de la société, 1931), vol.XXIII, Fasciscule 2, p.339.

in each canoe's supplies, consisting of '11 kitchen kettles weighing 102 *livres*', '11 kettles for water weighing 98½ *livres*,' and '11 kettles for gum weighing 11¾ *livres*', along with other essentials. It appears each canoe had three types of kettles: one for cooking, one for water, and smaller ones for melting spruce gum to repair canoes.[63] Five years later, 112 colonial soldiers, cadets, and militiamen attacking the Chickasaws were supplied with 18 canoes, equipped with '18 kitchen kettles', '18 gum kettles', and '18 kettles for water', meaning each set served about six men.[64] In that same year, a kettle weighing 7¼ *livres* was provided to a detachment of five cadets and two soldiers sent against the Chickasaws.[65] The previous year, Pierre Gaultier de Varennes et de La Vérendrye, a colonial officer, fur trader, and explorer, had issued kettles to his men, observing that they were 'useful in travels', serving multiple purposes like cooking, water transport, and canoe repairs.[66]

During King George's War, kettles with lids were occasionally distributed to colonial soldiers, such as when cadets and militiamen garrisoned at Prairie-de-la-Madeleine received '2 kettles, covered, weighing 25 *livres* [altogether]', suggesting that some kettles included lids.[67] By the Seven Years War, one copper kettle was typically issued for every four men, as reported by two French soldiers captured at Fort William-Henry in 1757, who remarked, 'every four men for cooking had a Copper kettle'.[68] According to French officer La Pause, officers, domestiques, regular and colonial soldiers, militiamen, and Native Americans were each supplied with one kettle per four men.[69] In contrast, records from Intendant Bigot's trial indicate that officers received 'one covered kettle' each, while domestiques, colonial soldiers, militiamen, and Natives were issued 'one kettle per five men', suggesting a distinction between the types of kettles issued to officers and those issued to the others.[70]

In fact, the kettles used by soldiers on detachment were likely the chaudière à la façon anglaise (English-style kettle) or chaudière évasé (flared kettle), terms used by French merchants for kettles with outward-flaring walls and no lids. A 1753 memo from the Rouffio brothers of Québec to their Amsterdam supplier indicates that these kettles were made in England and purchased through Holland:

…3 or 4 bales of flared kettle, meaning without a lid, of brass, that they be nestled. They are like cauldrons where the smallest holds a quart up to two or three cruches. These are the ones you were told about that came from Holland. We believe that we could purchase these from Villefranche at a cheaper price. We also believe that these are purchased from England. This is an essential merchandise for trading … we receive these articles in nests being stacked one in the other.[71]

The Gradis family, who secured significant contracts from the French government during the Seven Years War to supply Canada's storehouses, requested from La Rochelle in 1756: '30 brass kettles, English-style, from 8 to 10 *pots*', '30 brass kettles, ditto, 2 to 6 *pots*', and '400 brass kettles, English-style with brass lugs, the handles annealed. The said kettles with a flat bottom and deeper than the French ones.'[72] The following year, these dealers purchased '8,000 brass kettles, flared, assorted sizes, brass lugs, English-style, for the fur trade.'[73] These English-style or English-made kettles were also found at various forts, including '12 English kettles' at Fort Saint-Frédéric in 1748,[74] and '23 flared kettles, out of service' at Fort Carillon in 1758,[75] suggesting their use for detachments.

Colonial Officer's Kettles

Colonial officers, like soldiers, were supplied with cooking equipment for war parties or detachments, though their gear was typically of higher quality and often featured cooking vessels with lids. During the Fox wars and Chickasaw campaigns, for instance, the provided cooking pots included kitchen kettles with lids and kettles 'for water', possibly used as drinking vessels or water reserves. Prior to his departure at Montréal, M. de Noyelle, leading a war party against the Fox in 1734, received '2 kitchen kettles weighing [together] 21 *livres*'.[76] Five years later, Baron de Longueuil, commanding a Chickasaw campaign, was provided with '1 kettle of cuivre, 1 kettle for water, weighing together 17¾ *livres*', while his second in command, M. de Sabrevois, and other officers received '1 copper [or brass] kettle' and '1 kettle for water', though lighter than those given to De Longueuil.[77] Interestingly, De Noyelle's expedition canoes were allocated a 'kitchen kettle', 'kettle for

63 LAC, MG1-C11A, vol.61, f.151–151v.
64 LAC, MG1-C11A, vol.71, f.164–164v.
65 LAC, MG1-C11A, vol.71, f.156–179.
66 Pierre Gaultier de Varennes et de La Vérendrye, *Journals and Letters of Pierre Gaultier de Varennes de La Vérendrye and his Sons* (Toronto: The Champlain Society, 1927), p.309.
67 LAC, MG1-C11A, vol.117, f.208.
68 LOC, Colonial Office 5 folio 47, E. of Loudoun's Letter of April 25th. 1757, Declaration of two Prisoners taken the 23.d March 1757 at Fort Wm. Henry, Information of John Victor and Guillaume Chasse, two French Prisoners, Fort William Henry March 25th.
69 RAPQ, 1932–1933, p.210.
70 Bigot, *Mémoire Pour Messire François Bigot*, pp.39–40.

71 BAnQ-Q, P908, P9, Mémoire à accomplir par les frères Rouffio et Romagnac pour l'année 1753 relativement aux commandes de marchandises auprès de négociants de France et de Hollande, destinées à être envoyées au Québec… , 1752.
72 LAC, MG 18, H63, Fonds famille Gradis, F-1599, M. D. Goguet, La Rochelle, 6 octobre 1756.
73 LAC, MG 18, H63, Fonds famille Gradis, F-1600, M. D. Goguet, La Rochelle, 12 octobre 1757.
74 LAC, MG1-C11A, vol.92, f.36.
75 LAC, MG18, K9, vol.6, f.458.
76 LAC, MG1-C11A, vol.62, f.149.
77 LAC, MG1-C11A, vol.71, f.156, 157v.

water', and 'kettle for gum',[78] whereas Longueuil's canoes had only one 'kettle for water' and one 'kettle for gum'.[79]

Equipment lists dating from King George's War provide additional information about the kettles supplied to colonial officers on detachments. Many of these kettles, often described as having lids, weighed between 3½ *livres*,[80] and up to 13 *livres* for the 'large kettles.'[81] In 1746, officers Dubreuil and La Corne, along with *cadet* De la Saussaye and two Canadians heading to New England, received '1 covered kettle weighing 8 *livres*.'[82] The same year, officer Le Borgne and militia officers at Fort Saint-Frédéric were supplied with '1 covered kettle weighing 10½ *livres*,'[83] while *capitaine* de Linctot at Soulange received '1 kettle weighing 6½ *livres*.'[84] In 1747, '8 covered kettles for Messieurs the officers and the chaplain, weighing 64 livres' were sent with a war party led by Rigaud de Vaudreuil,[85] and officers La Corne, Dubreuil, and Bellestre, sent to the Pays-d'en-Haut, were given '3 covered kettles' and three smaller kettles totalling 25 *livres* in weight.[86]

Small brass or copper cooking vessels, referred to as marmites, were issued to officers of the regular troops who landed in Canada in 1755, with a shipment listing 'two hundred small marmites of cuivre of 4 *pintes* for officers.'[87]

À Montauban Kettles

The type of covered kettle issued to colonial officers in New France may have corresponded to two popular types of kettles of the period dubbed à Montauban (from the town of Mautauban) or 'de voyage' (for travel) by French merchants. In 1753, a memorandum by the Rouffio brothers of Québec described the à Montauban copper kettles, manufactured at Ville-Franche near Montauban, France, as having lids equipped with a single central ring and noted that these kettles were specifically requested for Canada and intended for the Native Americans:

> We have commissioned the Sieur Mothes of Villefranche. Copperware, to send from Villefranche … 10 kettles with their lids and without handles. Let there be a flexible ring in the middle to open the kettle … 50 small copper kettles that hold a little more than a bouteille and a half up to three quarters that we call 'à Montauban'. Let the greater part hold two bouteilles, in other words, a quart and that there be none of three quarters. No handle on the lid. There needs to be in

the middle of the lid a small handle-type ring to lift it…they must be thin, since these are, once again, for the Natives.[88]

Travelling Kettles (Chaudières de Voyage)

The second type of covered copper kettle, known as pour voyage or de voyage, translating to travel kettle or kettle for travels, was likely the most popular among colonial officers. These kettles were reportedly intended for French colonials living in Canada, as suggested by the contents of a letter written in 1753 by Québec-based merchants to wholesalers in France: '20 copper kettles, tinned, with their saucepan and handle like the ones we sent you for you to see. Observe that we need those that we ask for of a good third larger and that they be a little more solid as they will serve for the French inhabitants.'[89]

These types of kettles had in fact been shipped from France to Canada for many years and in 1745, 200 copper kettles with tinned linings and casserole lids, ranging from 3 to 8 *pots*, weighing 1,700 *livres*, were sent to Québec by the merchant Pascaud.[90] The following year, another 400 of these kettles were requested to be sent in 1747.[91] By the Seven Years War, large quantities of kettles with exterior-fitting lids and projecting handles were sent by the Gradis family, likely intended for the colonial troops. In 1755, for example, '500 copper kettles, tinned, with lids as casseroles from 8, 10 to 12 *pots*' and '150 kettles, ditto, from 2 to 4 *pots*' were shipped.[92] The next year, '800 copper kettles, tinned, with casserole lids of 10 *pots* each' were supplied by the same merchant for Gradis.[93]

These 'travelling kettles' frequently appear in the probate records of colonial and militia officers, with one example from 1740 listing Charles Renaud, Sieur de Dubuisson, as owning 'one small copper lid from a travel cooking pot (marmite)'.[94] In 1741, Jean-Baptiste Provancher dit Belleville, *capitaine en second* at Nicolet, had 'one travel kettle and its lid' valued at 6 livres,[95] while the colonial officer Charles Porcheron de Decombre left behind 'two

78 LAC, MG1-C11A, vol.62, f.151v
79 LAC, MG1-C11A, vol.71, f.164.
80 LAC, MG1-C11A, vol.117, f.196–196v.
81 LAC, MG1-C11A, vol.117, f.108–109.
82 LAC, MG1-C11A, vol 86, f.194v-195.
83 LAC, MG1-C11A, vol.117, f.188v.
84 LAC, MG1-C11A, vol.117, f.190-190v.
85 LAC, MG1-C11A, vol.117, f.22v.
86 LAC, MG1-C11A, vol.117, f.177.
87 LAC, MG1-C11A, vol.100, f.285v

88 BAnQ-Q, P908, P9, Mémoire à accomplir par les frères Rouffio et Romagnac pour l'année 1753 relativement aux commandes de marchandises auprès de négociants de France et de Hollande, destinées à être envoyées au Québec… , 1752.
89 BAnQ-Q, P908, P9, Mémoire à accomplir par les frères Rouffio et Romagnac pour l'année 1753 relativement aux commandes de marchandises auprès de négociants de France et de Hollande, destinées à être envoyées au Québec… , 1752.
90 LAC, MG1-C11A, vol.83, f.278v.
91 LAC, MG1-C11A, vol.86, f.12.
92 LAC, MG 18, H63, Fonds famille Gradis, F-1599, M. Horutener et compagnie, Rouen, 18 octobre 1755.
93 LAC, MG 18, H63, Fonds famille Gradis, F-1599, M. Horutener et compagnie, Rouen, 7 août 1756.
94 BAnQ-TR, Greffe du notaire Hyacinthe-Olivier Pressé, Inventaire de la communauté des biens de Louise Picard, veuve de feu Charles Renaud, écuyer, Sieur de Dubuisson, Major de la ville et Gouverneur des Trois-Rivières, 2 janvier 1740.
95 BAnQ-TR, Greffe du notaire Jean Leproust, Inventaire des biens de la communauté de Marie-Jeanne Lefebvre, veuve de

large copper kettles with their lids', 'a mid-sized kettle with its lid', and 'a small flared kettle' in Québec before leaving for Montréal.[96]

In 1755, François Delpée, a militia *capitaine*, had 'one copper travel kettle' also valued at 6 livres,[97] while in 1759, militia *capitaine* François Rochereau owned 'one small travel kettle with its lid' valued at 15 livres.[98] Finally, in 1761, Sieur Jean Jacques de St-Martin, a *capitaine* in the colonial troops, listed among his personal possessions 'one large travel kettle' worth 24 livres and 'two small travel kettles without their lids' valued at 2 livres.[99]

The Colonial Soldier's Eating Utensils

No military *ordonnance* from the period specifies the cutlery used by infantrymen, but it is reasonable to assume that, during campaigns or detachments, each colonial soldier likely carried his own personal eating utensils, which he used to eat from either his own bowl or a shared communal bowl or kettle. Since a colonial soldier's primary food consisted of soup made from a ration of peas and salted pork, accompanied by bread, this liquid meal was typically eaten with a spoon. Drier foods, such as meat, were initially consumed using a knife and fingers until the fork was adopted in military contexts at some point during the eighteenth century.

Spoons

Tablespoons have been an essential part of daily life for colonial soldiers in Canada since the 1680s, as highlighted in 1685 when Intendant De Meulles stated that soldiers expected their hosts to provide 'dishes, spoons, pepper', reflecting their use of the same utensils as the colonists.[100] A 1726 ruling further restricted inn owners from accepting 'clothing, glass bottles, earthenware or stoneware, dishes,

An illustration from Salmon's 1788 edition of *Art du potier d'étain* showing a worker pouring molten pewter into a spoon mould while holding it in place with his thighs.

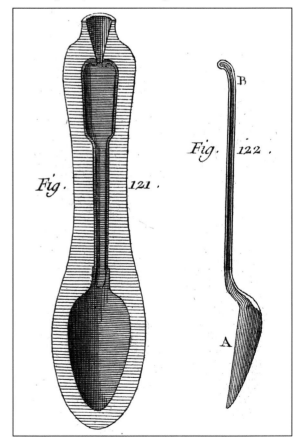

A half spoon mould and cast spoon featured in Diderot's *Potier d'étain*, as part of the 1771 edition of the *Encyclopédie*. This style of spoon, with a 'drop' style bowl attachment and slightly tapered fiddle back handle, was popular in France during the third quarter of the eighteenth century.

Jean-Baptiste Provancher dit Belleville, capitaine en second des milices, de Nicolet, 27 janvier, 1756.

96   BAnQ-Q, TL5, D1944. Procès de Charles Decombre (Porcheron dit Decombre), officier détaché des troupes de la Marine, contre Marie Couture, veuve de Simon Massy, 26 février 1758–28 mars 1759.

97   BAnQ-TR, Greffe du notaire Jean Leproust, Inventaire et partage des biens de la communauté des défunts François Delpée, capitaine de milice et Catherine Moriceau, du fief Tonnacour, 12 août 1755.

98   BAnQ-TR, Greffe du notaire Jean Leproust, Inventaire des biens de la communauté de Marguerite Provancher, veuve de François Rochereau, capitaine de milice, du Cap de la Madeleine, 22 janvier 1759.

99   BAnQ-TR, Greffe du notaire Louis Pillard, Inventaire et description des biens et meubles de Feu Gabrielle le Gardeur veuve de feu le Sieur Jean Jacques de St-Martin, Capitaine des troupes de la Marine, 10 mars, 1761.

100 Philippe Fournier, *La Nouvelle-France au fil des édits: chronologie reconstituée d'après les principaux édits, ordonnances, lois et règlements émis sous le Régime français* (Québec: ditions du Septentrion, 2011), p.189.

Left: Two corroded spoons recovered from the Fortress of Louisbourg. These spoons offer a glimpse into the style of common spoons used in French colonial North America. (Courtesy of National Historic Sites, Parks Canada. Photo Kevin Gélinas)

Right: A circa 1726–1727 drawing by Nicolas Delaunay depicting the King of France's spoon, likely showcasing the latest French fashion in cutlery at the time

Illustration from Surirey de Saint-Rémy's *Mémoires d'artillerie*, showing a wooden spoon used for serving mortar when proofing powder. This late seventeenth-century depiction of a trifid-handle spoon likely represents a common style of spoon from the period, one that may have also been used by French soldiers for eating.

Fiddle-pattern silver coffee and tablespoons engraved with the coat of arms of the Marquis de Montcalm on back of the spoons. The larger spoon is marked by Pierre Miston (1695–1757) of Montpellier, France. (Univers culturel de Saint-Sulpice. Photo Kevin Gélinas)

Left: French pewter spoon found at Fort Ouiatenon, bearing the King's coat of arms on the fiddle-shaped handle. The spoon features a thin rattail reinforcement where the bowl and handle meet, a common characteristic of pewter spoons from French sites such as Fort Senneville and Fort Michilimackinac. (Courtesy of Tippecanoe County Historical Society. Photo Thomas Wojcinski)

Right: Portion of an iron spoon found at Fort Ticonderoga, displaying a fiddle-shaped handle, possibly representing a fer blanchi (pewter-dipped iron) spoon, similar to those recorded at Québec during King George's War. (Collection of the Fort Ticonderoga Museum, New York)

plates, spoons, forks' from soldiers and officers,[101] and by the 1730s, pewter spoons were commonly found in outlying forts. In 1738, '2 pewter spoons' were recorded at Fort Niagara,[102] while '1 dozen ½ pewter spoons' were sent to Fort Ouiatenon; a decade later, '24 pewter spoons' were itemised at Fort Saint-Frédéric, likely for the garrison or redistribution to nearby forts.[103]

At the onset of King George's War, over five hundred spoons were purchased in Québec for the war effort, including '40 dozen iron spoons of fer blanchi' and '4 dozen pewter spoons.'[104] French period dictionaries explain that 'fer blanchi', literally translated as whitened iron, refers to iron beaten into blades and dipped in molten pewter to create a thin, rust-resistant coating.[105] It can be assumed that pewter and pewter-dipped iron tablespoons became the standard eating utensils used by colonial soldiers on the frontier.

In addition, many colonial soldiers carried their own personal spoons, either pewter or wooden. In 1754, 'one small wood tablespoon' and 'one wooden table spoon' were found in the pack and sack of the soldier Pierre de Monferand at Pointe-à-la-Caille near Québec.[106] Three years earlier, in Trois-Rivières, soldiers Cumberland, Beausoleil, and Sanssoucy were found to carry a tin cup, three boxwood-handled knives, a spring knife, and a pewter spoon, suggesting they may have shared both the spoon and the cup.[107]

Pewter spoons used by colonial soldiers were either imported from France, as recorded in merchant records, or cast locally. In 1740, Montréal merchant Ignace Gamelin imported '8 dozen fine pewter spoons' priced at 3 livres 10 sols per dozen,[108] and ordered another eight dozen two years later.[109] *Then again,* many spoons were

also made locally by craftsmen using bronze or cast-iron moulds. Swedish botanist Pehr Kalm, traveling through Canada in 1749, noted the widespread use of low-grade pewter spoons among French colonists, which he reported contained 'a lot of lead'.[110] In January 1755, 'pewter spoons' were urgently needed at Fort Duquesne and requested from Montréal to replenish supplies,[111] while shipments of equipment intended for the troops arriving at Québec that year included '3,000 pewter spoons for the soldiers,' '6 spoon moulds,' and 1,000 *livres* of pewter, likely intended for making additional spoons with the moulds.[112]

Forks

In France, the hand fork became fashionable in the seventeenth century, primarily for pricking pieces of food during meals, which were then brought to the mouth with the fingers. The custom took time to gain acceptance, as Louis XIV was still using his fingers for meat at the end of the century. According to a 1691 French treatise: 'It is an incivility to suck and lick your fingers. The plate should always be in front of oneself on the edge of the table; the knife and fork on the right, and the bread on the left. The bread is brought to the mouth with the hand, and the meat with the fork.'[113] By the eighteenth century, this practice extended beyond the upper classes to lower classes in France and its colonies, including their use amongst soldiers. In 1752, for instance, 'six steel forks' were found in a wood chest belonging to Louis Bonin, a *caporal* in the Lanaudière company at Québec.[114] Three years later, each soldier of the Troupes de terre arriving in Québec was issued 'one knife, one spoon, one fork', with the forks specifically noted as being made of iron, indicating that these utensils had become standard equipment for infantry during large-scale military campaigns in France.[115]

It is unclear when colonial soldiers first adopted forks, but by the 1740s, they were recorded in the inventories of several military outposts and forts. In 1740, Fort Saint-Frédéric listed '1 pewter spoon' and '1 steel fork,' both valued at 5 sols,[116] and the following year, '7 steel forks' were logged at Fort Niagara.[117] Between 1746 and 1747, large quantities of forks were purchased to replenish

101 Fournier, *La Nouvelle-France au fil des édits*, p.413.
102 LAC, MG1-C11A, vol.73, f.369.
103 LAC, MG1-C11A, vol.92, f.35v.
104 LAC, MG1-C11A, vol.117, f.54, 64v, 66.
105 Antoine Furetière, *Dictionnaire universel françois & latin...* (Paris: chez Estienne Ganeau, 1704), vol.1.
106 BAnQ-Q, TP1, S777, D178, Procès de Pierre de Monferand (Montferrand) dit Chevalier, 17 novembre 1754–17 mai 1755.
107 BAnQ-Q, TP1, S777, D174, Procès de Pierre Beaudouin (Baudouin) dit Cumberland, Joseph Ceilier dit Beausoleil, Ponsian Allé dit Sansoucy, François-Xavier Guernoté dit Latulippe et Joseph Gamin (Jamin) dit Saint-Louis, soldats, prisonniers, accusés d'avoir provoqué l'incendie de la Basse-Ville de Trois-Rivières, d'avoir commis plusieurs vols dans les maisons incendiées, et d'avoir blasphémé le Saint Nom de Dieu, 21 mai–28 août 1752
108 Division des archives (Université de Montréal, collection Louis-François-Georges Baby, G2/58 (mf 3114),Facture de marchandises chargées par J. Pascaud et consignées à Ignace Gamelin, La Rochelle, 28 mai 1740.
109 Division des archives (Université de Montréal, collection Louis-François-Georges Baby, G2/58 (mf 3112, 3113), Facture de marchandises chargées par Pascaud Frères, d'ordre de Mons. Guy et consignées à Ignace Gamelin, de Montréal, La Rochelle, 1er juin 1742.

110 Kalm et al, *Voyage de Pehr Kalm*, p.415, f.833.
111 Archives du Séminaire de Québec, Viger-Verreau, P32/002/164a, Papiers Contrecoeur, État des effets demandés à Montréal pour le Fort Duquesne, 15 janvier 1755.
112 LAC, MG1-C11A, vol.100, f.284v.
113 Étienne de Blégny, *Les élémens ou Premières instructions de la jeunesse* (Paris: Chez Charles Cabri, 1691).
114 BAnQ-Q, TL5, D1667. TL5, Procès criminel contre Louis Bonin, caporal de la compagnie de Lanaudière et soldat congédié; et Denis Lemoine dit Parisien, 14 ans, soldat de la compagnie de Lanaudière en garnison à Québec, logé à la caserne Dauphine, et complices, accusés de vol., 17 février–6 août 1752.
115 Société historique de Montréal, *Campagne de 1755*, p.4.
116 LAC, MG1-C11A, vol.73, f.156.
117 LAC, MG1-C11A, vol.75, f.265.

  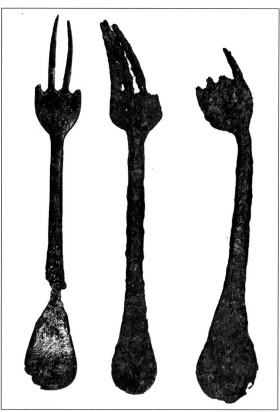

Left: Engraving of one of Louis XV's forks by Nicolas Delaunay, c. 1726–1727, showcasing the latest fashion in forks at the French court.

Centre: Three steel forks from Louisbourg Fortress, all displaying the typical French four-tine design. All of these forks feature a stem that gradually widens toward the curved terminal, a design often referred to as the 'Hanoverian Pattern' by British researchers. (Courtesy of National Historic Sites, Parks Canada. Photo Kevin Gélinas)

Right: Excavated examples include three steel or iron forks found at Fort Ticonderoga, each with four narrow tines. (Fort Ticonderoga Museum collection, New York. Photo Kevin Gélinas.)

Left: Three steel forks were also discovered at Fort Michilimackinac. (Mackinac State Historic Parks collection, Michigan. Photo Kevin Gélinas)

Right: Five silver forks with fiddle-pattern handles recovered from the wreck of L'Auguste. These likely belonged to high-ranking and wealthy passengers, including Jean Baptiste Le Ber de Saint Paul et de Senneville, a colonial officer whose coat of arms was engraved on one of the forks. A serving fork bearing the arms of Jacques-René Gaultier de Varennes, another colonial officer, was also found. (Courtesy of National Historic Sites, Parks Canada. Photo Kevin Gélinas)

Detail from *Le Goust* by Nicolas Arnoult, 1687, in *Recueil de Modes*. By the end of the seventeenth century, the use of the fork had become common among the French upper classes. These refined eating habits were closely tied to the courtly etiquette established under Louis XIV.

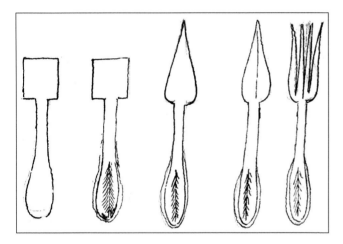

An excerpt from an unpublished 1763 manuscript by Fougeroux de Bondaroy, showing the production process of mass-produced forks at Saint-Étienne. Bondaroy notes that these four-tine forks underwent several manufacturing steps before finishing on the grindstone: 'The millstone removes the burrs on the handle. Along the part that has been ground, the handles are tapered and rounded.'

One half of a fork mould and a cast fork featured in Diderot's *Potier d'étain*, as part of the 1771 edition of the *Encyclopédie*. This style of four-tined fork with a slightly tapered fiddleback handle and narrow shoulders was common in France during the third quarter of the eighteenth century.

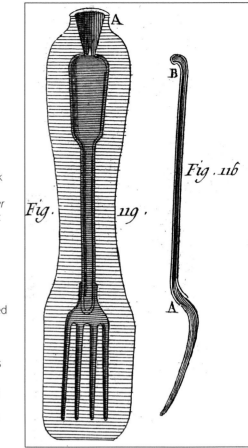

the King's storehouses, including '42 dozen forks of fer blanchi' priced at 13 livres 10 sols per dozen, '48 pewter spoons' at 4 livres per dozen, and '6 dozen iron forks' at 3 livres per dozen.[118] By 1748, Fort Saint-Frédéric recorded '30 steel (table) forks' and '2 large forks,' the latter likely used for lifting meat from cooking pots or serving it from dishes.[119] The following year, a task force led by Boishébert to Île Saint-Jean carried '6 forks' at 10 sols each and '6 pewter spoons' of equal value,[120] with steel forks requested at Fort Duquesne in early 1755.[121]

Table forks used by colonial soldiers were likely very similar to those used by French settlers in the St Lawrence Valley. In 1749, Pehr Kalm observed that '... folks that live in Canada use forks to eat; they are made of iron and have four tines.'[122] A decade later, John Knox noted that among Canadian colonists, 'every person was obliged to use his own knife and wine, there being only a spoon and a four-pronged fork laid with each napkin and plate.'[123] Shipping records reveal that most four-tine steel or iron forks came from Saint-Étienne, France, and were available in various grades of quality. For instance, in 1742, merchant Dugard shipped three grades of forks to Québec from Saint-Étienne: 'ordinary forks having 4 tines, No 1,' 'semi-fine forks, No 2,' and 'fine forks, No 3.'[124] The following year, additional shipments included '24 dozen steel forks, No 1'

118   LAC, MG1-C11A, vol.115, f.78.

119   LAC, MG1-C11A, vol.92, f.36v, 37.

120   LAC, MG1-C11A, vol.92, f.48v.

121   ASQ, Viger-Verreau, P32/002/164a, Papiers Contrecoeur, État des effets demandés à Montréal pour le Fort Duquesne, 15 janvier, 1755.

122   Kalm et al, *Voyage de Pehr Kalm*, p.415, f.833

123   John Knox, *An Historical Journal of the Campaigns in North America For the Years 1757, 1758, 1759, and 1760* (Toronto, Canada: Champlain Society, 1914), vol.9, p.236.

124   Centre des archives du monde du travail, Fonds Dugard, Série AQ, 62 AQ 41.

and '18 dozen finer forks,' once again sourced from Saint-Étienne for use in Canada.[125] Notably, an unpublished 1763 manuscript by Duhamel de Monceau described the fork-making workshops of Saint-Étienne, emphasizing their affordability and widespread availability: 'This is the manufactory of iron forks, which are given at such an inexpensive price that the less well-to-do artisans are not tempted to do without them … Their loss is so insignificant it is easy to compensate. These advantages make this utensil very common throughout the countryside.'[126]

Serving Bowls and Water Cans

In barracks, forts, or outposts, colonial soldiers typically ate from communal serving bowls or mess tins, known as gamelles in French, and used bidons to dispense beverages. The bidon was '…a kind of can or wooden vessel, containing four or five pintes, in which to hold the beverage intended for each meal for a crew of a ship.'[127] Both items were standard issue to the French Marine as per ordonnances from 6 October 1674, and 15 April 1689. By 15 April 1718, all troops, whether in garrison or on foot, were required to carry their own cooking pots, gamelles, and casks as if going into battle. The 1753 infantry ordonnance mandated that each tent or chamber of soldiers have 'a gamelle, a cask or [water] can'. In 1738, the colonial troops at Louisbourg were provided a gamelle for soup and a bidon for water per seven men.[128] However, these items were likely impractical for detachments or short campaigns, as they are rarely listed on official equipment lists and may have been burdensome to carry on foot or in a canoe.

French dictionaries of the time often describe gamelles used aboard ships as wooden bowls, with the Dictionnaire militaire defining them as 'a bowl of earthenware in which one puts the soup intended for three, five, or seven soldiers of a chamber. The bowls that serve for a ship's crew are made of wood.'[129] Another source further explains that

gamelles were 'usually a wooden bowl. Those of sailors are very hollow and without a rim; where we serve the soup, or what is intended for each dish of the men composing the crew.'[130] Wooden gamelles were likely preferred over earthenware to prevent breakage from the rough sea. As one account noted, infantry troops aboard ships should receive 'two wooden porringers with which to drink, two wooden bowls to eat from, because those of earthenware are broken from the first day.'[131]

Early records show that gamelle bowls, undoubtedly intended for military usage in New France, were initially made of wood. In 1688, for instance, '400 wooden gamelles or dishes' were dispatched from Rochefort to Canada,[132] followed by a request for an additional 200 in 1692,[133] and another 400 the following year.[134] By 1692, '500 strong wooden gamelles' were needed in Canada, suggesting that earlier examples may have been too thin or brittle.[135] In 1706, Lamothe Cadillac requested '40 dishes of wood or pewter' for Fort Pontchartrain,[136] while 38 wooden dishes remained in the King's storehouses at Louisbourg in 1742.[137]

During King George's War, Québec artisans crafted numerous gamelles for military use, likely smaller and intended for individual soldiers. By 1747, they had supplied 1,082 gamelles and 519 bidons, which were probably made of wood due to the prevalence of barrel-making expertise in the region.[138] However, by the late 1740s, pewter gamelles were increasingly needed for troops in Québec. In 1750, '20 pewter gamelles to make soup' were asked for,[139] and in 1751, Intendant Bigot requested '12 pewter basins or gamelles for soup', likely intended for use in barracks at Québec.[140]

When French regular troops arrived in Québec in 1755, they were issued '400 tin gamelles' and '400 tin bidons,'[141] four per company.[142] According to La Porterie's Institutions militaires for French cavalry and dragoons, these tin items included a bidon with a 12-pint capacity and a gamelle weighing 1 livre 6 onces.[143] By 1760, due to

125 Centre des archives du monde du travail, Fonds Dugard, Série AQ, 62 AQ 41.

126 Houghton Library, Harvard Library, Harvard University. Call No.: MS Typ 432.1. Descriptions des Arts et Métiers, 1721–1787. Duhamel du Monceau, Fabrique des fourchettes de fer à Saint-Étienne, 1763 (manuscrit). f.1, recto-verso.; Auguste Denis Fougeroux de Bondaroy, Lion et le Forez. Voyage fait en 1763 par Auguste Denis Fougeroux de Bondaroy, membre de l'Académie des sciences, MS ANC A156, Médiathèques municipales Saint-Étienne…Partie de l'art du taillandier : de la fabrique des fourchettes de fer.

127 Dictionnaire militaire, portatif, contenant tous les termes propres à la Guerre (Paris: Chez Gissez, 1758), vol.1, p.216.

128 LAC, C11B. vol.20, f.318.

129 François Alexandre Aubert de La Chesnaye-Desbois, Dictionnaire militaire: ou, Recueil alphabetique de tous les termes propres … (Paris: Chez David fils, 1745), p.513.

130 Encyclopédie ou dictionnaire raisonné des sciences, des arts (Paris: chez Briasson, 1757), vol.7, p.457.

131 P. A. Bardet de Villeneuve, La tactique ou l'art de ranger des bataillons (À La Haye: J. van Duren, 1740) p.313.

132 LAC, MG1-B, vol.15, f.26v.

133 LAC, MG1-B, vol.16, f.78.

134 LAC, MG1-B, vol.16, f.142v.

135 LAC, MG1-B, vol.19, f.130.

136 LAC, MG1-C11A, F-24, f.272

137 LAC, C11B, vol.24, f.259v.

138 LAC, MG1-C11A, vol.117, f.95–116.

139 LAC, MG1-C11A, vol.93, f.342.

140 AR, Série D3, État des munitions, marchandises et petit habillement qu'il est nécessaire d'envoyer de France pour garnir les magasins du Roi à Québec pour l'année mille-sept-cent-cinquante-et-un, Québec, 31 octobre 1750.

141 LAC, MG1-C11A, vol.100, f.264v-265.

142 RAPQ, 1933–1934, p.68.

143 François de La Porterie, Institutions militaires pour la cavalerie et les dragons (Paris: Guillyn, 1754), p.337.

Illustration from the 1702 edition of *Dictionnaire de marine* showing a bidon or water can used in the French navy. It is described as, 'a kind of can or wooden vessel, containing four or five pintes, used to hold the beverage intended for each meal for a ship's crew.'

Scene from an engraving showing French soldiers drinking and smoking in Paris while celebrating the victory at the Battle of Lutterberg in 1758. One soldier holds a pitcher decorated with what could be the King's coat of arms, while another pours himself a drink from a bottle. (Jacques-Philippe Le Bas, *Décoration du feu d'artifice tiré devant l'Hôtel de ville de Paris le 28 octobre 1758*, Bibliothèque de l'Institut National d'Histoire de l'Art, Collections Jacques Doucet, OC 34)

equipment shortages, Chevalier de Lévis recorded in his journal that bidons, gamelles, and ladles had to be fabricated locally from wood.[144]

Silverware of the Colonial Officers

Colonial officers often brought their own personal tableware on large-scale campaigns, where a tent and table would be set up for dining. An ordonnance dated April 1, 1705, specified that during campaigns, 'no infantry colonel, cavalry or dragoons camp master, nor any captain, junior officer or volunteer, may have in his equipment, other silverware than spoons, forks and goblets',[145] reflecting the widespread use of luxurious utensils among French officers. However, the King regarded such items as unnecessary for military service. As a result, high-ranking officials on North American campaigns likely used personal silverware as a status symbol, while officers leading smaller detachments may have opted for inexpensive imitation silver utensils, leaving their more valuable silverware at home.

By the summer of 1755, '200 spoons of métal' and '200 steel forks' were issued to the metropolitan officers under Dieskau.[146] The term métal, also recorded as métail, referred to a hard, white pewter alloy made from Babbitt alloy, copper, and bismuth, used in making 'spoons and forks that we polish in the way of silver'.[147] According to Salmon's *Art du potier d'étain*, 'métail de prince' is a pewter alloy with antimony used for various utensils. The *Encyclopédie méthodique* defines métal as an alloy of pewter with antimony spelter, bismuth, and red copper.[148] These officers, therefore, received higher-quality imitation silver spoons and steel forks, far superior to the iron forks and common pewter spoons provided to soldiers. La Pause noted that in July 1755, each officer was equipped with a silver spoon (likely of métail), a small cooking pot, two pewter plates, and an iron fork.[149]

Officers may have also used utensils made of what the French termed 'composition', likely referring to white tombac, a copper alloy 'whitened using arsenic and resembling silver'.[150] As outlined in *Règlemens des maîtres potiers d'étain de Lyon*, 'fine pewter composé, or alloyed with

144 Henri-Raymond Casgrain, *Collection des manuscrits du maréchal de Lévis, vol.II, Lettres du chevalier de Lévis concernant la guerre du Canada (1756–1760)* (Montréal: C.O. Beauchemin & Fils, 1889), p.275.

145 *Code militaire, ou Compilation des reglemens et ordonnances de Louis XIV, roy de France et de Navarre, faites pour les gens de guerre depuis 1651 jusques à present...* (Paris: chez Denys Mariette, 1708), p.232.

146 LAC, MG1-C11A, vol.100, f.284v.

147 *Dictionnaire portatif de commerce, contenant la connoissance des ...* (Copenhague: C. et A. Philibert, 1760), vol.3, p.24.

148 Pierre-Augustin Salmon, *Art du potier d'étain, première et seconde partie* (Paris: Chez Moutard, 1788), p.138; *Encyclopédie méthodique* (Paris: Chez Panckoucke, 1784), vol.3, p.172.

149 *RAPQ, 1933–1934, p.68.*

150 Pierre Jaubert, *Dictionnaire raisonné universel des arts et métiers, contenant l'histoire, la description, la police des fabriques & manufactures de France et des pays étrangers ...* (Paris: p.f.Didot, 1773), p.293.

Detail from a c. 1745 engraving titled *Halte d'officiers* by Ravenet, depicting French officers at rest. Note the larger platter at the centre surrounded by smaller plates, likely made of pewter, although the tumblers from which they drink were probably silver, as permitted by the 15 April 1705 ordinance. (Gravé par Ravenet. À Paris chez Roguié, rue S. Jacques au Boisseau d'Or)

copper and a ninth of antimony (pewter which is ordinarily called composition), is of one grain.'[151] During the 1750s, the merchant Augé received '2 dozen pewter spoons' priced at 50 sols per dozen as well as '6 dozen composition spoons' at 40 sols.[152] Colonial records also reveal that Paris was a main supply source for these spoons, as established by '6 dozen composition spoons' requested from Parisian wholesalers by Québec merchants in 1753.[153] As for forks,

a Québec merchant's 1752 invoice included '9 dozen steel forks, in the silver-style, dipped [in pewter]',[154] and in 1753, Québec merchants requested '18 dozen steel forks, in the silver style' from the Thiolière brothers of Saint-Étienne.[155]

Probate records suggest that many colonial officers owned considerable silverware. In 1742, Henry Albert,

151 *Reglemens des maitres potiers d'étain de la ville de Lyon...avec le Reglement Général fait pour l'essai de l'Etain, par l'Edit du mois de Mai 1691* (Lyon: Chez Claude-André Vialon, 1769), p.69.

152 LAC, Étienne Augé, 1750-1780, Fonds sur le commerce, Bobine M-859, No 5, Facture de Meynardie à Madame Augé.

153 BAnQ-Q, P908, P9, Mémoire à accomplir par les frères Rouffio et Romagnac pour l'année 1753 relativement aux commandes de

marchandises auprès de négociants de France et de Hollande, destinées à être envoyées au Québec... , 1752.

154 BAnQ-Q, P908,P4, Factures générales des marchandises envoyées à Québec par la société Rouffio pour l'année 1752... , 1752.

155 BAnQ-Q, P908, P9, Mémoire à accomplir par les frères Rouffio et Romagnac pour l'année 1753 relativement aux commandes de marchandises auprès de négociants de France et de Hollande, destinées à être envoyées au Québec... , 1752.

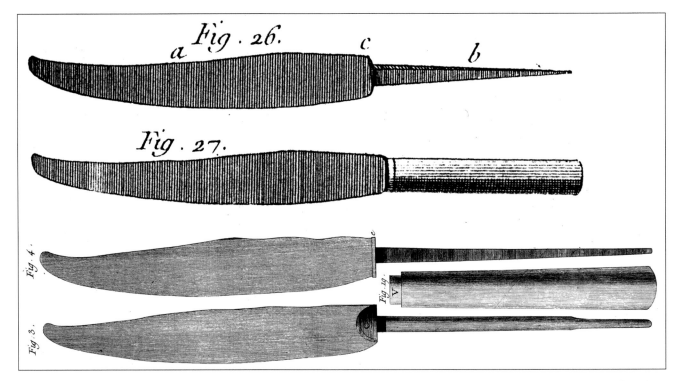

Detail taken from L'Art du coutelier en ouvrages communs featuring what Fougeroux de Bondaroy refers to as a table or sheath knife and blade; (Bottom) From Perret's *L'art du coutelier*, showing 'sheath knives' or table knives.

French table knife blade found at the Fortress of Louisbourg. Note the 'dorsal ridge' along the back of the blade, with a gentle curve that intensifies toward the pointed tip, characteristic of many French table knife blades from the first half of the eighteenth century. (Courtesy of National Historic Sites, Parks Canada. Photo Kevin Gélinas)

an officer at the Ouiatenon post, was the owner of six silver spoons and six forks.[156] In 1757, Claude Drouin, écuyer de Carqueville, possessed several silver spoons and forks,[157] while that same year, *capitaine* Louis Coulon de Villiers' estate inventory listed large quantities of silver cutlery, including 'six tablespoons, six forks, six coffee spoons.'[158]

Dishware of the Colonial Officers

On large European-style military campaigns, French officers typically dined under a tent with a full table setting for each guest, observing contemporary table manners. By the early eighteenth century, these officers were carrying lavish tableware, leading Louis XIV to decree on April 15, 1705, that no officer 'have in his equipment any silverware other than spoons, forks and goblets … that fruit be served in common dishes and not those of porcelains, crystals or other vases of this nature.'[159] When stationed at remote outposts, high-ranking officers were supplied with various kitchen items. At Fort Niagara in 1738, its commandant, chaplain, and officers received two red copper kettles, three frying pans, four iron pots with lids, six pewter dishes, 27 pewter plates, three pewter basins,

---

156 BAnQ-Q, Greffe du notaire Nicolas Boisseau, à la requête de M.M. Guillaume Estèbe, conseiller du Roi au conseil supérieur de ce pays au nom et comme fondé de la procuration d'Henry Albert, écuyer, sieur de St-Vincent, officier des troupes de la Marine entretenues en ce pays et commandant du poste des 8atanons (Ouiatenons)… , 23 juin, 1742.

157 BAnQ-M, Greffe du notaire Danré de Blanzy, Feu Claude Drouin, écuyer de Carqueville, lieutenant d'infanterie demeurant à Montréal rue Notre-Dame…, 16 juin 1757.

158 BAnQ-M, Greffe du notaire Danré de Blanzy, Inventaire des biens de feu Louis Coulon écuyer Sieur de Villiers, capitaine d'infanterie demeurant Montréal rue Saint-Paul…, 17 novembre 1757.

---

159 *Code militaire, ou Compilation des reglemens et ordonnances de Louis XIV, roi de France et de Navarre* (Paris: chez Denys Mariette, 1707), pp.327–329.

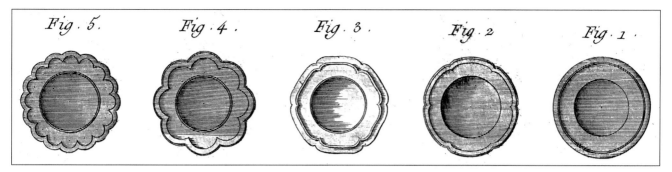

A series of French pewter plates with various contours, taken from Diderot's *Potier d'étain bimblotier*.

two pewter spoons, one serving spoon, two forks, one copper saucepan and six Mesley linen napkins.[160]

During the 1755 campaign, officer De la Pause detailed the equipment allocated to each officer serving with the regular troops under Dieskau, including two pewter plates, along with 'a platter per four men, and 6 table napkins, 12 for the commandant.'[161] Equipment inventories from the same year listed '200 pewter platters' and '770 pewter plates' designated for the officers.[162] In a letter written that year, Dieskau reminded senior officers of their obligations, noting that 'the commander and the other senior officers are required to keep certain records ... to be proportionally placed in a crew, both as far as table linen as well as tableware, pots and pans.'[163] This meticulous attention to the distribution of tableware and linen reflects the structured organisation of officer provisioning during the campaign but also the French tradition of refinement and etiquette, deeply rooted in the practices of noblemen and the upper class of the time.

Pewter plates were a staple at frontier forts, often reserved for high-ranking officers or privileged personnel. In 1741, Fort Niagara reported an inventory of '33 pewter plates',[164] while Fort Saint-Frédéric, in 1748, held an impressive collection that included 60 plates, 24 spoons, five porringers, and various other pewter items.[165] Following the surrender of Fort de Chartres in 1765, the inventory reflected more modest holdings, listing '1 large pewter soup dish', '2 pewter plates', and a small basin.[166] By the close of the Seven Years War, a 3 June 1758 ordonnance imposed restrictions on tableware, declaring that 'all silverware is forbidden, except place settings, ladles, and goblets; and crystals, porcelain, faience or

Pewter plate discovered at Fort Michilimackinac, possibly of French or British origin. Officers of the troupes de terre serving in New France during the Seven Years War were issued two pewter plates each. (Mackinac State Park collection. Photo Kevin Gélinas)

earthenware.'[167] In New France, colonial officers dining under tents during large-scale campaigns likely relied on their personal plates, a mark of their rank and refinement. However, on smaller detachments, practicality prevailed, and they would have carried only the most essential dishware, prioritising utility over luxury.

Portable Beverage Containers and Drinkware

Detailed accounts of water canteens and drinking vessels used by colonial troops in New France are scarce. Unlike European campaigns, French period accounts note that troops travelling through the vast forests of North America often fetched their water directly from nearby sources. This practice, likely influenced by Indigenous customs, was an efficient adaptation to the abundant natural watercourses

160 LAC, MG1-C11A, vol.69, f.274v-275.
161 RAPQ, 1933–1934, p.68.
162 LAC, MG1-C11A, vol.100, f.264v-265.
163 AG, MG4, B1, série A1, vol.3404, f.6.
164 LAC, MG1-C11A, vol.75, f.265.
165 LAC, MG1-C11A, vol.92, f.35v, 36, 37, 37v, 38.
166 *Transactions of the Illinois State Historical Society for the Year 1907. Publication Number Twelve* (Springfield, Illinois: Illinois State Historical Library. Phillips Bros., State Printers. 1908), p.215.

167 De Montandre-Lonchamps, René Louis de Roussel, *État militaire de France* (Paris: Chez Guillyn, 1759), p.382.

of the region. Officer Dumont de Montigny captured this reliance on nature in a poem about the construction of Fort St Francis in 1738, writing, 'the river, in a word, was the real cistern, where we drew water'.[168] Similarly, in July 1757, Royal Roussillon grenadier *capitaine* de Poularies observed:

> We were in this order about a league in great heat and stopped at a stream. We did not do a quarter of a lieue in most places without finding water … we made another lieue and a half after resting twice at creeks with streams whose beautiful water we had to drink despite ourselves: never did the troops drink so much without having been inconvenienced.[169]

By 1758, at Fort Carillon, efforts to ensure water availability became more structured. It was ordered that barrels of potable water be placed behind each battalion, and that each officer major '…will identify the streams and springs that may be behind the camp, which may provide water for the soldiers.[170]

Canteens or Water Flasks

Colonial soldiers on detachments or campaigns, particularly in warm regions like Louisiana, likely carried portable beverage containers such as calabash gourds, canteens, or flasks. French military guidelines from 1755 highlight the importance of water reserves: 'It would be good in dry countries that every soldier have a leather flask, or a small canteen filled with water to quench his thirst, or refresh himself in the heat of battle.'[171] According to eighteenth-century French dictionaries, a canteen, termed gourde in French, was a 'calabash, dried and drained squash used by soldiers and pilgrims to carry water, wine, or other liquor.'[172] Jean Bernard Bossu, a colonial officer in Louisiana, noted that one of his soldiers left with 'his musket, provisions in his haversack, and water in a calabash or gourd'.[173]

References to calabash gourds in Canada are scarce, though one notable mention comes from Montréal in 1733, where two drummers serving in the Compagnies franches

Plate and porringer excavated at Louisbourg. (Courtesy of National Historic Sites, Parks Canada. Photo Kevin Gélinas)

de la Marine were observed with 'a bottle and a gourde (gourd) near the house of the late M. de Callière'.[174] At Fort Frontenac in 1757, Marine carpenter Hervé Leroux's inventory listed 'a gourd' which may have been a calabash gourd.[175] Similarly, a chest discovered at Joseph Ladrière's house in Québec in 1750, likely belonging to a colonial soldier based on its contents of two soldiers' uniforms and a pair of canvas garters, also contained 'one gourd, two horns, and a shot bag.'[176]

Drinking Kettles, Tin Cups and Pewter Tumblers

Primary records indicate that colonial soldiers often used a small brass kettle as their main drinking cup during detachments or while stationed in barracks, forts, or outposts. These versatile containers, known in colonial documents as a 'kettle with which to drink from',

168 Marc de Villiers du Terrage, *Les dernières années de la Louisiane française* (Paris: Librairie orientale & américaine, 1904), p.359.

169 RAPQ, 1931–1932, p.10-11.

170 Charles-Nicolas Gabriel, *Le Maréchal de Camp Desandrouins, 1729–1792: Guerre Du Canada 1756–1760; Guerre de l'Indépendance Américaine 1780-1782* (Verdun: Renvé-Lallement, 1887), p.170.

171 *Essai sur les grandes operations de la guerre, ou Recueil des observations de différens auteurs, sur la maniere de les perfectionner* (Paris: chez Garneau, 1755), vol.3, p.353.

172 *Le grand vocabulaire françois: contenant l'explication de chaque mot… , les loix de l'orthographe…* (Paris: Panckoucke, 1770), p.177.

173 Jean Bernard Bossu, *Nouveaux voyages dans l'Amérique Septentrionale…* (Paris: Veuve Duchesne, 1778), p.300.

174 BAnQ-M, TL4, S1, D4076, Procès contre Bastien dit Canadien, tambour de la Compagnie DuFiguier, accusé du meurtre de Tourangeau, tambour de la Compagnie de Budemont, 18 septembre 1733–7 juin 1734.

175 BAnQ-Q, NF18, Mic. 6309, Pièces 32–34, Inventaire de feu Hervé Leroux, vivant Charpentier de marine, employé à la construction, décédé au fort Frontenac le deux février dernier, 25 janvier 1757.

176 BAnQ-Q, Greffe du notaire Jean-Claude Panet, Inventaire des biens de la succession de Joseph Ladrière (perruquier, de Québec)…veuf de Marie-Anne Lemieux, 14 janvier 1750.

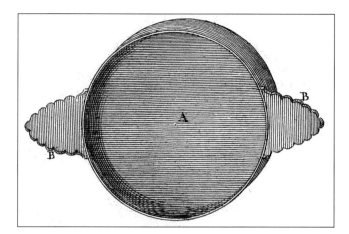

French pewter porringer from Diderot's *Potier d'étain*. Note the traditional form with simple flat-shaped lobed ears or handles.

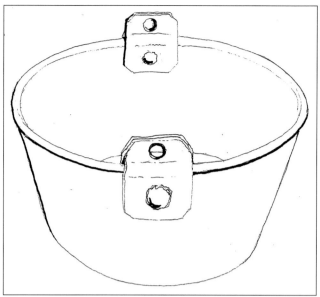

Artist's rendition of a very small brass kettle found at Fort St-Joseph, possibly corresponding to a chaudière à boire (drinking kettle) or chaudière à gomme (gum kettle). This versatile, lightweight vessel likely served colonial soldiers as both a water dipper and a cup or as a kettle for heating pitch used to repair birchbark canoes. (Line drawing by Michel Pétard)

a 'drinking kettle' (chaudière à boire), or a 'gum kettle' (chaudière à gomme), were favoured for their lightweight design and sturdiness as drinking vessels. For example, a probate record from Montréal in 1750 shows that these small kettles also functioned as tumblers, with one man owning 'one small kettle which serves as a tumbler from which to drink',[177] while the inventory of voyageur Jean-Baptiste Baron in 1748 included 'a small pot which serves as a drinking cup', highlighting their widespread use in New France.[178]

It is important to note that gum kettles, used to melt pitch or gum for mending birchbark canoes, were an essential part of every canoe's outfit during the period, as corroborated by De Noyelles' 1734 expedition against the Fox, where 11 canoes were each equipped with '11 gum kettles weighing 11¾ *livres* [each],' averaging 1.06 *livre* per kettle.[179] In 1746, the equipment for a war party heading to New England, which included officers Dubreuil, La Corne, *cadet* De La Saussaye, and two Canadian volunteers, included '1 gum kettle [weighing] 1½ *livre*', likely used both as a cup and for melting spruce gum for canoe repairs.[180] The following year, colonial officers La Corne, Dubreuil, and Bellestre, sent to the Upper Country, were provided with '3 small water kettles (chaudières à eau)', which undoubtedly refers to the popular 'drinking kettle', indicating that each officer received one small kettle for drinking during their detachments.[181]

During a criminal trial in Montréal in 1728, colonial soldier Pierre Richard dit Bonvouloir was noted for taking the communal drinking kettle from the guardhouse, indicating its common use in military settings:

> Asked if it is not true that being detained in the guardhouse he escaped, and that in leaving he did not take the drinking kettle (chaudière à boire) from the said guardhouse. He said that he held the kettle in his hands when he escaped, and carried away the said kettle, but that he was caught in this escape, and that the soldiers took back the said kettle.[182]

In 1738, a 'small brass kettle used for drinking' was recorded in the guardhouse and barracks at Fort Niagara,[183] and by 1740 'two small [copper or brass] kettles to drink from' were listed at Fort Saint-Frédéric, likely used by garrisoned soldiers.[184] Additionally, in 1765, the inventory of the guard room at Fort de Chartres included '1 bucket & a brass cup,' suggesting the bucket for water and the brass cup as a small drinking kettle.[185]

Large quantities of these kettles were imported from French merchants, including this particular shipment in 1746 consisting of '20 dozen small brass drinking kettles, weighing together 65 livres', averaging 0.27 livre each.[186] A decade later, '2 douzaine, 6 kettles of 3 pouces' were

177 BAnQ-M, Greffe du notaire G. Hodiesne, Inventaire des biens de Jean-Baptiste Monet, 9 mars 1752.

178 Kaskaskia Manuscripts (Randolph County Courthouse, Chester, Illinois), Inventaire de Jean-Baptiste Baron, voyageur et négociant au Pays des Illinois..., 6 juillet, 1748.

179 LAC, MG1-C11A, vol.62, f.151–151v.

180 LAC, MG1-C11A, vol.86, f.194v,195.

181 LAC, MG1-C11A, vol.117, f.177.

182 BAnQ-M, TL4, S1, D3478. Procès contre Pierre Richard dit Bonvouloir, alias Pierre Élie, soldat de la Compagnie Leverrier, fils de François Richard, ébéniste de la rue Saint-Antoine à Paris, accusé de vol de couverture aux sauvages, 3 octobre–18 octobre 1728.

183 LAC, MG1-C11A, vol.69, f.275v.

184 LAC, MG1-C11A, vol.73, f.341v.

185 *Illinois State Historical Library, Publications of the Illinois State Historical Library, Numéro 12* (Springfield, Illinois: Phillips Bros., State Printers, 1908), p.215.

186 LAC, MG1-C11A, vol.86, f.349.

seized from the merchant ship *La Renommé* en route from France to Québec, indicating these kettles may have had a 3 pouces (8.1 cm) diameter.[187]

These vessels are frequently mentioned in probate records of militia and colonial officers, such as the 1738 estate inventory of militia *capitaine* Alexis Marchand of Batiscan, which included a 'small drinking kettle of brass' valued at 1 livre.[188] Likewise, Nicolas Lesage, a militia *capitaine* at Cap-Santé, had a 'small kettle of brass to drink from.'[189] The following year, Joseph Dubois de Beaucours, colonial officer and governor of Montréal, was the owner of a 'small drinking kettle of brass' appraised at 15 sols.[190] In 1758, colonial officer Charles Decombre left behind a 'small flared kettle' in Québec, possibly a drinking kettle,[191] while two years later, militia *capitaines* Maurice Déry and Louis Marchand were both recorded as owning 'one small drinking kettle' each.[192]

Pewter tumblers, known as gobelets in French, were quite popular among colonial soldiers, particularly in the Québec area, reflecting a degree of refinement and accessibility to European goods. In 1749, for example, a 'pewter tumbler' was found in a cassette trunk belonging to Louis Daurizon dit Larose, accused of falsifying ordonnances in Québec,[193] whereas a 'pewter tumbler' was listed among items found in a pine chest at a colonist's home in Québec in 1752, along with a soldier's vest and brass buttons.[194] That same year at Trois-Rivières, a 'tin cup' was confiscated from three soldiers on trial, suggesting it was

Silver tumbler bearing the coat of arms of the Marquis de Montcalm. Many colonial officers may have carried their own personnel silver tumbler, which would have been identified with their heraldic symbol when participating in certain military operations or campaigns in Canada (Gobelet, 1725–1756, 18th century, M4839, Musée McCord, Montréal)

shared among them.[195] A few years later, a witness testified in a burglary trial in Québec that a soldier had 'a pewter tumbler … a tin cup, several packs of cards', indicating the popularity of tin cups (tasse de fer blanc) among colonial soldiers.[196] Tin cups also appeared on official equipment lists, such as a single 'tin cup' priced at 10 sols which was provided to a man returning to Canada from Acadia and Île-Royale in 1745 while serving under colonial officer Marin.[197] That same year, a list of equipment supplied for the war efforts at Québec, included nine 'tin cups, hollandé [in the Dutch-style or crafted in a sturdy manner],' each priced at 20 sols.[198]

During King George's War, tin cups were among the equipment supplied to *commandants* and *majors* of large war parties, likely serving to uphold utility while still adhering to the refinement expected of French officers,

187 TNA, High Court of Admiralty, 32–238. PT.2. La Renommé, 1757.

188 BAnQ-TR, Greffe du notaire A.-B. Pollet, Inventaire de la communauté des biens de Dianne Tetard veuve de feu Le Sieur Alexis Marchand, Capitaine de milice, 25 juin 1738.

189 BAnQ-Q, Greffe du notaire Jean-Baptiste Guyard de Fleury, Inventaire contenant acte de partage fait par Nicolas Lesage (habitant de Cap-Santé, capitaine de milice) et Maire-Françoise Paris,sa femme.., 11 juin 1756.

190 BAnQ-M, Greffe du notaire Danré de Blanzy, Inventaire de feu Joseph Dubois de Beaucours, gouverneur du Roi, 15 mars 1757.

191 BAnQ-Q, TL5, D1944. Procès de Charles Decombre (Porcheron dit Decombre), officier détaché des troupes de la Marine, contre Marie Couture, veuve de Simon Massy.–26 février 1758–28 mars 1759.

192 BAnQ-TR, Greffe du notaire Jean Leproust, Inventaire des biens de la communauté de la veuve Marie Vanas et feu Maurice Déry, Capitaine de milice, 14 mars 1760.; BAnQ-TR, Greffe du notaire Jean Leproust, Inventaire des biens de la communauté de Louis Marchand, capitaine de milice, veuf de Marie-Josèphe dit Montendre, de Batiscan., 5 mars 1760.

193 BAnQ-Q, TL5, D1640. Procès criminel contre Claude du Retour (Duretour) de Monsy, seigneur de Neuville et autres terres, environ 31 ans, soldat de la compagnie de Beaujeu, et Louis Daurizon (Dorizon) dit Larose, soldat de la compagnie de Beaujeu, environ 39 ans, pour falsification d'ordonnances, 1er janvier 1749–5 novembre 1751.

194 BAnQ-Q, TL5, D1667. Procès criminel contre Louis Bonin, caporal de la compagnie de Lanaudière et soldat congédié, et Denis Lemoine dit Parisien, 14 ans, soldat de la compagnie de Lanaudière en garnison à Québec, logé à la caserne Dauphine, et complices, accusés de vol.17 février–6 août 1752.

195 BAnQ-Q, TP1, S777, D174. Procès de Pierre Beaudouin (Baudouin) dit Cumberland, Joseph Ceilier dit Beausoleil, Ponsian Allé dit Sansoucy, François-Xavier Guernoté dit Latulippe et Joseph Gamin (Jamin) dit Saint-Louis, soldats, prisonniers, accusés d'avoir provoqué l'incendie de la Basse-Ville de Trois-Rivières, d'avoir commis plusieurs vols dans les maisons incendiées, et d'avoir blasphémé le Saint Nom de Dieu, 21 mai–28 août 1752.

196 BAnQ-Q, TL5, D1966. Procès criminel contre Conrad Raner, 33 ans, allemand de nation, soldat du régiment de la Reine, accusé de vol chez Gaffé. Jean Joseph Lob, grenadier, est nommé d'office comme interprète, 31 janvier–3 mars 1758.

197 LAC, MG1-C11A, vol.84, f.146.

198 LAC, MG1-C11A, vol.84, f.123.

even during the harsh conditions of military life on large wilderness campaigns. In 1747, the expenses for the war party led by *commandant* M. Rigaud de Vaudreuil included one tin cup and one tin coffeepot for Rigaud himself, along with another tin coffeepot and six tin cups designated for the *majors*, suggesting these cups were primarily used for coffee.[199] On the other hand, colonial officer Bossu, who explored the Mississippi region in the 1750s, remarked on the use of calabash cups by his men for coffee: 'I had prepared a kettle of coffee of which I had brought from the city, where each [man] drank a small calabash full (which serves as a cup for the Natives).'[200]

French officers, however, often preferred more refined drinking vessels, such as silver goblets adorned with their crests of arms, in keeping with the 15 April 1705 ordonnance permitting the use of silverware limited to goblets, spoons, and forks. Nicolas-Thomas de Joncaire, a *lieutenant* in the colonial troops who died at Fort Niagara in 1739, had in his possession both a silver cup and tumbler,[201] while Louis Coulon de Villiers of Montréal owned 'one spoon and one fork of silver, two tumblers, also of silver' at the time of his death in 1757.[202] In 1761, Luc de La Corne, a colonial officer and survivor of the *Auguste* wreck, carried 'a silver cup…' during his journey from Cape Breton to Québec.[203]

Rare tin cup of French, British, or American manufacture, found at Fort Ouiatenon (1717–1791). High-ranking Canadian officers participating in expeditions during King George's War were often supplied with tin coffee cups and coffeepots. (Courtesy of Tippecanoe County Historical Association collection, Lafayette, Indiana. Photo Kevin Gélinas)

199 LAC, MG1-C11A, vol.117, f.20v, 22v.
200 Jean Bernard Bossu, *Nouveaux voyages dans l'Amérique Septentrionale…* (Paris, Chez la Veuve Duchesne: 1778), p.92.
201 BAnQ-M, Greffe du notaire C.J. Porlier, Inventaire des biens de feu Nicolas-Thomas de Joncaire, lieutenant d'une compagnie du détachement de la Marine et interprète pour le Roi des langues iroquoises, 31 juillet 1739.
202 BAnQ-M, Greffe du notaire Danré de Blanzy, Inventaire des biens de feu Louis Coulon écuyer Sieur de Villiers, capitaine d'infanterie demeurant Montréal rue Saint-Paul…, 17 novembre 1757.
203 *Journal du voyage de M. Saint-Luc de La Corne, Écr. dans le navire l'Auguste en l'an 1761. Seconde édition* (Québec: A. Côté et Cie, 1863), p.21.

A depiction from a military camp scene showing a cook serving soup from a cast iron pot into a large bowl (gamelle) shared by several men. Colonial soldiers in Canada often ate from the same bowls such as sailors or common folk in France. The cast iron cooking pots used in garrison contexts in New France typically came with iron ladles for stirring and serving. (Troops at rest. Jean-Baptiste Joseph Pater, c.1725. Metropolitan Museum of Art.)

Detail from a painting by William Hogarth depicting soldiers of the Compagnies franches de la Marine serving at the port of Calais in 1748. This satirical view shows two soldiers in sabots carrying a cooking kettle, presumably full of soup. The soldiers hold what are likely wooden bowls and pewter spoons. (William Hogarth, *O the Roast Beef of Old England* ('The Gate of Calais'), 1748. Creative Commons)

Above: Copper kettle with two 'dog-ear' lugs made of folded sheet copper, designed to attach iron rod handles. Discovered underwater by divers in Ontario's French River in the 1960s, this vessel likely belonged to a trade kettle lost from an overturned French canoe. Records from 1740 show a Montréal merchant listing both brass and copper 'English-style kettles', suggesting that such flared kettles were commonly produced in both materials. (With permission of the Royal Ontario Museum © ROM)

Left: A depiction of a French infantry soldier on campaign carrying what appears to be an iron cooking pot from the butt of his musket. This type of iron cooking pot, likely similar to the tin-plated marmites brought to Canada by regular troops in 1756, had pans that served as lids. Taken from *Vue de la rade d'Antibes* by Joseph Vernet, 1756. (Courtesy of the Musée de la Marine, Paris. Photo Kevin Gélinas)

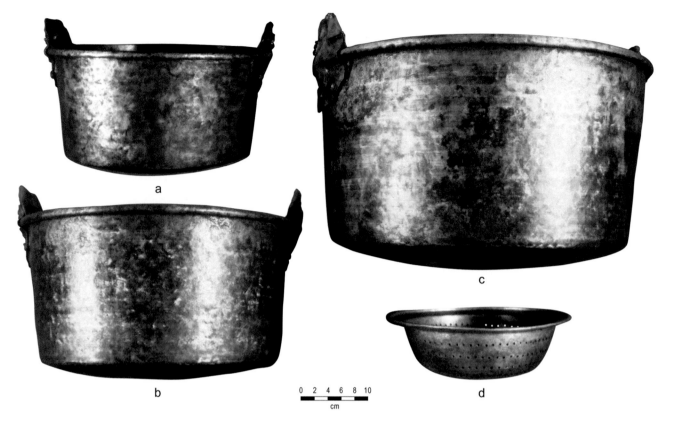

a

b

c

d

0 2 4 6 8 10
cm

Brass kettles excavated from the *La Belle* with rolled rims over an iron wire rim support. The bail ears are of the typical seventeenth- and eighteenth-century kettles found throughout French colonial North American sites. (James E. Bruseth, Amy A. Borgens, Bradfort M. Jones, Eric D. Ray, *La Belle: The Archaeology of a Seventeenth Century Ship of New World Colonization*, Texas A&M University Press. (Photo by the Conservation Research Laboratory, Texas A&M University))

Two sheet brass kettles excavated from the wreck of *Le Machault*, a French supply ship that sailed for New France in 1760. These kettles, with 'dog-ear' lugs for attaching wrought iron bails, were shipped in compact nested bundles called balots. A 1749 letter from Rochefort to Québec mentioned that each balot of kettles weighed about 100 *livres* and contained 25 to 30 nested kettles. By 1753, such kettles were manufactured in England and imported to France, labelled à la façon anglaise (English-style). These kettles, popular as trade goods, were likely used by colonial troops. (Courtesy of National Historic Sites, Parks Canada. Photo Kevin Gélinas)

Left: Copper kettle lid excavated at Fort Ticonderoga, likely from a Montauban-type kettle featuring a cover with a central ring. The lid bears a maker's mark with decipherable letters N and S, and a floral motif within an oval cartouche. (Collection of the Fort Ticonderoga Museum, New York. Photo Kevin Gélinas)

Right: Fully preserved copper kettle with a central ring on its lid, found at Fort St Joseph (1700–1781). According to a 1753 merchant's memo, these French-made kettles were primarily trade items produced at Villefranche-de-Rouergue, a kettle-making centre in southern France. The interiors were typically tinned to prevent the formation of verdigris, a toxic substance. French merchants referred to this lid style as 'À Montauban', as they were manufactured near the town of Montauban, France. (Fort St Joseph Museum collection, Niles, Michigan)

A copper kettle with a central ring lid, similar to the example excavated from Fort Saint-Joseph, as depicted by Jean-Baptiste-Siméon Chardin. (Still Life with Copper Pot, Cheese, and Eggs, circa 1730-1735. Creative Commons)

Detail from Vernet's *Vue du Port de Rochefort* (c. 1762) showing the three most popular types of cooking vessels used in the French colonies of North America. On the left, a nest of tinned copper kettles, likely English-style chaudières. In the middle, a pile of chaudières de voyage (travelling kettles), fitted with covers that double as saucepans or frying pans. On the right, a stack of tripod cast iron cooking pots (marmites) with outward-protruding rings around their upper bodies, similar to those requested for the colonial troops at Louisbourg in 1756. Note the lids, likely made of sheet metal, piled on the ground next to the cast-iron marmites. (Courtesy of the Musée de la Marine, Paris. Photo Kevin Gélinas)

Brass spoon mould excavated from the ship *L'Auguste*, which sank in 1761 near Cape Breton Island. Spoon moulds like this one were used in well-to-do Canadian households to cast pewter spoons. The mould bears an illegible family coat of arms, which would have appeared as a raised design on the spoon handle. One or more of the pewter spoons discovered at this shipwreck site may have been cast using this mould. (Courtesy of National Historic Sites, Parks Canada. Photo Kevin Gélinas)

Detail of a military camp scene showing typical eating utensils, including a large gamelle bowl, porringer, spoon, and bidon jug, all likely made of pewter and used by soldiers for their daily meals. In the background, a cast iron marmite cooking pot is hung over a fire, in which the soup was likely prepared. (Antoine Watteau, *Camp volant*, 1710-11. Creative Commons)

French Grenadiers taking a halt, with officers gathered around a drum, eating and drinking. A knife and a piece of ham can be seen on a platter, with the plates and platters likely made of pewter, while the goblets are possibly silver. (Halte de grenadiers à cheval de la maison du roi, Charles Parrocel, 1737. Musée de l'Armée, Paris, France. ©RMN-Grand Palais/Art Resource, NY)

A rare French table knife with its original wooden handle found during the Place Royale archaeological dig in Québec City. The blade measures 18cm, and the handle is 10cm. (Laboratoire et Réserve d'archéologie du Québec, Québec. Photo Kevin Gélinas)

Porringer bearing the coat of arms of Chevalier Michel Dagneau Douville, a French officer in the colonial troops, circa 1729–1749, silver. (Les prêtres de Saint-Sulpice de Montréal. Photo Kevin Gélinas)

Pewter table service excavated from the *Machault*, a French ship sunk off the banks of the Restigouche River in 1760. An écuelle (porringer), cup, plate, and coffee spoons were likely used at the captain's table. The porringer is strikingly similar to the one illustrated in Diderot's Potier d'étain. (Courtesy of National Historic Sites, Parks Canada)

As part of the equipment accompanying an eighteenth-century model canoe from the Trésor de la Cathédrale de Chartres collection were a wooden barrel and what appear to be two wine bottles, the first on the left distinguished by its unique shape, featuring a flared body and long narrow neck, typical of eighteenth-century French wine bottles. Note the cord attached to this bottle, suggesting it may have been used as a flask. (Courtesy of the Musée des Beaux-Arts de Chartres)

Canot cups, carried by fur traders, were used to collect fresh drinking water from lakes and rivers while travelling. The small barrel attached to the cup by string was tied to a sash worn around the waist. This example features sturgeon and heart motifs. It is possible that colonial soldiers adopted the use of these cups while travelling long distances by canoe. (Château Ramezay - Musée et site historique de Montréal)

Gourd belonging to *Lieutenant* De Lassuderie of the Régiment de Bourbonnois, 1775. This vessel, equipped with a brass spout, is engraved with flowers, foliage, and the King's arms, set against a background of military flags. (Collection and photo Bertrand Malvaux)

Gourd, c. 1610, given by Mi'kmaq chief Membertou to Charles Robin, a member of the Poutrincourt-Champlain expedition to Port Royal in 1604, who brought it back to France. This artefact is carved with decorative motifs, the Robin family coat of arms, and depictions of family exploits. (Gourde-calebasse, 1610, 17th century, 1976.58.1, Musée McCord, Montréal)

Left: Calabash gourd of the Régiment d'Enghien, c. 1770. (©Musée de l'Armée/Dist. RMN-Grand Palais/Art Resource, NY)

Right: Detail from Jean-Baptiste Joseph Pater's *Troops at Rest*, illustrating an infantry soldier with a haversack, hat, musket, and what appears to be a brass water dipper with a projecting handle. Historical records occasionally reference small brass kettles as 'drinking kettles', owned by militia and colonial officers as well as colonial soldiers. (Metropolitan Museum of Art)

Detail showing a soldier from the Royal Roussillon regiment camping in the Piedmont, c. 1745–1748, drinking from a calabash gourd, known as a calebasse in French. According to period French dictionaries, this type of gourd was a common beverage container among soldiers serving in France. (Fort Ticonderoga Museum collection, New York)

An eighteenth-century earthenware bottle gourd marked 'BOY', meaning drink in old French, likely made in Nevers, France. This bottle, with two top loops and base holes for carrying a cord, resembles an extant example in the Canadian Museum of History collection, which has four loopholes. According to Poole family lore, this later gourd belonged to a French soldier defending Québec during the 1759 siege. During a brief lull in fighting, the French soldier reportedly offered the gourd, filled with wine or eau de vie, to a British soldier taking cover from the near-constant firing. Later, apparently, another French soldier mistook the British soldier as an enemy and fired, causing the bottle to fall. It was eventually collected by Sergeant Poole. The Poole family preserved the gourd for generations before donating it to the Canadian Museum of History in 1967. (Private collection)

An eighteenth-century Nevers earthenware gourd fitted with four loops. One side bears the inscription 'Simion. Henry. / Officier. du. Roy.', indicating that the bottle gourd belonged to an officer serving under the King of France. (©Osenat)v

Above: Portable wooden campaign writing field desk box said to have belonged to Count de Maurès de Malartic. (Château Ramezay –Musée et site historique de Montréal)

Left: Silver tumbler with the coat of arms of Anne-Joseph-Hippolyte de Maurès de Malartic, an officer in the French regular infantry who accompanied the Régiment de Béarn to Canada in 1755. Malartic took part in several campaigns and battles in Canada before returning to France in 1760. His arms feature three stars surmounted by a crown, along with the insignia of the Order of St Louis. He was awarded the Cross of St Louis in 1758. (Courtesy of Maxime Champion)

Campaign Shelters of the Colonial Troops

Prior to the large-scale European-style campaigns during the Seven Years War in Canada, the colonial troops serving throughout the St Lawrence Valley mostly performed raids or small-scale tactical operations upon hostile Native nations or New England frontier towns. While taking part in summer-month campaigns, these men had to travel light carrying only a tarpaulin to be used as a temporary protective covering, which was typically allocated to their canoes, whereas one or more tents were traditionally brought along for the use of the commanding officers. For winter campaigns, these men carried along lightweight tarpaulins to be used as a make-shift lean-to shelter in winter environments to stay out of the wind and snow. Once the French regulars reached Canada in 1755, the colonial troops were issued tents and campaign kit in compliance with French infantry regulations. According to Michel-Jean-Hugues Péan, *capitaine* in the colonial regular troops and adjutant at Québec: 'when the European troops arrived, we changed our ways. We had to have tents, crews, rations.'[1]

Military Shelters in New France (1730–1755)

Traditionally, tents were provided to the officers taking part in large-scale expeditions or campaigns against hostile Native American nations or while leading excursions to attack British settlements. As part of a proposed expedition aimed at defeating the Fox nation in 1731, for example, the colonial officer Nicolas-Joseph de Noyelles had accounted for five tents at 30 livres each for the officers who led 150 soldiers.[2] During the final major campaign against the unruly Foxes in 1734, *commandant* De Noyelles was provided with 'one fully fitted tent', while the accompanying officers shared one tent for every three men, and the soldiers probably slept under basic canvas shelters.[3]

On rare occasions where European-style larger-scale offensive campaigns were needed such as during the Chickasaw campaign, a force from Louisiana composed of soldiers of the Compagnies franches de la Marine were said to make use of tents for encampments. On the first expedition that Governor Jean-Baptiste le Moyne de Bienville organised in 1736, the colonial officer Dumont de Montigny observed that, 'in the morning, at the first light of day, when the drum roll sounded, the men were to strike their tents. Each tent had seven to eight men in it'.[4] This colonial officer goes on to describe in detail living conditions and the laying out of their camps along the way: 'At last, near nightfall, we revert to the ground, we chop, cut, level ash wood, shrubs, to spend the night in tents that the whole army purposely sets up. Bienville is in the middle, the others all around.'[5]

Some three years later, archival documents show that the commandant and officers who took part in the 1739 campaign in continuation of the Chickasaw Wars now received fully fitted tents with their iron-capped poles and ropes. For instance, the Baron de Longueuil, as well as the accompanying officers, were each supplied with a fully fitted tent for a total of '16 fully fitted tents with their iron-capped poles' along with '3 skeins of rope weighing 19¾ livres for the tents', while Longueuil also received one tarpaulin measuring 9 *aunes*.[6]

Throughout King George's War, lists of supplies provided to the colonial troops serving on several expeditions include references to fully fitted tents intended for the exclusive use of the officers, indicating that they likely came with their stakes, rope, and poles, and possibly included a separate canvas cover for additional protection. On one such occasion, the campaign equipment delivered to colonial officers sent off to wage war on New England

---

1   Michel-Jean-Hugues Péan, *Mémoire pour Michel-Jean-Hugues Péan, chevalier, capitaine-aide-major des ville & gouvernement de Québec & des troupes détachées de la Marine…* (Paris: Imprimerie de G. Desprez, 1763), p.100.
2   LAC, MG1-C11A, vol.56, f.310-316v, f.314v.
3   LAC, MG1-C11A, vol.62, f.149, 150.
4   Jean-Francois-Benjamin Dumont de Montigny, *The Memoir of Lieutenant Dumont, 1715–1747: A Sojourner in the French Atlantic* (Chapel Hill, NC: The University of North Carolina Press, 2012), p.258.
5   Dumont de Montigny, *Regards sur le monde atlantique 1715–1747* (Sillery, Québec: Les éditions du Septentrion, 2008), p.339.
6   LAC, MG1-C11A, vol.71, f.1556v, 158v, 164–164v, 175v.

Detail from *Veuë du camp de la concession de Monseigneur Law au nouveau Biloxy*, 1720, by Jean Baptiste Michel Le Bouteaux, showing John Law's Concession at Nouveau Biloxi. This ink drawing shows an encampment of large square wall tents (*tentes à murailles*) covered by marquises (outer fly covers) housing the camp's directors (B, C, D), surgeon (E), and chaplain (F). These tents may have resembled those used by colonial officers in Canada, with marquises suspended above the tent roofs, overlapping slightly and extending down the sides. The marquises protected against moisture, rain, and sun while people ate, rested, or slept. To the left, labelled M, is the corps de garde, likely made up of smaller canonnière or single bell wedge tents for soldiers. (Courtesy of the Newberry Library, Chicago)

in 1746 included '6 fully fitted tents.'[7] The chaplains and surgeons accompanying colonial troops on raids were also provided with tents, as seen during François-Pierre de Rigaud de Vaudreuil's 1746 summer raids into New England, where six fully fitted tents were supplied to seven officers, two chaplains, and one surgeon.[8] Three years later, '1 tent of coutil' priced at 150 livres, was taken along with a detachment of soldiers and Habitants headed to Acadia in 1749 and likely intended for the commanding officer.[9] Coutil was a 'a very strong and tight type of canvas, usually made using hemp thread … it is also used to make tents for the army.'[10] That same year, '1 tent of coutil, quite old, esteemed at 10 livres' was recorded on the post-mortem inventory of the colonial officer Pierre Gauthier de La Vérendrye, highlighting the widespread use of such tents among colonial officers during this period.

Céleron's 1749 campaign journal at La Belle-Rivière (Ohio) provides further evidence of officers using tents during campaigns, as he noted, 'Monsieur de Joncaire brought the [Native] chiefs to my tent.'[11] Fascinatingly, a letter addressed by the Marquis Ange Duquesne de Menneville to the colonial officer Jacques Legardeur de Saint-Pierre in the summer of 1752 discloses the importance of such a piece of equipment for a high-ranking military man traveling in the interior. Duquesne remarks, 'that you find yourself forced to proceed into the interior without having but a tent to serve you well'.[12]

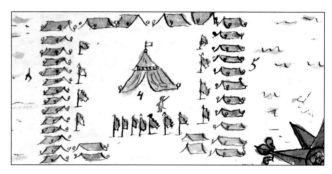

Detail from *Campement de l'armée à Tombecbe* by Dumont de Montigny, showing the 1736 camp of French colonial troops during their campaign against the Chickasaw nation near Fort Tombecbe. The large tent at the centre, possibly a rare depiction of a dome-shaped pavillon tent in New France, is said to be *général* Bienville's tent, surrounded by single bell wedge tents (canonnières), marked with the number 5, identified as soldier's tents. Dumont de Montigny described how the army would set up camp upon arrival: '..the first boat that was ahead chose a nice place to camp or to pitch the tents. The army disembarked; sentinels were placed in the woods for fear of surprise attacks, others at the landing, in front of the weapons or the General's tent.' (Campement de l'armée à Tombecbe, Dumont de Montigny, 1747. Ayer MS 257 map 10, Norman B. Leventhal Map & Education Center at the Boston Public Library)

We may add that prior to 1755, most tents and their respective accessories were likely locally made by various workers such as seamstresses or sailmakers working out of the St Lawrence Valley. At Québec, the sailmakers named Barthélémy Rosa and Jean Pierre were recorded as making a fair number of tents of coutil fabric in 1746, each priced at 15 livres apiece, while Marie Daniau, a seamstress at Montréal, was said to have made another 13 such tents.[13] That same year, supplies purchased directly from private merchants for the war efforts included two sets of tent fittings priced at 12 livres each.[14] Some 10 years later, the colonial officer Michel-Jean-Hugues

7   LAC, MG1-C11A, vol.115, f.254v.
8   LAC, MG1-C11A, vol.115, f.254–254v.
9   LAC, MG1-C11A, vol.119, f.6v.
10 Jacques Savary des Bruslons, *Dictionnaire universel de commerce d'histoire naturelle et des arts et métiers; divise en III volumes & en IV parties* (Genève: Chez les héritiers Cramer et Frères Philibert, 1742), vol.1, p.1179.
11 LAC, MG1, F3, Collection Moreau de Saint-Méry: C-10528, f.473.
12 ASQ, Viger-Verreau, P32/005/038a, Lettre du secrétaire du marquis Ange Duquesne de Menneville, Québec, à Jacques Legardeur de Saint-Pierre, en réponse à deux lettres…, 15 mai 1752.

13 LAC, MG1-C11A, vol.115, f.159v, 160, 162v.
14 LAC, MG1-C11A, vol.115, f.84v.

Péan had apparently 'distributed to all of the women of this town [Montréal] and many others, canvas to make bags, sails, tents, etc.'[15] This reafirms that prior to this time, many tents as well as canvas sails which doubled as tarpaulins, were made in Canada rather than purchased from France. By 1757, a quantity of 10,000 *aunes* of 'coutil, strong and common, wide, for tents' were to be sent to Canada by the merchant Gradis,[16] suggesting that a few of these shelters were still made onsite during the Seven Years War.

On the other hand, colonial officers, cadets and soldiers were also documented as using only a prélat (the French term designating a tarpaulin) as their only means of shelter when 'raiding' or travelling light over long distances. During the Chickasaw campaign of 1739, a cadet and two colonial soldiers were documented as receiving two prélats of 15 *aunes* of Mélis (a type of sailcloth fabricated at Mélis, France) for their voyage which meant that each canvass piece would have measured 7½ *aunes*.[17] Some six years later, one tarpaulin measuring 10 *aunes* as well as another 48 such canvasses, each respectively measuring 8 *aunes* were included on a list of supplies distributed to a party of Canadians and Native Americans who accompanied the colonial officer Paul Marin de La Malgue on an expedition from Québec against Annapolis Royal.[18] In 1747, an account listing supplies distributed to a large war party under the command of Rigaud de Vaudreuil, which was heading to Fort Saint-Frédéric, included the exact length of each of these canvass pieces. These were referenced as '69 prélats of 7½ *aunes*' along with 36 sails each measuring 9 *aunes*.[19] When the officers named La Corne, Dubreuil and Bellestre were detached to the upper countries to engage allied Native nations to fight alongside the French that same year, a portion of their equipment included '3 prélats, new, of Beaufort canvas' indicating that this was their main means of protection against the elements.[20] Two militia officers detached to garrison at Fort St-Frédéric received two such tarpaulins fabricated using this exact same type of material.[21] In addition to Mélis, Beaufort canvas, named after the French town where it was manufactured, appears to have been another popular fabric for making prélats.

Engraving from La Porterie's *Institution militaire pour la cavalerie et les dragons*, showing a canonnière tent according to the 1753 regulation. Beneath the tent is a bell-of-arms (faisceaux d'armes), where soldiers stored their muskets at night. The canvas cloak covering the muskets would be removed during the day or remain in place during rain. In 1723, colonial officer Dumont de Montigny described an incident during the Natchez war where his men rushed to retrieve their muskets 'at the bell-of-arms'.

Military Shelters in New France After 1755 for Summer Campaigns

With the arrival of the French Troupes de terre in 1755, the longstanding practice of colonial soldiers setting up camp under provisional shelters using a prélat, a method traditionally suited for short expeditions, came under scrutiny by the newly arrived military authorities in Canada. These officials were concerned because military campaigns had grown significantly longer, often lasting several months, leaving many soldiers vulnerable to illness due to prolonged exposure to the elements. A 1757 memo from the French minister succinctly captures the colonial soldiers' persistent reliance on tarps, even when encamped for extended campaigns:

> Among other things, he requested 500 canonnières [soldier's wedge tents] for the Canadians and 60 tents for the colonial officers. He had made the same request last year, and it had not been considered, since it had never been the custom to make supplies of this kind for the detachments of Canada. But he indicates that they are necessary in the present war, and that the Canadians, or even the colonial officers, do not require them for ordinary excursions in the woods. But when they camp, as they have done this year for seven months in a row, they cannot be

15   Péan, *Mémoire pour Michel-Jean-Hugues Péan*, p.93.
16   LAC, MG 18, H63, Fonds famille Gradis, F-1600, M. Chantecaille ainé, Niort, 12 octobre 1757.
17   LAC, MG1-C11A, vol.71, f.156v, 162v.
18   LAC, MG1-C11A, vol.84, f.149v.; LAC, MG1-C11A, vol.84, f.146.
19   AN. MG1-C11A, vol.117, f.28v, 29v
20   LAC, MG1-C11A, vol.117, f.177.
21   LAC, MG1-C11A, vol.117, f.188–188v.

exposed to the rain, and the lack of tents has indeed caused many diseases among them.[22]

Throughout the war, various types of tents were supplied to both regular and colonial troops for encampments, reflecting the differing needs of soldiers and officers. A significant number of tents listed as canonnières de soldat (soldiers' wedge tents) and canonnières d'officier (officers' wedge tents) were inlcuded on a 1755 general statement of equipment for the use of six regular battalions being shipped from France to Canada, clearly distinguishing the tents intended for soldiers from those reserved for officers.[23] During that year's campaign, the French officer La Pause indicated that each commanding officer would receive one canonnière per two men while each officer was given a single canonnière along with a tarpaulin per four men.[24] Malartic, however, observed the following: 'one cooking pot per officer, one tent per four [officers], two per battalion for the domestiques, and four tents and cooking pots for each company.'[25] As that year's campaign drew to a close, a military report revealed a pressing shortage of tents for the officers. The author of the report requests:

> …tents and marquises [outer tents] for the officers that it is necessary to send, or at least the canvas with which to make some. They [officers] have had, and still have, only one tent per four, and when I wanted to have marquises sent at the Frontenac camp at the end of September for the battalions of Guyenne and Béarn who were beginning to suffer from the cold nights, there were only nine in the storehouses.[26]

This shortage highlights the logistical challenges faced during the campaign, particularly as colder weather set in.

At Oswego the following year, Bougainville had observed that the officers were now required to carry one canonnière per two men,[27] while the French officer d'Aleyrac echoes the same observations for the siege of Fort George.[28] The practice of distributing a tent per two

A 1748 plate depicting what is likely a French single bell wedge tent (canonnière). According to Puysegur in 1748, the tent measured eight square *pieds* without including the back bell. Eight of the nine soldiers in this scene use their justaucorps as blankets, with their feet tucked into their haversacks for warmth. A ninth soldier, lying near the tent's entrance, appears fully dressed with a waist belt, sword, shoes, and garters, likely awaiting his turn for guard duty. In 1757, Montcalm issued instructions requiring 10 soldiers to share one canonnière tent. (*Plan pour faire voir la manière dont neuf Soldats sont couchez sous une tente*, M. le Maréchal de Puysegur, *Art de la guerre par principes et par règles*, Paris, 1748, plate 10)

officers continued during the William-Henry campaign in 1757 when Montcalm remarks that the officers were to be provided with a canonnière made of coutil while soldiers were to be given one canonnière tent per 10 soldiers.[29] In May of that year, the colonial officer Charles Porcheron dit Decombre had left behind at Québec, 'a tent of coutil with its poles', which may have represented his own personal campaign tent.[30] By the battle of St-Foy in 1760, there appeared to be a serious lack of tents in the colony since an official memo indicated a limited number of large wall tents (grandes tentes à murailles) were to be provided for each battalion at Québec: 'We can only provide but three large wall tents to each battalion that campaigned at Québec; we could place four officers in each [tent]; there are no questions about a tarpaulin. We must inform you of the officers who have tents, and have the old ones repaired.'[31]

22 LAC, MG 8, A1, vol.13, f.77–78.

23 LAC, MG1-C11A, vol.100, f.284.

24 RAPQ, 1933–1934, pp.68, 73.

25 De Malartic, *Journal des campagnes au Canada de 1755 à 1760*, p.13.

26 AG, MG-4, B1, Série A1, vol.3405, f.356–359.

27 Louis-Antoine de Bougainville, *Écrits sur le Canada: mémoires-journal-lettres* (Sillery, Québec: Les éditions du Septentrion, 2003), p.118.

28 BAnQ-M, ZF8, Fonds Jean Baptiste d'Aleyrac.

29 Le R. p.f.Martin, *Le marquis de Montcalm et les dernières années de la colonie française au Canada* (Paris: G. Tequi, Libraire-Éditeur, 1879), pp.85–86.

30 BAnQ-Q, TL5, D1944. Procès de Charles Decombre (Porcheron dit Decombre), officier détaché des troupes de la Marine, contre Marie Couture, veuve de Simon Massy, 26 février 1758–28 mars 1759.

31 Henri-Raymond Casgrain, *Collection des manuscrits du maréchal de Lévis, Lettres du Chevalier de Lévis concernant la guerre du Canada 1756–1760* (Québec: C.O. Beauchemin & Fils, Lib.-Imprimeurs, 1889), p.275.

Winter Campaign Shelters in New France After 1755

Since canvas tents may have been cumbersome to carry on toboggans and difficult to set up on the snow-covered ground during winter expeditions, period accounts indicate that one tarpaulin was provided for each officer for shelter while soldiers were required to share one per four or five men. For example, a list of equipment to be distributed for the winter campaign of 1756 included 'one prélat per four men used as tents',[32] while officers were provided with one prélat at Fort Saint-Jean in the winter of 1757.[33] In his journal, Malartic recounts delivering several prélats to Canadian or colonial soldiers camping in the woods near the same fort in February 1757: 'They managed it very well by making great holes in the snow, placing branches on the ground, and covering these branches with bear skins, creating warm bedding. They were shielded from the rain by a prélat, which is issued for every four men.'[34] That same month, a winter campaign against Fort William Henry, comprising 50 grenadiers from various army regiments, 600 Canadians, 100 Native Americans, and 250 colonial soldiers, recorded the use of a voile (sail) as their sole shelter during their journey, 'with a simple sail that serves as shelter against the wind.'[35] It is worth noting that the term voile used in this context may have referred instead to a prélat (tarpaulin). Later that year, a soldier from the Régiment du Languedoc, taken prisoner at Fort William Henry, stated that each French soldier carried, among other items, 'a Large Piece of Canvas, each four for a Covering by Way of a Tent.'[36] In *Mémoire Pour Messire François Bigot*, published in 1763, it is specified that one tarpaulin was provided per five colonial soldiers, which may have been due to the restrictions on such items due to their scarcity.[37]

Types of Tents

Primary source records indicate that four distinct types of military tents were employed in New France, each tailored to specific ranks and purposes. These included the practical and compact soldier's bell wedge tents, the slightly larger and more refined officer's bell wedge tents, the spacious and versatile wall tents, and the grand and imposing general's tents, which reflected the stature and authority of the commanding officers.

Soldier's Single Bell Wedge Tents (*Cannonnières de Soldat*)

The types of tents provided to the regular and colonial soldiers serving in summer campaigns during the Seven Years War in New France would have followed the army regulation of 1753 for encampment:

> The tents shall be of good linen canvas, their height shall be five *pieds* eight *pouces*, having from the bottom on the front six *pieds* six *pouces* from one corner to the other, so that the door may cross six *pouces* and each side shall be six *pieds* nine *pouces* in length, not including the cul-de-lamp [bell], which shall be ten *pieds* six *pouces* from the bottom, so that the depth from the fork of the inlet to the bottom of the cul-de-lamp, will be ten *pieds* four *pouces*.[38]

This regulation also specified that each company of 40 men was to receive five tents, while each grenadier company of 45 men was allocated six tents. If the companies were augmented, the number of tents would be increased proportionally. Each tent was to be marked in black characters with the name of the regiment and the number of the company.[39]

The term canonnière appears to have entered colonial documents related to New France around 1755. The 1756 edition of the *Dictionnaire languedocien-françois* defines a canonnière as 'a type of canvas tent having two poles and roof-shaped',[40] while Le Blond notes that 'these types of tents, particular to soldiers, are called canonnière.'[41] Canonnière tents provided to colonial soldiers in Canada in 1757 were seemingly identical to those described in the 1753 regulations. This is evident from a French merchant's invoice listing 1,200 of these tents for shipment to Canada in 1757, described as follows: '1,200 canonnières of light and well-beaten (battue) canvas, suitable to hold ten men,

---

32 Centre d'histoire La Presqu'île, P03/F.089, Fonds De Beaujeu, 28 novembre 1756.

33 Casgrain, *Journal du marquis de Montcalm*, pp.156–157.

34 De Malartic, *Journal des campagnes au Canada de 1755 à 1760*, p.95.

35 Henri-Raymond Casgrain, *Collection des manuscrits du Maréchal de Lévis. Guerre du Canada. Relation et journaux de différentes expéditions faites durant les années 1755–56 57–58–59–60* (Québec: imprimerie de L.-J. Demers et Frère, 1895), p.74.

36 LOC, Colonial Office 5 folio 47, E. of Loudoun's Letter of April 25th. 1757, Declaration of two Prisoners taken the 23.d March 1757 at Fort Wm. Henry, Information of John Victor and Guillaume Chasse, two French Prisoners, Fort William Henry March 25th.

37 Bigot, *Mémoire Pour Messire François Bigot*, pp.39–40.

38 *Ordonnance du Roi portant règlement sur le service de l'Infanterie en Campagne. Du 17 février 1753* (Strasbourg: Chez Jean-François Le Roux, 1753), p.2.

39 *Ordonnance du Roi … 17 février 1753*, pp.3–4.

40 Pierre-Augustin L'Abbé Boissier de Sauvages, *Dictionnaire languedocien-françois, ou, Choix des mots languedociens les plus difficiles a rendre en François…* (Nimes: Chez Michel Gaude, libraire, 1756), p.119.

41 Guillaume Le Blond, *Elémens de tactique: ouvrage dans lequel on traite de l'arrangement et de la formation des troupes, des évolutions de l'infanterie et de la cavalerie* (Paris: Chez Charles-Antoine Jomber, 1758), p.334.

Above: Regiment of the Grenadiers Royaux, 1757. This scene, depicting French military camp life of the period, shows several soldiers engaging in activities, such as gambling and drinking, which were common among troops serving in Canada. Two soldiers under a tent appear to be arguing over the outcome of a dice roll while their companions enjoy a pipe and drink around a table. (© Musée de l'Armée/Dist. RMN-Grand Palais/Art Resource, NY)

Right: Detail from a c. 1748 painting showing a bell-of-arms filled with soldiers' muskets from the Régiment royal du Roussillon. The muskets are arranged with the butt ends on the ground and the muzzles pointing upwards. There was typically one bell-of-arms for each company. (Fort Ticonderoga Museum Collection)

Rare map showing the siege of Québec from July to September 1759. One of the three French encampments at Beauport, labelled B in the bottom left corner, represents the one under the command of the Marquis de Montcalm (Camp des français commandé par Mr. de Montcalm), while the letter D indicates the location of a flying camp under Bougainville's command. Montcalm's forces comprised five battalions, each represented by two flags and several tents: the Régiments du Languedoc, La Sarre, Royal Roussillon, Guyenne, and Béarn. This map may represent one of the only surviving French-made maps of the siege, as indicated by

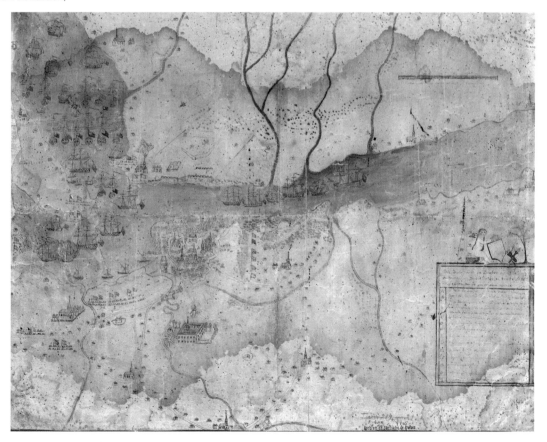

its orientation, with the top directed south, reflecting the French position on the north shore of the St Lawrence. (*Idée de la ville de Québec assiégée du 12 du mois de juillet 1759 et rendue le 18 de septembre de la même année.* Archives du séminaire de Québec)

Detail from a circa 1748 painting of the Régiment royal du Roussillon's camp, providing a glimpse into French military encampments of the time. The lower half of the painting shows rows of soldiers' wedge tents, while the middle row displays officers' square wall tents, likely covered by a waterproof marquise. The *général-majeur* on the left would have encamped in a tente de général. According to Bougainville, while gathered at Fort Carillon for the siege of Fort William Henry in July 1757, Montcalm was camped in a tent next to colonial commandant Rigaud. Bougainville wrote: 'In the evening, young men sang war songs opposite the tents of Messieurs de Montcalm and Rigaud, which earned them a few bottles of wine.' (Fort Ticonderoga Museum Collection, New York)

The Carillon Banner, measuring 213cm in width and 307cm in length. It is believed to have flown for the first time during Montcalm's victory at the Battle of Carillon in 1758. Its eighteenth-century origin is undisputed, bearing the arms of Beauharnois, a Madonna with Child at its centre, and fleur-de-lis pointing inward from each corner. However, the original colour remains uncertain, possibly white or pale yellow. Restored in the 1990s, it became a symbol for Québécois and made its public debut in 1848 during the Saint-Jean-Baptiste parade. This banner inspired Quebec's first official flag, representing the identity quest of Québécois and Quebec's evolution as a nation. (Musée de la civilisation, collection du Séminaire de Québec, photographe: Julien Auger - Icône, 1997.12008.0.1.)

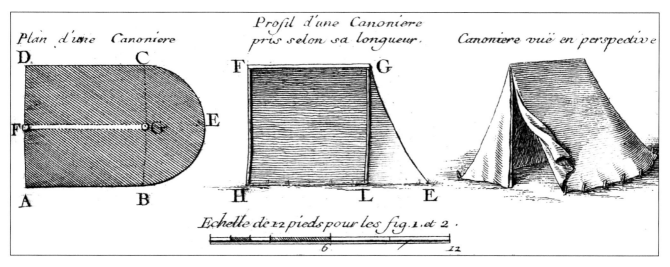

Illustration from *Elémens de tactique* (1758), showing the footing, profile, and perspective view of a canonnière tent. Le Blond noted that a canonnière tent typically housed seven or eight soldiers, while, according to Le Blond, there are '…only six or seven men in the **sergent**'s tents,', at the rear of the camp.

Three types of large tents with a marquise outer tent, featured in Diderot's *L'Art du tapissier*, plate 6. According to Diderot, this tent shape provided more space and comfort but required more fabric, rope, and time to set up. The tents vary in shape, with two cul de lampe (ends) for entrance and equipment storage. The octagonal-shaped wall tents, known as tentes à la Turque (Turkish-style tents), were perfectly cylindrical. The tents illustrated as figures No. 3 and No. 4 likely correspond to the officer's large wedge tents (canonnières d'officier) brought to Canada with regular troops in 1755, while figure No. 2 represents a wall tent (tente à murailles). The descriptions of the three tents shown on plate 6 of *L'Art du tapissier* are: 'No. 4. Measurements and proportions of a soldier's wedge tent and its walled marquise, with two gables and two cul de lampe, the rear one closed, the front one serving as a door … height of the upright fork, 6 *pieds* 6 *pouces*. No. 3. Measurements and proportions of a soldier's wedge tent with ridge and cul de lampe, with crow's feet on the body of the wedge tent and cul de lampe, allowing for ventilation by rolling up the tent bottom in hot weather … height of the upright fork, 7 *pieds*. No. 2. Measurements and proportions of a wall tent (tente à murailles) with two cul de lampe, one at the front forming an umbrella-shaped entrance and the rear set aside for equipment storage … height of the upright fork, 9 *pieds*.' A circular letter sent to battalion commanders during the 1760 campaign at Québec specified that each battalion would receive three wall tents to accommodate four officers, likely corresponding to one of the types shown in this illustration.

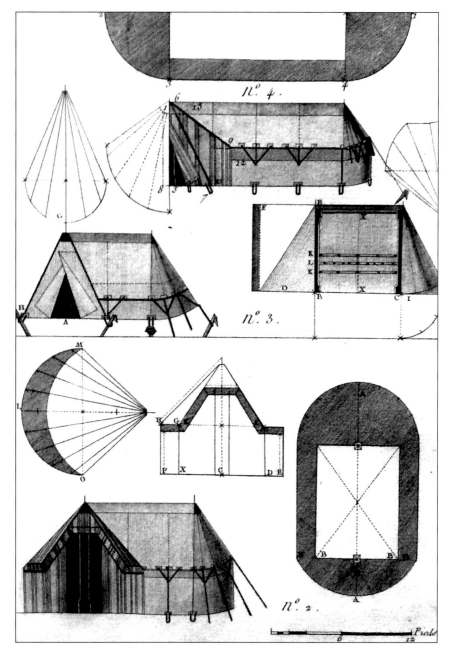

taken from the model of those given to the Troupes de terre.[42]

Officer's Large Wedge Tents

Period sources provide little detail about the specific types of tents supplied to French officers serving in Canada after 1755, as these are not described in the official army regulations of the time. However, a 1755 document requesting military equipment for the regulars included '30 officers' canonnières' alongside '300 soldiers' canonnières' suggests that officers' tents were distinct from those issued to soldiers.[43] Guillaume le Blond's 1758 edition of *Elémens de tactique* provides further insight, describing officers' tents as significantly larger than soldiers' wedge tents, likely their most notable feature:

> The officers' tents are much larger than those of the soldiers. They are wide on top, and we can stand up conveniently. The small pieces of wood which serve as forks are called masts (mâts), and the ridge is a cross-piece (faîtière). They are stretched with ropes attached to stakes like the canonnières … The tents of the officers are at the back of the camps… [44]

In 1754, Jacques-François Forget Duverger, a French priest traveling from Québec to his new post among the Tamaroas people at Cahokia in the Illinois country, offered a rare description of one of these larger tents. His account appears to depict an oversized canonnière tent, featuring a second canvas sheet or marquise draped over the structure:

> This portable dwelling is set up on two large sticks about 7 or 8 *pieds* high, a crossbar of the same length is attached, and then a canvas is laid there; This canvas is closed on one side by a kind of cul-de-lampe (the round bottom of a lamp) to support this canvas and render it impenetrable to the rain; It is secured to the ground by small pegs, which are fastened to roughly twenty rings, and in order to better protect ourselves against heavy rain, we place on top of this small transparent house a second well-tended canvas that does not come in contact with the one underneath other than by the top of the stakes to which it is subjected, being much higher than those of the first canvas. To complete this portable apartment, we have a folding camp bed (lit de sangles) which can be dismounted with screws.[45]

Officer's Wall Tents

Wall tents, known as tentes à murailles, were prominently used by officers during the campaigns of the Seven Years War in Canada. In 1760, for example, each battalion that had campaigned at Québec was to be supplied with three 'large wall tents' for every four officers.[46] These tents, distinct in their structure, are elegantly described in *L'Art du tapissier* as: 'those whose surface, instead of forming an oblique line from the ridge to the bottom, which extends further and further away from the centre, have this form only up to two-thirds or one-half of their height, at which point it drops perpendicularly.'[47] Their design offered both practicality and refinement, befitting the needs of high-ranking officers in the field.

General's Tents

Commanding officers or generals leading large-scale campaigns in New France likely sheltered under grand wall tents made of coutil fabric and supported by three vertical poles. For instance, '50 wall tents of coutil, with the marquises, for the general officers' were listed on a merchant's commercial invoices from 1757, suggesting these larger tents were accompanied by their corresponding outer tents (marquises).[48] Known in France as tentes de général, these structures were far larger than standard wall tents. As described in *L'Art du tapissier*, the general's tent was supported by three upright poles, featuring two cul de lampe sections, an alcove, an antechamber, and a central dining area, offering both spaciousness and sophistication befitting high-ranking officers.[49]

Pavillon Tents

In France, the term pavillon, often used interchangeably with tente, refers to a variety of large shelters characterised by a single dome or conical-shaped roof. While no documented evidence of such tents has yet been uncovered as part of this research, *général* Bienville's tent, as illustrated by Dumont de Montigny in 1736, may offer one of the rare depictions of a pavillon tent in North America. In France, these tents were described as large, portable dwellings used for the encampment of military personnel, 'made square or round and terminating in a point at the top, unlike tents that are long and wide and whose top is made in the form of a roof ridge. The pavilions are usually

42   LAC, MG 18, H63, Fonds famille Gradis, F-1600, M. de la Rivière, À la cour, 11 octobre 1757.
43   LAC, MG1-C11A, vol.100. f.284.
44   Le Blond, *Elémens de tactique*, pp.334–335.
45   LAC, MG 18, 314, Archives de la Marine 3JJ, Inventaire du Service hydrographique, F-651, François Forget Duverger, Relation d'un voyage au Canada, 1754.
46   Henri-Raymond Casgrain, *Collection des manuscrits du maréchal de Lévis, Journal des campagnes du chevalier de Lévis en Canada de 1756 à 1760* (Montréal: C.O. Beauchemin & Fils, 1889), p.275.
47   *Encyclopédie méthodique. Manufactures et arts* (Paris: Panckoucke, 1785), vol.2, p.225.
48   LAC, MG 18, H63, Fonds famille Gradis, F-1600, M. de la Rivière, 11 octobre, 1757.
49   *Encyclopédie méthodique. Manufactures et arts*, vol.2, p.226.

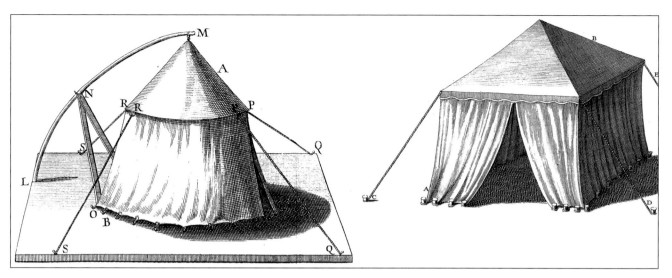

These pavilion tents, one circular and one square, illustrate a style with a single dome or conical roof, distinct from wedge or wall tents. The term 'pavilion' suggests a flag at the peak, often seen on French military tents of the period. Left: Engraving detail of a circular pavilion tent, also known as a marquise or tente pavillon, with a distinctive dome shape and rain fly. The suspension method shown here is conceptual, reflecting one of the alternative designs by inventor M. Marius, whose innovations were endorsed by the Académie Royale des Sciences. Right: A retractable square wall tent also designed by M. Marius, showcasing another popular military tent form of the time. (*Machines et inventions approuvées par l'Académie Royale des Sciences*, 1735)

A Native traveling party camping near Sorel, Québec. While some gather around a campfire, others rest under an upturned canoe. It is possible that colonial soldiers, when participating in small expeditions by canoe, used upturned canoes or tarpaulins as shelters. *Capitaine* Pouchot observed that a canoe 'also serves as a shelter; one side is raised, supported by one or two paddles, then we lie down under it for shelter against the wind. It is the usual shelter during voyages or when hunting'. (Library of Congress. A View of St. Johns upon the River Sorell, in Canada, with the Redoubts Works, etc. Taken in the Year 1776)

made of coutil.'[50] According to the *Dictionnaire militaire*, a pavillon is defined as 'a tent of canvas or of coutil, which is raised using poles for lodging during campaigns and wars,'[51] and where the 'the rooftop in pavillons finishes in a cone or dome, and those of the tents with a chevron-type roof.'[52]

Marquee Tents (Marquise)

The term marquise in French appears to denote a rain fly or outer covering designed to shield the actual tent

---

50   *Le grand vocabulaire françois* (Paris: C. Panckoucke, 1772), vol.21, p.250.

51   *Dictionnaire militaire, portatif: contenant tous les termes propres a la guerre ...* (Paris: La Veuve Bordelet, 1758), p.92.

52   François-Alexandre Aubert de La Chesnaye des Bois, *Dictionnaire militaire, portatif, contenant tous les termes ...* (Paris: chez Gissey, 1758), vol.3, p.455.

from water rather than a distinct type of tent. A period dictionary defines a marquise as 'the upper canvas of an officer's tent, so that the rain does not penetrate as much,'[53] while another source notes that such coverings were stretched over soldiers' bell wedge tents for added protection.[54] According to the *Dissertation sur les tentes ou pavillons de guerre*, the origin of the term marquise traces back to a certain marquis who revived the practice of draping a coarse canvas outer tent over a finer inner tent:

> The most magnificent [tents] were preserved with care, to prevent them from getting spoiled. A tent showed its splendour only on a fine day, and in bad weather it was covered with another, which was of more common fabric: thus, only having distinguished officers who had these double pavilions, from this perhaps came among us the custom to have similar ones for the same person, and to identify, by the name of marquise, a tent of coarse canvas which covers another fine canvas, and the marquise will have been thus named by some Marquis, a man of knowledge and taste, who has re-established the fashion in recent times.[55]

Various period sources suggest that these outer canvas covers were blue, possibly made from striped white and blue cloth. The 1784 edition of *Manufactures, arts et métiers* describes such a fly being used over a soldier's bell tent: 'the whole of which is covered over with a blue cloth of the same shape as the tent, and which is held over it leaving a gap all around, leaving a passage or gallery between the tent and this general envelope, which is called marquise.'[56] Further evidence is found in a shipping invoice from *La Renommée*, a French ship seized en route to Québec in 1757, which listed 40 bales of 'canonnières, tentes and marquises', confirming foremost that marquises did not refer to a distinct type of tent.[57] In 1761, the post-mortem inventory of Jean Jacques de St-Martin, a *capitaine* in the colonial troops, listed 'one tent with its marquise' valued at 24 livres,[58] whereas a publication dealing with the Intendant Bigot's trial in France, observed that the summer equipment of colonial officers consisted of a tent with its marquise.[59]

Although this scene takes place nearly 80 years after the conquest of New France, it provides a glimpse into the shelter-building techniques that likely had not changed much since the early colonial days. Here, we likely see Canadians and Indigenous peoples engaged in the process of setting up a camp during a winter expedition. Note the arrangement of Y-shaped forked sticks supporting a wooden crosspiece, over which a tarpaulin would have been stretched, a method probably used during the French regime when Canadians and their Indigenous allies sought shelter from the elements during their journeys through the wilderness. (James Hope-Wallace, Construction d'un abri. Collection du Musée national des beaux-arts du Québec, 1840)

Tarpaulin (Prélat)

The term prélat, also spelled prélart, is defined in the *Dictionnaire de Marine* as 'a large tarred canvas that we put over openings on a ship, such as slatted flooring, the breastwork of the quarter deck, panels and stairs.'[60] A 1757 scientific report by the *Académie royale des sciences* describes it as a 'canvas made with large tow fibre, which is first wetted and then painted on one side only, with red ochre crushed with oil.'[61] French engineer Louis Franquet, who visited Canada in 1752, states: 'We call a prélat a large piece of canvas painted with oil, in red, with which we cover the awning, to offer shelter from the rain.'[62] Malartic noted that soldiers traveling to Montréal in 1755 camped under boat sails or prélats, which he described as 'two pieces of canvas of five or six *aunes* in length, to protect the supplies that are in the boats from the rain.'[63] Colonial records from the Seven Years War also reveal that prélats were locally produced, such as a quantity of 22 prélats made in 1759 by la Veuve Niagara for the King's clerk at

53 Abel Boyer, *The Royal Dictionary, French and English, and English and French...* (London: Osborne, 1764)

54 *Manufactures, arts et métiers* (Paris: Panckoucke, 1784), vol.2, p.225.

55 Beneton de Perrin, *Dissertation on Tents or War Pavilion*, 1734.

56 Manufactures, arts et métiers (Paris: Panckoucke, 1784), vol.2, p.225.

57 TNA, HCA, 32, vol.238, La Renommé, 1757.

58 BAnQ-TR, Greffe du notaire J. Pillard, Inventaire et description des biens et meubles de feue Gabrielle Le Gardeur, veuve de feu Sieur Jean-Jacques de Saint-Martin, capitaine des troupes de la Marine, 10 mars 1761.

59 Bigot, *Mémoire Pour Messire François Bigot*, p.40.

60 *Dictionnaire de marine contenant les termes de la navigation et de l'architecture navale ... enrichi des figures etc* (Amsterdam: Pierre Brunel, 1702), p.642.

61 Jean Berryat, *Recueil de mémoires: ou, Collection de pièces académiques ...* (Paris: f.Desventes, 1786), vol.12, p.30

62 Louis Franquet, *Voyages et mémoires sur le Canada* (Québec: Imprimerie générale A. Coté et cie., 1889), p.5.

63 De Malartic, *Journal des campagnes au Canada de 1755 à 1760*, p.8.

Detroit,[64] and another 50 prélats by the widow Laderoute that same year.[65]

One prélat and one sail was traditionally included as part of the equipment allocated to each canoe serving either for military expeditions or for the fur trade and would have served to shelter both the supplies and the men from the elements. For instance, 11 eight-place canoes provided as part of the war party led by M. de Noyelles to attack the Fox nation, which included colonial officers as well as soldiers, were outfitted with '11 sails' and '11 prélats'.[66] Five years later, the 1739 expedition against the Chickasaw under the command of the Baron de Longueuil included 18 eight-place canoes as well as '18 sails' and '18 prélats' while one of these sets of sail and prélat was recorded as made using '15 *aunes* of Mélis' indicating that each piece measured 7½ aunes of canvas.[67] Sixteen of these canoes were referenced as assigned to 112 cadets, soldiers, and Canadians 'at a rate of seven men per canoe', which meant that these men likely shared one of these tarred canvas pieces as a provisional shelter when required.[68] Bougainville, Montcalm's aide-of-camp, had commented on the fact that when travelling in the upper countries or on the frontier near Fort Saint-Frédéric 'we camp in small canvas tents or prélats, and often voyageurs use only their canoes.'[69]

It is likely that, early on, colonial troops adopted a form of lean-to shelter inspired by Native practices, modifying it by replacing the branches, foliage, or reeds with tarred canvas, a waterproof yet lightweight material well-suited for travel on foot through the woods. Pierre Pouchot notes that this method of encamping was preferable to using a tent, particularly in cold conditions:

> They [Natives]… construct a shelter on the side towards the wind, by forming a half-roof with two sticks holding up little poles which they cover with branches of conifers, flattened foliage or reeds gathered from the marshes. In front of this shelter, they light a good fire. This arrangement, although simple, is preferable to a tent or a canonnière where you would freeze because you are more or less cut off from the heat…[70]

A 1756 supply list issued to colonial and regular soldiers describes shelters resembling Native-style lean-tos, adapted with tarpaulins. Intended for winter expeditions, these tarred canvases were likely set up using two Y-shaped forked sticks supporting a makeshift wooden crosspiece to form the frame, over which the canvas was stretched at the back: 'Prélat, per 4 men with which to camp. It is a sail canvas that we place on two forks.'[71]

64   AM, G.239, pièce numéro 30.
65   AM, G.239, pièce numéro 81.
66   LAC, MG1-C11A, vol.62, f.151.
67   LAC, MG1-C11A, vol.71, f.161v.
68   LAC, MG1-C11A, vol.71, f.164–164v.
69   Louis-Antoine de Bougainville, *Écrits sur le Canada: mémoires-journal-lettres* (Sillery, Québec: Les éditions du Septentrion, 2003), p.118.
70   Pierre Pouchot, *Memoirs on the late war in North America between France and England* (Old Fort Niagara Association, 1994), p.458.

71   SHD, Archives de la guerre, A1, vol.3417, f.404.

6

Non-regulation Weapons and Equipment of the Colonial Officers

Shoulder Weapons of the Colonial Officers

While officers of the Compagnies franches de la Marine were traditionally armed with a sword or spontoon, many opted early on to purchase a fusil, as it was far more practical than a pole arm for bush fighting in New France. During campaigns, these officers did not lead their men with archaic weapons like spontoons but instead engaged the enemy and defended themselves with firearms. The practice of officers carrying shoulder weapons is supported by numerous period documents, which indicate that they were issued gun-related equipment and ammunition before expeditions or wilderness campaigns. Colonial officers typically purchased their own shoulder weapons, as confirmed by probate records that reflect a wide variety of muskets and hunting guns, with or without bayonets. Finer hunting guns were common, and it is likely that some officers chose these stylish, high-quality firearms to distinguish themselves from the enlisted ranks.

With the arrival of regular troops in Canada at the onset of the Seven Years War, period records show that hunting guns supplied by the King became standard issue for all officers on detachment and during operations. This shift can be attributed to the fact that, by the late 1740s, many officers in France were already carrying firearms into combat instead of spontoons. This trend ultimately led to the introduction of a regulation-pattern officers' musket in 1758 and the official abandonment of the spontoon that same year.

French Regulation Model Officers' Musket

From an early period, French officers serving in infantry or dragoon regiments were equipped exclusively with a half-pike, and later with a spontoon, as mandated by the 10 May 1690 ordonnance. However, this weapon was widely regarded as impractical in combat. During the War of the Spanish Succession, officers stationed in the mountainous regions of Bavaria and Dauphiné, where polearms proved cumbersome, armed themselves with muskets of the same calibre and length as those carried by the soldiers. In a letter written in May 1710, the Marquis de Broglie remarked, 'For the service of the mountains, the musket is more convenient.'[1] A few months later, the King decreed that all subordinate officers, except those in the Suisse and Gardes françaises, were to be armed with muskets fitted with bayonets, a practice that continued until the war's conclusion in 1714. While no specific shoulder weapons were prescribed for officers at this time, the muskets they carried were distinguished from those of the soldiers by their finer craftsmanship and lighter weight.[2] With the return of peace in 1715, officers resumed carrying the spontoon.

Maréchal de Puysegur points out in his *Art de la guerre* that, after the war of the Austrian Succession in 1748, officers were at this point consistently arming themselves with muskets and leaving behind their polearms:

> There is no compelling reason to arm officers differently from soldiers when it is evident that the musket with a socket bayonet is the most effective and versatile weapon for all types of engagements. This is further demonstrated by the increasing number of officers who, in combat, choose to carry muskets with socket bayonets instead of spontoons, as well as by the fact that officers sent on detached duty for wartime operations consistently forgo spontoons altogether.[3]

De Puysegur further argued that officers and *sergents* could shoot alongside infantrymen without inconveniencing the company 'whereas, with the spontoon, they

---

1   François Bonnefoy, *Les Armes de guerre portatives en France, du début du règne de Louis XIV à la veille de la Révolution (1660-1789): de l'indépendance à la primauté* (Paris: Librairie de l'Inde, 1991), vol.1, p.65
2   Bonnefoy, *Les Armes de guerre portatives en France*, p.65
3   Jacques-François de Chastenet de Puységur, *Art de la guerre, par principes et par règles. Ouvrage de m. le maréchal de Puysegur. Mis au jour par m. le marquis de Puysegur son fils, maréchal des camps & armées du roy* (Paris: Chez Charles-Antoine Jombert, 1749), vol.1, p.221.

Detail taken from a map of North and South America published in 1755 on which a particular pictorial vignette depicts a contemporary representation of *commandant* Champlain shooting on a party of Iroquois warriors. While somewhat imaginary, it is however highly representative of what a French officer or nobleman of the period may have looked like while shooting a gun. (*L'Amérique : dressée sur les relations les plus récentes, rectifiées sur les dernières observations…* (Paris: Crépy, 1755))

are of little assistance'.[4] He further criticised the spontoon as impractical for performing the Manual of Arms, emphasizing that, equipped with muskets, 'the officers can themselves do the exercise, shoot, and perform all the military motions with their soldiers'.[5] He specified that the muskets carried by officers should match the calibre of those issued to the soldiers but be finer and lighter in construction. Regarding the maniement des armes, he advised that officers, like the soldiers, should rest the musket on the shoulder with the butt pointing forward.

D'Hericourt, *capitaine* of the Régiment du Roi, remarked that '…captains and other officers of the grenadier companies must be armed with muskets with bayonets. When war is waged in a hilly countryside, it is often the case that the Army General requires the subalterns to be armed in the same ways as grenadier officers.'[6] The 7 May 1750 ordonnance now made it mandatory that the officers of the grenadier companies be armed with a musket.[7]

Bonnefoy notes that, according to a 1754 memoir, officers at the time were armed with only very small muskets and even smaller bayonets, 'which is not suitable against the enemy.'[8] In response, a regulation was issued

to the three main arms production centres detailing the specifications for a grenadier officer's musket. This musket was to have a calibre of 16 balls to the *livre*, for a ball of 18 balls to the *livre*, match the construction of the soldiers' muskets, measure 4½ *pieds* in length, feature polished iron furniture, a walnut stock, weigh no more than 7 *livres*, and include an 8 *pouces* long bayonet versus the much longer regulation infantry bayonet issued to soldiers.[9] According to Boudriot, this first-generation officer's musket was limited to a production of 652 examples. It was otherwise identical to the later 1759 infantry officer's musket, of which 8,500 units were produced.[10]

The combat experiences of the Seven Years War underscored the benefits of equipping all officers, not just those of the grenadiers, with fusils. As a result, the Ordinance of 31 October 1758, extended the requirement to carry fusils to all officers of fusilier companies, both French and foreign. In short, the decision to arm French officers with muskets was likely part of a broader strategy to boost military effectiveness, assert authority in the field, and serve as a role model for the soldiers. This decision represented a particular view of the officer's role, one that was more in tune with the demands of combat, setting it apart from the practices adopted by other European armies. The decree mandated that their muskets be manufactured at the

---

4   De Puységur, *Art de la guerre, par principes et par règles*, vol.1, p.222.

5   De Puységur, *Art de la guerre, par principes et par règles*, vol.1, pp.227–228.

6   Nicolas d'Hericourt, *Élémens de l'art militaire* (À la Haye: Pierre Gosse, 1748), vol.1, p.168.

7   *Ordonnance du Roy sur le maniement des armes de l'infanterie du 7 mai 1750* (Lyon: p.Valfray, 1753), p.12.

8   Bonnefoy, *Les Armes de guerre portatives en France*, p.66

9   *Réglement pour la construction des espontons dont les officiers d'infanterie … du premier mai 1754* (Paris: Impr. royale, 1754), p.2.

10   Jean Boudriot, *Armes à feu françaises, modèles réglementaires: 1717–1836* (Cedex: Éditions du Portail, 1997), p.58.

factories of Saint-Étienne, Charleville, or Maubeuge and paired with bayonets from the Klingenthal factory: 'The officer's musket shall be of 4 *pieds* in length, of a calibre of 16 [balls to the *livre*], to receive the ball of 18 [balls to the *livre*]; it will weigh no more than 7 *livres*, equipped with its bayonet that shall have 8½ *pouces* with a hollowed blade.'[11]

These fusils came in two variations: a standard version for *lieutenants* and a more ornate, damascened version for *capitaines*, though both retained identical technical specifications.[12]

By November 1759, however, Marine officers stationed at French ports were still not equipped with a fusil and bayonet. This is evident in a letter from the Minister at Versailles to M. de Ruis, Intendant at Rochefort:

> …the officers of the former troops of Île-Royale currently serving at Rochefort ask to be armed with a fusil and bayonets like the officers of the Troupes de terre. This practice may be worthwhile; and I am not far away from introducing it among the troops of the Marine; but as there is no hurry in this respect, we must wait a little longer… [13]

This correspondence illustrates the gradual adoption of standardised arms across different branches of the military and hesitancy to extend the practice to Marine officers immediately.

Longarms Used by Colonial Officers on Campaigns

In the French colonies of North America, however, primary sources reveal that officers of the Compagnies franches de la Marine adopted fusils as early as the 1680s. The journal of Pierre de Troyes, a *capitaine* in the colonial troops, documents an overland expedition against Hudson's Bay Company trading posts in 1686 and includes numerous references to colonial officers armed with fusils. During the attack on Fort Monsipi (Moose Factory or Saint-Louis), Jacques le Moyne de Sainte-Hélène, the *premier lieutenant*, was credited with shooting an Englishman: 'There are some who attribute this shot to Monsieur de Sainte-Hélène, who is known to be a good marksman.'[14] His brother, Pierre Le Moyne d'Iberville, the second lieutenant, is described as having 'thrown himself at once, the sword in one hand and the fusil in the other … fighting

Detail taken from *Les Troupes françaises attaquant la forteresse de Colle dell Assietto dans le Piémont*, showing the Battle of Assietta, which was fought in the Italian campaign of the War of the Austrian Succession on 19 July 1747. Shown here in the foreground is a French infantry officer wearing a gorget and armed with a spontoon in hand, retreating with his men. This pole arm would have been utterly useless in a combat situation such as the one pictured here. (Les Troupes françaises attaquant la forteresse de Colle dell Assietto dans le Piémont, 1754. Private collection)

with his sword against all who presented themselves, wounded a few Englishmen in the face, and shot his fusil in a staircase.'[15]

The following century, Dumont de Montigny, a colonial officer serving in Louisiana in 1729, recounted arming himself with 'a good fusil de maître [master-made gun]' before escaping from Fort Rosalie for New Orleans.[16] References to colonial officers using shoulder weapons also turn up during the Fox wars, such as in 1730 when Sieur Coulon de Villier, the younger, was equipped with a fine master-style gun (un fusil fin de façon), valued at 70 livres, for his journey from Fort St-Joseph to Québec to deliver news of an attack on the Fox nation.[17] Three years later, during an assault on Fox warriors seeking refuge in a Sauk village near Green Bay, De Repentigny, *commandant* at Michilimackinac, avenged the death of his son using his fusil: 'he had the displeasure to see his son falling dead at his feet from a gunshot. He himself fired a gunshot with which he shot a man'.[18]

Gun-related equipment and ammunition issued to officers participating in various war parties against the Fox and the Chickasaw nations throughout the 1730s also indicate that many, if not all, officers were armed with flintlock shoulder weapons. During M. de Noyelles' expedition against the Fox nation in the winter of 1735,

11   Montandre-Longchamp, *Etat militaire de France* (Paris: Chez Guillyn, 1759), vol.2, p.384.

12   Bonnefoy, *Les Armes de guerre portatives en France*, p.66

13   LAC, MG1-B, vol.110, f.563v (137v), À M. de Ruis, À Versailles, le 23 novembre 1759.

14   Pierre de Troyes, *Journal de l'expédition du chevalier de Troyes à la baie d'Hudson, en 1686, édité et annoté par Ivanhoe Caron* (Beauceville, La Compagnie de l'éclaireur, 1918), p.67.

15   De Troyes, *Journal de l'expédition du chevalier de Troyes*, p.67.

16   Dumont de Montigny, *Regards sur les monde atlantique 1715–1747* (Sillery, Québec: Septentrion, 2008), p.226.

17   LAC, MG1-C11A, vol.52, f.162–162v.

18   Archives des Sulpiciens, dossier 20, numéro 4. 1733 au 23 janvier 1734 et d 6 avril au 21 mai 1734.

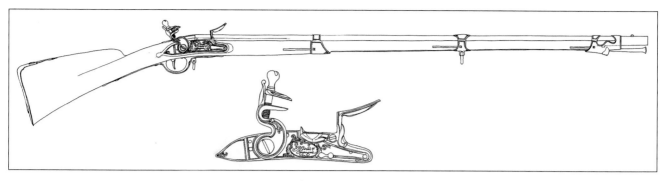

French model 1759 infantry officer's musket by Girard of Saint-Étienne, part of the 4,300 ordered from Girard, with only a few examples surviving. Unlikely to have reached Canada before 1760, its design reflects the weapon style favoured by French officers. Nearly identical to the French Dragoon officer's musket model 1752, which was studied as early as 1750, the model 1754 and 1759 grenadier and infantry officer's muskets exemplify the fashionable firearms of the time for officers in France and New France. Apart from being a ½ *pouce* shorter than the model 1754 grenadier officer's musket, the model 1759 infantry officer's musket shares nearly identical specifications, with only minor differences in bayonet length: 'The officer's musket shall be of 4 *pieds* in length, of a calibre of 16 [balls to the *livre*], to take a ball of 18 [balls to the *livre*]; it will weigh no more than 7 *livres*, equipped with its bayonet that shall have 8½ *pouces* with a hallowed blade.' (Drawing by Jean Boudriot)

colonial officers received gunflints, gunpowder, and lead balls, among other supplies.[19] Similarly, in 1739, officer De Sabrevois, accompanying Lemoyne de Longueuil against the Chickasaws, was supplied with 8 *livres* of gunpowder, 30 *livres* of lead balls, 15 *gunflints*, and one gun worm.[20] By 1738, at Fort Niagara, a 'fusil de Tulle' was listed among the supplies designated for the commandant, chaplain, and officers.[21]

By the time of King George's War, gun-related equipment appears to have become standard issue for colonial officers on campaigns and war parties. In 1746, for example, supplies issued to seven officers en route to attack Fort Massachusetts included 20 *livres* of gunpowder, 80 *livres* of lead balls, 120 gunflints, and 20 gun worms.[22] Additionally, the commanding officer, Rigaud de Vaudreuil, and a *capitaine* were each provided with a gun case made from ⅔ *aunes* of molleton. These records offer further evidence that shoulder arms were the primary weapons carried by officers during campaigns.[23]

Shoulder weapons were sometimes supplied to officers to replace those lost, damaged, or rendered unusable during service, providing us with valuable insight into the type of guns they were using while bush fighting. In 1746, Monsieur De St-Ours, an officer of the colonial troops, received a fusil de Tulle 'in replacement of the fusil he lost while on campaign in Acadia as part of the King's service.'[24] In 1747, while campaigning along the New England coast, the officer De Belestre was provided with a master-style hunting gun (fusil de façon), while the Chevalier de Repentigny was issued a Tulle fusil de chasse (hunting gun made in Tulle) 'in replacement of his fusil

Rare Tulle-made hunting gunlock marked A. TVLLE, probably of the 1729 or 1734 contract pattern. This would have been the type of lock which would have been used on a Tulle fusil de chasse as per those given to the colonial officer De St-Ours and De Repentigny to replace the firearms they had lost while on campaign in the late 1740s. Excavated at the Tenailles des nouvelles casernes at Québec. (Courtesy of National Historic Sites, Parks Canada. Photo Kevin Gélinas)

French officer's socket bayonet c. 1750 missing its blade, excavated from Fort de Chartres. This artefact displays a decorative swell on the shank, providing evidence that these weapons were privately purchased by colonial officers and finer than those of the soldier's pattern. An assortment of fine hunting guns equipped with bayonets were purchased by colonial officers serving in Canada in 1748, which may have had very similar bayonets. In essence, the officers' bayonets followed the same development as those of enlisted men but could accommodate either top or bottom bayonet studs, with variations in dimensions and decorative details. (Courtesy of the Illinois Historic Preservation Division. Photo René Chartrand)

19 LAC, MG1-C11A, vol.62, f.149–149v.
20 LAC, MG1-C11A, vol.71, f.157v.
21 LAC, MG1-C11A, vol.69, f.274v-275.
22 LAC, MG1-C11A, vol.115, f.254–254v.
23 LAC, MG1-C11A, vol.115, f.255–255v.
24 LAC, MG1-C11A, vol.86, f.206.

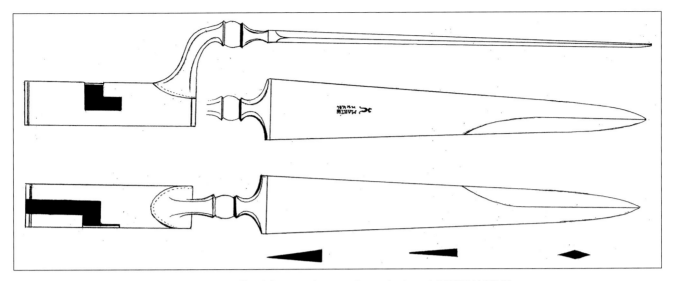

Illustration representing an ornate c.1735–1750 officer's bayonet, bearing the marker's mark MARTIN MICHEL.

Example of an extant French officer's bayonet bearing a partial marking of MICHEL on the top of its blade, likely representing the mark of one of the members of the Michel family of blacksmiths working out of the town of Saint-Étienne, France. (Bob Speelman collection. Photo Kevin Gélinas)

which he broke and put out of service in the said discoveries he made on the enemy country.'[25] In February of that same year, Louis Liénard de Beaujeu de Villemonde, who fought in the Battle of Grand-Pré in Nova Scotia, offers a vivid and rare description of a colonial officer using his fusil in close combat. After entering a house occupied by 25 Englishmen, De Beaujeu recounts: 'I gave the sergeant a blow to his stomach. And I thrust my gun through his body. He fell, the guts came out of his belly, and I withdrew my broken gun.'[26] This account suggests that De Beaujeu may have been armed with a musket or hunting gun equipped with a bayonet, as such a weapon would allow for both shooting and thrusting.

During the final year of the war, the cargo list of a seized French ship on its way to Québec in the spring of 1748 offers a rare glimpse into the type of shoulder weapons privately purchased for colonial officers serving in Canada. The inventory included '8 fusils with bayonets, spare cock and frizzen, for officers, fine, at 19 livres apiece', possibly referring to fine hunting guns equipped with socket or hunting plug bayonets.[27]

The Seven Years War

In 1755, French infantry officers who crossed the Atlantic under the command of Baron de Dieskau were equipped with hunting guns, a few years before the official ordonnance mandated that all infantry officers carry muskets. A supply statement for six battalions, loaded onto a squadron of ships departing Paris in March 1755, recorded 200 'hunting guns for officers … The guns in question have not been inspected in Paris, and some boxes must be unpacked to ascertain whether this supply is in serviceable condition.'[28]

It remains unclear whether these weapons were issued with bayonets. According to the officer La Pause, Baron Dieskau strictly ordered all infantry *capitaines* and *lieutenants* of the Régiment de Guyenne to take hunting guns from the storehouses prior to their departure from Montréal: 'There were many officers who took guns from the storehouses by a precise order from Monsieur le Baron de Dieskau, who wanted all the officers to take one.'[29]

An important memoir drafted in October 1755 confirms that officers of the regular troops were expected to procure their own shoulder weapons, although the cost of these guns would not be deducted from their wages. The hunting guns sent with the Troupes de terre in 1755

25 LAC, MG1-C11A, vol.117, f.177, 205.
26 Gagné, Joseph (2014), 'Fidèle à Dieu, à la France, et au Roi' Les retraites militaires de La Chapelle et de Beaujeu vers la Louisiane après la perte du Canada 1760-1762 (Mémoire de maitrise, Université Laval), pp.46–47.
27 TNA, HCA, 32, vol.99, pt 2, La Bien-Aimée de Bordeaux, 1748.

28 LAC, MG1-C11A, vol.100, f.287v.
29 RAPQ, 1933–1934, p.69.

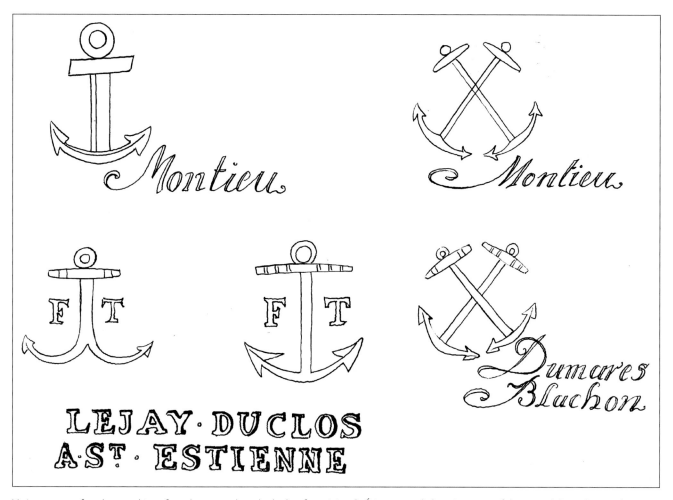

Various types of anchor markings found engraved on the locks of surviving St-Étienne-made hunting guns of the period. (Line drawing by Michel Pétard)

appear to have been issued to colonial officers as needed: 'We provide guns to the colonial officers only when they need them to go on detachments or for other service operations. The same will be done for the two battalions as per the occasion. Let guns be given to the officers of the said battalions, without any restraint on their salaries.'[30]

Two years later, the ship *Le Beauharnois*, carrying military supplies for the colonial troops at Québec, transported 'two hundred fusils de chasse (hunting guns) with iron furniture and wooden ramrods without bayonets.' These weapons were likely intended to equip officers of the Compagnies franches de la Marine in Canada.[31] Interestingly, in the same year, the French merchant Sieur de Boisroger purchased 600 fusils from Saint-Étienne to arm the colonial troops. This record confirms that the hunting guns sent to New France in 1757 were manufactured in Saint-Étienne and may have been copies of the Tulle fusil de chasse.[32] Further evidence of officers carrying hunting guns rather than soldiers' muskets comes from Pouchot's account of the 1759 siege of Fort Niagara, where

he noted: 'a few English officers and soldiers removed a few hunting guns from officers and militiamen'.[33]

Throughout the Seven Years War, colonial officers were typically issued standardised campaign equipment that included a gun case, a gun worm, and six gunflints. During the summer campaigns of 1756 and 1757, officers of the Compagnies franches de la Marine were distributed six gunflints and one gun worm.[34] A memoir published in 1763 during Bigot's trial in France adds further detail, listing the standard winter equipment issued to colonial officers, which included a gun case, a gun worm, gunflints, and a ball pouch (sac à balles).[35]

Probate Records

Postmortem inventory records of colonial officers serving in the French colonies of North America reveal a remarkable diversity of shoulder arms among their possessions. While some officers were listed as owning one or multiple

30   SHD, Archives de la guerre, série A1, vol.3405, f.360.
31   TNA, HCA, 32, vol.169, Le Beauharnois de la Rochelle, 1757.
32   LAC, MG1-B, vol.106, f.263v.

33   Pouchot, *Mémoires sur la dernière guerre de l'Amérique septentrionale*, p.125.
34   Centre d'histoire La Presqu'île, P03/F.089, Fonds De Beaujeu, 28 novembre 1756.; LAC, MG18-K9, vol.6, f.469–472.
35   Bigot, *Mémoire Pour Messire François Bigot*, p.39.

firearms, others appeared to possess none at the time of their deaths. This absence may be attributed to the practice of passing such weapons on to their children, a transfer often omitted from the records maintained by the acting notary. Moreover, since these weapons were documented as part of their personal belongings, it is challenging to discern their specific purposes, whether they served as personal hunting arms, equipment for expeditions, or items intended for sale or trade.

Hunting Guns (Fusils de Chasse)

Highly ornate hunting guns, known as fusils de façon, appear to have been quite popular among colonial officers. The term fusil de façon likely derives from the phrase 'façon de maître' ('master-style' or 'masterfully made'), which refers to firearms crafted with exceptional skill and high quality, as clarified by a newly uncovered merchant's invoice from the early 1740s describing '3 long fusils with 4-*pied* barrels, very fine, master-style [façon de maître], with silver sights and thumb pieces with relief, brass furniture, barrels bronzés', purchased from Saint-Étienne for Canada.[36]

For instance, in 1703, *capitaine* Jacques de Joibert owned a fusil de façon valued at 50 livres,[37] while seven years later, *capitaine* Daniel de Grelon owned a similar gun, also valued at 50 livres.[38] Philippe D'Amour, an officer of the colonial troops residing in Québec, possessed two such guns in 1726, each valued at 30 livres.[39] An intriguing example is found in the 1739 household inventory of *lieutenant* Nicolas Blaise des Bergères, commandant of Fort Niagara from 1730 to 1736, whose firearm was described as 'one fusil de façon, left-handed', indicating he owned a rare left-handed gun.[40] Six years later, *lieutenant* Louis Aubert de la Chesnay was also recorded as owning a fusil de façon

Miniature painting c.1780 representing the Canadian officer La Corne Saint-Luc, who owned a double-barrelled hunting gun in 1747.(Creative Commons).

among his personal assets in Québec.[41] The majority of these master-style guns imported to the French colonies in North America appear to have been made in Saint-Étienne, as indicated by numerous archival records.

Alongside these elegant hunting guns, a slightly less refined variation, known as fusils fins (fine guns), rarely appears in the probate records of officers reviewed during this research. One such firearm, valued at 17 livres, was listed among the personal belongings of Charles-Denis Regnard Duplessis de Morampont, an officer in the colonial regular troops and provost marshal residing in Québec in 1757.[42]

Several hunting guns bearing the names of craftsmen or distinctive marks associated with weapon production in Saint-Étienne, such as Thiollière, Girard, or anchor motifs, are

36   ANMT, Fonds Dugard, Série AQ, 62 AQ 41, De St-Étienne le 7 avril 1744, p.733.

37   BAnQ-M, Greffe du notaire Louis Chamballon, Inventaire des biens de feu M. Jacques de Joibert, chevalier seigneur de Soulanges, enseigne sur les vaisseaux du Roi et capitaine d'une compagnie franche des troupes du détachement de la marine, 2 mai 1703.

38   BAnQ-M, Greffe du notaire Michel Lepailleur, Inventaire de feu Sieur Daniel de Grelon, écuyer Sieur Duluth, capitaine d'une compagnie des troupes de la marine, 27 février 1710.

39   BAnQ-Q, Greffe du notaire Jacques Barel, Inventaire des biens après le décès de la dame D'Amour La Morendière, auparavant veuve du feu Sieur Pierre Gauvreau (vivant armurier) … épouse en seconde noce de Philippe D'Amour, écuyer Sieur de la Morendière, officier des troupes du détachement de la Marine entretenu pour le service du Roi en ce pays de présent en l'ancienne France… , 25 avril 1726.

40   In essence, the difference between a left-side and right-side flintlock shoulder weapon is based on the placement of the ignition system to suit the shooter's dominant hand and prevent dangerous flash exposure. BAnQ-Q, Greffe du notaire Abel

Michel, Inventaire après-décès de Nicolas Blaise de Berger (Des Bergères), écuyer, seigneur de Rigauville, 22 septembre 1739.

41   BAnQ-Q, Greffe du notaire Jacques-Nicolas Pinguet de Vaucour, Inventaire des biens de Louis Aubert Lachesnay, écuyer, vivant lieutenant dans les dites troupes, 25 octobre 1745.

42   BAnQ-Q, Greffe du notaire Jean-Antoine Saillant, Procès-verbal des meubles et effets de Sieur Charles Duplessis, écuyer Sieur de Monrampon, grand prévôt de Messieurs les Maréchaux de France en ce pays…, 31 juin 1757.

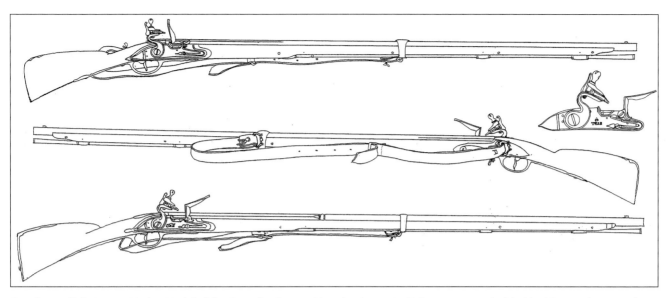

French 1716 Tulle Marine Musket Model of the Grenadier Pattern. Note the distinctive Tulle marine swivel of the 'double curve' type used on contract marine grenadier muskets versus the standard circular infantry-style ring of the models 1717-1746 regulation muskets. (Line drawing by Michel Pétard)

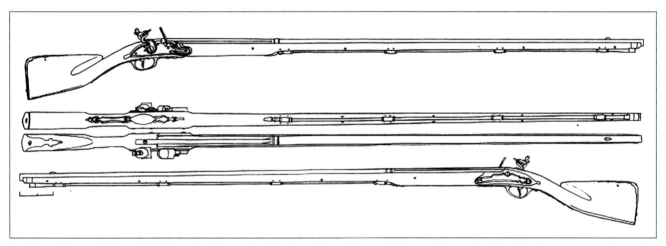

French Boucanier musket, c. 1725–1750. (Line drawing by Michel Pétard)

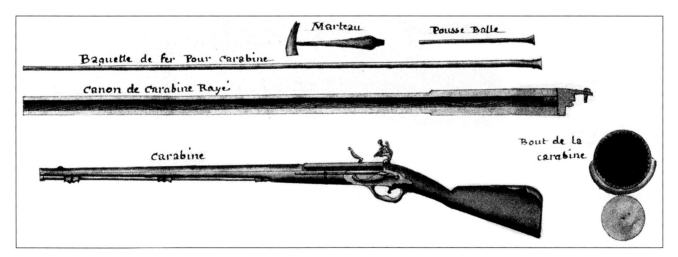

Detail of a rifled carabine and its various components taken from a treatise on French artillery written in 1721. This illustration shows a hammer (marteau), rammer (pousse-balle), the sharp edges of the interior of the barrel's bore as well as a cross-section of the barrel. This type of carabine (carbine) may have been quite similar to the 'one rifled carbine' that the colonial officer Jacques Leber of Montreal owned in 1706. (*Traité d'artillerie. Dessinée & écrit par Monsieur de Lepine.*. Ancienne bibliothèque Brunon)

documented in the possessions of colonial officers. A notable example is a gun crafted by Thiollière of Saint-Étienne, featuring a silver thumbpiece and its original gun case, listed among the belongings of officer Joseph Dejourdy de Cabanac of Montréal in 1737.[43] Eleven years later, Jean-Baptiste Montbrun de Saint-Laurent, a *lieutenant* of the Compagnies franches in the Illinois Territory, owned a total of 10 guns, including a Thiollière firearm valued at 26 livres, a Girard-marked gun appraised at 23 livres, and a firearm bearing a small anchor mark (fusils à l'ancre).[44] This latter type, also produced in Saint-Étienne, featured engraved anchor motifs on the lockplate and was a popular lower-grade hunting gun among Native Americans and voyageurs. In 1730, the colonial officer Dustiné, residing in the Illinois Territory, was recorded as owning four such guns with anchor designs on their locks. These firearms may have been trade goods rather than personal hunting weapons, reflecting their broader utility in the colonial fur trade economy.[45]

Double-barrelled hunting guns were an unexpected yet intriguing find among the personal possessions of several colonial officers serving in Canada. During a detachment against Fort Clinton in 1747, the colonial officer La Corne Saint-Luc famously promised his own double-barrelled hunting gun to an allied Native American, stating: 'Not having any porcelain necklaces, I promised my double-barrelled gun to the one that would bring me a prisoner from that Nation [Mohawk].'[46] In 1756, a double-barrelled gun described as having 'a broken stock' and valued at 15 *livres* was listed among the personal belongings of *enseigne* François Sarrobert in Montréal.[47]

The French treatise *Traités de vénerie et de chasses* provides valuable insight into the design of these particular firearms, noting: 'There are two types of double-barrelled guns, the fixed type and the turning type. The barrels of the latter are placed one above the other … instead of the fixed ones, where the barrels are side by side: each barrel has its own lock… '[48] The advanced hunting weapons owned by military officers in Canada undoubtedly featured side-by-side barrels with soldered ribs, as

this innovative technique had been introduced at Saint-Étienne in the 1730s. The text further states: 'It was only in 1740 that we began to use, while hunting, double-barrelled guns with soldered barrels. It is in Saint-Étienne that the first were made a few years earlier; and Jean Leclerc had built some in Paris in 1738.'[49]

Primary source records reveal that these types of hunting guns, which are in use in Canada as early as 1747 by many high-ranking or wealthy individuals in the colony, are generally coined 'fusils à deux coups' and 'fusils double' which can be translated to 'guns having two shots' or 'double guns'. This innovative type of hunting gun often came with their respective bayonets such as the one sent from France for the merchant-trader Etienne Augé in 1756 which was described as a 'double-barrelled gun with its bayonet' estimated at a very high price of 90 livres.[50] These hunting bayonets would have likely had a double socket and a shorter and wider blade than their military counterpart. Additionally, a few high-end varieties of these guns were also imported to Canada, such as the two following guns sent to Canada in 1757: 'one gun, double barrel master-made, damascened in gold at 77 livres … one master-made double barrel, damascened in gold and having a silver escutcheon in relief at 77 livres.'[51] These lavish guns were also in used in the interior, such as the 'fusil double' sold for 60 livres by a man named Fayot to the clerk at the King's storehouses at Detroit in 1760, which may possibly have served to arm a colonial officer or high-ranking individual in this town.[52] Lastly, in 1712, a reference to a fusil firing five shots (fusil à cinq coup) esteemed at 30 livres along with 'two poor pistols' were recorded as part of the personal belongings of François Lefebvre, Sieur Duplessis Fabert, a *capitaine* in the colonial troops.[53] This fusil probably represented a rare five-barrelled turnover flintlock hunting gun of the period.

Tulle Muskets or Guns

Shoulder weapons produced at the Tulle arsenal appear to have been a favoured choice among colonial officers for their personal armaments. However, since the French term fusil

43 BAnQ-Q, Greffe du notaire Charles René Gauchon de Chevremont, Inventaire des biens de feu Sieur Joseph Dejourdy de Cabanac, lieutenant d'une compagnie des troupes de ce pays, 27 mars 1737.

44 Kaskaskia Manuscripts, Randolph County Courthouse, Chester, Illinois, Testament de Jean-Baptiste Montbrun de Saint-Laurent, écuyer, vivant lieutenant des Compagnies franches pour la Louisiane, 20 janvier 1748.

45 Kaskaskia Manuscripts, Randolph County Courthouse, Chester, Illinois, Inventaire de feu Monsieur Dustiné, père, de Kaskaskia, officier… 17 mai 1730.

46 LAC, MG1-E, vol.243, p.11

47 BAnQ-M, Greffe du notaire Louis-Claude Danré de Blanzy, Inventaire de feu François de Sarrobert, enseigne dans les Cies Franches, 8 janvier 1756.

48 Charles-Jean Goury de Champgrand, *Traité de vénerie et de chasses. Première partie* (Paris: C.-J.-B. Hérissant, 1769), p.100.

49 Anon., *Traité complet de la chasse au fusil…* (Paris: Audot, 1823), p.5.

50 Division des archives (Université de Montréal, collection Louis-François-Georges Baby, G2/83 (mf 3091, 3092), Facture des effets chargés par Paillet et Maynardie pour le compte de Étienne Augé, de Montréal, La Rochelle, 24 avril 1756.

51 LAC, Q3-2277, M-859, file 24. 'Facture de Paillet et Meynardie, La Rochelle, à Augé, Montréal, 29 avril,1757.'; LAC, Q3-2277, M-859, file 26.'Facture de Paillet et Meynardie, La Rochelle, à Augé, Montréal, 30 avril, 1757.'

52 AM, G.239, pièce no. 10, Arrêts relatifs à la liquidation des dettes du Canada, 1767.

53 BAnQ-M, Greffe du notaire Michel Lepailleur, Inventaire de feu François Lefebvre, Sieur Duplessis Fabert, 24 novembre, 1712.

could denote either a musket or a hunting gun, colonial records do not always clarify whether a Tulle-made fusil was a civilian hunting firearm or a Marine contract musket.

The following examples of Tulle firearms in the possession of colonial officers likely represent a mix of fusils de chasse, fusils ordinaires (common muskets), or fusils grenadiers produced at the Tulle manufactory. In 1732, Pierre de Rivon de Budemont, *capitaine* in the colonial troops, had privately purchased a Tulle-made fusil from the merchant Monière at Montréal, which may have either served as his main firearm while leading a detachment or again as his personal hunting gun while hunting.[54] In 1748, the officer Montbrun de Saint-Laurent serving in the Illinois Territory owned a Tulle fusil valued at 37 livres among a number of other longarms,[55] while five years later an infantry *capitaine*, Jean-Baptiste Jarret, was recorded as possessing and old Tulle fusil valued at 10 livres.[56] The postmortem inventory list of the personal effects belonging to the *enseigne* François-Marie Bouat living in the district of Montréal included one Tulle fusil, a pistol and a powder horn assessed together at 12 livres,[57] while the officer Charles Decombre living at Québec in 1758, was the owner of three Tulle fusils.[58]

At least one of these Tulle firearms appears to have been a pre-1734 Marine musket, as it included a bayonet, suggesting compatibility with a socket bayonet. For instance, in 1732, Nicolas Bailly de Messein, a colonial officer residing in Québec, owned a 'Tulle fusil with its bayonet and without a ramrod.'[59]

Carbines, Boucaniers and Service Muskets

While uncommon, a limited number of colonial officers were the owners of carbines (carabines), which were a short military flintlock with a rifled barrel generally issued to carabineers (experienced cavalrymen) or to the King's guards. In 1706, the officer Jacques Leber of Montréal owned 'one rifled carbine' assessed at 2 livres,[60] whereas some two years later, *capitaine* Paul Lemoine was the owner of five longarms as part of his personal assets, amongst which was a carbine.[61] These short muskets were also recorded as late as the 1750s since *capitaine* Jean-Baptiste Jarret, had in his personal possession in 1752 two shoulder weapons which included a short carbine.[62] In New France, carbines may have also represented short or cut-down flintlock guns, frequently documented for civilian and Native usage, which may or may not have had rifled barrels as smoothbore is suggested by their inexpensive value in the records. As part of Jean Magnan dit l'Espérance's post-mortem inventory at Montréal in 1694, the notary added 'Four carbines or cut-down fusils' revealing that in Canada, the term carabine also referenced, in certain cases, shortened guns or muskets.[63] Although unusual in the hands of a fusilier serving in New France, this type of rifled firearm was apparently carried by a Swiss or colonial soldier who had fought alongside the officer Dumont de Montigny during the 1736 Chickasaw campaign: 'a soldier asked to take my place, saying he would not miss his shot. His musket being, in addition, rifled'.[64]

The very few carbines recorded on official government-related inventory lists in Canada seem to be specific to Québec and Fort Saint-Frédéric starting in the 1740s, which we can assume were used for their potential accuracy in defending strongholds from elevated fortifications, as both locations featured such defensive structures. The rifles shipped from the port of Rochefort to Canada in 1746 were described as 'infantry rifled carbines',[65] while a military supply invoice sent to Québec that same year listed '6 carbines, rifled, with their hammers and rammers.'[66] These references likely pertain to the same weapons, which may have been Model 1733 French cavalry carbines.

A single reference to a 'boucanier muket' (fusil boucanier) musket in the possession of a colonial officer

54 Marie Gérin-Lajoie, Montreal Merchant's Records Project, (microfilm copy of M496 Montreal Merchants Records Project, Research Files, 1971–1975, 1 roll — St. Paul: Minnesota Historical Society Library Copy Services), MG 23/GIII 25, Monière, vol.4, p.161, 23 juin, 1732.

55 Kaskaskia Manuscripts, Randolph County Courthouse, Chester, Illinois,…Lafrance demeurant en la paroisse de l'Immaculé Conception exécuteur du testament de Messire Jean-Baptiste Montbrun de Saint-Laurent, écuyer, vivant lieutenant des Compagnies franches pour la Louisiane…, 20 janvier 1748.

56 BAnQ-M, Greffe du notaire Louis-Claude Danré de Blanzy, Inventaire des biens de feu Jean-Baptiste Jarret, Sieur de Verchères, chevalier de l'ordre militaire de St-Louis, capitaine d'infanterie, 8 août, 1752.

57 BAnQ-M, Greffe du notaire Henri Bouron, Inventaire du défunt sieur de Bouat, sieur François Marie Bouat, enseigne d'infanterie au détachement de la marine en ce pays, 12 décembre, 1753.

58 BAnQ-Q, TL5, D1944. TL5, Procès de Charles Decombre (Porcheron dit Decombre), officier détaché des troupes de la Marine, contre Marie Couture, veuve de Simon Massy, 26 février 1758–28 mars 1759.

59 BAnQ-Q, Greffe du notaire Nicolas Boisseau, Inventaire de Catherine Trifflé, épouse du sieur Bailly (Nicolas Bailly de Messein), officier dans les troupes de ce pays…, 6 mars 1732.

60 BAnQ-M, Greffe du notaire Pierre Raimbault, Inventaire des biens du feu Sieur Jacques Leber, écuyer, Sieur de Fonville, 1 décembre 1706.

61 BAnQ-M, Greffe du notaire Antoine Adhémard, Inventaire de feu Paul Lemoine, vivant écuyer, Sieur de Maricourt, capitaine d'une compagnie des troupes du détachement de la marine…, 20 août 1708.

62 BAnQ-M, Greffe du notaire Louis-Claude Danré de Blanzy, Inventaire des biens de feu Jean-Baptiste Jarret, Sieur de Verchères, chevalier de l'ordre militaire de St-Louis, capitaine d'infanterie, 8 août 1752.

63 BAnQ-M, Greffe du notaire Antoine Adhémard, Montréal, 17–18 mars 1684.

64 Dumont de Montigny, *Regards sur les monde atlantique 1715–1747* (Sillery, Québec: Septentrion, 2008), p.280.

65 AR, 1E, vol.139.

66 LAC, MG1-C11A, vol.86, f.355v.

may trace its origins to his wife's first husband. The 1726 postmortem inventory of the personal assets of Philippe D'Amour, Sieur de la Morendière, and his wife, Lady D'Amour de la Morendière, notes that she was the widow of gunsmith Pierre Gauvreau, likely the musket's original owner, which may have passed to the officer through marriage.[67] Fusils boucaniers, characterised by their long, club-butt stocks and large-calibre barrels, were exclusively manufactured for the French Marine and colonies. Such a weapon, however, would have been inconvenient and overly heavy for an officer to use in the field.

A fusil de service (service musket) also appears in the 1745 inventory of *lieutenant* Louis Aubert de la Chesnay, listed alongside a fusil de façon and an old pistol. Valued at 10 livres, this military weapon likely represents a standard-issue musket for duty.[68] Contrary to modern interpretations, the term fusil de service does not denote a specific model but instead refers to a regulation musket or any other shoulder weapon issued for military use or assigned to a post or fort.

Colonial Officer's Personal Hunting Equipment

Many officers serving in the colonial regular troops owned hunting-related equipment such as powder horns, shot bags, and gun cases, likely carried during hunts on their seigneurie or while off duty at a fort or outpost. The colonial officer Dumont de Montigny, stationed at the Yazoo fort, recorded one of his deer hunts: 'having adjusted my fusil … I went to the place where I had seen this animal the night before.'[69] In 1753, a letter addressed to officer Jean Daniel Dumas at Fort Le Boeuf reveals that some officers and cadets at the post prioritised hunting over their assigned duties: 'I have deferred until today to tell you the discontent that I have in seeing that there is not daily an officer and cadets performing work. They must be continually employed rather than hunting.'[70]

By the Seven Years War, hunting by officers during service was frequently documented. In 1756, two officers of the Régiment de la Reine were scalped and killed by

The sculpture depicts two full-length Indian figures, modelled after a Choctaw boy captured by the British, supporting the central relief of the dying figure of Lieutenant Roger Townshend. One figure holds a hatchet while the other carries a musket, both adorned with powder horns and sheathed knives, wearing mitasses and a brayet. These sculptures, part of Townshend's monument at Westminster Abbey, feature three fleur-de-lis symbols on the powder horns, raising the intriguing question of whether these specific powder vessels were provided by the French from their storehouses and marked accordingly. (Creative Commons)

Mohawk warriors while hunting near Fort Carillon.[71] The following year, a *caporal* from the fort's garrison 'had left to go hunting and borrowed a fusil from an Habitant.'[72] In the spring of 1760, during the defence of Montréal, Jean-Baptiste Levrault de Langis Montegron drowned near Île Saint-Paul (present-day Île des Sœurs) under tragic circumstances: 'M. de Montegron, a famous proponent who was highly esteemed, drowned while hunting, a slab of ice having capsized the canoe which carried him.'[73]

Powder Horns

The primary gunpowder container among the personal belongings of colonial officers was typically the powder

67 BAnQ-Q, Greffe du notaire Jacques Barbel, Inventaire des biens après le décès de la dame D'Amour La Morendière, auparavant veuve du feu Sieur Pierre Gauvreau (vivant armurier) … épouse en seconde noce de Philippe D'Amour, écuyer Sieur de la Morendière, officier des troupes du détachement de la Marine entretenu pour le service du Roi en ce pays de présent en l'ancienne France… , Québec, 25 March 1726.

68 BAnQ-Q, Greffe du notaire Jacques-Nicolas Pinguet de Vaucour, Testament de feu Louis Aubert Lachesnay, écuyer, vivant lieutenant dans lesdites troupes… , Québec, 25 octobre 1745.

69 De Montigny, *Regards sur les monde atlantique 1715–1747*, p.193.

70 ASQ, V-V 5 :60 :21, Copie de la lettre que j'ai écrite à Monsieur Dumas du 26e août 1753.

71 Henri-Raymond Casgrain, *Collection des manuscrits du maréchal de Lévis, Journal du marquis de Montcalm durant ses campagnes en Canada de 1756 à 1759* (Québec: Imprimerie de L.-J. Demers & Frère, 1895), p.77.

72 Henri-Raymond Casgrain, *Collection des manuscrits du maréchal de Lévis, Lettres du chevalier de Lévis concernant la guerre du Canada (1756–1760)* (Montréal: C.O. Beauchemin & Fils, 1889), p.123.

73 De Malartic, *Journal des campagnes au Canada de 1755 à 1760*, p.313.

horn, a vessel crafted from a cow horn. Praised for its practicality, the powder horn was spark-proof, water-proof, and made from a material valued for its durability and resilience.

While soldiers were generally issued regulation brass-mounted powder flasks, colonial officers were occasionally outfitted with powder horns. For example, in 1746, the equipment issued to *capitaine* de Linctot of the colonial troops stationed at Soulange, included a gun worm, six gunflints, one *livre* of gunpowder, four *livres* of shot, and a powder horn.[74] In addition to powder horns, high-ranking officers were sometimes provided with gunpowder containers made of tin or tinplate. For instance, in 1716, when Rigaud de Vaudreuil dispatched forces to impose peace on the Foxes, *lieutenant* La Porte de Louvigny and several officers were supplied with '4 tin poulverins [priming flasks],' each priced at 4 livres.[75]

Personal powder horns, though rarely mentioned in probate records or accounts of notable events, were likely owned by many colonial officers, as they were indispensable yet often considered too ordinary or insignificant to document in detail. The officers Nicolas-Thomas de Joncaire and Sieur François-Marie Bouat both owned powder horns,[76] while another two of these gunpowder containers were noted in the possession of *capitaine* d'Arrazola at New-Orléans in 1755.[77] Further, the officer La Corne de Saint-Luc had on him his faithful powder horn, fire steel and gun flint when he miraculously escaped the sinking of the ship *L'Auguste* in 1761.[78]

Many of the powder horns owned by colonial officers were likely relatively plain, featuring a simple wooden plug at the base and a wooden stopper at the tip, much like those issued to Canadian militiamen. These horns were often described as having a one-*livre* capacity,[79] making them larger than the smaller, horn-mounted powder flasks commonly used by hunters in France. Such larger-capacity powder horns were likely referred to as cornes à la Canadienne (Canadian-style powder horns). In 1719, '400

[powder] horns in the Canadian style with their thong' were requested for Louisbourg,[80] and another '1,000 [powder] horns, in the Canadian style, for the detachments' were requisitioned for the same fortress in 1736.[81]

According to primary sources, these distinctive horns were large, dark in colour, and scraped to translucent thinness. In 1757, for instance, '4,000 powder horns, large and dark,' were ordered by Gradis from the Rouen-based merchant Horutener for Canada.[82] However, the horns supplied by the same dealer previously were criticised as 'small and neither scraped nor dark',[83] suggesting that they lacked the required powder capacity and were not thinned enough to allow the powder level to be seen. By contrast, in 1758, the merchant-trader Étienne Augé of Montréal requested 'two dozen horns, white, for powder' from his supplier in France, likely referring to creamy-white powder horns that were translucent enough for the powder inside to be clearly visible.[84]

Shot Bags or Pouches

Shot bags or pouches were evidently among the personal possessions of some officers serving in North America, reflecting the French hunting traditions of the period. However, it remains unclear whether these bags were European-style sportsman's pouches or Native-American-style slit pouches, as most descriptions are nonspecific, typically listing a sac à balles or sac à plomb, literally translated as 'ball bag' or 'shot bag'. Probate records referencing shot bags include Nicolas Blaise des Bergères, who owned a sac à plomb in 1739;[85] D'Arrazola of New Orleans, listed as having 'one shot bag full of balls' (un sac à plomb plein de balles) in 1755; and *enseigne* Sarrobert, who in 1756 was recorded as possessing 'three molleton shot bags' (trois sacs à plomb de molleton).[86]

It is likely that officers in the colonial regular troops, particularly those serving in the interior, adopted the Native American practice of wearing a slit pouch over a belt or sash, especially while on detachment or hunting off duty, as these types of small pouches were practical due to

74   LAC, MG1-C11A, vol.86, f.220.
75   LAC, MG1-C11A, vol.38, f.188.
76   BAnQ-M, Greffe du notaire C.-C.-J. Porlier, Inventaire des biens de feu Nicolas-Thomas de Joncaire, lieutenant d'une compagnie du détachement de la Marine et interprète pour le Roi des langues iroquoises, décédé ce jourd'hui vingt et neuf juin 1739..., 31 juillet 1739; BAnQ-M, Greffe du notaire H. Bouron, Inventaire du défunt Sieur de Bouat, Sieur François Marie Bouat, enseigne d'infanterie au détachement de la marine en ce pays, 14–15 décembre 1753.
77   LAC, MG1-E, vol.9, f.25, Inventaire d'Arrazola, capitaine des troupes de la colonie et aide-major à la Nouvelle-Orléans, mort noyé dans le fleuve le 12 ou 13 avril 1755... 19 avril, 1755.
78   Saint-Luc de La Corne, *Journal du voyage de M. Saint-Luc de La Corne, ecuyer dans le navire l'Auguste, en l'an 1761* (Montréal : Chez Fleury Mesplet, Imprimeur & libraire, 1778), p.18.
79   LAC, MG1-C11A, vol.100, f.192v.

80   LAC, F1, vol.21, f.77.
81   LAC, MG1-C11B, vol.18, f.226–227.
82   LAC, MG 18, H63, Fonds famille Gradis, F-1600, Horutener et compagnie, Rouen, 10 octobre 1757.
83   LAC, MG 18, H63, Fonds famille Gradis, F-1600, Horutener et compagnie, Rouen, 10 octobre 1757.
84   Division des archives de l'Université de Montréal, collection Louis-François-Georges Baby, P0058U00302, Lettre d'Étienne Augé à Nicolas Paillet et Jean Meynardi, 1758.
85   BAnQ-Q, Greffe du notaire Abel Michon, ... à la requête de Dame Marie Viennoy, veuve de défunt Monseigneur Nicolas Blaise de Berger (des bergères), écuyer Seigneur de Riguauville Bellechasse... lieutenant... capitaine d'une compagnie des troupes de la Marine... pour le service du Roi, 22 septembre 1739.
86   BAnQ-M, Greffe du notaire Louis-Claude Danré de Blanzy, Inventaire des biens de feu Sieur François de Sarrobert, enseigne d'infanterie, 8 janvier 1756. LAC, MG1-E, vol. 9, f. 25.

Detail taken from Bacqueville de La Potherie's *Histoire de l'Amerique Septentrionale* showing a Canadian on snowshoes heading off to war. According to the 1709 edition of the *Mercure Français*, the dress of the Canadians who attacked Haverhill in 1708 consisted of 'a powder horn that serves as a fourniment and the shot in a type of gibecière'. The author of this account likely used 'type of gibecière' for lack of a better term to describe what were likely slit pouches, for the sake of his European readers. (Claude-Charles Le Roy Bacqueville de La Potherie, *Histoire de l'Amérique Septentrionale*, 1722)

Watercolour and wash dating to c.1730 showing a Canadian voyageur wearing a Native-style slit pouch over his sash at the front and at the back in which he would have stored gunflints, lead balls, shot or other small personal items. (Habillemens des Coureurs de Bois Canadiens, no. 2, Anonymous, c. 1730, Beinecke Rare Book and Manuscript Library, Yale University Library, New Haven, CT, USA, WA MSS S-2412)

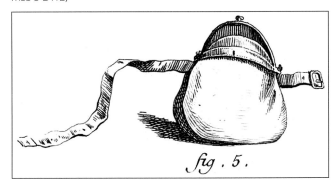

A hunting pouch, referred to as a gibecière de chasse, is depicted in Diderot's *Boursier* (*Encyclopédie, Boursier*, Planche II). Some of the shot or ball bags owned by colonial officers may have resembled the widely popular gibecière worn on a belt. A small hunting pouch frequently seen in eighteenth-century French hunting portraits and considered fashionable in France. A much larger gibercière made of knitted fabric was also used by French hunters of the period to carry their game. The post-mortem inventory prepared by the notary Danré de Blanzy on September 29, 1746, for officer François Degannes, residing in Montréal, included 'an old fusil with a faulty lock... with a powder horn and an old sailcloth gibecière...'

their accessibility, durability, multipurpose use, and light-weight design. Cultural appropriation of several Native American articles by French colonists in Canada, which likely also included slit pouches, was notably documented by Pehr Kalm in 1749:

> Though many nations imitate the French customs, yet I observed on the contrary, that the French in Canada in many respects follow the customs of the Indians, with whom they converse every day. They make use of the tobacco pipes, shoes, garters, and girdles of the Indians. They follow the Indian way of waging war with exactness. They mix the same things with tobacco; they make use of the Indian bark boats and row them in the Indian way; they wrap a square piece of cloth around their feet, instead of stockings, and have adopted many other Indian fashions.[87]

An inventory of items sold on behalf of Monsieur de Franchomme, an officer at Fort de Chartres in 1728, included a pair of Native stockings (mitasses) and 'one black deerskin shot pouch ornamented with porcupine quills', undoubtedly a Native-style slit pouch.[88] Similarly, in 1749, *lieutenant* Milon of the Compagnies franches de la Marine was recorded as owning a 'small hunting bag' (petit sac de chasse) at the time of his death in Green Bay.[89] Given its small size and the officer's frequent interaction with Native nations in the interior, this item was likely a slit pouch. Intendant Bigot also noted a ball bag or pouch (sac à balles) as part of the summer equipment list issued to the colonial officers which may also suggest the use of these smaller, practical Native-style pouches as shot and ball

---

87 Pehr Kalm, *Travels Into North America: Containing Its Natural History, and a Circumstantial Account of Its Plantations and Agriculture in General, with the Civil, Ecclesiastical and Commercial State of the Country, the Manners of the Inhabitants, and Several Curious and Important Remarks on Various Subjects* (London: The editor, 1771), vol.3, p.254.

88 Kaskaskia Manuscripts, Randolph County Courthouse, Chester, Illinois, Vente (délavé) de Monsieur de Franchomme, officier de la garnison, fait au fort de Chartres, 6 août 1728.

89 LAC, MG1-E, vol.314, p.4.

holders.[90] Such pouches appear to have been both functional and popular. Notably, during the Raid on Haverhill in 1708, which involved 100 Canadian militiamen and colonial soldiers, participants were described as carrying their powder in 'a horn which serves as a fourniment [powder reserve], and the lead balls in a type of pouch.'[91]

A detailed account of a colonial officer's shot bag, issued as part of a detachment, offers valuable insight into its size and design. In 1746, the supplies for officer Saint-Blain, who was to campaign alongside the Ho-Chunk in New England, included '1 shot bag (sac à plomb) [made] of ⅛ [of 1 *aune*] of molleton.' The fabric required for this pouch would have amounted to a very small square, approximately 14cm by 14cm, suggesting an ideal size for a slit pouch rather than a larger shot bag swung over the shoulder by a strap.[92]

Commandant Pierre Pouchot appears to describe this type of compact slit pouch when referring to the French Native American allies: 'they also have a shot bag [sac à plomb] that is made as a besace, where they put their balls and lead shot for war or hunting.'[93] A 1743 French dictionary defines a besace as a large bag carried over the shoulder, made from a long piece of cloth sewn into a pouch open at the centre, where one end hangs in front and the other at the back.[94] These Native-made slit pouches would have been highly practical for traversing dense woods and brush-covered terrain, where a larger pouch with a shoulder strap might have bounced around or become entangled in branches. Pouchot's description aligns with the functional design and practicality of such pouches for combat or long-distance travel in the wilderness.

On certain occasions, militiamen and allied Native Americans serving under a colonial officer were issued shot pouches of woollen fabric prior to expeditions. These pouches were likely of the slit-pouch variety, given their low cost and the fact that some were distributed to Native warriors. During a campaign led by Paul Marin de La Malgue against the British at Annapolis Royal, supplies included '201 shroud shot pouches' priced at 25 sols each, provided to a war party of Canadians, Abenakis, and Huron warriors.[95] Two years later, munitions sent from Québec to equip a party under Rigaud de Vaudreuil included, among other items, '200 fire steels', '200 gun worms', and '200 shot pouches', ensuring that each man was equipped with one pouch.[96] By 1750, '18 woollen cloth [étoffe] shot pouches' priced at 15 sols each were issued from the Québec storehouses to colonial soldiers, militiamen, Native Americans, and Habitants stationed or taking refuge at the Saint-Jean River and Shediac.[97]

Additionally, these shot bags appear to have been stockpiled in the King's storehouses at Québec and have also been found to be in the hands of colonial soldiers serving in the colony. Records from 1752 reveal that shot pouches made from two types of fabric were available at Québec, including '34 woollen cloth [drap] shot pouches' valued at 15 sols each and '1,887 shot pouches of canvas' priced at 5 sols per pouch.[98] That same year, 'one red woollen cloth pouch in which were found five musket balls and a few lead shots' was confiscated from three colonial soldiers accused of starting a fire at Trois-Rivières.[99] Also, in 1754, 'a canvas pouch (or bag) in which was found a gun worm, a fire steel, gun flints and two balls' was seized from soldiers implicated in a theft at Fort Saint-Frédéric.[100] It is plausible that most, if not all, of these pouches were slit-pouch designs, inspired by their widespread use among Native Americans and embraced by the French for their practicality, cost-effectiveness, and ideal functionality during wilderness expeditions.

Colonial Officers' Pistols

Long-range accuracy with firearms was crucial for hunting on foot and for executing both offensive and defensive manoeuvres, which explains the predominance of shoulder weapons in colonial warfare and survival practices. In contrast, pistols, while generally unsuitable for long-range shooting due to their lack of precision, could prove highly effective in close combat. By the late seventeenth century, French sources categorised pistols into three main types: 'those that cavalrymen wear at the saddle-bow of the saddle … belt pistols, and pocket pistols.'[101]

Probate records of colonial officers serving in Canada suggest that approximately 40 percent of these men owned pistols or related accessories (holsters, pistol bags etc.), many of which likely conformed to contemporary French

90   Bigot, *Mémoire Pour Messire François Bigot*, p.39.
91   *Mercure Galant*, 1709, vol.377, p.56
92   LAC, MG1-C11A, vol.86, f.191.
93   Pouchot, *Mémoires sur la dernière guerre de l'Amérique septentrionale*, pp.279–280.
94   *Dictionnaire universel françois et latin* (Paris: Veuve Delaune, 1743), vol.1, p.1183.
95   LAC, MG1-C11A, vol.84, f.150.
96   LAC, MG1-C11A, vol.117, f.25v.

97   LAC, MG1-C11A, vol.96, f.124v.
98   LAC, MG1-C11A, vol.98, f.246v.
99   BAnQ-Q, TP1, S777, D174, Procès de Pierre Beaudouin (Baudouin) dit Cumberland, Joseph Ceilier dit Beausoleil, Ponsian Allé dit Sansoucy, François-Xavier Guernoté dit Latulippe et Joseph Gamin (Jamin) dit Saint-Louis, soldats…, 21 mai–28 août 1752.
100   BAnQ-M, TL4, S1, D5921, Procès contre Menin Pouteau dit Parisien, sculpteur, soldat d'Herbin, Michel Dufeu dit Flame, soldat de la Compagnie de Villemonde, et Guillaume Goursol dit Lagiroflée, soldat de la Compagnie Debonne, accusés de vols dans la chambre de distribution du fort Saint-Frédéric, 9 septembre 1754–26 février 1755.
101   *Dictionnaire universel, contenant généralement tous les mots …* (À la Haye et à Amsterdam: Arnout & Reinier Leers, 1690), vol.3.

French cavalry officer by Parrocel featured in De La Guérinière's *École de cavalerie*. Note the chaperon or holster-cap draped over the leather holsters at the front of the saddle where the cavalrymen's pistols were placed.

Detail from a 1705 map illustrating a scene where armed Frenchmen stand by Illinois Natives, who are presenting a calumet as a token of peace. Note how the pistols are carried through the men's belts. We may suppose that the man at the far right, armed with two pistols and a musket, may represent a colonial officer. (*L'Amérique divisée selon l'étendue de ses principales parties*, N. de Fer)

Cartouche from a wall map of the Americas showing what could be a on the left, a French Marine officer shooting a pistol in one hand and holding a sword in the other. (*L'Amérique dressée sur les relations les plus récentes* … (Paris: Crépy, 1755))#

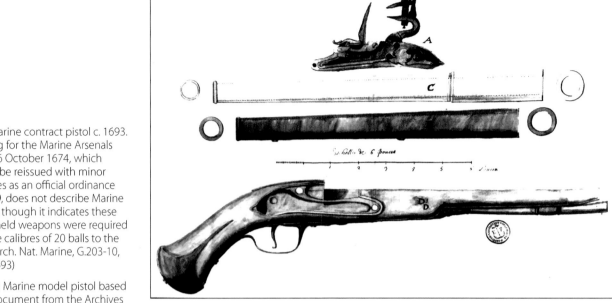

Top: Marine contract pistol c. 1693. A ruling for the Marine Arsenals dated 6 October 1674, which would be reissued with minor changes as an official ordinance in 1689, does not describe Marine pistols, though it indicates these hand-held weapons were required to have calibres of 20 balls to the *livre*. (Arch. Nat. Marine, G.203-10, nov. 1693)

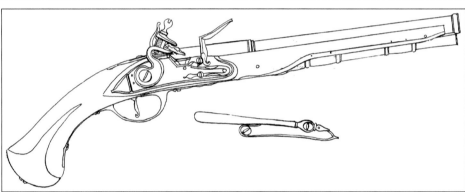

Centre: Marine model pistol based on a document from the Archives nationales, Marine, G.203-10, nov. 1693. These iron-mounted pistols were in use until the 1729 Tulle contract. Most pistols manufactured under contract by the Marine came from the Saint-Étienne or Tulle arsenals. At Tulle, early contracts dating from 1691 to 1696 specified pistols with 14 *pouces* barrels with convex shape locks, whereas from 1697 to 1734, the barrel length was reduced to 12 p*ouces*. (Line drawing by Michel Pétard)

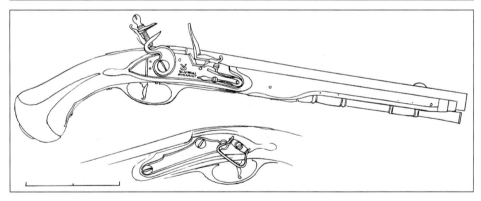

Bottom: Model 1729 marine pistol manufactured at Tulle. Iron furniture with a flat lock. Buckle-type swing swivel to be carried with a shoulder strap. In 1734, the hook was reintroduced while maintaining the sling swivel, which was probably optional. The 1729/1734 contract specified 12 *pouces* barrels of a calibre of 20 balls to the *livre*, the weight being about 1½ *livre*, with a flat lock and a flat along the top of the barrel. (Line drawing by Michel Pétard)

Brass French pistol trigger guard fragments having decorated motifs found at the site of the Tenaille des nouvelles casernes. This particular guard was likely mounted on a fine cavalry pistol of the period. (Courtesy of National Historic Sites, Parks Canada. Artifact number: 18G39E47-1Q. Photo Kevin Gélinas)

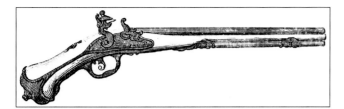

Detail from Surirey de Saint-Remy's Mémoires d'Artillerie first published in 1697 showing a late seventeenth-century cavalry pistol.

Detail from François Robichon de La Guérinière's treatise L'École de Cavalerie showing a cavalryman performing training exercises using a pistol on horseback. In eighteenth-century France, particular schools were established to educate noble sons in the arts and sciences necessary for royal service. Equestrian academies of the period were devoted to educating officers for the infantry and cavalry. Many Canadian officers had been sent to France for their military training, such as Olivier Morel de La Durantaye, who was sent to a military school at Rochefort in the 1680s where he '…performed firearm exercises, learned open-face fencing, practiced riding'.

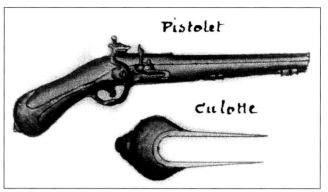

Detail of a pistol taken from a treatise on French artillery written in 1721. (Traité d'artillerie… Ancienne bibliothèque Brunon)

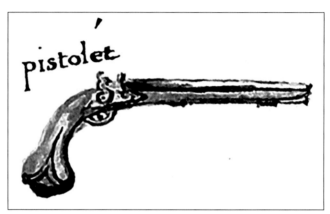

Detail taken from a series of illustrations showing the type of pistol found at a French seaport arsenal in 1738. (SHD-Brest, bibliothèque R 3415. Photo Christian Lemasson)

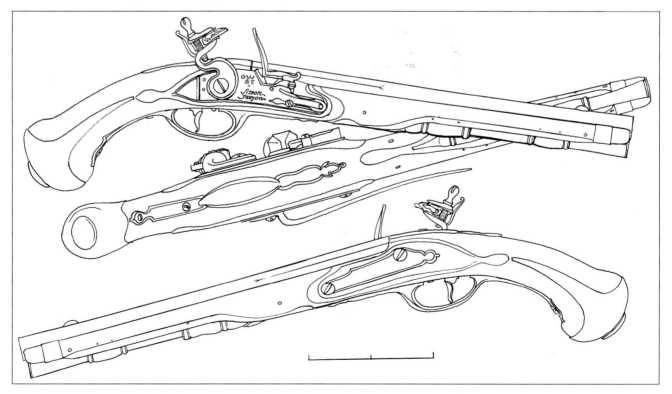

Cavalry/Dragoon model 1733 regulation French pistol, with a belt hook for dragoon and naval use. Issued to cavalry, dragoons and Gardes de la marine as well as Gardes du pavillon. The official regulation specified that weapons were to have barrels of 11 pouces 6 lignes in length, with a calibre of 14 lignes to be able to accept balls of 18 to the livre and of an overall length of 18 pouces 6 lignes. (Line drawing by Michel Pétard)

Portrait of l'Abbé Joseph-Marie De La Corne de Chaptes (1714–1779), brother of the colonial officer La Corne Saint-Luc. As part of the Affaire du Canada, a letter describing the events at La Bastille in Paris in 1760 included the following with regards to this ecclesiastic: 'He is a very good rider, he is very good on horseback ... I think he did his academy'. (Portrait of l'abbé Joseph-Marie De La Corne de Chaptes (1714–1779), Anon. 1750–1800, M22335, Musée McCord, Montréal)

styles. The heavier, bulkier cavalry pistols were likely used during travel on horseback, mirroring practices in France. Meanwhile, pocket pistols or shortened cavalry pistols offered a more practical alternative for campaign use. Their lighter weight and compact design made them ideal for close-range personal protection or hand-to-hand combat, particularly for officers travelling on foot along the frontier.

Early Accounts of Pistols in New France

Pistols were used in New France and its frontier regions from an early period, serving as both weapons and symbols of authority. As early as 1634, Jean Nicolet, the French interpreter and clerk of the Compagnie de la Nouvelle-France, made a dramatic entrance on the shores of Green Bay. Dressed in a Chinese robe, he fired the pistols he held in both hands, reloaded, and fired repeatedly, prompting awe and fear among the local population: 'As soon as we

saw him, all of the women and children fled, seeing a man carrying thunder in his two hands.'[102]

A decade later, Paul de Chomedey de Maisonneuve, the first governor of the island of Montréal, wielded pistols during an Iroquois attack in March 1644. Having missed his mark with his first shot, de Maisonneuve, 'took his other pistol and fired it so promptly and so luckily that he [the Iroquois] dropped dead.'[103] About 15 years later, the renowned fur traders and explorers Sieur des Groseilliers and Pierre Radisson carried an arsenal that included three pairs of large pistols and two pairs of pocket pistols, which left a strong impression on the Native Americans of Lake Superior. Radisson boasted of their commanding presence, stating, 'We were Caesars, being nobody to contradict us.'[104] In 1682, Cavelier de La Salle, writing from Michilimackinac about his expedition down the Mississippi, described his men approaching hostile Native Americans armed with 'only a hatchet or a pistol at the belt', while two years earlier, he noted that each man in his party was equipped with 'two guns, a pistol and a sword, powder and ball, and some knives and hatchets' to serve both as weaponry and as diplomatic gifts for the Illinois nation.[105]

Native Usage of Pistols

Native nations frequently received pistols from the French as gifts during peace and alliance negotiations, highlighting the widespread use and availability of these weapons in New France. In 1669, when Galinée and Dollier de Casson accompanied La Salle, they presented a Seneca chief with an ornate 'double-barrelled pistol' valued at 60 livres.[106] A 1692 statement of goods destined for Canada listed 30 pistols intended as gifts for Native groups in the St Lawrence Valley and interior.[107] Two years later, an inventory of munitions at Fort Bourbon on Hudson Bay included '4 pairs of service pistols, old', '3 pairs of pistols, half worn down', and '49 pairs of pistols for trade', indicating their use as trade goods.[108] In 1735, '1 pocket pistol' was sent to Michipicoten post, and in 1741, 'four cavalry pistols' and '2 pocket pistols' were listed among supplies

102 Auguste Gosselin, *Les Normands Au Canada: Jean Nicolet, 1618–1642* (Évreux: l'Eure, 1893), p.34

103 François Dollier de Casson, *Histoire du Montréal* (Montréal: Eusèbe Sénécal, 1871), p.30.

104 Grace Lee Nute, *Caesars of the Wilderness: Médard Chouart, Sieur Des Groseilliers and Pierre Esprit Radisson, 1618–1710* (St-Paul: Minnesota Historical Society Press, 1978), p.61.

105 Pierre Margry, *Lettres de Cavelier de La Salle et correspondance relative à ses entreprises (1678–1685)* (Paris: D. Jouaust, 1877), pp.131, 291.

106 Pierre Margry, *Mémoires et documents pour servirà l'histoire des origines francaises des ...* (Paris: Maisonneuve et cie., 1879), p.130.

107 LAC, B, MG1–2, vol.16, f.180.

108 LAC, A2, MG 6, NC, Liasse 5912, Inventaire des marchandises et munitions du Fort Bourbon, 1694.

for Rainy Lake post.[109] The use of pistols by Native warriors in combat is well-documented, reflecting their integration into both warfare and diplomacy. During Vaudreuil's 1739 campaign against the Chickasaw, Native allies were issued at least one pistol.[110] A few years later, a Nipissing chief avenged his brother's death by killing the British commander with a pistol before striking down another with a tomahawk.[111] In 1760, *commandant* Pouchot noted that five Iroquois warriors at la Présentation were armed with pistols, guns, and tomahawks.[112]

Pistols in Military Campaigns and Expeditions

From a military perspective, pistols were regularly issued for large-scale expeditions and campaigns in Canada from an early period, equipping various military personnel, including officers. While 100 pistols priced at 5 livres apiece were supplied to the Carignan-Salières regiment in 1666 to wage war on the Iroquois,[113] '200 belt pistols' were to be sent from La Rochelle in 1684 to arm the men who would accompany De La Barre on his expedition against this same Confederacy.[114]

Throughout the following decades, only a limited number of pistols were sent to New France. However, in 1734, a statement outlining the munitions necessary for the defence of the colony, and inventorying those currently in the King's storehouses, included '1200 pistols' as well as '4000 livres of balls for pistols.'[115] By the 1740s, these firearms increasingly turn up in the King's storehouses and were subsequently reallocated to the arsenal of various forts. In 1743, 50 pairs of pistols were supplied to Fort Saint-Frédéric,[116] and by the onset King George's War, '300 pairs of pistols, to be maintained and used only when needed',[117] were sent to Québec, where they appear to have been redistributed to military outposts throughout the colony.

The majority of pistols arriving from France tended to be kept in the storehouses at Québec. In 1750, an inventory recorded 483 pistols with a calibre of 18 balls to the *livre*, a number that grew by 1752 to include '504 cavalry and belt pistols' and '18 pocket pistols.'[118] By the Seven Years War, the greater part of the forts on the Lake Champlain and the Richelieu River corridor, as well as those bordering on Lake Ontario, counted a number of pistols in their storehouses. In 1757, for example, '3 cavalry pistols' were accounted for at Fort Carillon,[119] as well as another 65 at Fort Saint-Frédéric,[120] while the British Lieutenant Colonel John Bradstreet found 46 pairs of pistols after the capture of Fort Frontenac two years later.[121] Furthermore, the numerous line regiments serving with Baron Dieskau, who arrived in Canada in 1755, had brought along with them '100 pairs of pistols' which were to be 'handed over at Québec to be delivered to the troops as they need them.'[122]

Historical accounts as early as 1686 indicate that colonial officers were frequently armed with pistols during expeditions. Pierre Le Moyne d'Iberville, accompanying Pierre de Troyes to Hudson's Bay, reportedly used a pistol during an attack on an English fort: 'having a pistol in hand, fired it randomly, which scared off the siege men.'[123] Similarly, Nicolas Daneau de Muy, participating in Denonville's 1687 expedition against the Iroquois, 'got carried away and fired a pistol on one of the canotiers [boaters]' who had disobeyed his order to return to the fort.[124] In 1698, D'Iberville, his brother Jean-Baptiste le Moyne de Bienville, and several Canadians and freebooters were documented as being armed with 'fusils, pistols, cutlasses, bayonets, swords' during their search for the mouth of the Mississippi.[125] During the Natchez War in Louisiana, the colonial officer D'Etchepare, *commandant* near present-day Natchez, Mississippi, reportedly used a whistle to alert his troops during a surprise night attack rather than arming himself with a pistol or fusil. This incident highlights the frontier practice of officers relying on handguns for self-defence, contrasting with D'Etchepare's reaction: 'He stands, but like a fool, rather than grab a pistol or fusil'.[126]

A letter from Louis Liénard de Beaujeu de Villemonde, recounting his leadership during the 1747 attack on British forces at Grand-Pré, offers a vivid example of a colonial officer using his pistol in close-quarters combat, an approach well-suited to the confined and intense nature of such engagements: 'I entered the house, they fired

109 LAC, M-847, Account books of eighteenth-century merchants of Montreal, Monière, vol.4, pp.582–586; vol.8, pp.230-233.

110 LAC, MG1-C11A, vol.71,f.163v.

111 Séminaire de Saint-Sulpice, Montréal, MG-17, A 7–2, série 11, vol.2, f.866.

112 Pouchot, *Mémoires sur la dernière guerre de l'Amérique septentrionale*, p.162.

113 LAC, MG1-C11A, vol.2, f.274.

114 LAC, MG1-C11A, vol.11, f.20v.

115 LAC, MG1-C11A, vol.61, f.333v.

116 LAC, MG1-C11A, vol.82, f.169v.

117 LAC, MG1-C11A, vol.83, f.254.

118 LAC, MG1-C11A, vol.98, f.245v.

119 LAC, MG1-C11A, vol.102, f.213.

120 LAC, MG1-C11A, vol.102, f.214v.

121 John Bradstreet, *An impartial account of Lieut. Col. Bradstreet's expedition to Fort Frontenac...* (London: T. Wilcox, 1759), p.48.

122 LAC, MG1-C11A, vol.100, f.286v.

123 Pierre de Troyes, *Journal de l'expédition du chevalier de Troyes à la baie d'Hudson, en 1686, édité et annoté par Ivanhoe Caron* (Beauceville, La Compagnie de l'éclaireur, 1918), p.67.

124 *Collection de manuscrits contenant lettres, mémoires, et autres documents historiques relatif à la Nouvelle-France...* (Québec: Imprimerie A. Coté et cie., 1883), p.563.

125 Pierre Margry, *Découvertes et établissements des Français dans l'ouest et dans le sud de l'Amérique Septentrionale. Quatrième partie (1614–1754): mémoires et documents originaux* (Paris: Imprimerier D. Jouaust, 1880), p.242.

126 Dumont de Montigny, *The Memoir of Lieutenant Dumont, 1715–1747: A Sojourner in the French Atlantic* (Williamsburg: UNC Press Books, 2013), p.233.

immediately three or four musket shots at me that merely went through my capot, I fired my pistol on the captain, which I killed.'[127] Two years later, Jean-Baptiste Céloron de Blainville, a Canadian officer, reportedly had his pistol repaired at Fort Miami before his return to Montréal in the early fall of 1749 after an expedition through the Ohio Valley, suggesting that his personal firearm endured significant wear during the voyage.[128]

By the following decade, pistols remained a critical tool for colonial officers in the field. Bourlamaque wrote of Jean-Baptiste Levrault de Langis Montegron, an officer in the colonial troops, returning to Fort Carillon 'his arm in a sling, a pistol in his hand', while also remarking that 'emulation came for this type of war', highlighting the distinctive and adaptive methods employed by officers during expeditions of this period.[129] In 1760, Kerlerec, governor of Louisiana, related a duel between a Swiss officer named Debisseau and an *enseigne* in the colonial troops, Paul Rastel de Rocheblave, at New Orleans. According to Debisseau's testimony:

> Rocheblave presented him with two pistols, with their barrels resting on his chest, and declared, 'Monsieur, there are not two ways about it, you must take one.' I said to him, 'Monsieur, we are not offended to the point where either one of us wishes to blow each other's brains out, but I will fight with my ordinary weapon, which is my sword.' He further insisted for some time in pressing him to take one, and in the end, he fired them both on each side, one of which fired, the other merely burned its primer, and he placed them on the ground.[130]

Although sword duels were commonly documented in the French colonies of North America, this incident may represent one of the earliest recorded attempts at a pistol duel among military men in New France.

Archival records indicate that colonial soldiers stationed in towns or on the frontier occasionally owned or used pistols. In 1716, for example, a *sergent* of the colonial troops accused of stealing money in Québec was reported by the storekeeper Desnoyers to possess a 'brass-mounted pocket pistol.'[131] During the Chickasaw campaign of 1739, the equipment issued to a drummer in a detachment led by

Baron de Longueuil included '1 drum case, 2 drum skins, and 1 pistol.'[132] Similarly, a 1752 criminal trial concerning deserters at Fort Sandosky revealed that a soldier named Joseph Gorelle, known as dit Prêt-à-boire, used a pistol to fire at Sieur Sacquépée, a cadet. One witness testified that 'he knew that the pistol of the said Prêt-à-boire was only loaded with gunpowder.'[133]

Probate Records

French colonial probate records reveal that colonial officers serving in Canada often owned a range of pistols, including cavalry pistols, pocket pistols, and related accessories. At the time, pistols were regarded as a weapon of distinction, primarily associated with the nobility. Their exclusivity stemmed from their design and intended use: pistols were crafted for mounted combat, with holsters (or fontes) traditionally secured at the saddle bow, referred to in French as the arçon, a feature that lent the cavalry pistol its name, pistolet d'arçon. Ownership and use of a horse, along with the pistols that accompanied it, symbolized status and privilege, being largely confined to noblemen and the wealthier members of the bourgeoisie.

Holster Pistols

Many colonial officers in New France appear to have owned holsters (fontes) and pistol bags (faux fourreaux), whether or not they retained the pistols they were designed to hold. These items are closely associated with French cavalry pistols of the period, indicating their intended use while on horseback. For instance, *capitaine* Daniel de Grelon, who passed away in Montréal in 1710, owned a pair of pistols along with their pistol bag, suggesting they were likely cavalry pistols.[134] Fourteen years later, Étienne de Veniard, Sieur de Bourgmont, was reportedly hunting bison on horseback near present-day Kansas using saddle pistols, before presenting a Padouca chief with his 'blue coat … lined with red and adorned with a row of brass buttons on each side, and one of his saddle pistols.'[135] In 1737, *lieutenant* Joseph Dejourdy de Cabanac owned a cavalry pistol (pistolet d'arçon), valued alongside a pocket

127 Joseph Gagné, , 'Fidèle à Dieu, à la France, et au Roi' Les retraites militaires de La Chapelle et de Beaujeu vers la Louisiane après la perte du Canada 1760-1762 (Mémoire de maitrise, Université Laval, 2014), pp.46–47.

128 LAC, MG1-C11A, vol.119, f.143.

129 Henri-Raymond Casgrain, Collection des manuscrits du maréchal de Lévis, Lettres de M. de Bourlamaque au maréchal de Lévis (Québec: Imprimerie de L.-J. Demers & Frère, 1891), p.267.

130 LAC, MG1-E, vol.355, pp.7–8, 13–16.

131 BAnQ-M, TL4, S1, D1864, Procès contre Jacques Bonin dit Laforet, sergent de la compagnie d'Esgly, accusé de vol d'argent chez le trésorier de la marine à Québec, 19 février–19 mai 1716.

132 LAC, MG1-C11A, vol.71, f.161.

133 BAnQ-M, TL4, S1, D5667, Procès devant le Conseil de guerre contre François Boirond dit St-François… , 10 janvier 1752–1 février 1752; BAnQ-Q, P1000, S3, D220, Accusation envers François Boisron et d'autres pour désertion, 22 June 1752.

134 BAnQ-M, Greffe du notaire M. Lepailleur, Inventaire de feu Sieur Daniel de Grelon, écuyer Sieur Duluth, capitaine d'une compagnie des troupes de la marine. Demeure chez le Sieur Launay, tanneur… , 27 février 1710.

135 Frank Norall, Bourgmont, Explorer of the Missouri, 1698–1725 (University of Nebraska Press, 1988), pp.66, 149, 157.

pistol at 8 livres,[136] while De la Buissonnière, *commandant* at the Illinois, possessed two pairs of pistols, one identified as cavalry pistols.[137] Henri-Albert de St-Vincent, an officer of the colonial troops and *commandant* at Fort Ouiatenon, owned 'one pair of saddle pistols' (pistolets de selle) along with 'two pistol bags for saddle pistols' at the time of his death in 1742, further supporting their association with cavalry models.[138] The 1760 inventory of Thomas Philippe Dagnaux, Sieur de La Saussaye, drawn up in Montréal, included 'one saddle mounted with a blanket having a silver braid and two pistol holsters', indicating these cases likely held cavalry pistols.[139] Two years later, the belongings of Chevalier deLa Corne, who perished at sea aboard *L'Auguste*, included two pistol holsters valued at 2 livres.[140]

These probate records suggest that several officers of the Compagnies franches de la Marine indeed carried cavalry pistols when travelling on horseback, whether on or off duty. For example, the journal of Paul Marin's raid on Saratoga in 1745 takes note of many colonial officers travelling on horseback from one fort to another in the Montréal area, where many may have had saddle holsters and cavalry pistols. In one instance, it is written that 'Monsieur Marin and all of the officers mounted their horses and proceeded to the Saint-Thérèse camp' while further in this journal, it is said that many of the officers had left Fort Chambly on horseback for Fort Laprairie.[141] While in Acadia in October of 1757, British officer John Knox appears to have recognised the colonial officer Boishébert, who was travelling on horseback: 'A Frenchman has appeared on horseback (with a white uniform, supposed to be Monsieur Boi Hibert) on the shore westward of our fort'. It is, therefore, quite probable that De Boishébert carried cavalry pistols in holsters upon his horse's saddle.[142]

The widespread use of cavalry pistols among colonial officers extended to officers of the Troupes de terre in Canada during the Seven Years War, indicating that they may have prepared for warfare modelled after European military campaigns. Among Baron de Dieskau's belongings, inventoried in 1755, were a horse saddle and an 'embroidered pistol bag for horseback',[143] while the personal effects of the Régiment de Béarn officer De Jambert that were sold off at Fort Carillon in 1758 included a pair of pistol holsters valued at 1 livres 10 sols.[144] The following year, François de Marillac, *capitaine* in the Régiment du Languedoc who had died following the injuries sustained after the siege of Québec in 1759, was the owner of 'two pistols, old, for a saddle' valued at 12 livres.[145]

During the 1740s, a range of cavalry pistols (pistolets d'arçon) were shipped to Canada, reflecting both standard and modified designs suited to the specific needs of colonial forces. Among these shipments, the Rouen-based merchant Dugard supplied 'six pairs of cavalry pistols, old and for cavalrymen, cleaned, at 7 livres 10 sols apiece,'[146] alongside 'six cavalry pistols, restocked in new, at 8 livres 10 sols apiece', which had been refurbished in France prior to export.[147] All the while, a shorter variation known as demi-arçon or mi-arçon, interpreted as a half-length cavalry pistol, was also in use in New France.[148] In 1743, Dugard shipped '3 pairs of demi-arçon pistols' valued at 8 livres 10 sols per pair,[149] and by 1748, an invoice sent to a Montréal based merchant included pistolets d'arçon with 'barrels of 8 pouces in length',[150] significantly shorter than the standard 11½ *pouces* barrels of regulation cavalry or dragoon models. In 1751, '15 pairs of pistols mi-arçon, fine, at 25 livres each' coming out of Saint-Étienne were shipped to Canada.[151] In line with the French practice of shortening cavalry pistols during this period, it can be inferred that these shorter horse pistols were lighter and,

---

136 BAnQ-Q, Greffe du notaire Charles René Gauchon de Chevremont, Inventaire des biens de feu Sieur Joseph Dejourdy de Cabanac, lieutenant d'une compagnie des troupes de ce pays, 27 mars 1737.

137 Kaskaskia Manuscripts, Randolph County Courthouse, Chester, Illinois, Inventaire de Monsieur de La Buissonnière (Commandant aux Illinois) et Dame Marie-Thérèse Trudeau, sa femme, 12 décembre 1740.

138 BAnQ-Q, Greffe du notaire Nicolas Boisseau, Inventaire d'Henry Albert, écuyer, sieur de St-Vincent, officier des troupes de la Marine entretenues en ce pays et commandant du poste des 8atanons (Ouiatenons)… , 23 juin 1742.

139 BAnQ-M, Greffe du notaire Louis-Claude Danré de Blanzy, Inventaire de Dame Marie-Anne Jarret de Verchères et de feu Thomas Philippe Dagnaux, Sieur de la Saussaye, 11 avril 1760.

140 BAnQ-M, Greffe du notaire Pierre Panet, Inventaire des biens de la communauté d'entre dame Marie-Anne Hubert, veuve de Sieur Chevalier de la Corne, dit Sieur De la Corne, vivant chevalier de l'ordre Royal et militaire de St-Louis, capitaine d'infanterie de sa majesté, 19 avril 1762.

141 LAC, MG 18, N 48, Paul Marin. Microfilm, 1745.

142 John Knox, *An Historical Journal of The Campaigns in North-America…* (London: W. Johnston, J. Dodsley, 1769), vol.1, p.51.

143 BAnQ-Q, Mic.6309, NF 18, Registres de l'Amirauté de Québec, Inventaire des biens du Baron de Dieskau par Jacques Bréard, contrôleur de la marine, 17 septembre 1755.

144 ASQ, Fonds Casgrain, document divers, vol.1, doc. 2, État des effets de M. de Jambert, lieutenant au Régiment de Béarn… qui y ont été vendus à Carillon, 22 septembre 1758.

145 BAnQ-M, Greffe du notaire Pierre Panet, Inventaire de la communauté d'entre Marie-Anne de Villeray d'Artigny, veuve de Messire Chabert, François de Marillac décédé à l'hôpital général de Québec suite aux blessures reçues suite au siège de la ville par les anglais…, 19 octobre 1759.

146 ANMT, Fonds Dugard, Série AQ, 62 AQ 41, Cargaisons pour Québec, p.198.

147 ANMT, Fonds Dugard, Série AQ, 62 AQ 41, Cargaisons pour Québec, p.198.

148 A. Paulin-Désormeaux, *Manuel de l'armurier, du fourbisseur et de l'arquebusier…* (Paris: Roret, 1832) p.184.

149 ANMT, Fonds Dugard, Série AQ, 62 AQ 41, Cargaisons pour Québec, p.483.

150 LAC, Bobine M-859. Pierre Guy, Facture des marchandises reçues de l'envoi de Messieurs Pascaud frères, Jean Veyssière, veuve Charly de La Rochelle et Hermains de Paris à feu Sieur Pierre Guy…27 avril 1748.

151 Archives de la Bastille, Bibliothèque de l'Arsenal, MG 7, II, vol.12148, p.5.

as a result, more practical and less cumbersome to handle, whether on horseback or on foot.

Marine Contract Pistols

The first regulation Marine pistol was adopted in 1779. Prior to this time, the 6 October 1674 ruling (reissued in the 15 April 1689 ordonnance) for the Marine Arsenals described the Marine pistol as having a calibre of 20 balls to the livre and equipped with a flintlock 'according to the models which will be given to the Masters and Directors of the manufactories.'[152] No official regulation officially defined these naval firearms other than descriptions contained within Marine contracts, which needed to conform to the ordonnance of the period. These pistols, termed pistolet de ceinture (belt pistol) or pistolet de bord (boarding pistol), served mainly as a hand-to-hand combat weapon when boarding ships where each sailor was said to place 'one or two at the belt area.'[153] A number of these pistols, equipped with a hook, were designed to slip over a belt or waistband and were mostly manufactured at the Tulle and Saint-Étienne weapons production centres. Interestingly enough, from the probate records that were consulted as part of this research, no such pistols specifically described as being of the naval or belt pistol style were found in an officer's personal possessions. However, this does not exclude this type of weapon from having been owned by a member of the military service. An official memo written in 1757 in France regarding newly recruited soldiers and officers of the Compagnies franches de la Marine, which were to board ships for Canada, reveals that the commissary of the Marine was unable to provide each of these officers with pistols, which may indicate that officers possibly received Marine contract pistols as part of their armament prior to embarking for Canada: 'he could not distribute ahead of time 25 or 30 pistols to each of the officers'.[154]

These Marine pistols may have been much more suited for boarding at sea than for use on land and seem to have been much more frequent at Louisbourg and in the district of Québec, likely owing to the increased naval activity in these regions since these types of pistols generally remained aboard ships. For example, a statement of the weapons available at Louisbourg fortress in 1728 included a quantity of '16 pistols with hooks' as well as '16 pistols without hooks', which were deemed unfit for service.[155] Such pistols may, in fact, have served in certain circumstances to arm the detached troops at Louisbourg since a statement of munitions requested for 1742 included '100 pairs of belt pistols to arm the detached troops.'[156] Interestingly enough, 'two pairs of belt pistols, bronzed barrels' were also referenced on a private merchant's merchandise statement at Québec in 1752, indicating that these belt pistols, possibly of the Marine or dragoon models, may have had barrels which were browned to resist rust.[157]

Pocket Pistols (Pistolets de Poche)

Pocket pistols had been used in New France for a very long time. In 1642, Jean Nicolet had in his estate, amongst other firearms, two saddle pistols (deux pistolets d'arçon) as well as a wheel-lock pocket pistol (un pistolet de poche à rouet),[158] whereas officer Paul Le Moyne de Maricourt, had two fine pocket pistols priced at 10 livres in his store at Montréal in 1685.[159] Father Du Peron, a Jesuit who was appointed chaplain to Fort Saint-Louis in 1665, was said to have always carried a pocket pistol that he named 'his first punch'.[160]

In fact, a number of these smaller concealable pistols are also found in colonial officers' probate records. François-Marie Renaud d'Avène de Des Méloizes, who acquired a company in the colonial regular troops and arrived at Québec in August of 1685, owned 'two old pistols, one of the pocket types, the other of the cavalry (d'arçon) type.'[161] In 1716, enseigne Simon Dupuis was the owner of 'a small pocket pistol with its holster',[162] while lieutenant Jean-Baptiste Montbrun de Saint-Laurent, serving in the Illinois Territory, was recorded has having a pocket pistol amongst various other personal effects in 1748.[163] François de Sarrobert, enseigne in the colonial troops, owned 'two

152 Jean-Baptiste Torchet de Boismêlé, Histoire générale de la marine contenant son origine chez tous les peuples du monde... (Paris: Chez Antoine Bouder, 1758), vol.3, pp.46, 56.
153 De Boismêlé, Histoire générale de la marine, vol.3, planche XVI.
154 LAC, MG1-C11A, vol.102, f.247.
155 LAC, MG1-C11B, vol.10, f.38–39.
156 LAC, MG1-C11B, vol.24, f.174.
157 BAnQ-Q, P908, P4, Factures générales des marchandises envoyées à Québec par la société Rouffio pour l'année 1752..., 1752.
158 BAnQ-Q, Greffe du notaire Martial Piraube, Inventaire de feu Jean Nicollet, commis et interprète de la compagnie de la Nouvelle-France, 7 décembre 1642.
159 BAnQ-M, Greffe du notaire B. Basset, Inventaire de Chabert Lemoyne..., 27 mars 1685.
160 Pierre Margry, Mémoires et documents pour servir à l'histoire des origines françaises des pays d'outre-mer (Paris: Maisonneuve, 1879), p.384.
161 BAnQ-Q, Greffe du notaire L. Chamballon, Inventaire de feu F-M Renaud d'Avesne, lieutenant de vaisseau, capitaine de compagnies franches et de feue Marie Thérèse Dupont, 16 mai 1699.
162 Jean-Marie Lemieux, L'Île aux Grues et l'Île aux Oies: les îles, les seigneurs, les habitants, les sites et monuments historiques (Montréal: Éditions Lemeac, 1978), p.176.
163 Kaskaskia Manuscripts, Randolph County Courthouse, Chester, Illinois, ...testament de Messire Jean-Baptiste Montbrun de Saint-Laurent, écuyer, vivant lieutenant des Compagnies franches pour la Louisiane..., 20 janvier 1748.

leather holsters and two pocket pistols' valued together at 6 livres in 1756, which may have suggested that these pistols came with holsters.[164] That same year, the inventory list of the effects that had belonged to officer Antoine Denis de Saint-Simon included 'one pair of pocket pistols, very old, broken' valued at 2 livres.'[165]

These small, single-shot flintlock pistols were likely quite practical, as they could be easily concealed in a justaucorps or vest pocket, or in a pouch, making them useful for self-defence or close-quarters combat. Their compact size may have made them more suitable for many officers of the colonial regular troops on campaign than the larger, bulkier cavalry pistols. In a trial held at Montréal in 1741, a royal bailiff was recorded as threatening one of the King's surgeons over a land dispute using a pocket pistol concealed in one of his pockets, which reveals that the practice of carrying these small firearms in New France was certainly not uncommon. Many of these concealed weapons came in pairs and records reveal that they were for the most part manufactured in the town of Saint-Étienne. For example, '10 pairs of fine pocket pistols at 9 livres, 10 sols [apiece]' were sent from Saint-Étienne to Canada in 1751.[166] Certain pocket pistols were also called 'pistolet de bidet' back in France, from the French word bidet (small horse), such as the 'three pairs [pistolet] de bidet, common, at 5 livres each' as well as '1 pair ditto, finer, 7 livres 15 sols each' shipped to Québec by the Rouen-based merchant Dugard in 1744.[167]

Fine Pistols

The quality and craftsmanship of pistols owned by officers in the colonial troops varied significantly, with some standing out as remarkable examples of craftsmanship and refinement. Among these, François Mariocheau Digny, Chevalier of St Louis and King's *lieutenant* at Trois-Rivières, owned 'two master-made cavalry pistols' valued at 40 livres in 1730.[168] *Capitaine* Jean-Baptiste Jarret of Montréal possessed a 'pair of fine pistols' appraised at

15 livres in 1752.[169] While highly ornate pistols were relatively uncommon among colonial officers, exceptional examples occasionally appeared. In 1722, a pair of 'master-made pistols' (pistolets de maître), valued at an extraordinary 125 livres, were sold as part of the estate of Jacques Leprovost, *chirurgien major* of the troops at Fort de Chartres.[170] Likewise, in 1760, a 'silver-mounted pistol' assessed at the substantial sum of 100 livres was recorded among the personal belongings of Jean-Baptiste Levrault de Langis Montegron, an officer of the colonial troops.[171]

During the mid-seventeenth century, European gunsmiths developed flintlock arms capable of firing multiple shots in rapid succession using rotating barrels, commonly referred to as 'Wender' pistols, a term derived from the German word for to turn. One such pistol, featuring four rotating barrels, was presented to the Taensa nation on the Mississippi River by Louis Hennepin in 1680. Hennepin recounted how he had instructed his men to 'wear their best clothes, arm themselves from head to foot, and display a pistol capable of firing four consecutive blows.'[172] In 1724, a notarial record from Kaskaskia concerning Charles Danis noted the bequeathing of a double-barrelled flintlock pistol to his children, likely corresponding to a Wender-type pistol, as the technique of soldering barrels together did not emerge until later in the eighteenth century.[173]

Edged-Weapons of the Colonial Officer: Cutlasses, Sabres and Hunting Swords

The French sabre of the first half of the eighteenth century, a term in French often used to refer to either a sabre or a cutlass, was a type of sword commonly associated with light cavalry, grenadiers, and naval boarding actions. The key difference between the French sabre and a traditional sword is that the sabre was designed primarily for hacking or slashing, whereas a sword was intended for thrusting. Typically, sabres featured a single-edged, curved blade, whereas swords were double-edged. Another advantage of

164 BAnQ-M, Greffe du notaire Louis-Claude Danré de Blanzy, Inventaire des biens de feu Sieur François de Sarrobert, enseigne d'infanterie, 8 janvier 1756.

165 BAnQ-Q, Greffe du notaire Jean-Antoine Saillant, Inventaire des meubles et effets de la veuve Denis de St-Simon, 19 octobre 1756.

166 Archives de la Bastille, Bibliothèque de l'Arsenal-MG 7, II, vol.12148, p.5.

167 ANMT, Fonds Dugard, Série AQ, 62 AQ 41, p.733, Cargaisons pour Québec, 7 avril 1744.

168 BAnQ-Q, Greffe du notaire Jacques-Nicolas Pinguet de Vaucour, Inventaire des biens de la communauté des défunts François Mariocheau Digny, chevalier de l'Ordre militaire et de St-Louis et lieutenant du Roi de la ville et gouvernement des Trois-Rivières..., 20 mai 1730.

169 BAnQ-M, Greffe du notaire Louis-Claude Danré de Blanzy, Inventaire des biens de feu Jean-Baptiste Jarret, Sieur de Verchères, chevalier de l'ordre militaire de St-Louis, capitaine d'infanterie, 8 août 1752.

170 Kaskaskia Manuscripts, Randolph County Courthouse, Chester, Illinois, Vente des effets de M. Jacques Leprevost, 23 septembre 1722.

171 BAnQ-M, Greffe du notaire Louis-Claude Danré de Blanzy, Inventaire de Catherine d'Ailleboust du Manthet et de Jean-Baptiste Levreau écuyer Sieur de Langy, officier demeurant aux Outaouais, 26 April 1760.

172 Louis Hennepin, *Nouvelle decouverte d'un tres grand pays situé dans l'Amérique: entre le Nouveau Mexique...* (Amsterdam: Chez A. van Someren, 1698), p.265.

173 Kaskaskia Manuscripts, Randolph County Courthouse, Chester, Illinois, Suite du partage pour la vente, Sieur Charles Danis, 26 juillet, 1724.

the sabre or cutlass was its relative simplicity in use, requiring less training compared to the more complex techniques needed for a rapier or small sword.

The sabre d'abordage, or boarding cutlass, of this period corresponded to a hanger or sabre having a short or half-length curved blade favouring the cutting edge. These cutlasses were used as a close combat weapon and remained the sailor's weapon of choice since they were robust enough to hack through wood, canvas and rope and ideal for use in combat at close quarters in the restricted space of a ship's deck. Sabres used by the French cavalry or by specialized units, generally required a longer weapon for slicing down foot soldiers.

The grenadier's sabre, which was a weapon distinguishing these elite soldiers, had either a long or short curved blade prioritising the cutting edge, while those used by cavalrymen were functional combat weapons with a long straight blade, favouring the thrust.

Boarding Cutlasses

In the French colonies of North America, the boarding cutlass was common and widespread since it was a part of the armament of each ship crossing the Atlantic and remained a weapon of choice for the troops of the Compagnies franches de la Marine bound to serve at sea. Over time, cutlasses were eagerly adopted by various Native American nations, who adapted them for use on land, incorporating them into their traditional armament. The French, in turn, occasionally followed this trend, employing cutlasses in contexts beyond their original naval purpose.

Historical records indicate that while certain elite or specialised military units stationed in Canada were fully equipped with regulation sabres, colonial officers often chose cutlasses or sabres for expeditions and campaigns. Several factors likely influenced this choice, including the practical advantages of these weapons in specific combat scenarios, such as their utility in close-quarters engagements, as well as the possibility that they were simply selected as an alternative to

Above right: Detail of an engraving showing the famous corsair Jean Bart, who was a *chef d'escadre* in the French navy. This officer is seen here with a naval cutlass in hand and pistol tucked in his sash. Much like Bart, the French-Canadian privateer and colonial officer Pierre Le Moyne d'Iberville, who had an extraordinary career at sea and on land, was recorded as carrying a cutlass when he took part in an expedition to Hudson's Bay in 1686. (Portrait de Jean Bart, en pied, A Paris, chez N. Arnoult, avec privilége du Roy, 1702)

Right: Allegorical engraving, c.1700, by Nicolas Guérard featuring a French Marine officer holding what is clearly a cutlass in his right hand. A motto at the top of the engraving reads 'Always in between the arms of death.'

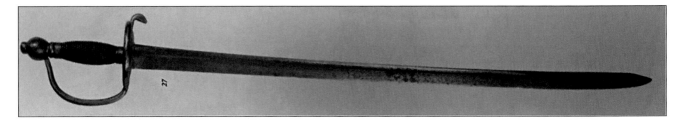

Above and right: Naval cutlass of the Louvois type, late seventeenth century. This type of cutlass, which likely appeared around 1670–1680, is recorded in French Marine arms contracts from 1700 onward. This model, manufactured at the Tulle manufactory, was consistently in use until its replacement by the model 1779 boarding sabre, nicknamed Sartines. Iron mounted, this cutlass has a hilt with a double shell counterguard bearing a fleur-de-lis mark on its blade. This type of weapon was intended for shipboard use and would have been quite similar, if not nearly identical, to the ones used in New France. (Private collection. Photo Michel Pétard)

Detail of a cartouche at the top of a map by Nicolas de Fer likely shows La Salle wearing a red justaucorps while one of his men shown shooting a musket wears what appears to be a cutlass from his waist belt. In September of 1679, it was recorded that La Salle and a small party of his men who voyaged down the shores of Lake Michigan were 'armed with guns, pistols and cutlasses'.

Detail taken from a series of illustrations showing the type of boarding cutlasses found at a French seaport arsenal in 1738. (SHD-Brest, bibliothèque R 3415. Photo Christian Lemasson)

A sword hilt with a complete faceted bone grip and a fragmentary scabbard, recovered from the Machault wreck. It is nearly identical to the common brass-mounted cutlass or boarding saber with a horn grip and half-shell counterguard decorated with a bust of King Louis XV, found at various French-context sites.(Courtesy of National Historic Sites, Parks Canada.)

Detail of a cutlass taken from a c. 1703 illustration listing the weapons available aboard a Royal French Galley. This weapon is described as 'Cutlass, 24, used by the sailors of rambades in case of boarding.' (Document Archives Nationales, Archives de la Marine, France, Série G)

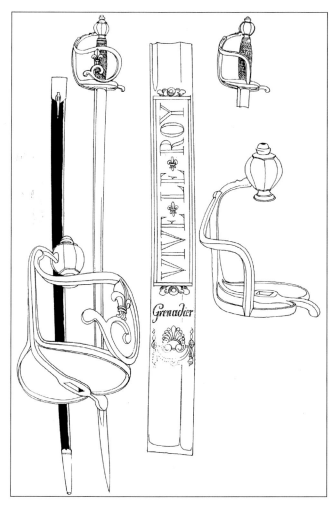

Two possible configurations of the Contrecoeur sabre, reportedly owned by colonial officer François-Antoine Pécaudy de Contrecoeur. Illustrated by Michel Pétard.

the small sword, serving both as a functional tool and a marker of rank.

Native Usage of Cutlasses

As early as the 1630s, the French recognised cutlasses as the ideal weapon for countering certain enemy Native nations, particularly the Iroquois. In a letter to Cardinal Richelieu in 1634, Champlain proposed arming all his men with 'short but very sharp' cutlasses, intending to reclaim much of the countryside south of the St Lawrence River by striking decisively against the Iroquois.[174] Notably, the Iroquois were armed with cutlasses from an early period, and by 1680, 500 Iroquois warriors, who had been attacked by Henri de Tonty along with his Illinois allies, were fully equipped with 'fusils, pistols, and cutlasses.'[175]

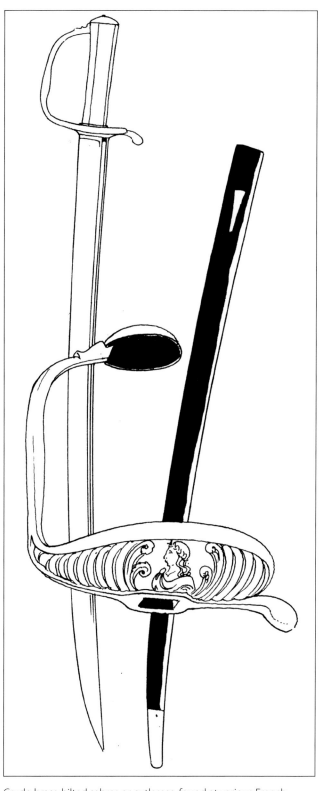

Crude brass-hilted sabres or cutlasses, found at various French archaeological sites in North America, appear to have been more common than other types of French sabre fragments. These may have been issued to officers, cadets, and allied Natives before raids during King George's War, as well as those sent by merchant Gradis during the Seven Years War. Identical decorated examples were found at sites such as Old Mobile (1702–1711), Fort Carillon (1756–1759), Fort Beauséjour (1750–1755), Fort St-Frédéric (1727–1759), the *Machault* wreck (1760), and Fort de Chartres (1720–1765). This illustration by Michel Pétard depicts this type of sabre with scabbard, showing the relief wreathed-head decoration on the brass counterguard and its simple knuckle-bow pontet.

---

174   David Hackett Fischer, *Champlain's Dream* (Toronto: Knopf Canada, 2009), p.461.

175   Pierre Margry, *Découvertes et établissements des Français dans l'ouest et dans le sud de l'Amérique Septentrionale. Quatrième partie (1614–1754)... Deuxième partie. Lettres de Cavelier de La Salle et correspondance relative à ses entreprises (1678–1685)* (Paris: D. Jouaust, 1877), p.121.

The effectiveness of cutlasses in combat was further highlighted during Denonville's 1687 campaign against the Seneca. A Native warrior from Sault St-Louis, fighting alongside French forces, reportedly killed one of his adversaries with a cutlass. This prompted Denonville to write to the minister, stating: 'All our brave Natives ask for cutlasses. We beseech you that they be of good quality. If you wanted to send us a hundred, it would give them great pleasure.'[176]

By the early 1730s, a proposed plan to attack the Fox nation, outlined by the colonial officer Payen de Noyan, recommended equipping the domiciled Native allies with '400 sabres [cutlasses]' priced at 40 sols each.[177] As King George's War loomed, cutlasses were among the weapons distributed to Native allies of the French. For instance, a group of Abenaki warriors from Bécancour received six cutlasses as part of their armament for the conflict,[178] while the following year, an inventory of items issued from the Montréal storehouses to Native allies included one cutlass valued at 5 livres.[179]

In many cases, cutlasses supplied to Native warriors were forged locally by colonial blacksmiths. In 1745, Pierre Belleperche, a blacksmith stationed at Michilimackinac, was paid 30 livres to craft five cutlasses for the Odawa tribe on the orders of M. de Longueuil.[180] That same year, Jean-Baptiste Marquis, a blacksmith at Detroit, produced a cutlass for a party of Nippissing warriors, further emphasising the popularity of cutlasses among Indigenous groups in the furthest reaches of the interior.[181]

French cutlasses were also highly valued both as prestigious gifts to seal alliances and as arms for allied Native nations along the Atlantic coast, particularly during King William's War (1688–1697). In 1692, '100 cutlasses with brass hilts' were provided as presents to the Native Americans of Acadia,[182] while some 13 years later the famous Abenaki chief Nescambiouit had received a cutlass that Louis XIV had presented to him at Versailles as a present, which he used alongside of the officers Jean-Baptiste de Saint-Ours Deschaillons and Jean-Baptiste Hertel de Rouville when ravaging Haverhill on the Merrimack River the following year.[183] According to the officer Baron de Lahontan, 'a few cutlasses' were typically included among a trader's supply of goods in Canada in the late 1680s.[184] The Jesuit Pierre-Michel Laure, on the other hand, noted the symbolic representation of this weapon in his relation of 1730, where the funeral rites of the Innu chief Maratchikatik included his cutlass and gun laid out crosswise.[185]

Shipments of Cutlasses and Sabers to Canada

Major shipments of sabres, which undoubtedly represented French boarding cutlasses, intended for the French colonies of North America extend back to the seventeenth century. Among the goods and munitions requisitioned for Canada in the late 1680s and early 1690s were edged weapons such as '100 sabres, of the best in the storehouses', transported from Rochefort to Québec in 1688,[186] and '200 sabres with brass hilts', prepared for shipment in 1693.[187] According to historical records, shipments of sabres for Canada seem to have dwindled in the following decades, whereas in 1734, a statement which included war munitions necessary for the defence of the colony and to sort the ones currently in the King's storehouses included '1000 sabres.'[188] Many of the boarding cutlasses dispatched to Canada during this period were likely intended to arm ships stationed at Québec or be held in military depots. By the 1740s, however, many of these cutlasses were transported into the interior and likely intended for land usage.

By 1745, a significant number of sabres, described as 'following a model,' along with their scabbards, were designated by the Ministry of the Marine for shipment to Québec the following year.[189] In 1746, the president of the Marine Council acknowledged that nearly 1,500 sabres were slated for delivery to Québec, although official records indicate that 1,088 ultimately arrived.[190] It is plausible that these weapons may have been dispatched to arm a portion of the militia, reinforcing the colony's defences against a potential British attack, especially considering that Louisbourg had been captured in 1745. A ship's manifest offers detailed descriptions of some of these arms: '500 sabres with grips and hilts of brass fitted with their scabbards of calfskin, tips of brass and iron hooks at 3 livres 10 sols each', accompanied by waist belts noted as 'buff waist belts for sabres with simple stitching, fitted with brass buckles and iron chaps at 50 sols each.'[191]

176 LAC, MG1-C11A, vol.9, f.18.
177 LAC, MG1-C11A, vol.56, f.314v.
178 LAC, MG1-C11A, vol.86, f.215.
179 LAC, MG1-C11A, vol.89, f.214v.
180 LAC, MG1-C11A, vol.83, f.310.
181 LAC, MG1-C11A, vol.83, f.303.
182 LAC, MG1-C11A, vol.16, f.74v.
183 Pierre-François-Xavier de Charlevoix, *Histoire et description generale de la nouvelle France, avec le journal historique d'un voyage fait par ordre du roi dans l'Amerique septentrionnale...* (Paris: Chez Didot, 1744), vol.2, , p.326.

184 Louis Armand de Lom d'Arce La Hontan, *Voyages du baron de Lahontan dans l'Amérique septentrionale* (Amsterdam: f.L'Honoré, 1741), p.75.
185 Anon., *The Jesuit Relations and Allied Documents: Travels and Explorations of the Jesuit Missionaries in New France, 1610-1791, volumes 68 à 69* (New York: Pageant Book Company, 1959), p.64.
186 LAC, MG1-B, vol.15, f.27.
187 LAC, MG1-B, vol.16, f.10.
188 LAC, MG1-C11A, vol.61, f.333v.
189 LAC, MG1-C11A, vol.84, f.278–278v.
190 LAC, MG1-C11A, vol.81, f.269.
191 LAC, MG1-C11A, vol.86, f.342–342v.

In 1749, 609 'sabres and cutlasses' from the original shipment of 1,088 remained in the King's storehouses at Québec.[192] Over subsequent years, the remaining sabres were distributed to Trois-Rivières, Montréal, and various forts such as Fort St-Frédéric. These weapons were often listed in the 'Clothing and weapons of the troops' sections of inventory records, suggesting they were intended for land-based military use rather than naval operations. By 1750, all sabres in the storehouses at Montréal were noted as having wooden core grips,[193] and by 1752, 50 sabres were stockpiled in the magazine at Fort St-Frédéric.[194]

Within the following two years, a few more shipments of sabres were sent for the colonial troops by official Marine suppliers in the mother country, which were undoubtedly intended for the Canonniers-Bombardiers serving in Canada. For instance, a quantity of '60 sabres mounted in gilded brass' as well as '90 sabres with grips and hilts or washed brass' were sent respectively in 1750 and 1752.[195] Further, the French regular troops who arrived in Canada in 1755 were recorded as bringing a number of sabre parts along with them that included '440 sabre blades for grenadiers' as well as '100 sabre grips', which most likely served as spare parts for the grenadiers.[196]

During the Seven Years War, the Bordeaux-based merchant family Gradis emerged as a key supplier of cutlasses for Canada, sourcing substantial quantities from Antoine Robert from the town of Saint-Étienne over a few years. Their shipments included '200 curved cutlasses' in 1755, another identical order the following year, and 96 cutlasses in 1757 described as 'having hilts', priced at 24 livres per dozen.[197] That same year, the ship *La Renommé*, contracted by Gradis and his son and later seized at sea by the British, was documented as carrying a bale of merchandise from Saint-Étienne that included brass and iron-mounted cutlasses:

6 dozen cutlasses with brass grips
1½ dozen ditto mounted in iron…No 1
4 dozen ditto… No 2½
2 dozen ditto… No 3
2 dozen ditto… No 4[198]

Sabres

Sabres used in a military context in Canada likely aligned with regulation models issued to specific units, such as the Canonniers-Bombardiers company, an artillery group established in 1750, or the Corps de cavalerie raised in Québec between the spring of 1759 and 1760 (see volume 1). They were also employed by the Grenadiers of the Troupes de terre from 1755 to 1760 and aboard ships as naval cutlasses, where they were referred to as sabre de bord or sabre d'abordage. The regulation sabres that would have armed the Canonniers-Bombardier company serving in Canada from 1750 to 1760 were described as having a brass gilt guard having two branches. The armament and the equipment proposed by Vaudreuil and the Intendant Bigot for the Corps de cavalerie, a volunteer cavalry raised in 1759 and consisting of 200 Canadian volunteers and five French officers, included good muskets and sabres, the latter of which were not specified although we may suppose that they would have similar to the regulation cavalry model sabres of the period.[199]

Historical documents reveal that this militia cavalry were armed with sabres since one historical account records that during the siege of Québec, a French cavalryman was 'killed with sabre in hand by a grenadier from the Languedoc regiment.'[200] The grenadiers, belonging to the whole of the French infantry which arrived at Québec in 1755, would have brought over their regulation sabres, which were specified in the 17 January 1747 ordonnance as having 'a 30 to 31 *pouces* blade, following the model.'[201] Orders provided to these men at Montréal prior to the campaign of 1755, required them to carry their sabres, which is corroborated by the testimony of two French soldiers who were made prisoner in 1757 and who declared, 'The Grenadiers only had their Sabres.'[202]

192 LAC, MG1-C11A, vol.93, f.331v.
193 LAC, MG1-C11A, vol.96, f.145.
194 LAC, MG1-C11A, vol.98, f.44–46.
195 LAC, MG1-B, vol, 92, f.5.; LAC, MG1-B, vol.96, f.172.
196 LAC, MG1-C11A, vol.100, f.289.
197 LAC, MG 18, H63, Fonds famille Gradis, F-1598, M. Antoine Robert, St Etienne, 20 décembre 1755; LAC, MG 18, H63, Fonds famille Gradis, F-1599, M. Antoine Robert, St Etienne, 7 août 1756; LAC, MG 18, H63, Fonds famille Gradis, F-1621, 6 novembre 1757.
198 TNA, High Court of Admiralty, 32, vol.238, pt. 2, La Renommée vers Québec, 1757.

199 Henri-Raymond Casgrain, *Collection des manuscrits du maréchal de Lévis, Lettres du marquis de Montcalm au chevalier de Lévis* (Québec: Imprimerie de L.-J. Demers & Frère, 1894), pp.175–179.
200 Aegidius Fauteux, *Journal du Siège de Québec du 10 mai au 18 septembre 1759…* (Québec: Fauteux, 1922), p.23.
201 François de Chennevieres, *Détails militaires: dont la connoissance est nécessaire à tous les officiers, & principalement aux commissaires des guerres* (Versailles: Chez Charles-Antoine Jombert, 1750), p.4.
202 TNA, CO 5/47, E. of Loudoun's Letter of April 25th. 1757, Declaration of two Prisoners taken the 23.d March 1757 at Fort Wm. Henry, Information of John Victor and Guillaume Chasse, two French Prisoners, Fort William Henry March 25th.

Cutlasses Used on Detachments and Expeditions

From time to time, officers of the colonial troops were provided with what was likely a cutlass amongst the equipment they received on detachments or expeditions. The de Troyes expedition against the English posts of the Hudson Bay region in 1686 included '60 swords or cutlasses at 5 livres each' to arm the men while Pierre Le Moyne d'Iberville, a colonial officer who took part in this expedition, was said to have used his cutlass on more than one occasion.[203] For example, while capturing the Englishmen John Bridgar's vessel near Fort Charles in July of 1686, Iberville gave one of the enemy men 'a cutlass slash to the head' while this same man 'was stopped shortly by a blow of the same cutlass through his body.'[204]

During the tumultuous Natchez War in 1731, colonial officer Louis Juchereau de Saint-Denis, *commandant* of the Fort des Natchitoches, led a charge against the entrenched enemy, reportedly 'falling on them with cutlass in hand.' This account suggests that he likely favoured a cutlass over the traditional small sword.[205] Some 16 years later, Monsieur de La Chauvignery, a colonial officer who was detached with two Frenchmen and six Native Americans, received a cutlass prior to leaving Montréal in order to meet the Onondaga people regarding diplomatic affairs.[206] A year earlier, the officer Joseph Boucher de Niverville, accompanied by his son, a cadet in the colonial troops, was detached to replace Monsieur de Montesson as commander at Ste-Thérèse, receiving a cutlass and the customary equipment for leading the garrison before his departure from Montréal.[207] In an April 1747 letter, Nicolas-Antoine Coulon de Villiers, a *capitaine* in the colonial regular troops, recounted leading an assault on New England forces, charging with 'the cutlass and hatchet in hand.'[208] These weapons, occasionally issued to officers from the stockpile of what were likely low-grade boarding cutlasses held in the King's storehouses, particularly after 1745, may also have been privately acquired by some officers.

Some NCOs and cadets were also documented as carrying cutlasses during war parties. For instance, cadets Langy and St-Blin, both serving in the colonial troops, were each issued a cutlass to accompany an Abenaki war party on the New England coast in 1747.[209] A year earlier, a man named Laprairie, who was a *sergent* in the colonial troops serving at Montréal, was accused of wounding the hand of the concierge at the residence of the governor using a cutlass. One witness indicated that he had seen this sergent 'having a cutlass at his side with a small cane in his hand', indicating that it was likely kept in a scabbard on a waist belt.[210] In 1751, a certain Joseph Gorelle dit Prêtaboire, soldier in the Compagnies franches de la Marine who had deserted from Fort Sandusky, was noted as threatening a soldier named Jean-Marie Ballet de St-Amour while 'swearing, his sabre in hand'.[211]

Probate Records

Sabres are at times found referenced in the post-mortem inventory list of navigators, administrators, middle-class merchants, traders as well as colonists living in the St Lawrence Valley. Many of the weapons are described with grips made from a variety of materials such as 'horn', 'deer horn' or 'bone'. Notably, in 1747 at Québec, the unique cutlass belonging to François de Charles, inspector of the Compagnie des Indes in Canada, was described as 'one cutlass with a small pistol integrated into the handle.'[212]

According to probate records, fewer than five percent of colonial officials in Canada owned a sabre or cutlass, and most of these references appear only after 1760. References to sabres in probate records concerning colonial officers are rare, suggesting that these weapons were privately purchased, often reflecting the personal tastes of their owners through a variety of decorative styles. For instance, prior to leaving for the Nipigon post in 1732, Paul Marin de La Malgue, an officer in the colonial troops, had purchased a very expensive sabre priced at 25 livres from the Montréal merchant named Monière.[213] An inventory list drawn up of the personal possessions belonging to the colonial officer Joseph Langy in 1760 included, among a number of items, 'one sabre with a brass guard' valued at 12 livres.[214] The following year, in December 1760, Sieur

203 LAC, MG1-C11A, vol.8, f.280.
204 Pierre de Troyes, *Journal de l'expédition du chevalier de Troyes à la baie d'Hudson, en 1686, édité et annoté par Ivanhoe Caron* (Beauceville: La Compagnie de l'éclaireur, 1918), pp.77, 111,
205 Dumont de Montigny, *Mémoires historiques sur la Louisiane…* (Paris: J. B. Bauche, 1753), vol.1, p.200.
206 LAC, MG1-C11A, vol.117, f.196–196v.
207 LAC, MG1-C11A, vol.86, f.231v-232.
208 LAC, MG1-E, vol.95, p.3.
209 LAC, MG1-C11A, vol.117, f.184v.
210 BAnQ-M, TL4, S1, D5201, Procès contre Laprairie, sergent, et Lajeunesse, soldat de la Compagnie de Noyan, accusés de voies de fait armées, 8–10 février 1746.
211 BAnQ-M, TL4, S1, D5667, Procès devant le Conseil de guerre contre François Boirond dit St-François, Caporal de la compagnie de Croizille, Henri Davoud dit Lasonde, soldat de la Compagnie Croizille, chirurgien, et Pierre Beauvais dit Léveillé, soldat, accusés de désertion, 10 janvier–1 février 1752.
212 BAnQ-Q, Greffe du notaire Claude Barolet, Inventaire des biens de feu M. François de Charles (vivant inspecteur de la compagnie des Indes en ce pays) … , 21 novembre 1747.
213 Marie Gérin-Lajoie, Montréal Merchant's Records Project, (microfilm copy of M496 Montréal Merchants Records Project, Research Files, 1971–1975, 1 roll —St. Paul: Minnesota Historical Society Library Copy Services), Monière, vol.4, p.161, MG23/GIII 25, Microfilm M-848, Journal No 3, 3 juin, 1732.
214 BAnQ-M, Greffe du notaire Louis-Claude Danré de Blanzy, Inventaire de Catherine d'Ailleboust du Manthet et de

de La Morendière, a *capitaine* and engineer for the King who had been present at the Battle of the Monongahela in 1755, left behind a 'regulation sabre' upon his death, which may have been a sabre corresponded to a cavalry, dragoon, or grenadier sabre.[215]

Hunting Swords

In past centuries, specialised hunting swords (couteaux de chasse) gained widespread popularity among Europe's aristocracy. These short, robust swords typically featured a slightly curved, single-edged blade designed to endure the demands of hunting. Renowned for their variety of designs, many were elaborately decorated and served as both functional tools and symbols of prestige. By the eighteenth century, hanger-style hunting swords were occasionally adopted by military officers as badges of rank. Like the fashionable small sword, hunting swords were practical yet refined, reflecting the status and elegance of their owners.

This plate, showing a man armed with a hunting sword, deals with hunting using dogs to chase the game. (*L'Encyclopédie*, Chasses, Plate II, Chasse, Venerie, la Chasse par Force, 1763)

By the 1730s, hunting swords had become a favoured alternative to traditional swords among the nobility of New France. A few examples also appear in the personal belongings of colonial officers, who may have carried them on military campaigns or as part of their hunting equipment. For these military men, the shorter hunting sword offered a practical, versatile, and stylish alternative to the small sword. Its compact design, easily carried on a waist belt, likely made it better suited for travel through the North American forests.

Hunting Swords in New France

French colonial documents from the period reveal that the couteau de chasse began gaining popularity in Canada during the 1730s and frequently appear among the personal possessions of individuals such as colonial militia *capitaines*, royal storekeepers, bureaucrats, and members of the bourgeoisie. For example, François Rochereau, a militia *capitaine* at Cap-de-la-Madeleine, owned an exceptionally valuable hunting sword with its accompanying

Sieur de La Chaumette charging at the Beast of Gévaudan in May of 1765. Note the short hunting sword hanging vertically at his side. (Représentation de la bête feroce nommée hiene. A Paris, chez Corbié, rue St-Severin aux Associés)

Jean-Baptiste Levreau écuyer Sieur de Langy, officier demeurant aux Outaouais, 26 avril, 1760.

215   BAnQ-M, Greffe du notaire Pierre Panet, Inventaire de feu Sieur de la Morandière, vivant capitaine ingénieur pour le Roi en cette ville..., 28 janvier, 1761.

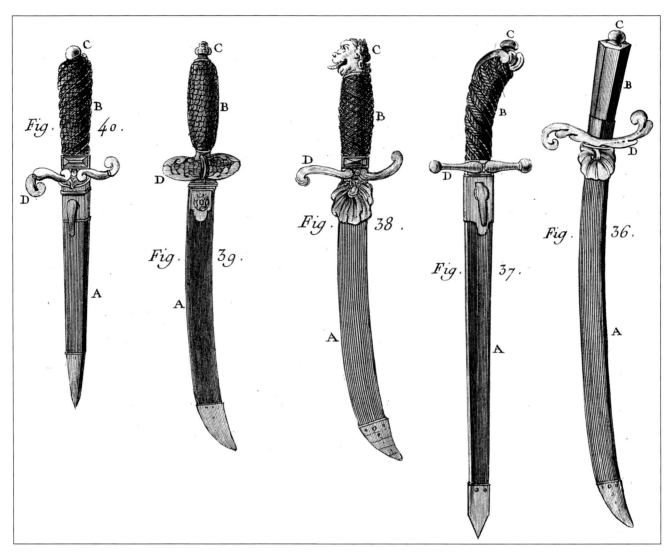

Taken from 'Fourbisseur' in Diderot's *L'Encyclopédie*, this illustration depicts five types of couteaux de chasse (hunting swords). Diderot notes that 'there are several kinds, some shorter than others; some with curved blades and others with straight blades.' A militia *capitaine* living in Charlesbourg near Québec in 1754 owned a hunting sword with a handle decorated with a sea dog, a decorative feature that may have been popular at the time, as seen in one of the examples. Diderot further describes the couteaux de chasse as 'a type of large, short, single-edged sword commonly used in hunting, from which it takes its name.' These hunting hangers were typically carried in a waist belt, as 'the gear of a hunter includes a large-brimmed hat, a hunting sword, and a sturdy waist belt, which we commonly wear over our garment or vest.'

waist belt, valued at 24 livres in 1759.[216] Similarly, in the previous year, Joseph-Étienne Nouchet, councilor of the Conseil Supérieur and director of the Domaine d'Occident, possessed a hunting sword described as having 'a green grip silver mounted',[217] suggesting that its grip may have been crafted from green-stained ivory.

Certain individuals, entitled by their profession or social standing to carry edged weapons such as hunting swords, often did so in and around urban areas. In 1759, for example, Augustin Viger, a master surgeon, drew his hunting sword from its scabbard to strike an British

servant who had physically threatened him upon his return to his home in Montréal.[218] Witness accounts suggest Viger may have been returning from a hunting trip in the countryside, as one observer noted: 'She saw Sir Viger returning from the country, as she believes, with his hunting sword at his side.'[219]

Commercial invoices provide compelling evidence of the wide variety of hunting swords and accompanying waist belts available in the colonies, most of which were imported from France to be sold on the colonial market. In 1748, for example, merchants in La Rochelle supplied

216 BAnQ-TR, Greffe du notaire Jean Leproust, Inventaire des biens de la communauté de Marguerite Provancher, veuve de François Rochereau, capitaine de milice, du Cap de la Madeleine, 22 janvier, 1759.

217 BAnQ-Q, Greffe du notaire Jean-Antoine Saillant, Inventaire des effets de feu Sieur Nouchet, Québec, 10 février 1758.

218 BAnQ-M, TL4, S1, D6276, Procès contre Augustin Viger, chirurgien de la rue Saint-Paul, accusé de voies de fait armées, 28 août–7 septembre, 1759.

219 BAnQ-M, TL4, S1, D6276, Procès contre Augustin Viger, chirurgien de la rue Saint-Paul, accusé de voies de fait armées, 28 août–7 septembre, 1759.

Print, c.1741, made by Jean Baptiste Guélard featuring a hunting sword with a simple counterguard and shell guard. Take note of its sheath and waistbelt buckle configuration. (Trofées de chasse dessinez par C. Hüet et gravez par Guélard. A Paris, chez Odieuvre)

'3 small hunting swords, blades in the style of sabres, with waist belts embroidered in yellow', priced at 7 livres each, along with '6 hunting swords, silver-gilt, neat', priced at 5 livres 15 sols each, complete with buff waist belts.[220] In 1754, Montréal merchants acquired '12 hunting swords, silver gilt…12 buff waist belts embroidered in silver for hunting swords',[221] followed a few years later by an additional shipment of '6 hunting swords, silver gilt brass hilts', and '12 hunting swords with silver-mounted ebony grips.'[222]

Common hunting swords also appeared on the tariff of duties to be levied in Canada under the edict of 1748, with values ranging from 6 to 9 livres and an average price of 7 livres 10 sols.[223] However, very few of these weapons are listed in the inventories of the King's storehouses in the St Lawrence Valley or the interior, suggesting they were speciality items primarily available through private colonial merchants.

220 Division des archives de l'Université de Montréal, collection Louis-François-Georges Baby, G2/65 (mf 1735, 1736), Facture de marchandises chargées d'ordre et pour compte de Monsieur Guy…, La Rochelle, 30 juin 1748.; LAC, Bobine M-859. Pierre Guy, Facture des marchandises… , 30 avril 1748.; LAC, Bobine M-859. Pierre Guy, Facture des marchandises… , 10 juin 1748.

221 Division des archives de l'Université de Montréal, collection Louis-François-Georges Baby, G2/81 (mf 1741), Facture de marchandises chargées à La Rochelle… , 7 novembre 1754.

222 Division des archives de l'Université de Montréal, collection Louis-François-Georges Baby, G2/92 (mf 1742, 1743) Facture des effets chargés pour le compte de Étienne Augé, par Maillet et Meynardie… , La Rochelle, 20 avril 1758.; LAC, Bobine M-859. Pierre Guy, Facture de Pascaud à Guy de Montréal, La Rochelle, 28 avril 1757.

223 LAC, MG1-C11A, vol.121, f.188v.

Hunting Swords: Better Suited than Military Swords

As early as the 1740s, *maréchal* de Puységur in his *Art de la guerre* had recognised the uselessness and inconvenience of the sword worn by French infantry officers, *sergents* and soldiers. He recommended instead that these be replaced with a hunting sword 'whose blade shall be of 21 *pouces* long and will be wide and sharpened on both sides up to half its length, the handle about 5 *pouces* long, strong, light and made of good wood.'[224] It was said that hunting swords would be 'of a great defence due to its position along the side [of the body], it cannot be a hindrance since it is laid out along the thigh.'[225]

This opinion was also echoed by Jean-Louis de Raymond, army officer and governor of Île-Royale, who in 1751, wrote that the manner of which the soldier's swords and bayonet were worn in a nearly horizontal fashion was too awkward in the woods and that, 'it would be advisable in this country, that they should be placed side-by-side along the thigh in the manner of a hunting sword.'[226]

De Puységur went even further, advocating for the complete replacement of the spontoon and gorget with a fusil and hunting sword, the latter being far more practical in combat. He suggested that, 'at least the officers, when ordered, whether to go on detachments, stand guard, or when the battalion takes up arms, be it for reviewing the troops, exercises, or action, will then leave their swords behind and take up the hunting sword along with a fusil, just as they do today with the gorget and spontoon.'[227]

By the 1740s, French military authorities had recognized the advantages of the hunting sword's length and placement along the thigh, a configuration that may have prompted some officers serving in Canada to adopt this weapon or its specific waist belt design. The practice of wearing hunting swords and their accompanying belts on campaigns appears to have been well established by King George's War. For instance, munitions drawn from the King's storehouses in Québec to arm a war party led by the colonial officer Marin de La Malgue in Acadia included 15 waist belts for hunting swords, each priced at 4 livres.[228] In 1750, an inventory of the King's storehouses at Montréal listed '444 waist belts for hunting swords', though no hunting swords were mentioned, suggesting these belts may have been surplus from earlier wartime distributions.[229] The exact use of these belts and their intended users remains a matter of speculation.

During the Seven Years War, several officers were recorded as carrying hunting swords on campaign. In 1758, Monsieur de Selles, a *capitaine* in the Régiment de la Sarre, used his hunting sword to strike an insolent Canadian at Québec.[230] That same year, De Massiac, a *lieutenant* in the Régiment de la Reine, raised his hunting sword to lure hostile Natives before defending himself with his fusil while on detachment near Fort Carillon.[231] The previous year, Antoine de Bellot, a *capitaine* in the Régiment de Guyenne, noted in his ledger that Monsieur de Sourche had purchased a hunting sword from him for 18 livres.[232] These weapons also served a practical role in hunting, particularly for finishing off game. In 1753, Joseph-Charles Bonin, a gunner in the Compagnie des canonniers-bombardiers in Canada who later became a storekeeper at Fort Duquesne, recorded that he had thrust his hunting sword into the belly of a bear during a hunt near the Ottawa River.[233]

Probate Records

Probate records reveal that nearly 15 percent of colonial officers owned one or more hunting swords, often of fine craftsmanship, with some featuring silver hilts and ornate waist belts. For example, in 1739, Nicolas Blaise de Berger, a *capitaine* of colonial troops residing in Québec, was recorded as owning a hunting sword valued at 3 livres.[234] In 1744, two hunting swords priced at 24 livres each were sold to Louis de La Corne by the Montréal merchant Pierre Guy, coinciding with la Corne's promotion to *capitaine*.[235] Nine years later, François-Marie Bouat, an *enseigne* in the colonial troops, owned two hunting swords, including 'an old hunting sword, silver gilt', valued at 3 livres.[236]

In 1755, *capitaine* and *aide-major* d'Arrazola, stationed in New Orleans, owned two hunting swords: 'a silver-mounted hunting sword with a waist belt trimmed in silver' and a 'mid-sized hunting sword'.[237] Three years

224 De Puységur, *Art de la guerre, par principes et par règles*, vol.1, p.120.

225 Raimondo Montecuccoli, *Memoires de Montecuculi, Généralissime des Armées, et Grand-Maitre de L'Artillerie de L'Empereur ...* (Amsterdam: Arkstée & Merkus, 1770), vol.1, pp.165–166.

226 LAC, MG1-C11B, vol.31, f.94–97.

227 De Puységur, *Art de la guerre, par principes et par règles*, vol.1,, pp.220-221.

228 LAC, MG1-C11A, vol.84, f.148v.

229 LAC, MG1-C11A, vol.96, f.144v.

230 Henri-Raymond Casgrain, *Collection des manuscrits du maréchal de Lévis, Lettres de M. de Bourlamaque au maréchal de Lévis* (Québec : Imprimerie de L.-J. Demers & Frère, 1891), p.207.

231 SHD, Archives de la guerre, MG4, B1, série A1, vol.3499, f.134.

232 LAC, MG18-H54 5/ p.2405, Cahier états de compte d'Antoine de Bellot, capitaine au régiment de Guyenne, 1758–1761.

233 Casgrain, *Voyage au Canada*, pp.91–92.

234 BAnQ-Q, Greffe du notaire Abel Michon, ... à la requête de Dame Marie Viennoy, veuve de défunt Monseigneur Nicolas Blaise de Berger (des bergères), écuyer Seigneur de Rigauville... 22 septembre, 1739.

235 LAC, Bobine M-851, Pierre Guy, Livre de comptes, p.229,1744.

236 BAnQ-M, Greffe du notaire H. Bouron, Inventaire du défunt Sieur de Bouat, Sieur François Marie Bouat, enseigne d'infanterie au détachement de la marine en ce pays, 12, 14–15 December 1753.

237 LAC, MG1-E, vol.9, 19 avril, 1755.

later, François de Sarrobert, an *enseigne* in the colonial troops living in Montréal, possessed 'a buff waist belt trimmed with false silver and gold lace with a horn grip hunting sword', valued together at 9 livres.[238] That same year, the inventory of *capitaine* Jacques de St-Martin's belongings at Trois-Rivières included 'one hunting knife with a waist belt,' valued at 8 livres.[239] As late as 1768, Joseph Damour des Plaines, a écuyer in the colonial troops, was recorded as owning 'a hunting sword with a deer-horn handle', valued at 1 livre.[240]

238 BAnQ-M, Greffe du notaire Louis-Claude Danré de Blanzy, Inventaire des biens de feu Sieur François de Sarrobert, enseigne d'infanterie, 8 janvier, 1756.

239 BAnQ-TR, Greffe du notaire Louis Pillard, Inventaire et description des biens et meubles de Feu Gabrielle le Gardeur, veuve de feu le Sieur Jean Jacques de St-Martin, capitaine des troupes de la marine, Trois-Rivières, 10 mars 1761.

240 BAnQ-Q, Greffe du notaire J.-C. Panet, Inventaire des biens de la communauté de Madeleine Coulon de Villier, veuve de Joseph Damour de Plaine, écuyer, 1 mars, 1768.

Circa 1760 French hunter shooting at birds and wearing a fashionable shoulder strap gibecière hunting pouch. Legally, hunting in seventeenth- and eighteenth-century France was the privilege of the landed aristocracy. (Courtesy of Le Louvre French Antiques)

Portrait of Pierre Le Moyne d'Iberville. (Creative Commons)

Portrait of Charles Le Moyne du Longueuil, 3rd Baron du Longueuil, who led a war party against the Chickasaw nation near Fort Assomption on the Mississippi in 1739. An equipment list enumerating what was provided to members of this party revealed that this commandant was issued 8 *livres* of gunpowder, 30 *livres* of lead balls as well as 15 gunflints for his personal use indicating that he opted for a firearm as his main armament when on a campaign. (Charles Le Moyne du Longueuil, troisième Baron du Longueuil, 1724-1755. Anonymous, c. 1753, M985.219, Musée McCord, Montréal)

Portrait of Jacques François de Chastenet Marquis de Puységur (1656–1743), *maréchal de France*. Between 1693 and 1743, he wrote on the principles and rules of the art of war and recognised as early as 1743, that French infantry officers should be armed with a musket and bayonet rather than with the cumbersome spontoon. (Musée de l'armée, Paris. Photo Kevin Gélinas)

Saint-Etienne copy of the Tulle fusil de chasse, c. 1745–1759, probably quite similar to the '200 fusils de chasse with iron furniture and wood ramrods without bayonets' sent aboard the *Le Beauharnois* in 1757, which were likely intended for the colonial officers serving in Canada. (Fusil Duclos Lejay, eighteenth century, 1974.24.183, Musée McCord, Montréal)

Iron-mounted hunting gun by Louis Jaley, Saint-Étienne, c. 1740. This type of very fine gun would have likely corresponded to the type of fusils de façon de maître in the possession of a few officers serving in the colonial regular troops. (The Metropolitan Museum of Art collection)

Thiollière Fusil, c.1720–1730. This example is possibly one of the earliest known Saint-Étienne trade guns, with a North American provenance still with its original European walnut stock. The top flat forward of the breech is marked with THIOLLIERE LAYNE, likely the mark of François or Jean-Claude Thiollière working out of Saint-Étienne c. 1730. (Private collection)

Fusil à l'ancre (c. 1745–1750) manufactured by Montieu of Saint-Étienne. (Private collection)

Circa 1740 barrel, which was once mounted on the Marquis de Montcalm's personal hunting gun. This exquisitely made barrel was signed 'Laroche – Paris' by Jean-Baptiste Laroche, who in 1743 became Louis XV's official gunsmith and resided at the Galleries du Louvre in Paris. With a calibre of 28 balls per *livre*, this profusely engraved work of art is inlaid using gold and silver and equipped with three silver ramrod pipes welded to the barrel's underside. The bracelet-type rear sight is engraved on its upper face with the following text: 'Ci devant la propriété du Général Montcalm mort le 14. Septembre 1759' (Here forth was the possession of General Montcalm who died on September 14, 1759). The gun on which this barrel was originally mounted was undoubtedly worthy of a *maréchal de camp* such as Montcalm. (Musée de la civilisation, 61-1)

French hunting gun by "Les Freres Penel" of Saint-Étienne, circa 1750. The name Frères Penel (Penel Brothers) refers to members of a Saint-Étienne arms merchant family, which were occasionally mentioned in period records related to gun descriptions in Canada. (William Basco collection)

This rare powder horn, which belonged to Jacques LeBlanc, bears a unique inscription reflecting his personal experiences and family history. LeBlanc, born in 1732 in Grand-Pré, was deported to Boston in 1755 during the Acadian expulsions and returned to the French territories of Saint-Pierre and Miquelon in 1763. He later moved to Chezzetcook, near Halifax, around 1766, where he is believed to have drowned in 1769. The inscription reads: 'Jacques LeBlanc, son of François La Petitcote. Made in Boston on March 23, the year 1762. Pray for us, Holy Mother of God, that we may be made worthy of the promises of Christ. Jesus and Mary.' (Collection Musée acadien de l'Université de Moncton)

Silver-mounted French fourniment powder flask with lever and porcupine quill strap. This rare piece may have belonged to a colonial officer, nobleman, or given as a presentation piece to a Native chief. (Robert Speelman collection)

Rare French powder horn attributed to Jean-Baptiste-Amable Adhémar, who was *garde-magasin* (chief clerk) at Fort Niagara from 1758 to 1759. He had signed a one-year contract with Joseph-Michel Cadet, purveyor general to the French forces in Canada, starting on April 14, 1758. This horn features a Native holding a French flag bearing three fleur-de-lis and is signed J.B.te ADHEMAR, 1759. (Photographer: Andrew Wilds, Hopkins Collection)

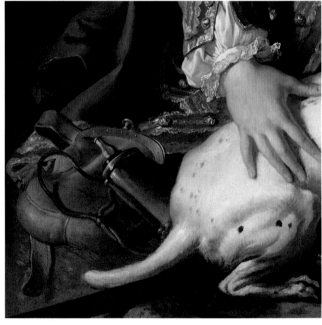

Detail from a hunting portrait of the Chevalier de Beringhen showing his belt hunting pouch and brass-mounted powder flasks. (National Gallery of Art, Jean-Baptiste Oudry's Henri Camille, Chevalier de Beringhen, 1722)

This painting entitled *Jeune chasseur et ses chiens* portrays a young French hunter with his fusil, fourniment, gibecière, and hunting bayonet. By mid-century, the gibecière is said to be worn with a shoulder strap rather than at the belt area when hunting. In New France, a gibecière of the type shown here may have been carried by officers while hunting on their Seigneurie in keeping up with the latest fashionable European hunting uniform of the Royal Hunt. Attributed to Jacques Charles Oudry (1720–1778). (Photo courtesy of Georges Rousset, Galerie Laury-Bailly)

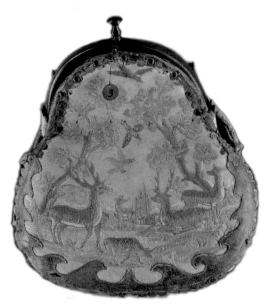

Left: Shot bag, France, eighteenth century. Embroidered hide with two flaps protecting the inside pockets. (Musée de la chasse et de la nature. Inv. 68.17.1. Photo Kevin Gélinas)

Right: Detail from *Picnic after the Hunt*, likely from c. 1735–1740 by Nicolas Lancret, showing a man in hunting attire resting on the ground. He is shown here wearing a traditional French waist pouch. By the 1750s, hunting pouches are now worn around the shoulder by means of a strap. (Samuel H. Kress Collection, 1952.2.22)

This mid-eighteenth-century leather bullet pouch or slit pouch, decorated with dyed porcupine quills and fringed ends, would have been draped over a belt or powder horn for carrying ammunition. It was probably made in Kahnawake, a Kanienkehaka (Mohawk) community on the Saint Lawrence River near Montréal. (Courtesy Pocumtuck Valley Memorial Association's Memorial Hall Museum, Deerfield, MA)

The man shown here holds over his shoulder a besace, a large cloth bag with a slit at its centre that officer Pouchot compares to the form of Native-made slit pouches. (L'homme à la besace, Françoise Duparc, Musée des beaux-arts de Marseille. Creative Commons)

One of 10 brass-mounted pistols found in the *Machault* shipwreck, which shows a side plate with a hole for attaching a hook, indicating that this pistol was not intended for a cavalryman but rather for a dragoon or the ship's crew. (Courtesy of National Historic Sites, Parks Canada. Photo Kevin Gélinas)

Iron mounted Marine contract pistol, c. 1740–1750, bearing crossed anchors and DUMARES/BLACHON on the front face of the lockplate. Antoine Blachon and Pierre-François Dumarest of Saint-Étienne were regular suppliers of arms to the French Marine. (Collection privée, Photos Alain Simon)

Detail from a c. 1748 painting depicting the Camp of the Régiment royal du Roussillon in the Piedmont region during the final campaigns of the War of Austrian Succession. This specific detail shows an officer of this regiment wearing his brass gorget and holding the reigns of a horse on which we can see the brass pommels of two cavalry pistols inserted into their red cloth pistol-bag and leather holster. (Photo courtesy of Michel Pétard)

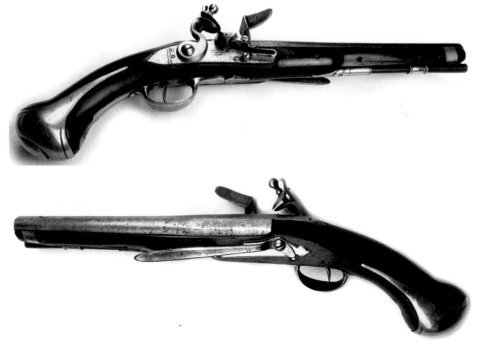

French dragoon pistol, Model 1733, c. 1750. This dragoon pistol features a walnut stock with brass fittings, an iron belt hook, and a reinforced muzzle band. The squared iron lockplate is marked with the crowned S.E. for Saint-Étienne, beneath which is inscribed GIRARD/COMP, referencing Pierre Girard, an entrepreneur active in Saint-Étienne 1740–1759. The 31cm barrel is engraved Reg. DRAGONS DE NICOLAI along the top, with a faint JL under a crown on the left side. Overall length: 49 cm. (Private Collection)

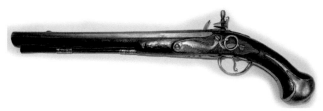

Toulon Archer de la Marine's Pistol, 1690–1703. This Marine pistol features a walnut stock with steel fittings, a rounded lockplate engraved with an anchor and ROVZET for Jean Rouzet, a naval contractor in Saint-Étienne, and a sideplate marked TOVLON with a thumb piece inscribed 2. Its slightly flared 35cm barrel is engraved ARCHER.DE.LA.MARINE, with the maker's mark THEZENAZ below. Used by port police under a *prévôt*, it includes a suspension ring for carrying. Total length: 53cm; calibre: 17 mm. (Private Collection)

French brass pistol pommel, c. 1700–1730, found at the Place royale in Québec City. Note the grotesque face design at the base of the pommel and the additional decorative ornamentation indicating that it may have been originally fitted on a fine pistol. (Aurélie Desgens, 2012 © Ministère de la Culture et des Communications du Québec, CeEt-8-1A7-614)

Above: Red fleur-de-lis marked pistol bags which had belonged to Louis Ferdinand of France (1729–1769), then passed on to the Duke of Berry. The bags came with two ornate pistols and a red velour-covered cleaning rod. These types of bags would have been used by colonial officers serving in North America. (Musée de la chasse et de la nature. Photo Kevin Gélinas)

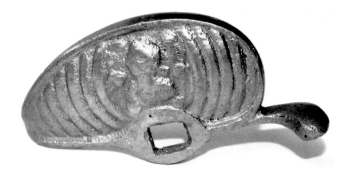

Left: One of several sabre or boarding cutlass half shell counter-guard fragments found aboard the *Machault*, an eighteenth-century French frigate sunk in action in the Battle of Restigouche (New Brunswick) in 1760 showing what is the bust of King Louis XV wearing a laurel wreath. (Courtesy of National Historic Sites, Parks Canada. Photo Kevin Gélinas)

Double-barreled pistol, reportedly belonging to Philippe Louis Baudelart, the King's surgeon in Montcalm's army in 1759. According to legend, a soldier named Fraser picked it up on the Plains of Abraham. These side-by-side flintlock pistols feature soldered barrels, a technology introduced in the 1730s. This pistol is marked with the word Paris on its lockplate. (Musée de la civilization, photographe: Amélie Breton – Perspective Photo, 34-14)

One of four Native kings painted by Jan Vereist, 1710. This Mohican chef named Etow Oh Koam is shown here armed with what is probably a British imported Indo-Persian cutlass hung at his belt. He visited Queen Anne in England in 1710 as part of a diplomatic visit. (Creative Commons)

Common sabre or boarding cutlass fragment with half-shell counterguard decorated with a bust of King Louis XV found at Fort Saint-Frédéric.. It is to be noted that this sabre was likely regripped using wood at some point, as it would originally have had an octagonal bone grip. (Photo courtesy of René Chartrand)

Surviving brass-mounted cutlass or boarding sabre, c. 1745–1760, with horn grip and single knuckle guard. This type of sabre may represent one of the 1,008 sabres sent to Québec in 1746, recorded as brass-mounted and following a specific model provided by French Marine officials. These were likely ships' arsenal arms intended for use as boarding sabres. Additional shipments of brass-mounted sabres in the 1750s, likely corresponding to this model, suggest that production was centred in Saint-Étienne. Excavated hilt examples show these were originally mounted with bone grips. (Courtesy of Don Troiani)

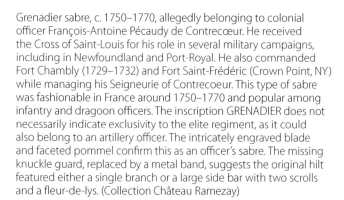

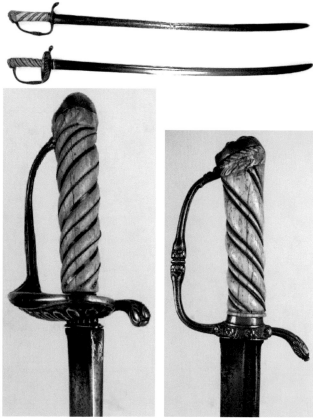

Grenadier sabre, c. 1750–1770, allegedly belonging to colonial officer François-Antoine Pécaudy de Contrecœur. He received the Cross of Saint-Louis for his role in several military campaigns, including in Newfoundland and Port-Royal. He also commanded Fort Chambly (1729–1732) and Fort Saint-Frédéric (Crown Point, NY) while managing his Seigneurie of Contrecoeur. This type of sabre was fashionable in France around 1750–1770 and popular among infantry and dragoon officers. The inscription GRENADIER does not necessarily indicate exclusivity to the elite regiment, as it could also belong to an artillery officer. The intricately engraved blade and faceted pommel confirm this as an officer's sabre. The missing knuckle guard, replaced by a metal band, suggests the original hilt featured either a single branch or a large side bar with two scrolls and a fleur-de-lys. (Collection Château Ramezay)

Two presumed French Marine officer's cutlasses. One displays an anchor marking on the blade's spine near the brass half-shell counterguard, while the other blade's atypical heel is indicative of blades made at the Tulle manufactory for the Marine. (Private collection, France)

Above: An exceedingly rare and presumably French-made hunting sword excavated at the Tenaille des Nouvelles Casernes in Québec city (1772–1837). Its blade is of the flat diamond cross-section, with a brass hilt, scallop-filed hilt, and wood grip, which shows vertical grooves on its entire length. (Courtesy of National Historic Sites, Parks Canada. Collection Tenaille des Nouvelles Casernes, 18G40B48-1Q. Photo Jean Jolin)

Right: Halt of the Hunt by Carle Vanloo, c. 1737. The French aristocrat holding a plate is wearing a typical hunting sword of the period. (The Metropolitan Museum of Art, New York)

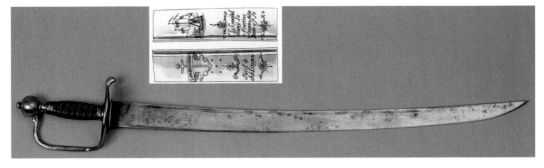

A customised boarding cutlass, c. 1745. This grenadier-type sabre has a brass hilt with a single branch and half-shell counterguard, and a wooden grip covered with iron wire. The curved blade with fuller, which was forged at Solingen, is engraved with a banner over an anchor in which we can read LAIMABLE GRENOT, the name of a frigate, while the other side reads C. Le Conardel Fournÿ la Marine Auprès Notre Dame a Saint Lo, the name of the furbisher to the Marine. (Courtesy of the Musée national de la marine, France)

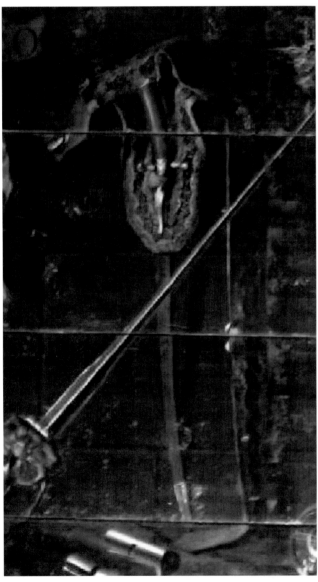

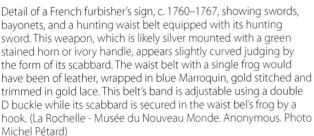

Detail of a French furbisher's sign, c. 1760–1767, showing swords, bayonets, and a hunting waist belt equipped with its hunting sword. This weapon, which is likely silver mounted with a green stained horn or ivory handle, appears slightly curved judging by the form of its scabbard. The waist belt with a single frog would have been of leather, wrapped in blue Marroquin, gold stitched and trimmed in gold lace. This belt's band is adjustable using a double D buckle while its scabbard is secured in the waist bel's frog by a hook. (La Rochelle - Musée du Nouveau Monde. Anonymous. Photo Michel Pétard)

Hunting suit given by Louis XV to King Christian VII of Denmark. This costume was given to Christian VII during a trip to France in 1768 on the occasion of a hunt. The presentation of foreign dignitaries to Louis XV was made during the King's hunts, especially the hunting of stags. Depending on their rank and birthright, they were or were not allowed to participate. This hunting attire comes complete with a silver trimmed waist belt in which is placed what appears to be a single-hilted silver mounted hunting sword with an ebony grip. (Courtesy of The Royal Danish Collections, Copenhague, Château de Rosenborg)

French hunting sword with a presumed provenance associated with François Vallé, a merchant and political leader of Upper Louisiana. Vallé was a *lieutenant* in the Sainte-Geneviève militia during the Anglo-Indian attack on St Louis in 1780. This weapon's blade is engraved with the words 'Milot marchand fournisseur rue Condé près le coin du miroir à Dijon' (Milot, arms dealer, Condé road, near the corner of the mirror in Dijon), an arms merchant working out of Dijon, France, in 1790. This hunting hanger was likely custom ordered via New Orléans by Vallé and represents a rare surviving relic that is representative of the French heritage and tradition very much in place on the North American frontier as late as 1800. Hunting swords were certainly in use in the Illinois territory from an early time since Jean-Baptiste Baron, a voyageur and merchant living at Cahokia was recorded as owning a hunting sword in 1748.

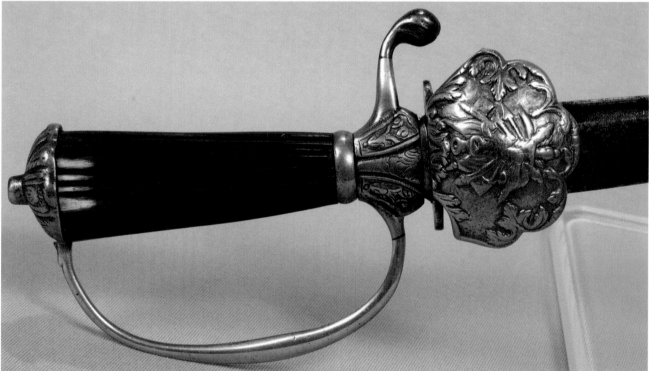

French hunting swords were made with a great variety of hilts, some very plain, others with ornate pommels and quillons. This better-quality example exhibits a military panoply of arms on the brass shell guard with a wooden grip with vertical fluting. The straight single-edged blade, with a fuller and a false edge, bears a large fleur-de-lis stamp on both faces. (Courtesy of Valley Forge National Historical Park)

Appendix

Selected Extracts of Winter and Summer Equipment Issued to the Colonial Troops Serving in Canada, 1686–1757

1686 – Statement of the expenditures and overheads made by the Compagnie du Nord, established by the orders of His Majesty, in Canada, supplied to the detachment made by Monseigneur le Marquis de Denonville Governor-General of the country, and under the command of Monsieur de Troyes, left Québec on the first day of March 1686, accompanied by Father René Silvie, Jesuit, for the enterprise of the Baie du Nord.

For the clothing provided to each of the aforementioned 31 soldiers, namely:
1 capot of blue cloth, trimmed in lace
2 shirts
1 tapabord
1 red cloth under-waistcoat (chemisette)
2 pairs of stockings
1 pair of French shoes
2 pairs of Native-style shoes
1 pair of molleton drawers

We provided three and a half months of food for each man, namely:
10 *pots* of eau-de-vie (for each man)

For all
2,000 *livres* of salted pork
8,000 *livres* of biscuit
1,000 *livres* of rice
6,000 *livres* in 120 *minots* of corn and peas
250 *livres* of ham …
For pepper, clove, salt, and other trivial needs …

Ammunition
1,500 *livres* of powder …
4,500 *livres* of lead …
1,200 *livres* of tobacco …

Weapons besides those of the 31 soldiers
130 fusils and their cases
50 pistols
100 bayonets fitted to insert at the end of the fusil
50 complete grenades
60 swords or sabres

Provided to the detachment of M. de Troyes
37 large and 37 small kettles, that is two kettles per canoe for voyageur's needs weighing 370 livres
80 large re-steeled axes
150 re-steeled mid-size axes
100 picks and spade shovels
100 *livres* camphor and sulphur
50 pairs of snowshoes to walk on the snow
2 rifled carbines
50 dog-pulled toboggans
37 sleds to carry canoes beyond Long Sault on the ice[1]

1696 – Projected expenses for provisions, ammunition, artillery, and officers.

(It is presumed that these projected expenses are directly associated with Count de Frontenac's expedition against the Onondagoes.)

In Québec, we will supply the necessary provisions to sustain one hundred soldiers participating in the expedition for two and a half months, as is customary in Canada.
25 barrels of wine …
[for 20 soldiers detached for six weeks] … a barrel of eau-de-vie in two *quarts*
Plus, ten barrels of vegetables, including four of broad beans, and six of peas
Plus, four barrels of eau-de-vie in *quarts*
Plus, 300 *livres* of Brazilian tobacco

---

1   LAC, MG1-C11A, vol.8, f.272v, 273v-274.

Plus, two barrels of common Bordeaux plums

25 birchbark canoes for the return trip of the one hundred soldiers

Plus, two *quarts* of salted pork … and a *quart* of lard

Ammunition

600 *livres* of fine powder

1,500 *livres* of ball

3,000 gunflints

50 hoes

50 shovels

20 picks

300 gun worms

It is necessary for the return of the hundred soldiers to Québec in their 25 canoes, 13 kettles of five *pots* each with their handles

And 25 bray kettles of three quarters of a *livre* each …

A half gross of awls

A piece of hemp fabric of 50 *aulnes* to make canoe sails

Plus, 100 battle axes, forgotten in the ammunition section.[2]

1702 – [Planned] Account of the operation against Boston by Monsieur de St-Castin:

As the one responsible for this operation, I propose to take 1,200 to 1,400 select men from Canada, including both soldiers and Native allies.

Account of the supplies needed at Québec to equip the expedition against New England, by Monsieur de Saint-Castin…

3,000 *livres* of powder,

8,000 *livres* of musket balls,

4,000 *livres* of lead shot,

20,000 selected gun flints,

2,000 jambette knives

1,000 boucheron knives,

3,000 *aulnes* of Melis for tents and sacks,

400 canons, [sic]

1,500 axes,

30 barrels of eau-de-vie,

150 *livres* of Poitou thread,

100 *livres* of Reims thread,

200 cod lines,

100 *quintaux* of fishing line,

125 barrels of salted pork,

5,000 *quintaux* of biscuit,

700 *boisseaux* of peas,

100 *boisseaux* of salt,

400 pitch kettles.

600 kettles at 5 d.

20 barrels of pitch[3]

1734 – Statement of what was supplied from the King's storehouse at Montréal for provisions, ammunition and utensils provided to a party commanded by M. de Noyelle going to war against the Fox savages

To Messieurs de La Corne, La Perrade, Herbin, St-Ours, Deschaillons, Lignery, Demuy, Chabert and the chaplain for the supplement and the ration issued to them.

675 *livres* of biscuits in 14 sacks

270 *pots* of wine in 18 barrels

108 *pots* of eau-de-vie in 9 barrels

90 *livres* of tobacco

54 *livres* of powder in 9 sacks of ¼ [*aunes*]

216 *livres* of lead

90 gunflints

9 kitchen kettles weighing 89 *livres*

18 deerskins

4½ *livres* of pepper

2 *minots* of salt in 9 sacks of ¼ [*aunes*]

18 *pots* of vinegar in 9 barrels

3 fully fitted tents

3 flags

And for all officers:

2 calves

50 *livres* of beef

100 *livres* of bread in 4 sacks

1 ham, 76 beans in 3 sacks

3 small axes

3 auger

3 funnels

10 *livres* of candles

15 *livres* of soap

1 *livre* of Rennes thread

1,000 sewing needles

6 *mains* of paper

6 *onces* of Spanish wax

Sixty days' worth of food to 22 Inhabitants who serve as guides and 56 men of the troops:

720 *livres* of biscuit in 141 sacks

2,340 *livres* of salted pork in 27 barrels

22 *minots* of peas in 22 sacks of ½ *aunes*

---

2   LAC, MG1-C11A, vol.2. f.97–98.

3   *Collection de manuscrits contenant lettres, mémoires, et autres documents historiques relatifs à la Nouvelle-France…* (Québec: Imprimerie A. Côté et Cie: 1884), vol.2, pp.399–400.

312 *pots* of eau-de-vie in 33 barrels
156 *livres* of tobacco
78 *livres* of powder in 11 sacks of ½ *aune*
234 *livres* of lead
312 gunflints
78 fire steels
78 gun worms
78 awls
78 tumplines
78 deerskins
78 small axes
56 pairs of mittens from 18⅔ *aunes* of Mazamet
56 pairs of mitasses from 56 *aunes* of molleton
56 pairs of chaussons from 18⅔ aunes of Mazamet
16 powder horns[4]

1739 – General statement of expenses incurred for equipping the party sent to war against the Chickasaw savages…

For the officers of the detachment's food and a three-month supplement:
1,400 *livres* of biscuits in 28 sacks
700 *livres* of fine flour in 14 sacks of ¼ of an *aune*
700 *livres* of salted pork in 14 barrels
14 *minots* of peas in 14 sacks of ¼ of an *aune*
560 *pots* of wine in 56 barrels
280 *pots* of eau-de-vie in 28 barrels
84 *livres* of tobacco
70 *livres* of powder in 14 sacks of ⅛
280 *livres* of lead balls in 14 sacks of ⅛
140 gunflints
14 copper kettles, 14 water kettles – weighing together 178¾ *livres*
3½ *minots* of salt in 14 sacks of ¼
28 *pots* of vinegar in 14 barrels
7 *livres* of pepper in 14 sacks of ⅛
14 fully fitted tents
420 *livres* of lard in 14 barrels
70 *livres* of candle
210 broad beans or tongues in 14 barrels
14 casse-têtes
14 fire steels
14 gun worms
28 awls
14 pairs of mitasses
1 cave of olive oil of 45 *livres*5
1 flag
2 cassettes

30 livres of bread
15 livres of beef

For three months' worth of food and supplements for 112 cadets, soldiers and Habitants comprising 16 canoes at a rate of 7 men per canoe:
6,720 *livres* of biscuit in 134 sacks
5,600 *livres* of flour in 112 sacks of ¼ of an *aune*
4,480 *livres* of salted pork in 112 barrels
112 *minots* of peas in 112 sacks of ¼ an *aune*
336 *pots* of eau-de-vie in 48 barrels
560 *livres* of tobacco
112 *livres* of powder
336 *livres* of lead
448 gunflints in 224 sacks of ⅛
112 casse-têtes
112 hafted swords
112 fire steels
112 gun worms
112 awls
112 pairs of mitasses
112 tumplines
28½ *aunes* of ribbon for cockades

By the name of Bellefleur, drummer of the detachment:
1 drum case
2 skins
1 pistol

Expenditure made at Niagara Fort following a report sent by the storekeeper of the said well-known French party, a *sergent* and five soldiers of the garrison of the said fort detached for the said war.
11 casse-têtes
11 boucherons knives
11 fire steels
33 gunflints
11 gun worms
11 awls
11 *livres* of powder
44 *livres* lead
11 *aunes* of molleton for mitasses[6]

1746 – Excerpt from the registers of the King's stores in Montréal, detailing expenditures related to Fort Saint-Frédéric for the current year of 1746.

Issued to M. Mercier, an officer detached to garrison the said fort…

---

4   LAC, MG1-C11A, vol.62, f.149v-150v.
5   'Cave' refers to a cellaret (a chest with compartments used for storing bottles).

---

6   LAC, MG1-C11A, vol.71, f.158v-160, 160v-161, 169–169v.

1 deerskin weighing 3 *livres*
1 bearskin
1 sealskin
1 pair of snowshoes
1 *aune* of molleton in 1 pair of mitasses
1 pair of mittens, 1 pair of chaussons – ⅔ of molleton
1 casse-tête
1 wood splint toboggan
1 tumpline
1 *livre* of tobacco
1 cradle blanket for nippes

Issued for 15 days' worth of supplements to a *sergent* and 17 soldiers detached to garrison at the said fort [Saint-Frédéric]:
135 *livres* of biscuit
39¼ *livres* of salted pork
20 *pots* of guildive [rum] in 26 barrels
18 *livres* of tobacco
2½ *livres* of gunpowder
5 *livres* of balls
36 gunflints
2 fire steels
2 gun worms
25 fishing hooks
2 *bottes* of fishing line
1 *minot* of peas in 2 sacks of ½ *aune*

Issued for the food and equipment of Messieurs De Longueuil and Mezière, officers, and Sieurs Porneuf and Dusablé, cadets detached to serve at this fort under the command of Monsieur Denoyer, commander of this place [Saint-Frédéric]:
4 boucherons knives
4 Siamois knives
4 fire steels
4 awls
25 gunflints
8 *livres* of tobacco
4 tumplines
4 bearskins
4 deerskins weighing 12 *livres*
4 casse-têtes
4 *aunes* of molleton in 4 pairs of mitasses
⅔ of molleton in 4 pairs of mittens and 4 pairs of slippers
4 cotton shirts
4 *livres* of chocolate
20 *pots* of wine and 2 barrels
12 *pots* of eau-de-vie in 4 barrels
1 *minot* of peas in 4 sacks of ¼
5 tongues, 5 broad beans (in 2 sacks)
100 *livres* of biscuits in 2 sacks
7 *livres* of salted pork
30 *livres* of white bread

30 *livres* of beef (in 3 sacks)
1 sheep[7]

1746 – Excerpt from the expenditures incurred at the King's stores in Montréal for equipment and various small parties sent to New England, along with other war-related expenses…

December 1st – Food and equipment distributed to Messieurs Deganne, Laplante [officers], Decombre, Demeloise [cadets], Quesnel, Chevallier [Canadians], Duplanty, Viger [Canadians], Roulleau, Lafausse [soldiers].
Detached to go to Fort Saint-Frédéric as part of the war efforts:
300 *livres* of biscuit
100 *livres* of salted pork (in 8 sacks)
6 tongues
6 broad beans
25 *livres* of lard in 1 barrel
1 sheep
20 *pots* of wine, 10 *pots* of eau-de-vie in 3 barrels
1 *minot* of peas in 1 sack of ½ an *aune*
10 bearskins
10 *livres* of powder
20 *livres* of lead in 2 sacks of an ⅛
10 deerskins weighing 27½ *livres*
10 *livres* of tobacco
10 casse-têtes
10 gun worms
10 awls
1 fire steel
60 gunflints
6⅔ *aunes* of Molleton for 10 pairs of mittens and 10 pairs of chaussons
10 *aunes* of Molleton in 10 pairs of mitasses
10 boucheron knives
4 Siamois knives
6 white bread weighing 18 *livres*
1 covered kettle
2 tarpaulins
5 *livres* of line
33 *livres* of powder in 1 barrel
66 *livres* of balls in 2 sacks of ⅛
75 *livres* of tobacco
20 deerskins weighing 55 *livres*
20 sealskins
20 bundles of roots
4 large axes[8]

---

7   LAC, MG1-C11A, vol.88, f.214–214v, 221–221v, 229–229v.
8   (LAC, MG1-C11A, vol 86. Folio 218–219.)

1747 – Excerpt from the expenditure that was incurred at the King's store in Montréal both for the equipment of various parties that were on the outskirts of New England and other expenses as part of the war efforts.

Issued for the food and equipment of Monsieur le Chevalier de Niverville, officer in command of a war party composed of three cadets, six Canadians and 45 Abenaki Natives of St Francis to strike New England:
2 *livres* of powder
4 *livres* of balls
2 boucherons knives
1 Siamois knife
1 awl
1 gun worm
6 gunflints
1 tumpline
1 bearskin
1 deerskin weighing 3 *livres*
1 pair of oxhide shoes
1 casse-tête
⅔ of Mazamet in 1 pair of mittens and for 1 pair of chaussons
1 *aune* of Molleton in 1 pair of mitasses
1 cotton shirt
1 pair of snowshoes
1 *livre* of chocolate
1 wood splint toboggan
2 *livres* of tobacco

Food and equipment issued to Monsieur de La Chauvignery, second officer, along with two Frenchmen and six Iroquois from the Sault and Lac des Deux Montagnes for war-related matters.

To Monsieur de La Chauvignery and the two Frenchmen:
3 *livres* of powder
6 *livres* of lead
3 boucherons knives
3 Siamois knives
3 fire steels
6 gun worms
6 awls
18 gunflints
6 *livres* of tobacco
3 tumplines
3 pairs of snowshoes
3 wood splint toboggans
3 bearskins
6 deerskins weighing 17 *livres*
3 pairs of oxhide shoes
3 casse-têtes
3 medium-size axes

2 *aunes* of Mazamet for 3 pairs of mittens and 3 pairs of chaussons
3 *aunes* of molleton in 3 pairs of mitasses
4 cotton shirts including 2 for the officer
3 crooked knives
16½ of Cadis / 4 *onces* of Rennes thread in 3 capots
3 three-point blankets
60 *livres* of biscuit
10 *livres* of lard in 1 barrel
½ *minot* of corn flour grilled in 1 sack of ½ *aune*
40 *livres* of wheat flour in 2 sacks of ¼
1 kettle weighing 3½ *livres*
½ calf
1 *main* of writing paper
1 *once* of Spanish wax
2 razors
1 lancet
1 box of Thériaque[9]
3 *livres* of vermillion
3 cutlasses
2 tarpaulins of Beaufort cloth
2 canoes
½ *aune* of Crépis
¼ of cloth for 1 breechcloth
1 hat
1 botte of line weighing 5 *livres*
2 deerskins used for 2 sacks weighing 3 *livres*
4 files

Food and equipment issued to the Sieur Mariette, cadet, who is going in the said party:
1 *livre* of gunpowder
2 *livres* of lead
1 boucheron knife
1 Siamois knife
1 fire steel
1 gun worm
1 awl
6 gunflints
1 *livre* of tobacco
1 tumpline
1 bear pelt
1 deer skin weighing 3 *livres*
1 casse-tête
2⅓ *aunes* of Mazamet for 1 pair of mitasses and 1 pair of chaussons
1 cotton shirt
¼ of cloth for a breechcloth
1 pair of snowshoes
1 *aune* of molleton for 1 pair of mitasses

---

9   A medicinal compound with around 50 ingredients, including a large proportion of opium.

(14 April) Equipment issued to a *sergent* and six soldiers detached to garrison at Fort Chateauguay:

7 *livres* of powder
14 *livres* of balls
7 tumplines
7 deerskins weighing 19 *livres*
7 casse-têtes
7 bearskins
1 botte of fishing line 4 *onces*
50 fishing hooks
25 gunflints
7 fire steels
7 gun worms
7 *livres* of tobacco
7 boucherons knives
7 awls

Equipment issued to 16 soldiers detached to garrison at Fort Sainte-Thérèse:

8 *livres* of powder
16 *livres* of balls in 2 sacks of ⅛
16 tumplines
16 casse-têtes
16 bearskins
16 deerskins weighing 43 *livres*
4 *once* of fishing line
36 fishing hooks
50 gunflints
16 fire steels
16 gun worms
16 awls
16 boucherons knives
33 *livres* of tobacco given to Monsieur de Vassant
2 *pots* of guildive [rum][10]

1747 – Statement of expenditures incurred at Montréal, Chambly, and Fort Saint-Frédéric for a French and Native war party commanded by Monsieur Rigaud de Vaudréuil, who departed from Montréal on June 8th of this year … Expedition against Saratoga

Officers of the troops … (for eight officers, a chaplain and two surgeons). For their food and equipment:

275 *livres* of white biscuit, 108 *livres* of white bread in 11 sacks
175 *livres* of salted pork, 40 tongues, 40 broad beans in 11 sacks
5 calves

156 *pots* of wine in 11 barrels
44 *pots* of eau-de-vie in 11 barrels
11 cotton shirts
11 pairs of mitasses
11 deerskins weighing 30 *livres*
11 fire steels
11 gun worms
11 awls
11 tumplines
11 boucherons knives
11 small knives
11 casse-têtes
11 bearskins
11 *livres* of chocolate
22 *livres* of tobacco

To Monsieur Rigaud in particular:

30 *pots* of wine in 2 barrels
16 *pots* of eau-de-vie in 1 barrel
8 tongues
8 broad beans
1 veal
2 *pots* of vinegar in 1 barrel
1 *livre* of pepper
100 *livres* of white biscuits in 2 sacks
1 *livre* of chocolate
1 cotton shirt
4 *mains* of paper
2 sticks of wax
1 penknife
4 *aunes* of cotton in ¾ for a waistcoat and breeches
1 coffee pot, 1 cup, 2 funnels, 1 tin box – from 3 sheets of tin

Rigging and utensils for boats and birchbark canoes:

6 new tents, fully fitted, for messieurs the officers
1 flag for the commandant
8 covered kettles for the officers and the chaplain weighing 64 *livres*

To the *major* of the said party:

6 *mains* of paper
2 Spanish wax sticks
1 penknife
1 coffee pot, 6 cups, 2 candleholders, 1 box – from 7 sheets of tin[11]

---

10   (LAC. MG1-C11A. Volume 117, f.191V-192, 196–196v, 202, 206v-207, 205v-206.

11   MG1-C11A. Volume 117, Fol. 20-20v, 22v.

1756 – An account of provisions and refreshments to be issued … to the officers and soldiers of the battalions and those of the colony.

(An anonymous list of supplies from the French Army Archives).

Observations:
Soldier's equipment for the summer campaign months:
1 blanket
1 capot (it is a short volant with a hood)
1 wool bonnet
cotton shirts
1 pair of mitasses (this serves as gaiters)
1 [pair] of breeches
1 [pair]drawers
1 skein of thread
6 needles
1 awl
1 fire steel
6 gunflints
1 boucheron knife
1 comb
1 gun worm
1 *pot* of eau-de-vie prior to leaving for the campaign
1 pair of tanned shoes per month
1 *livre* of tobacco per month

Troops taking part in winter expeditions:
2 pairs of slippers
1 vest
Nippes for shoes
Deerskin shoes and no tanned shoes (deerskin to be used for shoes in the way of Native shoes)
1 tumpline
1 toboggan
1 pair of snowshoes
1 sealskin
1 tarpaulin, per 4 men with which to camp. It is a sail canvas that we place on two forks.
Officers are provided with big dogs that pull the toboggan.
A sealskin to cover the food on the toboggans.

Note: All of this was distributed to the infantry battalions and colonial soldiers.[12]

1756 – Account of food and refreshments to be issued henceforth to the officers, the soldiers of the four battalions and those of the colony for each month of campaign.

(An anonymous inventory of supplies from the De Beaujeu family archives, dated March and November 1756.)

At Québec on November 28, 1756.
Soldier's equipment for the summer campaign months:
1 blanket
1 capot
1 wool bonnet
2 cotton shirts
1 pair of mitasses
1 [pair] of breeches
2 skeins of thread
6 needles
5 awls
1 fire steels
6 gunflints
1 boucheron knife
1 comb
1 gun worm
2 *pots* of eau-de-vie prior to the campaign
1 pair of tanned shoes per month
1 [*livre*] of tobacco per month

For the winter campaign in addition to the summer one:
2 pairs of slippers
1 pair of mittens
1 vest
Nippes for shoes
1 [pair] of deerskin shoes and no tanned shoes
1 tumpline
1 toboggan
1 pair of snowshoes
1 sealskin
a tarpaulin for four men for tents[13]

(Undated-likely from 1757) List of supplies, likely drafted by François-Charles de Bourlamaque, third in command after Maréchal-de-camp Montcalm and Brigadier François-Gaston de Lévis.

Officer's equipment for the summer months:
1 blanket … 25 livres
1 capot … 9 livres
1 wool bonnet … 3 livres

---

12   SHAT, Dossier A1, 3417, Pièce 144.

13   Centre d'histoire La Presqu'île, P03/F.089, Fonds De Beaujeu, 28 novembre 1756.;

2 cotton shirts at 8 livres each … 16 livres
1 pair of mittens … 5 livres
1 breechcloth … 2 livres 10 sols
2 skeins of thread
6 needles
6 awls
1 fire steel
6 gunflints
1 boucheron knife
1 comb
1 gun worm
1 pair of tanned shoes … per month
1 casse-tête

For the winter campaign in addition to the summer one:
1 bearskin
2 pairs of slippers
2 Siamois knives
1 pair of mittens
1 vest
½ cradle blanket to make nippes for shoes
2 pairs of deerskin shoes or 1 tanned deerskin – and no tanned shoes
2 tumplines
1 toboggan
1 pair of snowshoes

Soldier equipment for the summer campaign:
1 blanket
1 capot
1 bonnet
2 cotton shirts
1 pair of breeches and drawers
1 pair of mitasses
2 skeins of thread
6 needles
1 awl
1 fire steel
6 gunflints
1 boucheron knife
1 comb
1 casse-tête
For the summer – 1 pair of tanned shoes … per month

For winter equipment in addition to the summer one:
2 pairs of slippers
1 pair of mittens
1 vest
2 Siamois knives
½ covered with cradle for the nippes of the shoes
2 pairs of deer shoes or 1 deerskin passed – and no tanned shoes
2 tumplines
1 toboggan

1 pair of snowshoes
1 bearskin

In addition:
½ of powder – to each soldier and militiaman
1 *livre* of balls – to each soldier and militiaman
1 *livre* of tobacco – to each soldier and militiaman
1 axe per 2 men – to each soldier and militiaman
1 tarpaulin/1 kettle – per 4 men[14]

1757 – French Expeditions against Ft William Henry & Mohawk River

'Every man in the French army that came against Fort William Henry, was equipped in the following manner, viz. With two Pair of Indian Shoes, 2 Pair of Stockings, 1 Pair of Spatterdashes, 1 Pair of Breeches, 2 Jackets, 1 large Over Coat, 2 Shirts, 2 Caps, 1 Hat, 1 Pair of Mittens, 1 Tomahawk, 2 Pocket Knives, 1 Scalping-Knife, 1 Steel and Flint, every 2 Men an Axe, and every four a Kettle and Oil-cloth for a Tent, with one Blanket and a Bearskin, and 12 Days Provisions of Pork and Bread; all of which they drew on Hand-Sleighs.'[15]

1757 – Declaration of two French prisoners taken on March 23 1757 at Fort William-Henry

Liste de John Victor, prisonnier français et soldat des Troupes de la colonie

'Each man had two pair mocassans or Indian shoes, one pair of Indian stockings or Leg pieces, one pair of thick worsted mittons for their hands, two new cotton shirts, 1 pair of worsted stockings, 1 pair of woollen sox, one thick red woollen cap besides their hatts, one flannel waiscoat with sleeves, a blue coath vest & breeches, one upper coat, one watch coat or Great coat with a cap, one fine blanket, and every man in the army had a bear skin. Likewise each man had three knives given him, vizt. Two small knives for the pocket, and one large knife in a Cade [Case], to hang at their Brest (to fight as he was told), one Tomahack, one pair of Snow Shoes, a pair of Iron Creepers to walk on the Ice, a Steel and Flint, a Comb, a Show Aux, Six Needles and a Quantity of Thread, & half a pound of Tobacco, in a Bag. The Grenadiers only had their Sabres. 12 days of provisions at Carillon,vizt. Six days Bisket, & six Days bread, and half a pound of pork a day, no allowance of Spirits, Wine, nor Vinegar. All the Indians and a considerable number of the Troops besides were provided with sheats. 300 scaling

---

14   LAC, MG18, K9, vol.6, f.469–472.
15   *Boston Gazette*, 'From a Letter Dated March 26th, 1757'.

ladders, several boxes full of Combustibles with Machines and Implements for Setting on Fire Vessels, Store Houses &c. No horses or wheell carriages. Each man was provided with a hand sleys and a strong rope to draw by it.'

The list of Guillaume Chassé, French prisoner, soldier of the Régiment du Languedoc confirms John Victor's list and adds the following: 'every two man had a large axe for cutting wood, every four man for cooking had a Copper kettle, and likewise a Large Piece of Canvas each four for a Convering by Way of a Tent'[16]

1763 – François Bigot Trial Records

The (colonial) officer's winter equipment consisted of the following:
1 capot of Cadis
2 cotton shirts
1 woollen vest
1 pair of cloth mitasses
1 cloth breechcloth
1 gun case
1 deerskin
1 bearskin for bedding
1 wool bonnet
1 four-point wool blanket
1 cradle blanket for nippes to put in the shoes
1 pair of tanned shoes per month
1 covered kettle
1 casse-tête
1 axe for the camp
1 tarpaulin for tenting
1 livre of tobacco per month
2 boucherons knives
1 pair of snowshoes
1 fire steel
Thread
Needles
1 gun worm
Gun flint
Shot bag

Soldiers, the miliciens, domestiques, and Natives, had the same winter equipment as officers, except that the capot was made using Mazamet, and that they only had a seal-skin instead of a bearskin, and a tarpaulin and a kettle per five men.

The summer equipment for officers, domestiques, soldiers, militiamen, and Natives, was the same as the winter one, except that we removed the woollen vest and bearskin. But the officer had a camp bed, a tent with its marquis; and the milicien and Natives troops had canon-nière tents per six.[17]

---

16 LOC, Colonial Office 5 folio 47, E. of Loudoun's Letter of April 25th. 1757, Declaration of two Prisoners taken the 23.d March 1757 at Fort Wm. Henry, Information of John Victor and Guillaume Chasse, two French Prisoners, Fort William Henry March 25th.

17 Bigot, *Mémoire Pour Messire François Bigot*, pp.39–40.

Select Bibliography

Main Manuscript Primary Sources

Library and Archives Canada (LAC)
Manuscript records and illustrations.
C13A (Louisiana),
F1 (Fonds des Colonies)
F1A (Finances)
F3 (Moreau de Saint-Mery Collection)
MG1-B (Lettres envoyées)
MG1-C11A (Correspondance générale; Canada)
MG1-C11C (Correspondance générale; Amérique du Nord)
MG1-C11D (Correspondance générale; Acadie)
MG1-E (Dossiers personnels)
MG 4 (Archives de la Guerre)
MG 6 (Archives départementales, municipales, maritimes et de bibliothèques)
MG 7 (Bibliothéque Nationale, Fonds Français)
MG 11 (Colonial Office, London)
MG 18 (Pre-Conquest Papers)

Archives départementales du Tarn-et-Garonne à Montauban, Montauban, France
Manuscript records.

Archives du port de Rochefort (AR)
Séries C3, D3, 1E.

ANMT (Les Archives nationales du monde du travail)
Série AQ (Papiers de Dugard, négociants-armateurs)

Archives du Séminaire de Québec
Manuscript records.

Archives du Séminaire de Trois-Rivières
Manuscript records.

Bibliothèque et Archives nationales du Québec, Centre d'archives de Montréal, Montréal, Canada (BAnQ-M)
Probate and court records.

Bibliothèque et Archives nationales du Québec, Centre d'archives de Québec, Québec, Canada (BAnQ-Q)
Probate and court records.

Bibliothèque et Archives nationales du Québec, Centre d'archives de Trois-Rivières, Trois-Rivières, Canada, (BAnQ-TR)
Probate records.

Bibliotheque Nationale de France (BNF)
Manuscript and illustrations.

BRH Bulletin des recherches historiques.

Centre d'archives de Vaudreuil-Soulanges (Centre d'histoire La Presqu'île)
Manuscript records.

Library and Archives Canada (LAC)
Manuscript records and illustrations.

Library of Congress (LOC)

Randolph County Courthouse, Chester, Illinois (KM)
Kaskaskia Manuscripts.

The National Archives, UK (TNA)
HCA: High Court of Admiralty. Prize Papers; WO: War Office.

Service historique des Armées, France (SHAT)
Archives de la Guerre.

SHD (Service Historique de la Défense)

Universite de Montréal, Division des archives (UMCB)
Collection Louis Francois-Georges Baby.

Primary Printed Sources

Bossu, Jean Bernard, *Nouveaux voyages dans l'Amérique Septentrionale…* (Amsterdam: Veuve Duchesne, 1778)
Bougainville, Louis-Antoine, *Écrits sur le Canada: mémoires-journal-lettres* (Québec: Septentrion, 2003)
Casgrain, Henri-Raymond, *Journal du marquis de Montcalm durant ses campagnes en Canada de 1756*

à 1759 (Québec: Imprimerie de L.-J. Demers & frère, 1895)

Casgrain, Henri-Raymond, *Collection des manuscrits du maréchal de Lévis, vol.I, Journal des campagnes du chevalier de Lévis en Canada de 1756 à 1760* (Montréal: C.O. Beauchemin & Fils, 1889)

Casgrain, Henri-Raymond, *Collection des manuscrits du maréchal de Lévis, vol.II, Lettres du chevalier de Lévis concernant la guerre du Canada (1756–1760)* (Montréal: C.O. Beauchemin & Fils, 1889)

Casgrain, Henri-Raymond, *Collection des manuscrits du maréchal de Lévis, vol.V, Lettres de Bourlamaque au maréchal de Lévis* (Québec: Imprimerie de L.-J. Demers & Frère, 1891)

Casgrain, Henri-Raymond, *Collection des manuscrits du maréchal de Lévis, vol.IV, Lettres et pièces militaires : instructions, ordres, mémoires, plans de campagne et de défense, 1756–1760* (Québec : Imprimerie de L.-J. Demers & Frère, 1891)

Casgrain, Henri-Raymond, *Collection des manuscrits du maréchal de Lévis, vol.VII, Journal du marquis de Montcalm durant ses campagnes en Canada de 1756 à 1759* (Québec: Imprimerie de L.-J. Demers & Frère, 1895)

Casgrain, Henri-Raymond, *Collection des manuscrits du maréchal de Lévis, vol.XI, Relations et journaux de différentes expéditions faites durant les années 1755–56–57–58–59–60* (Québec: Imprimerie de L.-J. Demers & Frère, 1895)

Casgrain, Henri-Raymond, *Voyage au Canada: dans le nord de l'Amérique septentrionale: fait depuis l'an 1751 à 1761 / par J. C. B.* (Québec: Imprimerie Léger Brousseau, 1887).

de Charlevoix, Pierre-François-Xavier, *Histoire et description generale de la nouvelle France, avec le journal historique d'un voyage fait par ordre du roi dans l'Amerique septentrionnale … vol. 2* (Paris: Chez Didot, 1744)

de Courville, Sieur, *Mémoires sur le Canada depuis 1749 jusqu'à 1760* (Québec: Société littéraire et historique de Québec, 1873)

Dumont de Montigny, *Regards sur le monde atlantique 1715–1747* (Sillery, Québec: Les éditions du Septentrion, 2008)

Franquet, Louis, *Voyages et mémoires sur le Canada* (Québec: Imprimerie générale A. Coté et cie., 1889)

Gabriel, Charles-Nicolas, *Le Maréchal de Camp Desandrouins, 1729-1792: Guerre Du Canada 1756–1760; Guerre de l'Indépendance Américaine 1780-1782* (Verdun: Renvé-Lallement, 1887)

Hennepin, Louis, *Nouvelle decouverte d'un tres grand pays situé dans l'Amérique: entre le Nouveau Mexique, et la Mer Glaciale…* (Amsterdam: Chez A. van Someren, 1698)

Kalm, Pehr, Jacques Rousseau, Guy Béthune, Pierre Morisset, *Voyage de Pehr Kalm au Canada en 1749* (Montréal, Québec: Pierre Tisseyre, 1977)

Kalm, Pehr, *Travels into North America: Containing Its Natural History, and a Circumstantial Account of Its Plantations and Agriculture in General … vol.3* (London: The editor, 1771)

Le Beau, Claude, *Avantures du Sr. C. Le Beau, avocat en parlement, ou, Voyage curieux et nouveau parmi les sauvages de l'Amérique septentrionale…* (Amsterdam: Uytwerf, 1738)

Margry, Pierre, *Lettres de Cavelier de La Salle et correspondance relative à ses entreprises (1678–1685)* (Paris: D. Jouaust, 1877)

Margry, Pierre, *Mémoires et documents pour servir à l'histoire des origines françaises des pays d'outre-mer* (Paris: Maisonneuve et cie., 1879)

Margry, Pierre, *Découvertes et établissements des Français dans l'ouest et dans le sud de l'Amérique Septentrionale. Quatrième partie (1614–1754): mémoires et documents originaux* (Paris: Imprimerier D. Jouaust, 1880)

de Maurès de Malartic, Gabriel and Paul Gaffarel (eds), *Journal des Campagnes au Canada de 1756 à 1760 par le comte de Maurès de Malartic* (Dijon: L. Damidot, 1890)

Pouchot, Pierre, *Mémoires sur la dernière guerre de l'Amérique septentrionale entre la France et l'Angleterre* (Sillery, Québec: Les éditions du Septentrion, 2003)

de Troyes, Pierre, *Journal de l'expédition du chevalier de Troyes à la baie d'Hudson, en 1686 …* (Beauceville: La Compagnie de l'éclaireur, 1918)

Secondary Printed Sources

Back, Francis, 'S'habiller à la canadienne', *Cap-aux-Diamants*, 24 (1991), pp.38–41

Back, Francis, 'First Voyageurs, 1650–1715', *Museum of the Fur Trade Quarterly*, 36 (Summer 2000), pp.3–17

Back, Francis, 'Le costume des coureurs des bois: le mythe et la réalité', *Cap-aux-Diamants*, 76 (2004), pp.15–17

Back, Francis, 'Le capot canadien, origines et évolution', *Canadian Folklore*, vol.10, no. 2 (1988), pp.99–128

Back, Francis, 'Le tapabord', *Cap-aux-Diamants*, 60 (2000), p.50

Back, Francis, 'Tuque, teuge, toque ou bonnet à la Turque?', *Cap-aux-Diamants*, 53 (1998), p.56

Back, Francis, 'Le bonnet bleu des patriotes', *Cap-aux-Diamants*, 61 (2000), p.62

Back, Francis, 'Un commando en 1686', *Cap-aux-Diamants*, 69 (2002), p.52

Back, Francis, 'Des raquettes sur le sentier de la guerre', *Cap-aux-Diamants*, 75 (2003), p.58

Back, Francis, *Pour le christ et le roi: La vie au temps premier des montréalais* (Montréal: Libre Expression, 1992)

Borgens, Amy A., Bradfort, M. Jones, Eric D. Ray, *La Belle: The Archaeology of a Seventeenth-Century Ship of New World Colonization* (College Station, Texas: A&M University Press, 2017)

Bouchard, Russel, *Les fusils de Tulle en Nouvelle-France 1691–1741* (Chicoutimi: Imprimerie du Commerce, 1982)

Boudriot, Jean, 'Le fusil boucanier français', *Gazette des Armes*, no 40, juillet-août 1976, pp.24–30

Boudriot, Jean, 'Pistolet de bord', *Gazette des Armes*, no 15, avril 1974, pp.34–40

Brain, Jeffrey P., *Tunica Treasure* (Cambridge, Mass.: Peabody Museum of Archaeology and Ethnology, Harvard University; Salem, Mass. : Peabody Museum of Salem, 1979).

Chartrand, René, 'The Winter Costume of Soldiers in Canada', *Ethnologies*, 10 (1-2) (1988), pp.155–181

Chartrand, René, *French Military Arms and Armor in America, 1503–1783* (Woonsocket RI: Andrew Mowbray, 2016)

Chartrand, René, *Raiders from New France: North American Forest Warfare Tactics, 17th–18th Centuries* (Oxford: Osprey Publishing, 2019)

Dechêne, Louise, *Habitants et Marchands de Montréal au XVIIe siècle* (Montréal: Boréal, 1988)

Delisle, Steve, *The Equipment of New France Militia, 1740-1760* (Bel Air, MD: Kebeca Liber Ata Company, 1999)

Marie Gérin-Lajoie, *Montreal Merchant's Records Project* (microfilm copy of M496 Montreal Merchants Records Project, Research Files, 1971–1975)

Gladysz (Gélinas), Kevin, *The French Trade Gun in North America 1662-1759* (Woonsocket, RI: Mowbray Publishing, 2011).

Gladysz (Gélinas), Kevin, Hamilton, Ken, 'Axes in New France: Part I The Biscayan Axe', *Journal of the Early Americas*, vol.II, no.IV (2012), pp.6–18

Gladysz (Gélinas), Kevin, Hamilton, Ken, 'Axes in New France: Part II French Colonial-made Axes', *Journal of the Early Americas*, vol.II, no.V (2012), pp.6–15

Gladysz (Gélinas), Kevin, Hamilton, Ken, 'Axes in New France: Part III Casse-têtes (French Tomahawks)', *Journal of the Early Americas*, vol.II, no.VI (2012), pp.6–19

Gladysz (Gélinas), Kevin, Hamilton, Ken, 'French Knives in North America: Part I', *Journal of the Early Americas*, vol.I, no.IV (2011), pp.7–15

Gladysz (Gélinas), Kevin, Hamilton, Ken, 'French Knives in North America: Part II', *Journal of the Early Americas*, vol.I, no.V (2011), pp. 8–19

Gladysz (Gélinas), Kevin, Hamilton, Ken, 'French Knives in North America: Part III', *Journal of the Early Americas*, vol.I, no.VI (2011/12), pp.7–19

Gladysz (Gélinas), Kevin, Hamilton, Ken, 'French Knives in North America, Part III: Boucheron Knives', *Journal of the Early Americas*, vol.I: no.VI (2011/12), pp.6–17

Gousse, André, Suzanne, *Costume in New France from 1740 to 1760: A visual dictionary* (Québec: Fleur de Lyse, 1999)

Pétard, Michel, *Des Sabres et des Épées* (Nantes: Éditions du Canonnier, 1999)

Pétard, Michel, *Les équipements militaires de 1600 à 1870. Volume 1 (de 1600 à 1750)* (Nantes: chez l'auteur, 1984)

Stone, Lyle M., *Fort Michilimackinac, 1715–1781: An Archaeological Perspective on the Revolutionary Frontier* (East Lansing, Michigan: Michigan State University Museum, 1974)

Sullivan, Catherine, *Legacy of the Machault: a collection of 18th-century artifacts* (Ottawa: Canadian Heritage, 1986)

From Reason to Revolution – Warfare 1721-1815

http://www.helion.co.uk/series/from-reason-to-revolution-1721-1815.php

The 'From Reason to Revolution' series covers the period of military history 1721–1815, an era in which fortress-based strategy and linear battles gave way to the nation-in-arms and the beginnings of total war.

This era saw the evolution and growth of light troops of all arms, and of increasingly flexible command systems to cope with the growing armies fielded by nations able to mobilise far greater proportions of their manpower than ever before. Many of these developments were fired by the great political upheavals of the era, with revolutions in America and France bringing about social change which in turn fed back into the military sphere as whole nations readied themselves for war. Only in the closing years of the period, as the reactionary powers began to regain the upper hand, did a military synthesis of the best of the old and the new become possible.

The series examines the military and naval history of the period in a greater degree of detail than has hitherto been attempted, and has a very wide brief, with the intention of covering all aspects from the battles, campaigns, logistics, and tactics, to the personalities, armies, uniforms, and equipment.

Submissions
The publishers would be pleased to receive submissions for this series. Please email reasontorevolution@helion.co.uk, or write to Helion & Company Limited, Unit 8 Amherst Business Centre, Budbrooke Road, Warwick, CV34 5WE

You may also be interested in: